Deep
Care

Praise for *Deep Care*:

"This is a fearless and necessary work of history keyed to the dangerous days we live in. *Deep Care* draws on the deep wisdom of those who have been long in the struggle to defend bodily autonomy and radical self-determination. To transmit that knowledge across the generations is itself an act of revolution. Read this book—but more importantly, *use* this book. We all need to be down for the cause, more deeply now than ever."

Susan Stryker, author of *Transgender History: The Roots of Today's Revolution*

"An important record of the secret history of how an eclectic gathering of women poets, musicians, community-based health care workers, grassroots activists, and visionary volunteers created underground abortion service provision in Oakland and fought to defend clinics as *Roe v. Wade* was won and then eroded. Reminds and inspires us to see the treasure of creative collective solutions."

Sarah Schulman, author of *Let the Record Show: A Political History of ACT UP New York, 1987–1993*

"A well-researched historical book documenting that women will do whatever is necessary—legally or illegally—to control their bodies. A much-needed deep examination of the intersections of white supremacy, misogyny, and class not often offered in books about abortion politics. . . . Certainly worth the read and should be taught in every Gender and Women's Studies course."

Loretta Ross, cofounder of SisterSong Women of Color Reproductive Justice Collective and MacArthur Fellow

"*Deep Care* is a passionately researched, intimate look at the real work feminists did on the ground to create a standard of health care for people who need abortions. I felt so tremendously inspired learning about these grassroots champions and so grateful for both their dedication and for Angela Hume's telling of their story."

Michelle Tea, author of *Knocking Myself Up: A Memoir of My (In)fertility*

Deep Care

The Radical Activists Who Provided Abortions, Defied the Law, and Fought to Keep Clinics Open

Angela Hume

AK PRESS

Deep Care: The Radical Activists Who Provided Abortions,
Defied the Law, and Fought to Keep Clinics Open
© 2023 Angela Hume
This edition © 2023 AK Press (Chico / Edinburgh)

ISBN 978-1-84935-526-1
E-ISBN 978-1-84935-527-8
Library of Congress Control Number: 2023938361

AK Press   AK Press
370 Ryan Avenue #100   33 Tower Street
Chico, CA 95973   Edinburgh, EH6, 7BN
USA   Scotland
www.akpress.org   www.akuk.com
akpress@akpress.org   akuk@akpress.org

The addresses above would be delighted to provide you with the latest
AK Press catalog, featuring several thousand books, pamphlets, audio
and video products, and stylish apparel published and distributed
by AK Press. Alternatively, visit our websites for the complete
catalog, latest news and updates, events, and secure ordering.

Cover design by Crisis
Cover illustration by Juna Hume Clark

Printed in the United States of America on acid-free, recycled paper

Pat Parker's "maybe i should have been a teacher," in *Jonestown and Other Madness*
(Ithaca: Firebrand Books, 1985), is reprinted here as it appears in *The Complete
Works of Pat Parker* (Dover, FL: A Midsummer Night's Press, 2016), 211–15.

Descriptions of medical conditions and procedures in this book are
for educational purposes and are not intended as medical advice.

"We don't have to wait for permission. Sometimes we can claim the power we want by acting as if we already have it."
—Ninia Baehr, *Abortion without Apology*

Contents

Preface ix

Introduction: We Did It Before, and We'll Do It Again. 1

CHAPTER 1   Use All the Tools of Your Being. 11

CHAPTER 2   Allow Everyone to Become a Teacher 45

CHAPTER 3   The Self-Destruct Mechanism Is
             the Self-Help Clinic. 65

CHAPTER 4   Why Would You Not Want to Know
             What's Up in There? 79

CHAPTER 5   Become a Community Scientist. 113

CHAPTER 6   Your First Line of Defense Is Self-Defense . . 137

CHAPTER 7   No One Person Has the Power 175

CHAPTER 8   You Only Need to See the Front Line of
             Musclebound White Male Thugs to Know
             What This Struggle Is Really About 207

CHAPTER 9   Rage Is Your Bitter Fuel . . . . , . 233

CHAPTER 10   No Way to Learn Except to Do 263

CHAPTER 11   Everyone Deserves a Place . . . . . . , , ... 291

Conclusion: All Throughout Your Life You Learn 313

Acknowledgments 333

Notes 337

List of Interviews 383

Credits 385

Index 387

Preface

This is a story about revolutionary deep care—community care that transforms and empowers us from the inside out, through practice and over time.

It's the story of an independent abortion clinic, an abortion underground (or secretive network), and a clinic defense coalition that were active during some of the years that abortion was legal in all fifty United States.

The clinic practiced feminist sexual, reproductive, and abortion health care and taught people about body sovereignty, or how to have power in your body and in your life.

The underground "self-help" movement took from the clinic supplies and knowledge about how to provide abortions and seeded them throughout the community.

The clinic defense coalition fought to keep the clinic open and defend the community against anti-abortion extremists.

I think of them—the clinic, the underground, and the coalition—as a single, radical abortion defense movement history. And the lessons this history has to offer couldn't be more urgent today.

THIS STORY BEGINS and ends with the Supreme Court case *Dobbs v. Jackson Women's Health Organization*, but not because this book is a legal history—it's not. (Though it is in part a story about abortion and law.) I start with *Dobbs* because I was finishing this book as the decision was coming down—as the idea that a person should have the right to an abortion was being nullified by the state. In summer 2018, when I started researching radical abortion defense, it occurred to me that we could lose *Roe v. Wade* before I was finished. (Yet who were "we," and what was "*Roe*"?)

On December 1, 2021, I sat at my laptop with a mug of coffee and livestreamed the Supreme Court hearing of arguments in *Dobbs*. The case was about a Mississippi law that criminalized abortion after fifteen weeks and challenged the constitutional right to abortion enshrined by the 1973 ruling on *Roe v. Wade*. The Mississippi lawyer argued that the Court should uphold the law and overturn *Roe*, which had determined that a woman had the right to choose abortion under the Constitution's implied right to privacy, and *Planned Parenthood of Southeastern Pennsylvania v. Casey*, the 1992 ruling that had reaffirmed *Roe*'s "essential holding" under the doctrine of *stare decisis* (legal precedent).[1]

During the *Dobbs* hearing, regarding the Court's willingness to consider reversing *Roe*, Justice Sonia Sotomayor posed the question, "Will this institution survive the stench that this creates in the public perception that the Constitution and its reading are just political acts?" She continued, "I don't see how it's possible. . . . If people actually believe that it's all political."[2]

At the end of the hearing, the lawyer for the US government, Elizabeth Prelogar, suggested that the "profound liberty interests" of women were at stake. In reply, Justice Brett Kavanaugh cited "the other side": "There's also the interest in fetal life at stake as well."[3]

That phrase, I thought. The idea of "fetal life" represents not one but two entwined "other sides" to body sovereignty: One, the argument of the Christian Right, that fetuses deserve the same protection as human beings. Two, the interests of the state, invested not so much in fetal lives but rather fetal *life* in the abstract. The historian Michelle Murphy describes this abstract life as the pure potential for future populations. Controlling this potential life is a primary concern and shared project of the state and modern capitalism. As Murphy puts it: the state "govern[s] sex for the sake of economy."[4]

The phrase "fetal life" appears in the *Roe* decision, which said that after fetal viability, states could take actions to "protect fetal life." Immediately after the ruling on *Roe*, the Right began to pursue a constitutional amendment to ban abortion in the name of fetal rights.[5] Fast-forward to the wrecking-ball 1989 Supreme Court ruling on *Webster v. Reproductive Health Services*, which suggested that the state may have an interest in protecting fetal life *throughout* pregnancy, not just in later pregnancy. This idea was affirmed by *Casey*, which at the same time upheld *Roe*, in 1992.[6]

After the hearing, I got on the phone with Laura Weide, a longtime abortion defender. We talked about how forcing women to carry unwanted pregnancies to term could mean more maternal and infant deaths in groups of people with already disproportionately high numbers of deaths. Black, Indigenous, and poor women die more often due to pregnancy complications than white women, and infants born to Black, Indigenous, and poor women have higher mortality rates, too.[7] We talked about how forced births could also lead to more children in the foster system, if parents end up not being able to afford or to care for them. And about how the foster system props up the prison system, and capitalism needs the prison system, just as it needed slavery.[8] We talked about the Right's racist "replacement theory"—the idea that liberals aim to supplant white people with people of color by welcoming immigrants—and how the idea was being used to promote the attack on abortion rights in the name of saving white babies, just as pro-white, anti-immigrant platforms were used to criminalize abortion in the late nineteenth century.[9] It felt like a dire moment.

That afternoon, I put on a PlanCPills.org shirt that read "Abortion Pills by Mail Is a Reality in All 50 States" and took off to pick up Linci Comy, who was the director of the clinic I was writing about—Women's Choice—for three decades. We parked at BART and took the train into the city.

On the drab concrete outside of the San Francisco Federal Building, thirty-some people stood around in amoebic formation. Activists from a feminist group called Radical Women had organized the demonstration. While protesters spoke into the mic, I walked around and offered people PlanCPills.org stickers with a QR code that linked to information about how to order combination (mifepristone and misoprostol) abortion pills online, including advance provision pills, and have them mailed to you in any state.[10] Abortion law was about to implode, I thought. Why weren't there more people in the streets?

As the light started to go out of the sky, Linci made her way up to the mic. "My name is Linci Comy," she began. "I ran an abortion clinic in Oakland for thirty-two years." She continued:

> What we know is that fascism is alive and well in the Supreme Court of America. I'm a United States veteran. I swore to defend this country and these people from enemies external and internal. They have declared themselves the enemy of women. They have declared themselves the enemy of people of color. They have declared themselves the enemy of immigrants. They have declared themselves the enemy of children. They have declared *themselves*. Well, I declare back. I say: now is the time to rise. Because illegal abortion hurts women. Anyone with a cervix needs assistance at times. It's important to remember that trans men need assistance sometimes. Pregnancy is one of the most dangerous things we do with these bodies. Death and complications related to birth are significantly higher than those associated with pregnancy termination. The mythology that abortion is the highest risk is a lie.

She concluded, "We're here today because women deserve health care. Because the Supreme Court cannot make a law that says I lose my body sovereignty."

On the train ride home, Linci reminded me in a weary voice, "We've been doing this shit for forty years, and we're still here."

At home, I sat down to write. What had happened? How had a history I was studying become the tsunami of the present? What would happen next?

These were good questions. But what I want to begin with is a supposition: that state power will try to adapt past systems of control into current ones. Which leads me to a question that's been central for abortion defenders in this book: All along the way to revolution, how do we circumvent these systems?

Toward a politics of deep care

Even during the *Roe* era, when abortion could be accessed legally at clinics nationwide, women and others who could become pregnant studied and practiced abortion outside the walls of the medical institution. They called their movement "gynecological self-help." I will call it "gynecological and abortion self-help"—for short, "abortion self-help" or just "self-help."

When I say "self-help," I'm not talking about the popular culture idea grounded in the neoliberal principle that one can self-actualize through individual consumer choices. Rather, I'm talking about a West Coast–led political movement in which, starting in the early 1970s, ordinary people taught each other how to do suction abortions and defended the right to access abortion in a clinic. They fought for sexual and reproductive health care for their communities—poor people, people of color, and queer and trans people—because they knew that the state, along with an organized and zealous Christian Right, would try to deny them care at every turn. They fought for the kind of empowerment that comes from community self-reliance.

With an orientation toward our current and future struggles, I'm going to look back at history and tell you how some people survived the political maelstrom of the last fifty years and cultivated community power. As the state and the Right waged a war on reproductive rights, radical activists—revolutionary feminists, Black radicals, lesbian and queer anarchists, socialist feminists, LGBTQ+ activists, revolutionary communists, labor organizers, anticolonial healers, and others, too—put their bodies on the line to learn, practice, teach, and defend sexual and reproductive autonomy.

The struggle to defend abortion access and body autonomy was and is multipronged. It has included a network of feminist abortion clinics, a post-1973 abortion underground, and street resistance to defend clinics against attacks by the Christian Right. It's a struggle that's played out in every state, in urban and in rural places, all over the country.

You might ask: Why was there a need for an abortion underground and militant clinic defense movement during years when abortion was federally protected? Didn't *Roe* mean that underground networks like the Chicago-based Jane Collective were no longer necessary?[11]

Let me back up. When abortion was illegal—let's say from 1880, the year by which criminalization had been achieved in all states, to 1973, when abortion was decriminalized at the federal level—helping each other access abortion was an ordinary part of life for American women of all experiences of race and class.[12] Women would share stories with each other about how to self-abort, from taking herbs, to inserting objects (knitting needles, hairpins) into their vaginas, to irritating their cervixes with Q-tips or fingers, to injecting fluids like saline or vinegar.[13] These and other methods were often ineffective and sometimes deadly.[14] Women increasingly referred each other to doctors, midwives, and others who could do abortions and eventually developed sophisticated underground networks.[15]

It was often challenging to get an abortion before 1973, let alone a safe one, and *Roe* was a lifesaver for many women. But even so, the constitutional right to abortion from 1973 to 2022 was, for many, in name only. By the end of the 1970s, abortion opponents secured the Hyde Amendment, which prohibited federal funding for abortion and made abortion unaffordable for people on Medicaid and for many Indigenous women who accessed health care through the Indian Health Service.

In the decades that followed, abortion opponents passed more legislation and influenced Supreme Court rulings that further gutted access. In the 1980s and 1990s, the Christian Right escalated its terrorization of women seeking abortions and reproductive health care workers at clinics through the military-like execution of human blockades. The risks abortion seekers, along with abortion self-helpers and clinic defenders, were forced to take during years when abortion was ostensibly protected by constitutional law lay bare how symbolic that protection often was.

In this book, I focus primarily (though not exclusively) on activities in or near Oakland, California—the San Francisco Bay Area. By providing a case study of the multiracial, cross-class Bay Area self-help and clinic defense movement, I'm able to explore the nuances of how people organized and built new worlds together—as abortion defenders have in many different places over the last half century.

I spent years listening to self-helpers and clinic defenders share, in interviews, what they learned through their work. Learning about this history changed the way I think about relationships, revolution, and the meaning of body sovereignty. Now, I want to share some of what I learned, about what they learned, with you.

WHEN ENACTED, SUSTAINED, and transmitted over time, practices of what I call "deep care" cultivate community power and autonomy from the inside.[16] They involve learning how to do intimate relationships differently. These practices, central to the abortion defense history I write about, are about so much more than pregnancy and abortion. Practices of deep care are foundational to feminism—the recognition of each person's body sovereignty and the acknowledgment that the way we share power is by taking care of both ourselves and each other, each other and ourselves.

By studying abortion self-help and clinic defense, we begin to see that feminism is not the dream of some utopian future, but rather what we have the power to create *now*, what we *do* create, in and through our daily lives and relationships: around kitchen tables and in beds, at doorsteps and on sidewalks and in parking lots and streets, in exam rooms and infoshops and meeting halls and parks.

Abortion self-help and clinic defense ask how two or three people or a group of people together can unsettle the dynamics of dominance and submission, of policing and control, of received scripts for self/other recognition, and of enemy and state surveillance. These practices aspire to repudiate and to be inscrutable to enemies and the state. They fundamentally redistribute history, tools, knowledge, and power. They are revolutionary.

Self-help and clinic defense practices are embodied. What happens when you use your hands to support, hold, and care for the bodies that make up your community? What happens when you put your hands inside of your community's bodies? When you use your arms to lift your community's bodies up over other bodies and through embattled clinic doors? What happens to *the way you care*? To your sense of where your sovereign body ends and where your community's bodies begin? The deep care of self-help and clinic defense happens at these embodied thresholds.

The political wager of deep care is that by reaching across these thresholds, repeatedly and over sustained time, we begin to better understand our own embodied needs, which are not separate from the needs of our community. Through our active, daring, ordinary reaching across, we can meet each other's needs, and thus *meet each other*, in new and profound ways.[17] "Self-help is where the power is," one self-helper and clinic defender told me. She understood the seamless overlap of self-help and clinic defense. Moreover, her comment points toward how, in seeming contradiction, self-help isn't really about the "self" at all. Rather, self-help happens in moments of creative relationship and mutual care. In these moments, the power lies.

My hope is that, by disseminating primary-source self-help and clinic defense history and knowledge, this book models a practice of deep care. Within, you will learn concrete information about how, for example, people perform abortions in different settings and contexts. And you will also learn about the abstract qualities of what makes small affinity-group work challenging, powerful, and sustainable (or not).

Where I'm coming from

"They'll call you a traitor to theocracy," Linci once said to me. "And you'll say, 'Thank you. Of all the things in the world to be known for . . . thank you for giving me that.'"

I MYSELF WAS not an abortion self-helper or clinic defender during the period discussed in this book. My outsider's perspective is a strength and a weakness. It is a strength in that I bring a fresh lens and sense of discovery, and a weakness in that my analysis may not sync with that of self-helpers and clinic defenders who were there. Conscious of my outsider status, I questioned if I should write this book at all, but I decided that the survival history I assembled was too important not to share.

My nuclear family was a city-working-class religious white one, and in conservative St. Paul, Minnesota, I was raised to be a girl. When I was a young adult, I left home. For a long time, I thought of my hometown as all milk and corn, church and Catholic school plaids. I didn't know what I didn't know about its history: that in the nineteenth century, the settlers had waged a war against the Dakota people just blocks from where I grew up. That Indigenous women and children had been interned at a concentration camp by the river.

On Ford Parkway in St. Paul was a nondescript brick building, a Planned Parenthood. I remember being a child and coming out of the library across the street with my mom and my siblings and studying the scene. There were often anti-abortion protesters by the door, holding up signs with fake images of aborted fetuses. "Stop Abortion Here," they read. "Abortion Kills a Baby."

I was taught that abortion was wrong because it violated the fifth commandment: thou shall not kill. I learned this lesson from groups like Family Life (Catholic) and Focus on the Family (fundamentalist), whose publications had glossy photos of smiling, chaste teens, and from our priests and teachers at school. I remember feeling creeped out as I began to see what seemed like the Church's obsession with controlling girls and women. I couldn't have named it then; it was more of a body feeling. Later I was able to see that Christianity wanted to control the people who went into the clinic.

In my teens, I was taught little about sex other than that I should abstain from it. I didn't have sex with boys mostly because I wasn't that interested, and I had also started to realize that I had experienced abuse, but I didn't yet know how to tell that story, even to myself. I felt disconnected from my body. Eventually I decided I was pro-choice. It, too, was a body feeling—the lives of girls and women should be their own!

When I did have sex with some men, starting when I was about eighteen, I never became pregnant. Now, as a queer person in my forties, it's unlikely I'll ever have an abortion or give birth. You might wonder why someone who has never been pregnant would choose to write this book. For the first two decades of my life, I lived and breathed the Christian Right's repression of sex and sexuality along with its subjugation of women, girls, and queer and trans people. For me, writing this book has been about saying *no* to what I never thought I could. It's the biggest *no* of my life.

American anti-abortion ideology incorporates white supremacy, misogyny, class oppression, and fascism. It normalizes sexual violence and economic inequality. Anti-abortion ideology has been used by the Christian Right to consolidate a large extremist base that now dictates abortion law—not to mention laws governing the sexual and reproductive health care of women and queer and trans people broadly. The proliferation of the anti-abortion movement has been coextensive with the collapse of what some would call American democracy, what legal historian Mary Ziegler articulates as a partnership between anti-abortion forces and the Republican Party that has won control of both the Supreme Court and elections.[18]

Today anti-abortion ideology is as robust and tentacular as ever, and it's terrifying. In this context, *Deep Care* is my attempt to champion the acts of creative world-building by everyday revolutionaries who demanded, and still demand, that it be different. May they continue to inspire us.

The story of this book

Based on history that I largely pieced together from original interviews and primary-source material, *Deep Care* asks philosophical questions about archival engagement and the practice of feminist historiography—the study and theory of historical story-telling. What does it mean to give an account of a movement that has been repressed but that at the same time has resisted documentation? How do you tell stories about other people's lives in ways that are feminist? How do you make good on a commitment to keep your participants safe and, moreover, in the process of your research, honor people's dignity inside of their lives? I wrestled with these questions endlessly, and they shaped my approach to this project in every way.

I didn't set out to write a book about abortion self-help and clinic defense. Deeply interested in the work of feminist and queer American poets who were also health activists—Audre Lorde, Judy Grahn, Pat Parker, and more—I was researching an academic book about poets and poetry. It was (and is) compelling to me that these poets wrote about how their social and material environments had made them sick and how they imagined feminist medicine and healing as forms of empowerment and resistance.

This was how I learned that Pat Parker, a Black lesbian feminist revolutionary and poet, had worked at the Oakland Feminist Women's Health Center, also known as Women's Choice Clinic (which I'll refer to as OFWHC/Women's Choice). So I started researching the clinic. I learned that it was part of a network of feminist health centers and abortion clinics that grew out of a West Coast–led gynecological self-help movement. Thus began my journey into the self-help archives.

This journey took me to libraries around the country. It also led me to people's doorsteps. I went on to interview dozens of activists—clinic workers, underground lay health workers, and clinic defenders. Often they had folders or boxes full of literature and ephemera from their movement work: photos, videos, newsletters, posters, art, pamphlets, manuals, zines, news clippings, clothing, and much more. One of the stories I tell in this book is the story of encountering these bedroom-closet archives.

Deep Care follows the approximate lifetime of OFWHC/Women's Choice, which was redubbed the West Coast Feminist Health Project/Women's Choice in 1988: the early 1970s through the first decade of the twenty-first century. Importantly, self-helpers and clinic defenders in the Bay Area did not stop doing their work when the clinic closed in 2009.

In the course of my research, one thing that struck me was how many Bay Area abortion defenders were also poets and artists, beyond the poets whose work started me on this journey. The clinic's long-term director, Linci Comy, whom I interviewed extensively, is, in her own words, an orator. During our interviews, she would spontaneously spit poems. I transcribed a few of them, lineated them according to her cadence, and brought them into this book.

To find self-helpers and clinic defenders, I used a method that social scientists call "snowball research." I started by sitting down with Linci and then Judy Grahn, whose own activist history overlapped with the clinic's. Linci and Judy introduced me to more people, who in turn introduced me to more, who in turn introduced me to more. I met with these activists one-on-one and in small groups. Some I met with many times over years. We met in parks, at cafés and beaches, on front porches, in living rooms and bedrooms. We talked on the phone, cooked meals, went for walks, went to parties, went camping. People talked to each other before talking with me. They vetted and considered and strategized. How much would they share? Who would talk to me? Who would not?

A handful of self-helpers and clinic defenders became my friends. I got to know their families. They taught me about gardening, backpacking, raising chickens and goats, parenting, aging, caring for elders. They also taught me about feminist conversation, friendship, bias, discomfort, conflict, communication, group work, intimacy, play, grief, transition, stepping back, stepping up, organizing, communism, anarchism, revolution. Writing this book has been an immersive, shattering experience—the greatest privilege of my life.

The people I present in this book are real, as are the stories I tell and details I include. I worked closely with the activists I write about, and I tried to tell stories that would resonate with their experiences. News stories, books, and other published material helped me fill out the history, but I was also cautious of trusting published sources as much as the accounts and archives of my interview subjects. I was conscious that elevating published material could reproduce the ideology that suppresses the stories of women's, queer, and trans empowerment in the first place. I use pseudonyms for some activists (indicated with an asterisk on first mention)—in particular, for those who did underground work and asked that I not identify them. But these "characters" are not semi-fictional amalgamations; rather, they are *historical people* who intervened in the material conditions of their lives, with others, to demand the recognition of women's and other oppressed people's body sovereignty and to make their world more livable. Throughout, I refer to activists (some of whom I interviewed personally, and some whom I did not) by their first names, while I mostly refer to researchers, scholars, and antiabortion extremists by their last names.

That we live in a time when some of these activists still feel they need to withhold their identities for fear of surveillance, criminalization, or retaliatory violence, that we do not live in a world where they get to be widely recognized as heroes, makes me angry. It's unfair that it is so often radical feminist histories that remain in obscurity because it is too dangerous for those involved to come forward. They deserve better. We all deserve better.

I wrote this book knowing that our enemies would read it, too. By sharing their stories, the contributors to this book seemed to suggest that claiming their history, resisting erasure, and sharing their lessons and tools of survival with younger generations were more important to them than avoiding the attention of their enemies by staying quiet. Their storytelling makes clear: we, the people, are stronger than ever before.

DEEP CARE FOLLOWS Ninia Baehr's 1990 pamphlet *Abortion without Apology*, published just after the Supreme Court ruling on *Webster v. Reproductive Health Services*, which laid the groundwork for the gutting of *Roe*. Baehr's pamphlet offers a history of radical abortion activism from the 1960s to the 1990s, with a focus on organizing in California and New York. Like Baehr's, my book also comes after a major ruling in US abortion law and likewise includes firsthand accounts from activists. I think of *Deep Care*, like *Abortion without Apology*, as using "history to encourage a new generation of activists to envision what they really want, and to empower them to take action to get it."[19]

This book is about abortion defense and reproductive justice, certainly. Reproductive justice demands the right to choose abortion and also the right to choose parenthood, along with the right to resourced, healthy environments in which to raise children.[20] *Deep Care* is about sex, intimacy, family, and friendship—relationship politics. It's also about feminist consciousness-raising and institution-building. Black feminist critical social theory.[21] Reproductive labor. Multiracial, cross-class coalition work. Queer kin- and community-making. Fighting fascists. Poetry.

There are many things that *Deep Care* is not. While it is a book of history based on primary-source research, it's not intended to be academic. While sociologists or anthropologists may be interested in the analysis I provide, this book is not a social science study or an ethnography. It is not a legal history, nor is it a history of the pro-choice or anti-abortion movement. There are many other things that it is not.

Deep Care is a work of public historical scholarship and of radical political theory that is intended to educate, agitate, and inspire. It writes into history for the first time some courageous, revolutionary people. Throughout, I avoid taking other philosophers' concepts and applying them to the histories I chronicle. Instead, I draw theoretical insights from the words of my sources, who are brilliant philosophers and political theorists in their own right, and from the archives they assembled. They speak eloquently and for themselves.

Finally, I want to say that *Deep Care* is for revolutionaries and potential future revolutionaries everywhere. Which is to say: it is for everyone.

Revolutionaries Are Everyday People

The whole point about revolution
Is seeing the things that are intolerable
And insisting on making change
And it takes everyday people to do that

The people in power, they don't want change
They don't want to see it
It's the everyday people
That are the revolutionaries

You don't wake up one day and
Suddenly have this revolutionary fervor
That you're going to turn the world upside down
One day you wake up and realize
That you're just not going to do
The same thing again and again and again and
Expect a different outcome

And that you're going to start to feel in your soul
What place you want to live in
Where you want to be
And you're going to start to create that
With your community

So revolutionary fervor is really just that
Great space of change
And transition
That we learn to feel

Revolutionary people
That's just the We
We the people
That's the revolutionary you see

So welcome to the world
Just open your eyes
And revolution grows
That's how we change
Everything we know

—Linci Comy, October 26, 2020, Oakland

We Did It Before, and We'll Do It Again

This story of Bay Area radical abortion defense unfolds around a clinic: Oakland Feminist Women's Health Center / Women's Choice, which was renamed West Coast Feminist Health Project / Women's Choice in 1988. I first talked to Linci Comy, the clinic's director for more than thirty years, in the summer of 2018. I'd wanted to ask her about the Black feminist poet, health activist, and abortion defender Pat Parker, whose life I'd been learning about and whom Linci had worked with in the 1970s and 1980s.

You know how, if you're lucky, there are a few people who come into your life and blow up the story you've been telling yourself about the world? People who make your life a different one than it was before?

When I first met Linci, she had her blue eyebrows on. An elfin dyke witch with glittery eye makeup and hard turquoise eyes, she wore her silver hair short, punky, and queer. Among the tattoos on her arms was a rainbow-striped caduceus. She invited me inside her house and sat with me at the sunny kitchen table. My first question must have been something like, "Can you tell me about the clinic where you worked with Pat Parker?" I couldn't have known that it was the first of what would be thousands of questions that I would ask her.

Through our conversations, Linci helped me see that what activated and sustained the Bay Area radical abortion defense movement was the collaboration of three core components: feminist clinical practice, an abortion underground, and militant clinic defense. Abortion self-help—gynecological and abortion care provided in both clinic and non-clinic settings—took place in private spaces, such as exam rooms, living rooms, and bedrooms, while clinic defense played out in the public spaces of sidewalks and streets.

The gynecological and abortion self-help movement, which started in the early 1970s, is said to have grown out of civil rights and New Left organizing and to have been catalyzed by women's movement calls for feminists to "seize the means of reproduction."[1] Michelle Murphy argues that the conditions for this call were technologies that made it possible for people to "manipulate their very embodied relationship to sexed living-being," namely birth control and new abortion techniques.[2]

The conditions for this call also included the innovation of feminist consciousness-raising. Starting in the late 1960s, the consciousness-raising movement upheld small-group work as fundamental to liberation processes. Through "opening up, sharing, analyzing, and abstracting," group members created autonomous zones where learning from lived experiences empowered them to transcend the isolation that was patriarchy's primary tool for subjugating them.[3]

As they applied the tools of feminist consciousness-raising, self-helpers taught each other about gynecological health, anatomy, and fertility tracking. They also taught each other how to empty the uterus with a suction technology they developed called "menstrual extraction." Through these practices, they collectively produced body knowledge and helped others achieve reproductive autonomy.

Some early self-helpers argued that menstrual extraction was not abortion. They wanted to distinguish clinical abortion, a service for a fee in which the patient is passive, from at-home menstrual extraction, which was performed in a group of activists that centered the autonomy of the person receiving the procedure and that was most often offered for free.[4] Even so, I use the phrase "abortion self-help," and I do so to acknowledge that menstrual extraction was and is a form of pregnancy termination.

Also, I use the phrase "abortion self-help" when referring to both menstrual extraction *and* feminist clinical abortion as I see them as complementary. I want to name the simple fact that menstrual extraction and feminist clinical abortion were technically and philosophically similar, and each was made more groundbreaking in its relationship to the other. With abortion as criminalized as it is today and thus as hidden as ever, it is critical to name abortion where it has been and where it is performed to help people understand that abortion has always been and remains a widespread medical, social, and cultural practice.

By the time the abortion self-help movement emerged in the early 1970s, a broader nationwide progressive health movement was already underway. Scholar Alondra Nelson explains, "This multifaceted radical health community was a decentralized aggregate of groups, collectives, and organizations with distinct missions that sought to transform medicine, institutionally and interpersonally."[5] To ground their initiatives, activist groups experimented with the neighborhood health center model, established under Lyndon B. Johnson's War on Poverty. In 1965 the Office of Economic Opportunity began funding neighborhood health centers around the country.[6]

As well as a progressive health movement, abortion self-help was preceded by decades of Black health activism focused on overturning medical segregation and discrimination. From Booker T. Washington's Black health uplift campaign in the early twentieth century to the Student Nonviolent Coordinating Committee's Freedom Summer health initiatives in 1964 and the Black Panther Party's People's Free Medical Clinics in the 1970s, Black health advocacy was critical to what Nelson calls the "long medical civil rights movement."[7] Susan Smith refers to this as the "history of black 'self-help.'"[8]

As Smith chronicles, during the Jim Crow era (from the 1860s to the 1960s), Black women developed public health programs for their communities. Black women volunteers were critical to the opening of Chicago's first Black hospital and affiliated Nurses' Training School for women in 1891. In the 1920s and 1930s, before the New Deal or government-sponsored

neighborhood health centers, Black women's social clubs set up
and raised money for free clinics for poor children.[9]

Social theorist Patricia Hill Collins describes a longer "tradition of merging intellectual work and activism," in which Black
women have used "everyday actions and experiences" to inform
their politics; Black women's leadership in health activism in the
twentieth century exemplifies this tradition.[10]

Across the decades, abortion self-help has been a multiracial, cross-class movement. As first-generation self-helpers
noted to me, in the early 1970s the movement was made up of
mostly working-class white women. But due to its grounding
in the birthplace of the Black Panther Party, Bay Area abortion
self-help internalized and reflected Black radical ideas from the
beginning. In the 1980s, women of color were the leaders of
OFWHC / Women's Choice.

Abortion self-help extended the radical abortion activism
of the decade that preceded it. In the 1960s, the West Coast
feminist-led Society for Humane Abortion fought for the repeal
of laws restricting abortion, while helping women obtain safe illegal abortions in the meantime.

When community abortion care came under attack starting
in the late 1970s, health activists, including some self-helpers,
summoned a formidable clinic defense movement. As I will show,
when we historicize gynecological and abortion self-help (encompassing feminist clinical abortion and menstrual extraction) *with*
clinic defense, and not each separately, powerful lessons come
into sharp relief.

Toward revolutionary body talk

Some of us want to move away from binary understandings of
sex, sexuality, and gender. We want to abolish gender, a tool of
oppression. We also want to abolish the medical police who want
to control our health, our relationships to our bodies, and our
reproduction, and who draw on the punitive carceral powers of
the state to do so. To achieve our aims, we must demand gender

liberation and recognize the ways the state and economic system exploit and control our sexed being and our fertility. To do so, we have to keep talking about our bodies."" When it comes to gender and sex liberation, the revolutionary demand is the same: body sovereignty. This implies the abolition of capitalism, which precludes that sovereignty.

Today calls for gender liberation are being co-opted by liberalism. According to some, using gender-inclusive language is a political act in and of itself. But in our highly mediated, identity-obsessed culture, language remains mostly ideology, signaling partisanship ("I'm a Democrat, not a Republican") or liberal virtuousness ("I value diversity, equity, and inclusion" or "I'm queer- and trans-inclusive").

It is time to articulate both gender and sex liberation through a frame that accounts for the historically specific risks to physical bodies that queer and trans people have been forced to take or have courageously taken. I hope to contribute to this accounting in this book, which is about the lives of women, queer, and gender-nonconforming people who were oppressed for living their genders and sexes in ways that sought to destabilize, even shatter, norms.

When talking about reproductive justice, using gender-inclusive language is good politics, and here's why. Reproductive justice and queer and trans health justice are structurally similar, interconnected, and ongoing struggles against the body cops. They are sibling movements. Poor women and queer and trans people have fought and continue to fight for access to responsive, non-traumatic health care, and in many cases for access to care at all.[12]

Using gender-inclusive language is also a good thing to do because more young people, many of whom can get pregnant, are identifying as nonbinary or trans now, and reproductive justice is a movement for young people.[13] For all of these reasons, I often use gender-inclusive language in this book.

Because *Deep Care* is a historical book, I use gendered language when it is historically accurate to do so. While I sometimes use phrases like "people who can become pregnant," I also use "woman" and "women" in my historical storytelling simply because these are the words that the people I am writing about used and deeply identified with.

Toward revolutionary talk about care

"Care has reentered the zeitgeist," Hiʻilei Julia Kawehipuaakahaopulani Hobart and Tamara Kneese write in their introduction to a 2020 special issue of *Social Text* on "radical care."[14] They cite Angela Davis in 2016: "Self-care and healing and attention to the body and the spiritual dimension—all of this is now a part of radical social justice struggles. That wasn't the case before."[15] One could say that self-care, healing, and attention to the body have *always* been part of radical social justice work, as Davis's work with the Black Panther Party and Black feminist health activism attests. But I think what Davis is getting at is how, despite the long importance of care labor to political movements, only recently has care been explicitly recognized as integral to revolutionary struggle. For example, in 2022, Black feminist scholar Robyn Maynard theorized self-care as a form of resistance to settler colonialism, which commits itself to "evading wellness at any cost." She writes, "We cannot live in community or move toward political transformation if we are not able to commit, in the most intimate part of our lives, to authenticity within ourselves and to wellness."[16]

At the same time, the narrative around care continues to be co-opted by neoliberal capitalism, under which "self-care" is the moral imperative to both self-manage and self-police. This moral imperative serves, first, the state by relieving it of the obligation to provide welfare programs and, second, capitalism by ensuring a self-reliant and disciplined workforce.[17]

Against this backdrop, Hobart and Kneese (and Maynard, too) uphold the Black feminist insight that survival is a political activity. They define radical care as both a political theory and a practice or set of strategies for surviving precariousness.[18]

I titled this book *Deep Care* with the challenge of the phrase in mind. I recognize that trending words like "care" can lead us to adopt a kind of presentism. Yet there is a fair amount of despair right now amid intensifying economic and state oppression, and many people are asking, in earnest, "Does anyone care?" Care is on our minds, and for good reason.

The story of abortion self-help and clinic defense is the story of how, in times of particular devastation—or, as Linci once put it, "life under occupation"—people have gotten creative in and with their caring. They have risked caring deeply, which is the opposite of despair. Precisely the type of survival story we need today.

Learn, defy, fight

Deep Care braids three story threads. A first thread is about OFWHC / Women's Choice, for many years part of a network called the Federation of Feminist Women's Health Centers, and later renamed West Coast Feminist Health Project / Women's Choice. This thread chronicles moments in the clinic's near-forty-year struggle to keep its doors open and provide feminist abortion and sexual health care. In this thread, I track and theorize the influences of gay women's liberation, the Black Panther Party, and a longer tradition of Black women's health activism and self-help health care on clinic politics and philosophies of abortion counseling and abortion work. I tell stories about how this specific clinic transformed how people imagined reproductive health care—how, for example, it started the first sperm bank in the country to serve single women and lesbians as well as the first to offer a donor identity-release option. And how the clinic played a critical role in helping to get the abortion pill mifepristone approved in the United States.

Throughout this first thread, I explore the "participatory clinic" model of small-group care that distinguished Women's Choice from mainstream providers. The participatory clinic posited that sexual health care must be a nonhierarchical, shared undertaking. This story thread runs through chapters two, three, four, five, nine, and eleven.

A second story thread historicizes the underground gynecological and abortion self-help movement in California's Bay Area. The simple fact that abortion has been practiced intentionally, carefully, holistically, and near-constantly by skilled but unlicensed laypeople outside of the medical institution even during years that *Roe* stood has not been adequately grasped or theorized. In this thread, I offer stories and analysis of this movement. Drawing on interviews with underground self-helpers, I show how these activists took abortion care into their own hands, learning, practicing, and teaching manual-suction abortion beyond the walls of the clinic.

The work abortion self-helpers did both inside and outside of clinics was complementary and revolutionary. Underground self-help groups in the Bay Area relied on health workers at Women's Choice for access to medical knowledge and supplies. Critically, this thread reveals how these activists along with health workers at a licensed clinic together transferred restricted knowledge about gynecology and abortion to laypeople.[19] I tell stories about the abortion underground in chapters one, three, seven, and ten.

A third story thread chronicles Bay Area abortion defenders' central role in resisting the rise of the Christian Right's militant anti-abortion campaigns. In the 1980s and 1990s, the Bay Area Coalition for Our Reproductive Rights (BACORR)—which included Women's Choice, along with the feminist group Radical Women; the feminist collective Women Against Imperialism; the anti-imperialist group Roots Against War; a loose-knit group of queer antifascists; labor organizers and trade unionists; and others—executed a creative, tactically sophisticated, and highly effective clinic defense movement with nationwide reach. Bay Area abortion defenders also trained and led volunteers in clinic escorting over many decades. This thread unspools in chapters six, eight, and eleven.

Deep Care unfolds more or less chronologically. Chapters one through three are about the 1970s. Chapters four through six are largely about the 1980s. Chapters seven through ten are about the 1990s, and chapter eleven is about the first decade of the 2000s.

In my conclusion, I offer some final stories and reflections that respond to a question: What survival lessons do gynecological and abortion self-help and clinic defense offer us today, when reproductive justice and body sovereignty are less a legal reality in the United States than they were half a century ago? As I will show, self-helpers and clinic defenders made a world in which intimate knowing, of self and of community, was both possible and revolutionary. They did so by learning to provide abortions themselves, defying the law when necessary, and fighting to keep clinics open. As Linci put it, "We did it before, and we'll do it again."

Chapter 1

Use All the Tools of Your Being

Linci and I sat in the sun on the steps of her North Oakland house. She lived in the upstairs unit: a steep, brown-painted wood staircase led from the sidewalk up to a small porch alcove. From the alcove ceiling hung a pirate ship puppet. The beamy afternoon light of the flatlands seemed to swirl around our heads like thrown gold dust.

It was the summer of 2020, just months after the horrific murder of George Floyd in Minneapolis and nearing the end of a stretch of unprecedented mass uprisings. Not two years later, the Supreme Court would overturn *Roe v. Wade*, ending a half-century era of legal abortion nationwide.

I had sent Linci a draft of an article I'd written about Oakland Feminist Women's Health Center / Women's Choice (later West Coast Feminist Health Project / Women's Choice). From 1977 until its closure in 2009, Linci worked at the clinic, mostly as its director. At that point, I'd been interviewing her for a couple of years, and I'd interviewed other people who had worked at the clinic, too. In that crisis moment, early in the COVID-19 pandemic, it felt like one of the most important stories in the world—it was a story about public health defense.

"I showed it to a couple of my friends," Linci said, raising her blue eyebrows, two mischievous carets. "People you haven't met." Her eyes were bright as polished turquoise.

"Oh yeah?"

"They want to talk to you," she said. "The underground wants to talk." Linci paused and then continued, "People are starting to ask, is it time now to talk about what we did for forty years? If it is, is it to inspire people? Is it to make sure that it doesn't become debris of the past? People are starting to ask these questions."

As far as I knew then, what Linci and others in the self-help movement had done for forty-plus years was teach ordinary people about gynecology, fertility, and abortion care. Starting in the early 1970s, feminist women's health centers (FWHCs), run by laypeople, equipped laypeople with knowledge and skills to track their ovulatory cycles, diagnose common sexual health conditions, and participate in abortion care. Some FWHCs offered donor-insemination programs and housed sperm banks. Women's Choice led a feminist health education initiative that inspired many activists to become licensed providers.

I knew that the gynecological and abortion self-help movement had a history of being secretive, especially around the teaching of menstrual extraction, a procedure for manually suctioning out the contents of the uterus. Due to laws that defined what constituted "practicing medicine" and then regulated who could do it, self-helpers had been forced to practice menstrual extraction more or less, well, underground. What story did the underground want to tell, I wondered? What story could they tell that didn't already live in the self-help archives around the country: in the clinic records, correspondence, pamphlets, videos, zines, and other ephemera in library special collections?

I didn't realize then that this wasn't the right question. A better question would have been: What story will the underground tell that *already* lives in the subtexts of chosen language and of omission, the creases and folds, of the self-help archives? I didn't fully realize then that the story I was writing was about a militant struggle for body sovereignty and the lengths laypeople were willing to go to defend and reimagine that sovereignty.

"Once you know how to make a Del-Em out of a mason jar, a one-way valve, and some flexible tubing, you really can't go back," Linci said. I wasn't sure I understood what she was trying to tell me. But my ears were open. Because if there's one thing I'd learned about Linci, it's that she tells you exactly what it is she thinks you need to hear.

The body is a tool

"When I came to the clinic in 1977, self-help was an active part of the health center and the movement. I pushed for the development of self-help groups," Linci once told me. "I thought self-help was cool as fuck. When I'm excited about something, I share it."

IT WAS DECEMBER 1977 in Oakland, California, in the after-hours at OFWHC / Women's Choice. Cigarette smoke left over from the waiting room down the hall still hung lightly on the air. Only the table lamp was on. In the office, someone had put on Tui's album. With six people crowded into the small aftercare room, it was warm but not too warm.

Linci, just twenty-four years old, peeled her pants and underwear off but left her socks on. She sat on a disposable chux pad spread over a blue-cushioned bench. People were sitting on the carpet beside her. On the matching bench against the opposite wall, two other people were also pantless. She had only met everyone that Monday. Today was Thursday.

Linci leaned back into a cushion. Inhaling and clenching her square jaw, she separated her legs.

"Insert the speculum with the handle to the right, and when it's in all the way, twist it upright, squeeze the handle, and push down to lock it," instructed Laura from the other side of Linci's open legs. Linci felt slight pressure as she opened the speculum and clicked it into place. It occurred to her that she had never opened her legs for a group of women before had it not been sexual.

"Aim the flashlight at the mirror," Laura said. "Your cervix should pop into view." Linci brushed strands of sandy brown hair to the side of her angular face and pursed her lips in concentration. In the mirror, below a mess of wiry pubic hair and through the opening of her speculum, she could see the ridgy coral-pink walls of her vagina. But no cervix.

"Don't worry," Laura said. "Your cervix is just hanging out in a different position. I'll help you find it. Try moving the speculum a little to your left." Linci played with the angle and depth of the speculum. Eventually a pink knob with a bellybutton-like slit at the center did indeed come into view. It poked upward. She had never seen her own cervix before, and there it was.

A couple of others turned their attention to Linci and murmured affirmations. Laura leaned in close to make observations. "Your uterus is tilted back," she said. "That's why it's pointed up." Like Linci, some others in the room were also new clinic health workers doing self-exams for the first time. Most were still learning the language for navigating a speculum exam. But Laura was among their most experienced comrades.

"I had never thought of my body as a tool before," Linci told me. "I'd never considered the knowledge that the tools of my being could give me."

Linci grew up in a poor Catholic family in the Rust Belt city of Lorain, Ohio. Prior to coming to OFWHC / Women's Choice, she was a navy corpsmember who served as a medic in the Micronesian Islands, treating wounded Vietnamese refugees. Many were survivors of American chemical warfare. "When I went into the service, I thought I was going to do a good thing and be a medical person," she told me at one point. But her experience was disillusioning. "I mean, we dumped *white phosphorous* from the sky," she said. "We did that. That was a regular thing." When she got back, Linci wanted to find sanity. "For me, coming to the clinic after the war was about coming to a space about health."

When Linci told me the story about her first cervical self-exam, we were sitting under the leafy persimmon tree next to my Berkeley garden shack. It was Easter Sunday.

What Linci didn't know that day in 1977 was that she had just performed the first of what would be thousands of cervical self-exams in group settings.

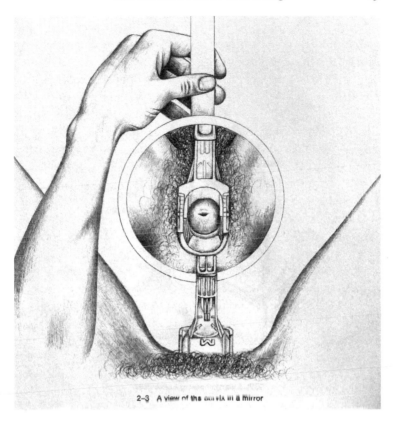

2–3   A view of the cervix in a mirror

"A view of the cervix in a mirror" by Suzann Gage. Federation of Feminist Women's Health Centers, *A New View of a Woman's Body: A Fully Illustrated Guide* (Los Angeles: Feminist Health Press, [1981] 1991), 24.

A first step in any surgical abortion procedure

There are many reasons why someone might want to locate and examine their cervix or the cervix of another person. The cervix is the entrance to the uterus, the mammalian organ in which offspring are conceived and developed, located in the pelvic area behind the bladder and in front of the colon. The cervix's round, firm face bulges into the vaginal canal. The opening at the center of the cervix is called the os. From the uterus, through the os, and through the vaginal canal come menstrual blood, secretions, and sometimes babies. For people in the gynecological and abortion self-help movement, examining one's cervix and the cervixes of others were ways to become familiar with cycles, explore differences among bodies, and learn to identify common conditions like yeast.[1] They were also the first steps in accessing the uterus.

Michelle Murphy writes, "While it might be tempting to dismiss vaginal self-exam as simply an expression of a privileged narcissism masquerading as radicalism in the 1970s—titillating but ultimately trivial—I want to take this practice seriously as a historically specific and influential form of technoscience that reassembled objectivity."[2] I also want to take cervical self-exam seriously as a material practice—locating the cervix is a first step in any surgical abortion procedure.

To do their work, self-helpers relied in part on the dominant culture's sexist assumption that a group of women crowded into a room to look at each other's parts couldn't possibly be doing anything all that subversive. But they were. Self-helpers practiced cervical exam so that they could learn how to provide abortions for themselves safely—to "directly challenge physicians' control of routine health care and healing," of which they considered abortion to be part.[3] They did so at a time when abortion access was restricted. As it is today.

Starting in the 1970s and continuing for decades, underground self-helpers formed small clandestine groups that taught and practiced routine gynecological care and at-home menstrual extractions and suction abortions. In the Bay Area, self-helpers accessed resources and supplies through community clinics, especially Women's Choice. Drawing on knowledge of the "tools of their being"—knowledge produced through direct practice on each other's bodies—self-helpers reimagined abortion care and abortion defense.

Murphy reads the self-help movement as an early expression of neoliberalism. She points out that self-help modeled small-group "protocol feminism," or scripted forms of talking, sharing information, and demonstrating procedures. This protocol feminism would, in institutionalized forms, be used by nongovernmental organization (NGO) women's health initiatives. Small-group work in the 1970s, she explains, was thought of by human-relations researchers as a technology for facilitating liberal self-actualization, a form of governmentality that would come to mark the neoliberal era.

Murphy also argues that cervical self-exam anticipates biomedicine, the moment when "research and care collapsed into one another." Biomedicine, she explains, is a form of technoscience, or science that attempts to engineer the world. Self-help worked *through* technoscience, just as it "crafted" itself as "a form of counter-conduct" to dominant scientific and medical practices.[4]

I read self-help groupwork differently. Murphy doesn't acknowledge the improvisatory and experimental nature of the intimate relationship practices that make up the social aspects of self-help. These dynamic, political-relational aspects are the ones I'm interested in. Perhaps Murphy is right that 1970s self-help registered an incipient neoliberalism. But for every technoscientific self-help "protocol," there was also a self-help swerve. It's in these adaptive responses—risks in intimacy that people took together—that I locate self-help's radical feminist politics. I read self-help as anticipating and ultimately resisting neoliberalism—a structure that atomizes people, precluding intimacy—from beneath that emerging structure.

Historians have suggested that underground self-help declined during the Reagan era. But underground self-help was practiced continuously and in fact more widely in the late 1980s, when abortion came under heavy attack.[5] As threats to legal abortion snowballed, underground self-helpers in the Bay Area ratcheted up their skills and reach. All along the way, they challenged social and medical definitions of the body's insides and outsides and the meaning of body sovereignty.

Once Linci told me that she thinks of self-help as a continuum, from learning cervical self-exam and fertility tracking to learning how to perform and then providing abortion care beyond the walls of the clinic. It was always the movement's course to teach simple practices with low risk and then gradually introduce more complicated practices, sometimes with more risk.

Underground self-help created an autonomous zone outside of the clinic and its norms, the law, and even established scientific and medical definitions of pregnancy. And this autonomous zone was predicated on a community of people coming together around the idea that these laws and definitions had to be abolished before women would be free.

The story of an invention

A mason jar, a one-way valve, and some flexible tubing. A cannula and a syringe. Let's go back to April 1971—I want to tell you the story of an invention.

Lorraine Rothman thumbed through her husband's science lab mail-order catalog. White and middle class with four kids, Lorraine sometimes also worked as an assistant to her husband, a biologist.[6] She lived in suburban Orange County and was thirty-nine years old.[7]

Through her local National Organization for Women (NOW) chapter, Lorraine started doing abortion activism. Under the Therapeutic Abortion Act, signed into law under Governor Ronald Reagan in 1967, abortion was legal in California but only when a pregnant person's life or mental health was determined, by multiple doctors, to be at risk.[8] That is to say, abortion was legal but still mostly inaccessible; thus, abortion law repeal was a critical issue.[9] Lorraine and some other feminists demanded that all laws that restricted and controlled women be repealed.[10]

Try to hold a picture of Lorraine leafing through her husband's catalog in your mind while I take you around a bit more. At that time, the abortion reform and repeal movements were in high gear. Thirty-some miles north of Lorraine, in Los Angeles, a white working-class activist named Carol Downer was also passionately engaged with the abortion struggle. Thirty-eight years old, Carol had six children. She had had two abortions, one illegal and one "therapeutic."[11] Since 1969 she'd been a member of the abortion committee for her NOW chapter, in which she and the others would visit local women's groups to talk about abortion. Lana Clarke Phelan of the Society for Humane Abortion was the committee head—and Carol's mentor. In addition to working with NOW, Carol in 1969 started organizing with a small group. Julie Barton, Elaine Heiman, Cheryl Libbey, Mary Petrinovich, and Carol were the "original five" who decided to take abortion into their own hands, she told me when I visited her in Los Angeles in 2019.

In 1969, the original five became acquainted with an abortion provider named Harvey Karman and his colleague, a doctor named John Gwynn, who together ran an illegal clinic on Santa Monica Boulevard. As Carol put it to me, she and the others started "hanging around" the clinic and observing Harvey and John at work. Harvey was not a licensed doctor (his degrees were in psychology and theater), but he had been performing abortions in the region for a decade and a half and was well known as a provider and an outspoken activist. By 1969 he had been arrested twice and imprisoned for two and a half years after being "convicted of abortion."[12]

By that time, Harvey had developed and begun to introduce a thin, flexible plastic cannula, a game changer for early-term suction abortions.[13] A cannula is like a straw. When connected to a syringe, it makes simple suction procedures possible. Suction abortion with a plastic cannula was a less invasive alternative to dilation and curettage (D&C) for early procedures, which required scraping the inside of the uterus with a metal instrument.[14]

When the original five realized Harvey's suction technique was simple enough for other laypeople to perform, they began to study it.[15] In this realization, Carol was inspired by her mentor Lana along with Pat Maginnis and Rowena Gurner, who through their work with the Society for Humane Abortion in the 1960s and early 1970s ran an extensive abortion referral service, in addition to teaching classes about how to self-abort.[16] Only a few months later, at a Los Angeles conference on abortion for physicians, presented by a company that sold aspirating machines, the original five marched onto the stage unannounced. With the others flanking her, Cheryl announced, "Doctors, we're going to do it ourselves. Women are going to take this back."

Around the same time, Carol organized a rally to support Harvey and abortion rights: five hundred people showed up at Hancock Park. On a battery-powered record player that she had brought from home, Carol put on "Land of Hope and Glory" and announced that they would be establishing the "Fellowship of Felons." She invited anyone who'd had an abortion to come forward if they wanted to. People did. One woman later told Carol that when she stood up, it was the first time she'd come out to her mother as having had an abortion.

Carol told me about a moment that contributed to her understanding that ordinary people could learn how to do abortions. In 1970, she had accompanied a friend and the friend's daughter to Harvey's clinic so that the daughter could have an IUD inserted. From behind her thick oval frames, Carol observed the daughter's cervix as she lay on the exam table with a speculum in place. Her cervix, she thought, was entirely accessible. It was right there.[17]

Then, in April 1971, Carol and some others from the original five called a meeting.[18] Held in the front office of a house in Venice, the home of Everywoman's Bookstore and *Everywoman's Newsletter*, the meeting was intended to be an informational event about starting an underground service. Thirty-some people attended, including Carol's precocious teenage daughter Laura Brown.[19]

Among them, also, was Lorraine.

Attendees crowded in shoulder-to-shoulder; some sat cross-legged on the office floor. One of the organizers had brought a manual-suction device Harvey had built—a cannula attached to a plastic syringe. Carol held up the device and tried to explain it. It made people visibly uncomfortable, "green in the gills," she told me. To ease their worry, she decided to show the group just how accessible, in fact, the cervix is.[20]

From on top of the office desk, she leaned back, pulled up her skirt, and spread (or "pried," as she remembered it) her legs apart. She angled the gooseneck desk lamp so that it illuminated her vulva and then inserted a plastic speculum into herself. Carol had taught herself how to perform a cervical self-exam with a mirror, speculum, and flashlight in the preceding months. She wanted to show them all how close the cervix is to the opening of the vagina.

People stood up, gathered around her, and leaned in, taking turns peering inside of Carol's body. Mary volunteered to do a cervical self-exam next. By the end of the meeting, six or so of the attendees had gotten on top of the desk. The room was electric. "How many children have you had?" people asked. "You look totally different!"

Lorraine was inspired by Carol's demonstration. "The fact that this particular area of the body that has been inaccessible to us is now *visualized*. . . . It was so revolutionary," Lorraine later said.[21] After the meeting, she couldn't stop thinking about Harvey's device. One problem with it was that it didn't have a mechanism to stop air from being pumped back into the uterus, which can cause an air embolism and be deadly. Another problem was that if the syringe were to fill up, the cannula would have to be taken out (so the syringe could be emptied) and reinserted.[22]

A gust of wind swept through the open window and caught the corners of pages as Lorraine scanned the industrial supply mail-order catalog. *There*, she thought. A one-way valve. The valve would prevent air from being pumped back through the tubing into the uterus.

After ordering the valve and gathering some equipment from hardware and grocery stores, an aquarium shop, and the lab where her husband worked, Lorraine set to work reimagining the device.[23] She laid out her supplies:

Sharp knife or razor
Cutting board
Four-millimeter cannula
Five-millimeter cannula
Six-millimeter cannula
Aquarium (Tygon) tubing (one fifteen-inch length and one
     thirty-inch length)
One-way valve

60cc syringe
Two-hole #13 rubber stopper (to seal the jar)
Half-pint mason jar
Toothpicks

First, Lorraine cut one-inch pieces off the five-millimeter cannula, creating two small adapter tubes that would be used to bridge together tubing of different widths. She attached one of these five-millimeter adapters to the valve post and connected the fifteen-inch length of aquarium tubing to it, then fit the valve to the 60cc syringe. When pulled, the syringe's plunger would create suction. Then, with the help of a toothpick, she pushed the six-millimeter cannula through one of the two holes of the rubber stopper until there was only an inch protruding out of the top of the stopper. Lorraine allowed a half inch of the cannula to stick out from the bottom of the stopper and cut off the excess. She fed the remainder of the six-millimeter cannula through the other hole of the rubber stopper, repeating the process to create two six-millimeter adapter tubes running through the stopper.

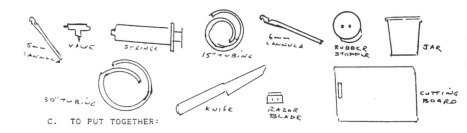

Del-Em supplies. Lorraine Rothman, "How to Put a Del-Em Menstrual Extraction Kit Together" handout, undated, RL.00427, box 62, folder 1, Feminist Women's Health Center Records, David M. Rubenstein Rare Book and Manuscript Library, Duke University, Durham, NC. Also from *Izabel's personal collection.

Next, she connected the free end of the fifteen-inch length of tubing to one of the six-millimeter adapters protruding from the top of the stopper. She attached the thirty-inch length of tubing to the stopper's other adapter tube protruding from the top, then fitted the stopper tightly into the mason jar, sealing it like a lid. The mason jar, supplied from Lorraine's kitchen, would serve as the receptacle for collecting the blood and tissue from the uterus.

Lorraine fit the remaining five-millimeter adapter to the free end of the longer, thirty-inch length of tubing. If the procedure was done using a small four-millimeter cannula inserted through the cervix, this five-millimeter adapter would ensure a tight fit, but if a larger five- or six-millimeter cannula were used instead, the adapter would not be needed. Finally, she tested the fit by inserting a thin four-millimeter cannula a half inch into the adapter. During an actual procedure, this last cannula to be fit in would need to be kept sterile so that its free end could be inserted directly through the os and into the uterus.[24]

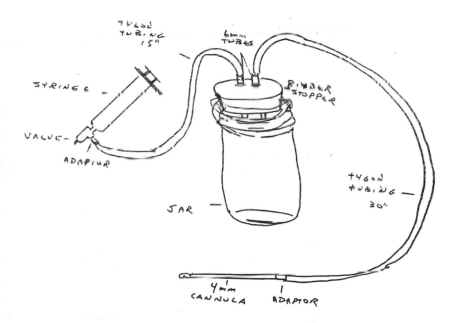

Del-Em. Rothman, "How to Put a Del-Em Menstrual Extraction Kit Together."

Pulling on the syringe attached to the set of tubing on one side of the stopper would create a vacuum inside the jar. The vacuum would then produce the suction needed to draw blood and tissue up through the set of tubing on the other side of the stopper, into the jar. The one-way safety valve would ensure that no air could travel the reverse direction back into the uterus.[25]

As she stood back to review her work, Lorraine's stomach did a flip. She couldn't help but smile.

Not long after, Lorraine would name her device the "Del-Em," a jab at a doctor who once called it a "dirty little machine."[26] She also patented it.[27] Lorraine and the others wanted to keep the device out of the wrong hands.

The simple answer to our need

Lorraine, Carol, and some other West Coast Sisters—a group that came together in 1971 to develop the "self-help clinic concept," as they started calling it—began practicing using the Del-Em on both people who were and were not pregnant.[28] The West Coast Sisters also began meeting regularly for "clinics," where they practiced cervical self-exam. By examining the consistency of their cervical mucus (slippery and stretchy meant fertile) and noting changes in the color and texture of their cervixes, they tracked their cycles. STI's, contraception, and abortion were all topics for inquiry and exploration.[29] They met at the bookstore, in people's houses, and eventually at the Los Angeles Women's Center on South Crenshaw Boulevard in South Los Angeles, out of which they began to run an abortion referral service, connecting women with providers.[30]

The West Coast Sisters transformed a couple of back rooms in the women's center into the Los Angeles Feminist Women's Health Center (LAFWHC).[31] The space was small and seemed always to be at least semi-crowded. There was a well-worn couch and chairs arranged in a circle, newspaper clippings and posters for political demos tacked up on the walls, and supplies for performing self-exam—speculums, mirrors, gloves, lube—cluttering tables.[32]

What happened next is fascinating: the West Coast Sisters decided to bring the Del-Em to the NOW conference taking place in Santa Monica that August 1971. But they didn't call the device and procedure "suction abortion"; instead, they called it "menstrual extraction," a concept that they had "evolved" in the months since the Del-Em's invention.[33] They distributed flyers inviting people to come to their hotel room to watch demonstrations, and dozens of people showed up for their "ME marathon."[34]

Starting from the time of the Del-Em's public debut at the conference, the West Coast Sisters told a story in which "menstrual extraction is not a euphemism for abortion." They emphasized, "When the Self-Help Clinic means abortion we refer to it as abortion. . . . Our advanced groups must not be misrepresented if they are going to continue to work effectively for all women."[35]

Lorraine later wrote, "We saw the possibilities of using the non-traumatic method for reasons other than early abortion. We had practiced on one another during our menstrual periods and we learned that introducing a four-millimeter cannula into the os of the cervix caused very little pain so that it was unnecessary to use any anesthetic. We learned that simple sterile techniques were sufficient, since there was no breaking of the skin or scraping of tissue. We also learned that it was possible to extract the major portion, or all, of the typical menstrual period."[36] They would write that, with a Del-Em, "Women could free themselves of heavy, crampy periods, or avoid having a period if it would interfere with travel, vacation or perhaps an athletic event, and could extract the contents of the uterus if there was the possibility of unwanted pregnancy."[37]

The West Coast Sisters knew they couldn't openly practice abortions, so they went to lengths to distinguish their practice from the one performed by physicians. Menstrual extraction was a form of "research into women's health needs."[38] It was a "home-care procedure" in which "the woman having her flow extracted controls all aspects of [it]," as opposed to a clinical procedure administered by a doctor.[39] It was practiced not by individuals but by groups of people working together to build skills.

The objective of menstrual extraction was not *necessarily* pregnancy termination, because, according to the story the West Coast Sisters told, it was usually performed on or around the first day of a person's expected period, before the person could know if they were pregnant.[40] Or before a person would think or choose to use the term "pregnant" to describe themselves. Of course, if a person didn't want to be, or didn't want to become *more*, pregnant, an extraction would ensure that they weren't, or wouldn't. And if a person suspected they *had* been pregnant, the group would check the contents of the jar for chorionic villi—yellowish tissue with branchlike structures, or products of conception—to confirm that the pregnancy had been removed.[41] But even so, for early self-helpers (and for some later self-helpers, too), an abortion resulting from an extraction was not so much an aim as a corollary to an action that people who could become pregnant could take to assert their right to bleed.

The story that menstrual extraction was "not a euphemism for abortion," at least in the beginning, was both a practical front and a challenge to mainstream definitions of pregnancy. Moreover, underground self-help understood itself as a form of collective knowledge production and shared care. The West Coast Sisters emphasized that "sisterhood is safety." As much as it was about learning a technical procedure, menstrual extraction was about "sisters learning from sisters and helping other sisters to fully realize their control over their own bodies."[42] West Coast Sister Debi Law said at one point, "Menstrual extraction is much more than the technique. It is also the setting, the close community of women, the information sharing, the simple answer to our need."[43]

Murphy observes, "ME [menstrual extraction] was out of time in relation to abortion. Abortion law did not apply to the first moments of a predicted missed period. . . . ME materialized its object as 'menses' indifferent to the presence or absence of a zygote."[44] Through its proclaimed "indifference" to whether the recipient of an extraction was pregnant according to the medical establishment, menstrual extraction, or underground abortion self-help, as I've argued, created an autonomous zone outside of the clinic, the law, the commodity (as Murphy points out, too), and mainstream medical definitions of the female reproductive system and cycle.

Practically speaking, however, underground self-helpers across the decades were *not* indifferent to the presence or absence of an embryo. Determining whether a potential recipient of an extraction could be or was pregnant affected how a group would measure risks and go forward (or not) with a procedure. In fact, determining how pregnant a person was using only eyes and hands was a skill that self-helpers worked to develop.

FOR PRACTICAL REASONS, the presence or absence of an embryo mattered. For political reasons, it did not. "Why did you decide to call the Del-Em procedure 'menstrual extraction' and not 'suction abortion'?" I asked Carol over the phone in May 2022. A draft of the *Dobbs* decision had just been leaked.[45] Carol's mind was going a million miles per hour. Here's what she told me:

> To practice the procedure, we had to start using ourselves, our own uteruses. [The concept of menstrual extraction] arose out of our gaining that familiarity. Lorraine pointed out that the way we think is When are we going to get our period? And if we don't get our period, we begin to think that maybe we're pregnant. And we keep wanting to have our period. If we can take some herb and bring it on or something, we think, well, good, I brought on my period. It's a seamless thing. We're not visualizing an embryo. We're just thinking, I'm pregnant, I don't want to be, how can I not be pregnant.
>
> It's not that people are ignorant. It's just that when it's your body, you're not caught up in these categories. It's the patriarchy that makes the categories. Lorraine was looking at it from *our* point of view. It was from that point that we proceeded.

The self-helpers' initial project of learning how to perform at-home abortions became also about learning how to extract their periods because extracting their periods was what they had to do to become proficient in a procedure that would help them help each other not be pregnant. To subscribe to a categorical distinction between abortion and menstrual extraction was to submit to a patriarchal understanding of the body, the female cycle, pregnancy, and fertility control. For the West Coast Sisters, to receive a menstrual extraction was simply to say: It's my body. It's normal for my body to bleed. And I assert my right to bleed.

THE CONCEPT OF bringing on one's period appears in many different cultures. Ann Hibner Koblitz points out that in Chinese, Colombian, Cuban, Indian, Mexican, and other societies, "bringing on" a late period through dietary changes, with herbs, or through some other regimen has been thought of as healthy. Many Indigenous peoples of the Americas along with some in Europe, Africa, and Asia have viewed delayed or missed periods as unhealthy and possibly an impediment to future conception.[46]

Koblitz emphasizes that many historical accounts of what is sometimes referred to as "menstrual regulation" do not refer to pregnancy or its possibility at all. This is likely because people did not believe that what they were removing from their uteruses was a pregnancy. Or, it's because they did not choose to describe what they removed as a pregnancy.[47] In the eighteenth and nineteenth centuries in the United States, women considered "blocked menses" to be a condition that was treatable with herbs and commercially available drugs.[48] The liminal space between not-pregnant and pregnant, between contraception and abortion—precisely the space recognized, inherited, and inhabited by abortion self-help—has long been its own ontology for women and others who can become pregnant, across time and geography.

In her philosophy dissertation about menstrual extraction, which she wrote under the direction of Judy Grahn, Carol's daughter Laura Brown interprets the practice as part of "a trend in western culture (that occurred in [the] second half of the twentieth century) toward bringing menstruation into the open."

Thus, menstrual extraction extends the cross-cultural tradition of reimagining the body through menstrual regulation and stands in stark contrast to the patriarchal idea of the body as simply pregnant or not. Laura argues that storytelling about the "liminal experience" of menstrual extraction can be transformative because "liminality is the state of being at the threshold of a transition. It is in being in between or in marginal areas where the boundaries between one stage and the next are permeable."[49]

The principles of abortion self-help are old and deep, and self-helpers tried to understand their practices in relationship to this history.[50] Claiming the liminal space between not-pregnant and pregnant continues to be not only a cultural project but a political one. As people who can become pregnant have long known, we have the power to tell our own stories, and thus summon worlds, in which our bodies and our bleeding are our own.

LATER IN 1971, Carol and Lorraine went on a cross-country Greyhound tour, visiting feminists they had met at the NOW conference.[51] In October 1972, they held a national meeting in Iowa City to give women resources to help them start their own clinics.[52]

At the meeting they also wanted to spread their critique of the International Planned Parenthood Federation. Self-helpers had begun to develop a political analysis in which they defined self-help against the practices, technologies, and policies of state population planners.

Confronting population planners

You can't start to wrap your head around the politics of abortion self-help until you look at the global population control movement that was happening at the same time. The history I offer here barely scratches the surface.

In the mid- to late-twentieth century, the United States–led population control movement helped liberalize ideas about birth control and abortion both inside and outside of the United States.[53] The concept of population planning was popularized by Thomas Malthus, who in 1798 argued in *An Essay on the Principle of Population* that the rate of food production would not be able to keep up with the rate of population growth. In May 2022, Carol wrote to me, "In the self-help movement in Los Angeles . . . we recognized that the population control movement existed, and we fashioned our strategy accordingly."

Self-helpers believed that the twentieth-century population control movement was a coercive imperialist project. It led them to develop positions on everything from international birth control, sterilization, and abortion—along with what they argued were key differences between menstrual extraction and "menstrual regulation"—to global travel, conversation, and collaboration. Ultimately, they advocated for women's, not states', control of contraception and abortion.

In the 1960s, many US abortion-repeal advocates were pro-population control.[54] At that time, environmentalists were pro-population control, too. An NGO called the Population Reference Bureau stated in 1968, "Those of us who live in North America are on the brink of a fundamental revolution in our understanding of environment. We are finally coming to realize that the resources of our continent are limited." The bureau named population growth one of the "greatest environmental forces of our age."[55] The population control movement was considered a liberal one.

Like the early-twentieth-century progressive movement for birth control in the United States, led by the activist Margaret Sanger, the population control movement drew on principles of the late-nineteenth- and early-twentieth-century eugenics movement. Eugenics promoted the reproduction of "fit" citizens.[56] Crucially, both the eugenics and population control movements were preceded by centuries of capitalist and Christian settler state violence enacted against African American and Indigenous women with the aim of controlling their fertility. As Loretta Ross and Rickie Solinger explain, from the seventeenth through nineteenth centuries, the plantation economy capitalized on the fertility of enslaved Black women. In the mid-seventeenth century, colonies established that children would follow the status (slave or free) of their mothers, ensuring the growth of the unfree Black population. And in the eighteenth and nineteenth centuries, to decimate the birth rate of Indigenous people, government officials waged war and enacted removal policies that destroyed Indigenous populations and lifeways. Additionally, US missionaries worked to erode the social influence of Native American women in their communities and therefore their power and reproductive autonomy. Meanwhile, by the late nineteenth century, the government had criminalized birth control and abortion to force white women to have more babies.[57]

While the eugenics, birth control, and population control movements were connected, they were also distinct, and it's important to understand their distinctions.[58] Matthew Connelly suggests that nineteenth-century anxieties about mass migrations catalyzed modern eugenics.[59] At that time, European states began to institutionalize citizenship and, in doing so, ushered in an era of "official nationalisms" and the science of demography.[60] In the early twentieth century in the United States, the eugenics idea that some populations' rates of growth were a problem became more prominent when waves of European immigrants arrived.[61] Eugenics advocated for the sterilization—tubal ligation or vasectomy—of "defective" people. In a tubal ligation, the fallopian tubes are cut, tied, or blocked to permanently prevent pregnancy; in a vasectomy, the tubes that carry sperm are cut and sealed.

The 1927 Supreme Court ruling on *Buck v. Bell* upheld a Virginia law that permitted the forced sterilization of "unfit" people, including those with cognitive disabilities, and marked the beginning of a new era of eugenic sterilizations. The majority of these sterilizations would be performed on women and would target poor people.[62]

By midcentury, the population control movement had started to go a different way. Unlike eugenicists, who sought to "improve" the citizenry, population controllers wanted to increase capitalist development and control around the world. Modernization through population control was posited as integral to the US war on communism.[63]

In 1955, a privately funded Population Council made up of demographers began developing birth control programs to take abroad, especially to Latin America.[64] Throughout the 1960s, the US Agency for International Development (US AID) funded population control work there. Starting in 1967, it began funding population research by the International Planned Parenthood Federation (IPPF), and soon IPFF had affiliates in fourteen Latin American countries. US AID supplied IPFF with oral contraceptives for dissemination that were known to be unsafe. Similarly, the Ford Foundation funded sterilization campaigns in Colombia, and the Rockefeller Foundation funded experimental IUD insertions in Chile.[65]

As the century wore on, Michelle Murphy argues, "Altering the fertility of poor people became a globalized US-funded project in the name of preventing an apocalyptic future." She recounts how, in the 1970s, the United States launched a campaign encouraging countries to conduct family-planning surveys and, in the process, generate demand among participants for birth control. With advocacy and research programs already in place for reaching their populations and collecting data, the former colonies of South Asia participated robustly, and soon they became the focus of the US-led population control movement.[66]

Bangladesh, amid and in the aftermath of a devastating war and famine, and committed to future development, furnished ample data. The United States supported an aggressive family-planning campaign there, which often involved door-to-door projects, such as contraceptive delivery.[67] IPPF set up clinics where manual-suction "menstrual regulation" procedures were offered to pregnant rape survivors. Because abortion was illegal in Bangladesh, menstrual regulation was described as a "form of nonabortion," an "interim method to establish nonpregnancy."[68]

Like Lorraine's Del-Em, the menstrual regulation device was a manual-suction technology for emptying the uterus.[69] Consequently, West Coast self-helpers worked to define menstrual extraction *against* menstrual regulation, to articulate a reproductive politics that was anti-imperialist. They emphasized that the Del-Em was "individually assembled," while menstrual regulation devices were "commercially produced and marketed."[70] As Murphy explains, "ME was fashioned as a *noncommodity*. . . . Rothman secured her patent, not to protect her individual ownership of ME, but to protect her movement's rearticulation of exchange relations as *sharing*."[71]

Self-helpers emphasized that population control policies aimed to control the fertility of *all* women. As Carol put it to me in early 2023, "While we saw that racism underlaid most of the politics of the Western world, and we were fully outraged by the social injustices these policies caused, we also saw that population control policies affected all females in the world of whatever ethnic group and whatever social class."

In December 1973, Laura Brown, not yet twenty years old, and some other self-helpers attended a Hawaii population planners' conference focused on promoting menstrual regulation as a simple, low-cost, low-complication abortion technology for use in the developing world.[72] Afterward, Laura reported that their "mere presence" was disruptive and helped create buzz about feminist-led self-help. "Several women physicians spoke out in support of us and Self-Help," she added, concluding that their attendance was a victory in their fight against misuses of technologies they believed should be controlled by women.[73]

By the time Harvey Karman developed his flexible cannula and suction device, patents for various manual-suction abortion technologies had been on file for at least a century in the United States.[74] But it was Harvey who promoted his device to researchers, NGOs, and state agencies, garnering the interest of both IPPF and US AID, which eventually used it as a model for developing menstrual regulation kits.[75]

The population control movement led self-helpers to argue that a "global woman power" movement was needed to counter the imperial motives of state-administered family planning. But Murphy argues that the self-help movement "fail[ed] to recognize non-Western women as nonidentical persons, or already as feminists; rather, they were perceived as masses in need." She continues, "I have not found a single person from the global South individually named in the ME literature despite the literature's global imaginary."[76]

Murphy's point gets at a seeming contradiction. Self-help required painstaking, durational local work. Yet to confront the politics of population control along with the imperial ideology that self-helpers believed motivated it, self-help had to understand itself in a transnational context. A revelation of the movement was that, just as the personal is political, the local is global.

In fall 1973, Carol and Debi went to Europe to talk about self-help, Lorraine went to New Zealand, and some other self-helpers went to Canada. While on tour, they led "abortion learn-ins."[77] In 1974, Debi wrote, "It became obvious to us that the political and territorial divisions that men have created—of country, state, province, city, household—have kept us isolated in our oppression."[78] Self-helpers saw traveling as a political action that subverted state attempts to atomize women.

The 1975 *FWHC Report* features an article on the "Japanese Eugenic Protection Law," in which Linda Curtis writes about four Japanese feminists—Tanaka Mitsu, Wakabayashi Naeko, Takeda Miyuki, and Fujisawa Noriko—who collaborated with US self-helpers. The article argues that in both countries "abortion has been made accessible for the wrong reason—that is population control." Japan allowed abortions for "economic reasons," and the American feminists identified a parallel between the Japanese law and the sterilization of poor women in the United States.[79]

The issue also includes an article decrying the "neo-colonial" Mexican economy, dominated by multinational corporations. The article tells of how West Coast feminists traveling to Mexico City to participate in the first United Nations conference on women in summer 1975 faced no opposition smuggling speculums "because immigration officials thought speculums were for birth control and that [the feminists] were agents of the population controllers."[80] Foreign interventions in Mexican women's fertility were so normalized, the article argued, that Americans entering the country with gynecological instruments were of no concern.

Self-helpers worked to learn what they could about women's experiences of reproductive coercion around the world. During an exchange about the question of whether self-helpers were Western-centric, Carol pointed out to me, "American institutions provided a whitewashed version of history and no education about foreign countries. We were trying to fill the gaps. We were careful not to make assumptions about women who lived in Third World countries."

The population control movement prompted self-helpers to distinguish their movement from the mainstream women's movement. In a handout Carol created titled "The Master's Plan," she reprinted a table published by Planned Parenthood in 1970, which listed "Examples of Proposed Measures to Reduce U.S. Fertility": "fertility control agents in water supply," "reduce / eliminate paid maternity leave or benefits," and "compulsory sterilization of all who have two children except for a few who would be allowed three," among others.[81] Alongside it, she wrote, "When the Supreme Court made the decision to reform abortion legislation, there were cries of thanks from many women in the women's movement. . . . Abortion will be accessible to a lot more women now. But we must be aware that the laws have not been changed for our benefit, but so that the government can have control over the population."[82]

The abortion self-help movement's critique of initiatives that sought to govern fertility in the name of economy, whether international or national, would continue to inform its opposition to state intervention in people's sexual and reproductive health care for decades to come.

TODAY HARVEY'S MENSTRUAL regulation device is still in use around the world. Known as a manual vacuum aspirator (MVA), it is industrially manufactured by the reproductive health services NGO Ipas, which also teaches health workers how to use it. In Bangladesh, menstrual regulation with the Ipas MVA is legal, even though abortion is not (with few exceptions). There, if a woman reports missing her period in the first twelve weeks, a health worker will "restore" it using the handheld aspirator, without first doing a pregnancy test; MVA remains an "interim method to establish nonpregnancy."[83]

The right to self-exam

One night in September 1972, shortly before the Iowa City national meeting, the California Department of Consumer Affairs of the Board of Medical Examiners raided LAFWHC. Colleen Wilson and Carol were arrested—Colleen for fitting a diaphragm, and Carol for teaching someone how to examine her cervix and apply yogurt to treat a yeast condition—and both charged with practicing medicine without a license.[84]

The LA feminists were outraged. They declared, "We are going to use this opportunity to . . . focus public attention on women's health needs."[85] Colleen pleaded guilty to fitting a diaphragm. But Carol fought the charge, and she was found not guilty with the defense that she had practiced a home remedy, not medicine. The feminist newspaper *off our backs* cavalierly named the incident the "great yogurt conspiracy."[86] But the implications were serious: Carol's acquittal was a win in that it helped establish a person's right to self-exam in California.[87] Moreover, the coordinated attack on the clinic by a nexus of regulatory agencies signaled the state's investment in policing the sexuality of women, even as the national discourse around abortion continued to liberalize.

Once the law stands trial . . . it will collapse

Abortion self-help was not the first radical abortion defense movement in the United States in the twentieth century. Surprisingly underacknowledged by contemporary activists is the Society for Humane Abortion / Association to Repeal Abortion Laws (SHA / ARAL), which was based in the Bay Area. That is to say, the work of Pat Maginnis, Rowena Gurner, and Lana Clarke Phelan.

Throughout the 1960s, Pat, Rowena, and Lana tried to get arrested for breaking abortion laws in hopes of jump-starting the process of repealing those laws. They also helped thousands of women access illegal abortions and taught some women how to induce their own. SHA was the aboveground advocacy arm of their work, and ARAL was the underground referral and illegal-activities arm. In an SHA newsletter, they explained their strategy:

> In December 1965 the idea was generated of testing the California abortion law in the courts. In order to do this a person must violate the law, undergo arrest and be tried. A lower court may declare a law unconstitutional, but if trial results in conviction, the defendant may appeal the conviction to a higher court on the grounds that the law is unconstitutional. In this case, the abortion law is believed to violate our constitutional guarantees of free speech, freedom of / from religion, freedom from invasion of privacy, freedom from cruel and unusual punishment, freedom from encroachment of the government on individual basic rights. The plan was to a) solicit women to obtain abortions and b) distribute a list of specialists who would perform the surgery [88]

SHA/ARAL wanted an appeal to work its way up through state and federal courts so that the law criminalizing abortion could ultimately be found unconstitutional. They also wanted people to be able to access safe illegal abortions in the meantime. It is astonishing how much work Pat, Rowena, and Lana did to meet their aims.

THE SKY OPENED up, and Pat Maginnis was suddenly wet as a drowned rat. Yellow leaflets slipped from her hand and fell to the slickening sidewalk. "Are You Pregnant?" asked one side of a bill. As she reached down to pick them up, holding her long peacoat against her body with one arm, Pat came face-to-face with a pair of smiling crescent eyes. Lana Phelan had beaten her to the task.

It was 1965 in downtown San Francisco.

Both Pat and Lana had grown up poor, Pat in New York and Lana in Florida, and both had had illegal abortions.[89] When Pat and Lana met on the street, Pat already had one other collaborator; they were about to become a trio.

It was in 1961 that Pat started an education campaign. She stood on corners and invited people to talk with her frankly about abortion and to help her spread the word about how common and dangerous illegal abortions were and how most people wanted to see the laws liberalized.[90] Pat had a dark mole on the side of her chin and was captivating and funny. People couldn't resist stopping when she flashed them a smile.

In 1962, Pat founded an advocacy group called the Citizens Committee for Humane Abortion Laws.[91] Her committee espoused a humanist platform: "In keeping with reverence for human life and a real concern for women and children, the present abortion law must be changed."[92] Pat argued that people deserved legal possession of their own internal organs; the right to abortion was the right to your body.[93] She gave and hosted talks, did media interviews, and conducted opinion polls.[94]

In addition to being an activist, Pat was an artist. Her sardonic political cartoons convey how draconian it is for institutions to attempt to control people's body parts. The cartoons point to the three-headed monster that women were up against when it came to accessing abortion: the state, the Vatican, and the medical establishment. Her drawings depict women or female reproductive organs being chased, grabbed, yanked, stretched, smothered, or overwhelmed by buffoonish politicians, theocrats, and other misogynistic institutions and forces.

In 1964, an activist named Rowena Gurner, then still a stranger to Pat, rang the bell at Pat's apartment. Rowena had been radicalized by her own experience obtaining an illegal abortion, and when she learned what Pat was doing, she sought her out. That same day, she started helping Pat type responses to letters from people writing to ask for abortion information.[95]

Together, Pat and Rowena campaigned for the repeal, as opposed to the reform, of abortion laws, with the view that, as Pat put it, reform "merely perpetuates the concept that abortion is wrong."[96] The existence of any abortion law implied that abortion needed to be regulated to prevent "abuse" and that women needed to be controlled by a paternalistic state. In contrast, Pat and Rowena argued that there was no need for abortion laws and that "as long as . . . 'the law' refuses to care for [pregnant women wanting abortions] there will continue to be unsafe self-abortion, and 'criminal abortionists' ready to meet the demand."[97]

Pat and Rowena started to build an abortion referral service. Through their underground arm ARAL, they distributed thousands of referral kits, officially known as "The List of Abortion Specialists."[98] The kits were updated frequently and included names and locations of providers in Mexico and Puerto Rico, where abortion was less expensive and easier to access, and Japan, where it was a routine procedure. They included detailed reviews authored by previous patients. The kits also contained extensive information about abortion procedures along with how to make travel plans, pack, cross the border ("Your appearance should be such that it will not attract attention"), prepare for a procedure, get to a provider ("If you direct a taxi driver to the address of a particular specialist, he may try to talk you into going to someone else who is 'much better'[,] who will probably give him a bonus for bringing in a customer. Tell the driver that unless he complies with your order you will take a different cab"), evaluate the safety of a provider upon arrival, pay for a procedure ("Always cash"), recover after a procedure, monitor for complications, and deal with the police if questioned ("Say absolutely nothing other than your name. . . . Do not admit that you had an abortion").[99]

Maintaining a referral service and list entailed tireless research, correspondence, and relationship maintenance. ARAL's correspondence with providers abroad was often cordial, but sometimes, when complaints were made, Pat and Rowena had to weigh the need for a provider's services against negligent or even violent behavior. In their words, "If we receive a 'bad' report we use our own judgment as to whether we remove the specialist's name from the list."[100]

Once Rowena confronted a doctor who had been accused of providing an incomplete abortion in addition to sexually assaulting two patients. Rowena demanded a refund for the patient, adding: "We shall have to warn people who contact us about your unprofessional conduct. We fervently hope there will be no such attempts at seduction or rape on your part in the future."[101] Sometimes she made threats, a tactic for maintaining control over an underground collaboration gone sour, such as in this letter to a specialist (different from the one above), who provided an incomplete abortion to a patient and also told the patient to have her doctor back home refer patients directly to him, circumventing ARAL:

> Inasmuch as you are violating the friendly terms of our agreement despite our many request[s], we are going to provide some further information on our List about you which you preferred us to omit. We will put your real name and your address on the List. This will be helpful to the women. If you have problems with the police . . . as a result, it's your own fault. If you make an agreement with us, we expect you to keep it. If you are nothing but a liar and a cheat, we will simply ignore any of our promises to you to protect you from discovery.[102]

As Rowena reminds this specialist, the stakes of working underground were high. People's bodies, health, careers, reputations, and futures were on the line. If a specialist broke their agreements, ARAL was punishing.

On that day in the rain in 1965, Lana enthusiastically joined up as SHA / ARAL's Los Angeles arm. Together, the three promoted "elective abortion"—the idea that anyone seeking an abortion was entitled to good care.[103] In the words of later activists: abortion on demand, without apology.

One way that Pat, Rowena, and Lana broke the law was by offering abortion classes with information about how to get abortions outside of the country and how to self-abort. One self-abortion technique they shared was the digital method, which involved using the tip of a finger to stretch the opening of the cervix.[104] They warned people that the method was risky. Best case, it would induce contractions and miscarriage; worst case, it would cause serious infection. The method required a pregnant person to stretch their cervix multiple times a day for as long as eight weeks. They instructed: "Squat on the floor. Push and strain as if you are about to have a bowel movement. This should bring the womb and cervix down close to the opening of the vagina where you can feel them easily. Insert your finger inside the vagina. The cervix is a somewhat movable, round appendage that feels like the end of your nose. There is an opening in the middle."[105]

Pat, Rowena, and Lana invited cops to attend their classes. In the SHA's winter 1967 newsletter, Pat, with her characteristic deadpan humor, tells stories of how police repeatedly passed up opportunities to arrest them. They were too busy directing traffic, she wrote, or even attending abortion classes with their friends for their own reasons, or reticent, apparently afraid of SHA. The real reason police refrained from arresting them, Pat argued, was because they "realize[d] that once the law stands trial in court, it will collapse."[106]

A year went by before Pat and Rowena were arrested teaching a class in San Mateo County, where they had passed out specialist lists and abortion kits and introduced attendees to specific methods for self-aborting.[107] The case wasn't settled until after the *Roe* decision six years later, but it did help move the state to declare the law prohibiting abortion to be unconstitutional.[108]

Exasperated with the abortion situation, in 1969, Pat and Lana published a satirical book called *The Abortion Handbook for Responsible Women*. Its sections range from humorous—"Naughty Poetry for Felonious Females" ("Please woman, stay ignorant, pregnant and weary / Gross National Product grows; the economy's cheery!")—to caustic—"Common Do-It-Yourself Abortion Methods or Suicide Routes for Women of No Value," with subsections such as "Turpentine, Kerosene or Gasoline Douche" ("This may work just fine, destroying the fetus, membrane, and you along with it").[109]

Brazenly, creatively, and with a dark sense of humor, Pat, Rowena, and Lana throughout the 1960s called on women to talk honestly with each other about their experiences and to bravely defy the law as a way of helping to change it, laying the foundation for the abortion self-help movement of the 1970s.

Politically, the self-help movement departed from SHA/ARAL in one critical way. Whereas SHA/ARAL was interested in confronting and changing the law by openly breaking it, self-helpers aimed to work simultaneously with and without the law—by running licensed aboveground clinics *and* underground self-help groups. The law had no power over them, they wanted to prove, and the rules were there to be exploited or abjured.

Just in case

On January 22, 1973, when the US Supreme Court issued its ruling on *Roe v. Wade*, Carol and the West Coast Sisters turned LAFWHC into an aboveground abortion clinic. Since they had been operating a referral service, they already had relationships with local doctors. They hired a doctor, who extended a line of credit so that they could buy equipment and supplies, and applied for a state license. In February, LAFWHC performed its first legal abortions.[110] Then Lorraine opened a clinic in Santa Ana in Orange County. The previous fall, Laura Brown had started a health center in Oakland, and in the spring of 1973, the Oakland Feminist Women's Health Center opened a licensed abortion clinic, too: Women's Choice.[111]

The West Coast Sisters established the group of FWHCs as a tax-exempt nonprofit organization.[112] According to their 1992 narrative in *A Woman's Book of Choices*, after the ruling on *Roe*, "Carol, Lorraine, and their cohorts focused their attention on managing legal abortion clinics and working on a broad range of reproductive health concerns. . . . Menstrual extraction went on the back burner. Women still learned the technique and a small number of them, perhaps as many as a thousand at any one time, maintained their skills, 'just in case.'"[113]

I interpret this to mean that the Los Angeles feminists' choice to focus on running licensed abortion clinics necessarily forced menstrual extraction underground. In reality, though, it was not the case that menstrual extraction "went on the back burner" or was practiced "just in case," as self-helpers claimed in public.

An FWHC pamphlet from 1973 suggests that self-helpers had no intention of tabling menstrual extraction and that these health centers hosted "Advanced Self Help Clinics research projects." These "advanced clinics," like their other programs, "provide[d] immediate[ly] needed services, help[ed] each woman change her perspective of her own power, and in actuality, change[d] the imbalance of power inherent in our society." The clinics and their programs were "power bases" that challenged "discriminating, sexist, and inadequate health care services."[114]

The pamphlet goes on to provide something like a menstrual extraction manifesto. Here are just a couple of sentences: "We would no longer passively accept the whole denigrating system of myths and disc rimination built around the fact that women monthly have a period and the misconception that she is therefore incapacitated several days each month. We would not even wait passively until a mysterious examination by a physician (usually male and usually 6 weeks too late) tells us that we are growing an unwanted mass of cells."

The West Coast Sisters emphasize the importance of acting on their own terms and outside of the medical institution. They define an embryo not as a pregnancy but as a "mass of cells." Self-help has to do with actions that you take, but it also requires a new paradigm. Bodies that can become pregnant are not passively subject to fertilization, as the patriarchy would have it; rather, they are fundamentally capable of controlling when and how they bleed.[115]

For decades to follow *Roe v. Wade*, self-helpers, both affiliated and unaffiliated with licensed feminist abortion clinics, would continue learning, practicing, and sharing self-help, including menstrual extraction, to have autonomy over their lives and offer other women a non-medicalized setting in which to end unwanted pregnancies.

Chapter 2

Allow Everyone to Become a Teacher

Laura Brown. I couldn't convince her to do an interview with me. I met her just once. She swept through the front room of her mother's house on a day I was there to interview Carol—a gust of loose hair and orange floral-print cotton. As I remember it, she smiled and greeted me, and then she was gone. We didn't talk that day, as much as I would have liked to, but the story of Oakland Feminist Women's Health Center / Women's Choice does start with Laura Brown.

In October 1972, a fearless nineteen-year-old Laura, "full of revolutionary zeal," as she described herself, sent a letter to her friends announcing that she had started a self-help clinic in Oakland. She told them that she had rented a house off Telegraph Avenue, at 444 48th Street. "Drive down Telegraph, turn left down a really grungy alley, go right past that collapsed building with the junked car in front of it," were her directions to the Oakland Feminist Women's Health Center.[1]

Almost a half century later, on my bike, I tried to follow her directions. But from a since-gentrified, built-up Telegraph, I didn't see an alley between 48th and 49th Streets, just a private parking lot.

"It was right off Telegraph?" I texted Linci. "Yep," she replied.

I turned left onto a quiet 48th Street and scanned the house numbers: 448, then 442, but no 444. "The numbers are out of order," a neighbor told me. "Go left into the driveway at 442. It's behind there." Sure enough, behind the multi-unit 442, two tiny box houses sat mostly hidden from street view. A short flight of blue-painted stairs led up to the doorway of 444, its front-facing windows red-trimmed. I wondered how many coats of paint the little house had seen over nearly half a century and how much it cost to rent now.

It was in that house on 48th Street that the Oakland gynecological and abortion self-help movement got its start.

In these next sections, I discuss OFWHC / Women's Choice and Oakland abortion self-help in the context of the movements to which they were most indebted: women's liberation, and gay women's liberation especially; and twentieth-century Black health activism, and Black Panther Party "self health" survival programs in particular.

We realized that the personal is political

At first, OFWHC was just Laura. When she called a meeting for people interested in starting a "self-help clinic," almost no one came. Laura told a local newspaper, "For the next three or four months I answered the phone using different voices so people would think there were lots of us working at the clinic. I'd say, '*We're* doing this, and *we're* doing that.'"[2]

Soon, though, Laura had collaborators. Within six months, two white lesbian activists from Iowa City, Boach Hanson and Debi Law, joined her, along with Fran Burgess and Lyn Tijerina from the Bay Area. OFWHC offered pregnancy screening, abortion referrals, and practical support for people seeking abortions, such as transportation, childcare, aftercare, and Medi-Cal enrollment help, Laura told the *Oakland Tribune*. It also hosted "clinics" for girls and women of different ages, including one on puberty and menstruation and another on menopause. "Our philosophy is that if we understand our bodies, things are not done to us," she said.[3]

Laura had personal experience with pregnancy and abortion. When she was seventeen and still in Los Angeles, she became pregnant. Carol took her to get an abortion at an underground clinic where she had been observing procedures. Laura went with her mom to the clinic other times, too, and learned about abortion work in the process. In 1971, when Laura moved to the Bay Area to go to college at University of California, Berkeley, she started practicing with a self-help group. So by the time she founded OFWHC, she was already knowledgeable about menstrual extraction and suction abortion.[4]

In 1973, Barbara Hoke, a white lesbian feminist from a working-class background, joined Laura in Oakland, too. Born and raised in Texas, Barbara had been living in Tampa and building the women's movement there. By 1973, she had cofounded the Tampa Women's Center, where she co-organized a Radical Feminist Conference.

Barbara was married to a Southern Baptist minister turned philosophy professor whose career had taken them to Tampa, she explained in her southern accent when I interviewed her at her home. Upon their arrival, Barbara was conscripted to play the part of hospitable wife for his male colleagues.

One night, in a house stuffed with loud men, an inebriated professor broke a chair and propositioned the host of the party. It marked a turning point, prompting the professors' wives to get together and write a statement essentially saying, "Until you put us on the payroll, we'll never host one of your parties again." And they didn't.

At that point, the women had started a consciousness-raising group. "We trusted each other and had the consciousness to refuse to be used," Barbara said of their boycott. The group met once a week. "We spent a year together in a closed group where all we did was testify about all kinds of personal stuff," she added. "And we realized that the personal is political. It revolutionized everything I thought. I've never been the same since."

The women who came together to form the Tampa feminist movement were, in Barbara's words, "hardcore" and "all in." "We did all kinds of mischief in Tampa. We broke into a live shock-jock radio program and stopped a misogynist from speaking. We did abortion referrals. I'm sure there were police informants among us," she said. "It was exciting."

Leading up to the 1973 Radical Feminist Conference at the Tampa Women's Center, Barbara and her co-organizers invited

Laura and Shelley Farber, who worked at LAFWHC, to come out and talk about the self-help clinic concept. During the conference, Barbara brought Laura and Shelley to her house so that they could demonstrate cervical self-exam and menstrual extraction. Barbara recalled: "First we all participated in self-examination. We all looked at, touched, and experienced our bodies as we never had before. We looked through a mirror at our own insides and saw that our cervixes were as unique as our faces." There was a shared feeling that what they were doing was radical.

That night, Barbara witnessed a menstrual extraction for the first time, and the person it was performed on was her. "It was subversive, profound, and life changing to proceed to liberate ourselves from fear and body shame," she continued. "I made the decision that night to join the radical women's health movement. I sold my house, got a divorce, quit my job, and moved to Oakland."

What makes a household a household?

Because the tiny house on 48th Street was, in addition to being a health center, home to four people, the space was always busy and crowded. Barbara explained the walk from the door through the front room and into the kitchen: "The walls were lined with Kotex boxes, and there were visitors staying with us 24-7. There were kids, lots of kids." In the evenings, Judy Grahn writes in her memoir, the housemates covered the boxes of pads with towels and used them as chairs.[5]

Even after the *Roe* ruling, OFWHC hosted weekly self-help groups. As Barbara put it, the health center *was* the self-help group. The new nationwide legal status of abortion did not deter self-helpers from learning, practicing, and teaching lay gynecology and abortion care. While they believed that "women in medicine" played an essential role in transforming the institution by shifting the emphasis from product to process and by encouraging skill sharing, self-helpers also maintained that ultimately the way to resist the "destructive professionalism" of "male-controlled medicine" was to take control of ordinary processes such as menstruation, birth, and early abortion and "restore [them] to [the] personal domain" (as Carol put it).[6]

During underground self-help meetings on 48th Street, participants would practice cervical self-exam and menstrual extraction. Before they performed a menstrual extraction on someone, they would do a pelvic exam, or uterine check, to determine the size and position of the uterus.[7] Barbara explained, "The goal was to have a group of women who were familiar with each other. We would regularly do pelvics on each other. We knew if one woman's uterus tended to move to one side, or if someone's tended to be harder or softer. The idea was to not do MEs on strangers. That was an essential part of making it safe."

They had started to crystallize a central tenet of underground self-help: that their practices were the most empowering and safe when done in small, intimate groups.

The health center also maintained an abortion hotline, which was a phone next to Barbara and Laura's bed. As far as Barbara knew, no other hotline existed in the East Bay at the time, so she and her housemates ended up offering crisis and rape support as well. "We were the only women offering telephone support, so we got all kinds of calls for all kinds of problems that local women and children had," she said.

One time, Barbara recalled, the entire household responded to a caller's report of domestic violence. "We went to her house where she had been beaten up by her partner and got all of her stuff out of the house and basically moved her before he returned."

In her memoir, Judy describes OFWHC as one of a handful of "households" that were most significant to the gay women's liberation movement in the Bay Area. Gay women's liberation emerged alongside—and ultimately distinguished itself from— the Gay Liberation Front that grew out of the June 1969 New York City Stonewall Riots, in which gay and transgender patrons fought back when police attacked them at the Stonewall Inn, and which catalyzed nationwide calls and uprisings for gay liberation.[8]

By summer 1969, gay and trans liberation activities were already underway in the Bay Area. The Committee for

Homosexual Freedom had started holding demos that spring to protest companies that discriminated against gays.[9] Three years before, in August 1966, trans patrons rioted at Compton's Cafeteria in San Francisco's Tenderloin red-light district in defiance of the police harassment trans customers regularly endured. The cafeteria was a popular gathering place for transfeminine people, many of whom were sex workers and youth, and when the cafeteria riot exploded out into the streets, hundreds of others joined in defense of their community.[10]

In 1969, the year she connected with the gay community in the Bay Area, Judy was a twenty-nine-year-old out lesbian, already an experienced activist who had organized with the Mattachine Society, picketed in Washington, DC, for gay rights, and published articles and poems that were read widely. But in the Bay Area gay community, she and others did not feel seen in their experiences as lesbians. "Who were women to each other, to anyone, to ourselves?" she asked herself. "We literally did not exist in any social sense." So Judy and her partner, Wendy Cadden, and some other lesbians began holding meetings. As their community grew, they organized poetry readings and all-women dances and formed "dyke households."[11]

"Lesbians made important contributions to the distinctive women's culture that blossomed in the early 1970s, a culture with its own music, literature, social theories, gathering places, community publications, fairs, and festivals," write Susan Stryker and Jim Van Buskirk in *Gay by the Bay*, a queer cultural history of the Bay Area.[12] From the beginning, Laura, Barbara, Judy, Wendy, and their friends were at the center of this movement.

What made a household a household in the lesbian community, Judy explains in her memoir, was that it "centered on particular aspects of women's existence needing reclamation," from self-defense to safety from battery and rape to health care and birth control and abortion information. Households, which were community centers, helped meet women's material needs by providing sanctuary and facilitating access to education, training, and resources. They allowed everyone to become a teacher. Judy explains: "Women taught their skills and gave each other a way to accomplish something or even gain a trade." And in the process, they built a "powerful economic, social, political, and familial network."[13] The lesbian household model informed the structure and culture of the health center and self-help clinic from the start.

You prepare yourself by being in control of yourself

In Oakland, the earliest abortion self-helpers were working-class white lesbians involved in the women's movement and gay women's liberation. Crucially, abortion self-help was shaped by Black-led health movements that emerged in the early 1970s, too. One Black health movement that influenced abortion self-help was the "self health" initiative of the Black Panther Party, a Black power organization founded in Oakland in 1966 that developed programs to support Black communities and help them achieve what we now call reproductive justice.[14]

By 1970 in Chicago, volunteer nurses associated with the newly established Black Panther Party People's Free Medical Clinic (PFMC) were teaching laypeople how to do lab urinalysis and bloodwork. They also sent laypeople into neighborhoods to take blood pressures and medical histories. Alondra Nelson writes, "Through such expansions of responsibility for health outreach and medical treatment from professionals to community members, the Party put a check on medical authority by transforming its standard practice. This course of demystification took at least two paths: first, the valorization of nonexperts' experience over physicians' expert knowledge, and second, and related to this, the promotion of the practice of self-help healthcare, or 'self health.'"[15]

The Panther concept of "self health" was an extension of the party's theory of self-defense: the idea that people needed to work within their community to protect and strengthen it against police occupations and white-on-Black violence and also help each other access jobs, housing, education, and health care.[16] "Self health" involved training laypeople to defend their

communities against structural health injustices, including mal-
nutrition, sickle cell anemia, and involuntary sterilization.
The Panthers advocated a multifaceted approach to self
health. In 1969, chapters began offering a free breakfast program
for children. Then, in April 1970, party cofounder Bobby Seale
made a statement that all chapters should have a PFMC.[17] While
modeled partially after the neighborhood health centers that
emerged during Lyndon B. Johnson's War on Poverty, PFMCs
were autonomous.[18] The Panthers described the PFMCs as a
"Survival Program."

In 1971, Panther survival programming began confronting
and anticipating what the party theorized as plots of genocide.
It ran a powerful sickle cell anemia research, education, and
screening campaign, calling the disease, which disproportionately
affects people of African descent, "Black genocide." The Panthers
made a connection between sick cell anemia and experimental
birth control campaigns, arguing that birth control, too, was
Black genocide.[19] Their anti-birth control rhetoric reflected a pronatalism that was characteristic of Black nationalism at the time,
which argued that Black women should have children to increase
the Black population and further the revolutionary struggle.[20]
This pronatalism, Loretta Ross explains, was the result of fears
among Black Americans of depopulation, instilled by a century
of racial violence and economic injustice.[21]

But just as Black nationalists like the Panthers argued that
birth control was genocide, Black women argued that their liberation was predicated on access to birth control, abortion, and
resources to support healthy pregnancies and families. Black
women began to chart, as historian Jennifer Nelson phrases it, a
"broad reproductive rights agenda" that refuted Black nationalism's condemnation of birth control along with white feminism's
primary emphasis on abortion rights.[22]

In fact, Black women's reproductive health activism began
much earlier. In the 1920s, many Black women advocated for the
establishment of family-planning clinics in their neighborhoods
and actively spread information about birth control.[23] But in 1927,
after the Supreme Court ruled in *Buck v. Bell* that states could

create laws that permitted forced sterilization, ushering in a new era of reproductive coercion, experimentation, and control aimed at poor women of color, Black women began to take pause.[24]

By the mid-1930s, some twenty thousand people in the United States had been involuntarily sterilized.[25] In Puerto Rico, between the 1930s and 1970s, a third of women were sterilized.[26] During this period, the Indian Health Service aggressively sterilized thousands of Indigenous women as well.[27] In total, more than sixty-three thousand people received eugenic sterilizations between the late 1920s and the mid-1970s. Historian Johanna Schoen writes, "The state . . . alternately offered and denied poor women access to birth control, sterilization, and abortion. . . . Poor women were rarely able to gain access to these technologies on their own terms."[28]

It was in this context, in the 1970s, that a Black feminist health movement that advocated birth control and abortion access, along with a holistic approach to care, emerged. Toni Cade Bambara's 1969 essay "The Pill: Genocide or Liberation?" in her anthology *The Black Woman* laid important groundwork. In it, she responds to the Black nationalist idea that Black women should "dump the pill." She writes,

It is a noble thing, the rearing of warriors for the revolution. I can find no fault with the idea. I do, however, find fault with the notion that dumping the pill is the way to do it. You don't prepare yourself for the raising of super-people by making yourself vulnerable—chance fertilization, chance support, chance tomorrow—nor by being celibate until you stumble across the right stock to breed with. You prepare yourself by being healthy and confident, by having options that give you confidence, by getting yourself together, by being together enough to attract a together cat whose notions of fatherhood rise above the Disney caliber of man-in-the-world-and-woman-in-the-home, by being committed to the new consciousness, by being intellectually and spiritually and financially self-sufficient to do the thing right. You prepare yourself by being in control of yourself. The pill gives the woman, as well as the man, some control.[29]

For Black women who want children, Bambara argues, birth control is essential to self-determination and integral to the whole health of women. Frances Beal also published an essay in *The Black Woman* that rejected the Black nationalist imperative that women have children and, moreover, called for women's access to contraception and abortion. The essay also denounced involuntary sterilization. She writes, "Black women have the right and the responsibility to determine when it is in the interest of the struggle to have children or not to have them, and this right must not be relinquished to anyone. . . . The lack of the availability of safe birth control methods, the forced sterilization practices, and the inability to obtain legal abortions are all symptoms of a decadent society that jeopardizes the health of black women (and thereby the entire black race) in its attempts to control the very life processes of human beings."[30] Beal argues that reproductive freedom for Black women is a necessary condition for the health and freedom of Black communities.

In response to and in support of Black women's increasing mobilization against forced sterilization, the Panthers developed their own critique. In their May 1, 1971, newsletter, they reprinted an article with a historical materialist lens titled "Sterilize Welfare Mothers?" The article opened, "When black women were first brought to this continent in bondage, part of their oppression entailed forced impregnation designed to insure future generations of chattel slaves. Now this situation is being transformed into its equally odious opposite through legislative campaigns for mass sterilization of women forced onto relief by capitalism's financial crises."[31]

The article was written in protest of a Tennessee bill that sought to force women on welfare to get sterilized or lose their benefits. The title page of the next newsletter on May 8 read "Sterilization—Another Part of the Plan of Black Genocide," and the feature article inside elaborated a critique of the "genocidal law," drawing parallels to Nazism and concluding that the US government intended to "commit genocide."[32] In this way, the Panthers redirected their argument about Black genocide away from birth control and toward involuntary sterilization specifically.

Jennifer Nelson describes the shift: "As the feminist message of a woman's fundamental right to abortion became more widespread, and as black women began to forge a feminism of their own, the Panthers refined their criticism to accept birth control and abortion when voluntarily chosen. This gradual transformation came at the behest of black women, both in the Party and outside of it, who rejected the total condemnation of reproductive control for people of color as genocidal."[33] By the time Elaine Brown was leading the party in 1973, Nelson argues, the Panthers recognized "the complementary nature of health care and abortion."[34]

The parallels between Panther self health and early abortion self-help are striking. "Own your own speculum. Do you own examinations," Oakland PFMC worker Norma Armour recalled advising her community.[35] Both Panthers and self-helpers prioritized the inclusion of laypeople in clinic operations. They did not seek to reject medical knowledge but rather, as Alondra Nelson argues about the Panthers, "provide and model respectful and reliable medical practice." As she writes, "This transmission of expert knowledge was central to the Panthers' health politics"— just as it was to the politics of abortion self-helpers.[36] Moreover, both critiqued medical policing: in the case of the Panthers, of policing through eugenic sterilizations, and in the case of abortion self-help, of policing through eugenic and coercive population control measures.

At OFWHC / Women's Choice, Black women were in leadership by the late 1970s. One health center director, Pat Parker, had herself been a Black Panther. As I will show in chapter four, these clinic workers took insights from Black radical and other Black health activist histories, inflected them with Black feminist perspectives from their own experience, and brought them to the clinic.

2930 McClure Street

In the Oakland Public Library History Room at the 14th Street Main branch, I learned that in spring 1973, shortly after the *Roe v. Wade* decision, Laura opened a licensed aboveground abortion clinic at 2930 McClure Street, a "proper" location on "Pill Hill" (in contrast to the tiny living room health center on 48th Street), home to a number of other medical buildings. A local doctor named Jane Wiley was to perform the abortions, and the abortion clinic, called Women's Choice, was to be under the umbrella of OFWHC. The clinic began offering abortions for $150, which Laura felt was too much. "We plan to lower the price as the number of women using the service increases," she said.[37]

Abortions were done with the same flexible plastic cannulas that self-helpers used when practicing menstrual extraction. The clinic talked about abortion in a way that aimed to destigmatize and normalize it. For example, Laura told the *Oakland Tribune*, "The procedure is so easy that we can't say it will be painful enough to deter a woman from having another abortion; and of course there will always be some who use this as a form of birth control."[38] The clinic provided each patient with an advocate, or counselor, who accompanied them into the exam room, and they were allowed to bring partners into the room, too.[39]

In the beginning, OFWHC / Women's Choice offered menstrual extraction to patients as well. They framed it as an option for people who hadn't yet missed a period but suspected they were pregnant. "They don't have to wait," Laura said. "We encourage them to come in as early as possible."[40]

Even after Laura and her comrades began offering professional abortion care at the clinic on McClure Street, they continued to practice menstrual extraction in a self-help group. Barbara explained the relationship between Women's Choice, which was the abortion clinic, and the health center on 48th Street, which was where they lived and practiced self-help as laypeople: "Self-help was the essence of what was important," she said. "Providing abortion services at Women's Choice was a means to an end. But the point was for women to learn how to take control of their bodies through self-help."

When they moved OFWHC from the living room space on 48th Street to the building on McClure Street, the feminists held their self-help group meetings at their various homes. "The self-help group was homey," Barbara said. "It was personal and closed."

Barbara remembered how women came to study with them on McClure Street, wanting to learn how to start a clinic, how to find and hire doctors, provide abortion counseling, deal with pathology, and more. "Women came to learn about what a feminist abortion entailed," Barbara said. "And the essence of feminist abortion was the self-help group and self-exam."

There, at the office on McClure Street, Women's Choice, along with its container organization, OFWHC, would operate for two more decades.

"How did it look and how did it feel?" Linci asked, repeating back my question to her in one of our interviews. "It looked like a nice place. It was clean. It was well kept. Everything was well-used, but it was spotless." She added, "You had one-on-one contact. All the way through, you were guided by a woman who was your ally. And that person was *with* you."

AS OF A few years ago, the building still housed medical offices. You followed the brick walkway to the side entrance, Linci explained. Right away, you went up a short flight of stairs. The first floor, she said, was home to a couple of admin offices, a childcare room, and the sperm bank (more about that in chapter five).

Another flight of stairs took you up to the second floor where the waiting room was, along with the exam rooms and lab. It was there that clients received counseling, physical exams, procedures, and aftercare. I handed Linci my research notebook and pen, and she drew me a detailed floor plan from memory.

When I visited McClure Street myself, the sectioning of the space looked different from in Linci's drawing. There had been a renovation. Standing in the light from the original semi-opaque glass windows that brightened the second-floor landing, I thought of all the health workers, doctors, patients, partners, family, friends of patients, and others who had stood in that spot, feeling tired or stressed out, or strong and grateful, or safe, less alone. But it wasn't a feminist women's health center anymore. So I walked down the stairs and out the door.

Confronting the mechanistic, chemical model

In April 1974, three years after the first self-help meeting in Venice, OFWHC hosted a conference on menstrual extraction. According to the facilitators—Carol, Lorraine, Shelley Farber, and Francie Hornstein from Los Angeles, and Laura and Debi from Oakland—the purpose was to give accurate information about menstrual extraction to the health care community and media.

The conference proceedings themselves, crammed with text, technical and anatomical illustrations, and black-and-white photographs, suggest a more ambitious agenda. It's clear that the facilitators aimed to show that menstrual extraction was essential to the larger project of transferring women's health care to women's hands. Laura was quoted in a conference news release saying, "We recognize that there are those who define what we are doing as illegal. . . . We, in the Women's Movement however, have never questioned our right to or the legality of controlling our own bodies."[41]

That morning in April, the San Francisco hotel conference room hummed as participants introduced themselves to each other and shuffled to find open seats. The air was bright and thick with the smell of brewing coffee. Francie, a director at LAFWHC, stood at the podium wearing a plaid suitcoat. She leaned in toward the microphone and gave a cordial welcome. Pat Maginnis and Lana Clarke Phelan from the Society for Humane Abortion were both in the room, Francie noted, before welcoming Carol, the day's first speaker, to the podium.

Even if they didn't know Carol personally, many people in the audience knew of her, thanks to the yogurt conspiracy. With her pointer finger, Carol nudged her thick oval frames into place and began to speak. The topic of Carol's talk was not menstrual extraction but the self-help clinic more broadly. She asserted that the aim of self-help was to wield collective force to gain control of women's medicine. She knew that she was speaking to a room where some people in attendance had power inside of the medical institution.

"It [isn't] enough to become more sophisticated consumers or to form lobbies to pressure delivery or to become more able to take care of our everyday health needs including the regulation of our menstrual periods," she said. "All of these are vital steps, but our eventual goal must be to control the institution." Carol noted that 80 percent of trained health workers were women. "The self-help movement and the women in medicine must join forces to challenge and displace the present medical authorities and bring a new age of enlightened and human health care," she argued.[42]

In her talk, Carol discussed diethylstilbestrol (DES), a drug prescribed to pregnant women from the 1940s to 1970s to prevent miscarriage, which was found, in 1971, to cause cancers in women whose mothers took it.[43] In 1974, the longer-term effects of widely used chemical compounds were just starting to be known, including their effects on reproductive organs. DDT had been banned in the United States just two years before, in 1972, ten years after the scientist Rachel Carson detailed its horrifying effects on the bodies of humans and other animals in her book *Silent Spring*. In this context, Carol described Western medicine as an "anti-human" institution whose primary purpose was to generate capital. Linking corporate science and medicine and state power, she called for the repudiation of "this mechanistic, chemical model" and of "medicine as a means of social control."[44]

Not long after, bright-eyed Laura, half her mother's age, stood in front of the room and held up a plastic speculum. Smiling, she said, "I just don't think I could talk to anybody if I didn't hold it in my hand."[45] The audience laughed. Some of them knew her; those who didn't were immediately won over.

Like Carol's, Laura's talk was incisive and had the room rapt. Laura argued that menstrual extraction was women-controlled research that directly challenged racist and sexist "conventional research." To communicate the reckless nature of this conventional research, she cited the profit-driven development and distribution of the Dalkon Shield, a crab-shaped IUD that caused numerous infections and even the deaths of seventeen people (it was taken off the market shortly after the conference) and that helped bring about the 1976 Medical Device Regulation Act.[46] Laura cited the charges of practicing medicine without a license that had been brought against self-helpers, pointing at the hypocrisy: "Education is illegal [while] experimentation is not."[47]

After the talks, the facilitators invited the audience up to the front to watch them perform a menstrual extraction. A volunteer named Mary lay on a disposable chux pad on top of a table, naked from the waist down. Another self-helper stood at her feet, holding a flashlight. First Laura demonstrated a pelvic exam on Mary. One facilitator narrated the exam as Laura performed it: "Putting your fingers underneath the cervix, very gently press in the upward direction because the uterus behind it is usually sensitive. With the hand on Mary's abdomen, she's going to very gently press down. By bringing the uterus upward and the fingers downward, we're trying to, and usually able to, locate the uterus between our fingers. A little rubber ball. This way we can find the position and the size."[48]

Then Laura performed the menstrual extraction. She detailed each step along with what she was feeling with her hands: "What I'm feeling is your uterus in a position being tipped downward, as opposed to angled to the back, which seems a very common position for many women." She explained the instruments and sterile technique before inserting the cannula through the os and into the uterus. Frequently she asked Mary whether she was in any pain. In turn, Mary described how each step felt for her. After the extraction, the facilitators fielded questions about the procedure and other birth control methods.[49]

At the end of the day, Debi spoke about how self-helpers actively collected data to ensure quality care, reiterating, "Not one of us is interested in continuing to extract our periods if it is harmful to us." She explained that in every self-help group, at least one person had studied with an even more experienced group. Thus, menstrual extraction was a "necessarily slow process of dissemination." Debi concluded, "The motto of the French midwives of the 18th century . . . clearly illustrates our respect for our bodies, 'Be careful to do no harm.' And this is how we have proceeded."[50]

Communication, a focus on process, quality control, cautious action, and the prevention of harm were the hallmarks of underground self-help, argued the facilitators. For some conference participants, these takeaways were what stuck in their minds. For others, it was the structural critiques and revolutionary calls to action of earlier in the day that resonated. For others still, it all came together in a synthesis, and it was these others who would seek out the self-help clinic again to learn more.

Simply the hardest work

Shortly before the conference on menstrual extraction, in March 1974, a representative from the Berkeley Food and Drug Administration office visited OFWHC / Women's Choice. He told Laura that their office had been contacted by the Office of Medical Devices in Maryland. He warned her that the Food and Drug Administration (FDA) could file lawsuits, make arrests, and seize menstrual extraction kits at the post office.[51]

State agencies harassed other clinics, too. In 1975 and 1976, the Los Angeles State Health Department and Department of Consumer Affairs alleged that LAFWHC was "exceeding the limits of their license" or operating without a license altogether, which the clinic denied.[52] Carol replied with letters to Consumer Affairs reporting harassment: "This covert investigation is tantamount to harassment of a legitimate organization which is in the forefront of change, changes which some people wish to hold back by any means, fair or foul."[53]

State intimidation efforts did not stop self-helpers. In 1975, OFWHC/Women's Choice, LAFWHC, and Orange County FWHC joined forces to form the Federation of Feminist Women's Health Centers—an umbrella organization under which they could collaborate on research, education, advocacy, and publishing projects.[54] Other FWHCs (Atlanta, Chico, and Detroit) would eventually join, too.

By the fall of 1974, OFWHC/Women's Choice was busy most days of the week. With throw pillows and used furniture in the waiting room, and art and ephemera decorating the walls, McClure Street had started to feel like a home. The health center held different clinics on different days of the week, on topics including abortion, gynecology, vasectomy, infertility, and STI screening. Abortion clinics were held three times a week, gynecology clinics twice weekly, and a vasectomy clinic once a week. A male urologist, assisted by two male advocates, performed the vasectomies while women health workers facilitated the vasectomy clinic itself.[55]

Barbara described how intense the work was: "Working for the health center was more than a full-time job. I had been a public school teacher and worked for the Farmworker Association of Florida. I coordinated the state grape boycott for the United Farm Workers. I knew about hard work and taking responsibility. But my work at the health center was simply the hardest work I ever did."

Barbara felt that the health center would not have been an antipatriarchal and antiracist group had it not paid its staff. "Paying salaries, as minimal as they were, made the health center an outlier in the broader Leftist women's movement," she said. "We charged for health care services in order exist as a feminist group, as well as to accomplish feminist goals."

According to Barbara, the health center used its revenues to help "fund women's liberation." One feminist project that OFWHC/Women's Choice supported in 1974 was the "Free Inez!" campaign that aimed to exonerate Inez García, a California farmworker who had been convicted of second-degree murder for shooting and killing a man after he and another man raped her.[56] The health center used some of its funds to finance the mailing of press releases and other materials about Inez's case to groups all over the world. Additionally, the health center paid staff to attend Inez's trial. "It was expensive," Barbara told me. "And it was the reason we existed."

Chapter 3

The Self-Destruct Mechanism Is the Self-Help Clinic

To understand the intimate relationship politics and worldbuild-ing power of gynecological and abortion self-help, you have to look closely at how the "self-help clinic" was being practiced and theorized in the 1970s.

From the beginning, self-helpers conceived of their move-ment as an act of resistance to the heterosexual nuclear family and economic dependence of women on men. The story I'm about to tell about feminist institution building is a case in point.

For Laura Brown, the self-help clinic was both a practice and a theory: the practice of body sovereignty and a theory of revo-lutionary change. I didn't know Laura was a philosopher until I came across a book she wrote, in the papers of Adrienne Rich Published by Diana Press in 1976, the book is titled *The Power of Valuenergy: A Theory of Feminist Economics.*

"*What?!*" I wanted to holler from the silent Schlesinger Library reading room at Harvard. It was sometime in 2019. I had been reading all about Laura Brown, sending her emails, trying to convince her to talk to me. (She wasn't replying.) I wanted to hear her in her own words, and this was my chance.

In *Valuenergy,* Laura theorizes the "self-help clinic." The book tells a story of a multiracial clan of women living together like "wild and healthy animals" in a post-revolutionary, not-so-distant future. (It is not clear, in the story, what has become of the men.) In a bucolic setting beside a creek, elders tell girls about "the days before the women discovered the power of valuenergy," when "men had godlike power over women and children."[1]

Laura interrupts the speculative narrative to ironically address the women's movement: "You, you Women's Movement, you revolutionaries, you radicals, you nuts, 'Where do you think you are going?' How will you get there?" On behalf of the movement, she asserts, "We are women that have every intention of creating a world based on Feminist principles and values. . . . We need no step-by-step plan to justify this struggle. In fact, such a plan would be supercilious to us since the basis of our struggle is anarchistic." She continues, "We are not bound by rules that require we predict herstory"; a "world based on Feminist principles" would not subscribe to a limiting determinism.[2] In it all people would be free.

It is the embodied practices of the self-help clinic, Laura then argues, that, through their embrace of open-endedness as opposed to determinism, provide a "format" for empowering and radicalizing people. She writes, "Once a woman has looked inside herself at her own body, she immediately turns her eyes and energies outward in an aggressive way. She is able to confront institutions that she once thought were out of her control entirely."[3]

Laura is talking about abortion self-help, but her comments reveal how self-help is much more widely applicable. This is because its principle is so basic: That you have to look inside before you can look out with the eyes of a revolutionary. The personal is political.

The self-help clinic teaches people to start with embodied body knowledge. Crucially, self-help is portable. In fact, for it to fulfill its purpose, it *must* travel. Laura explains, "In any reformist activity we involve ourselves in we must be prepared to build in a self-destruct aspect. In the case of the Feminist Women's Health Centers that offer services such as abortion and gynecological care in a clinic setting, the self-destruct mechanism is the Self-Help Clinic. . . . Creating Feminist Institutions will not free us, but they can be the mechanism that we use to build the kind of global communication necessarily to bring about total and real changes."[4]

Laura makes a distinction between the health center, which was a reformist institution, and the self-help clinic, which was a revolutionary technology. The health center is a building and a business that offers services such as abortion. The self-help clinic is a *process*, which sometimes happens at the health center but also travels beyond it, and by which people share information, produce new knowledge, and transform the social order.

Laura writes, "The self help clinic [is] a way for women to take care of each other and never go to a place other than their homes or their neighbors' homes for health care."[5] Self-help is a tool for demystification and deinstitutionalization. And the fact that self-help is ongoing, not an objective in and of itself, is why "the self-destruct mechanism *is* the Self-Help Clinic."

Once feminists deinstitutionalize health care, along with other institutions, the need for the health center will no longer exist. In the process of these institutions' dismantling, the feminized space of "home" will be transformed into its seeming opposite: the outdoors, "air . . . clean, fresh, sharp," with "sun . . . shining, bright, strong."[6] In this post-revolutionary world, all people will practice body sovereignty and mutual care: "each person is a whole unto itself and a part of the larger whole."[7]

To get there, Laura argues, feminists must harness the "power of valuenergy." In contrast to patriarchy's relative, quantitative system of valuing the world, feminists must revalue the world on their own terms. The multipronged solution, she suggests, involves not rejecting money, but rather using it to invest in each other to ensure everyone's needs are met. Investing in each other means supporting "feminist groups" such as the FWHCs. As Laura puts it, "When a woman invests her money, time or life to a feminist group, she is in fact investing . . . in the growth of the movement that will eventually free us all."[8] In the short term, the counter to patriarchal capitalist accumulation, Laura argues, is the accumulation of capital by women.

The book concludes with a section simply titled "FEN." The acronym is not explained. But the section reiterates the point that, by supporting feminist businesses, feminists contribute to the revolutionary project of spreading the self-help clinic and thus "build[ing] a Feminist world."[9]

Valuenergy's separatist claim that investing in "the movement" will "free us all" overlooks the fact that there was never a single "movement," let alone "us."[10] One could argue that Laura's politics exemplify what historian Alice Echols calls counter-revolutionary "cultural feminism," or a politics oriented toward "women's culture guided by 'female' values."[11] In the end, though, I go back to the material implications of the self-destruct mechanism. While Laura does call for a world based on "feminist values," the self-help clinic wasn't only cultural: it was material. Laura's and others' focus was on teaching laypeople how to do procedures and processes—cervical and pelvic exams and menstrual extractions in a group setting. Laura is talking about teaching people how to intervene in the material conditions of their lives.

It's not that Laura didn't understand that feminist capital was still capital. It's that she believed the only way to gain power from within the oppressive system was via capital itself. At a time when few women owned any means of production at all, she asked, how *could* capital in women's hands help redistribute power?

FEN

But wait. What was FEN?

Laura wrote *Valuenergy* to theorize the self-help clinic concept. She also wrote and disseminated it as an invitation for people to invest in a new venture of hers and her friends.

In February 1976, Laura, Barbara, and Oakland Feminist Women's Health Center / Women's Choice joined up with a couple of other feminist businesses to create the Feminist Economic Network Corporation, or FEN. Their collaborators were Coletta Reid and Casey Czarnik from Diana Press, a lesbian publishing house in Baltimore (and publisher of *Valuenergy*), and Joanne Parrent and Valerie Angers of the Feminist Federal Credit Union in Detroit, the first feminist financial institution.[12]

The group decided to form FEN at a conference for feminist businesses in Detroit in November 1975.[13] FEN could serve as a holding company for their businesses, allowing them to merge and leverage their assets and expand their projects.[14]

In fall 2020, I had a phone call with Coletta Reid from Diana Press. Coletta had been a member of the Furies, a radical lesbian collective in Washington, DC, which was active from 1971 to 1972. She also cofounded *off our backs*, a feminist newspaper that circulated from 1970 to 2008. When I talked to her, she was in her late seventies, living in Santa Fe.

Coletta had a razor-sharp memory and equally sharp analysis. She began by recounting when Laura visited Baltimore in the fall of 1975.

> I became very enamored of Laura's ideas. She introduced me to the idea that health care was not in the hands of women. I started looking at my own experiences. When I tried to get off contraceptives, the doctor refused [to let me]. My childbirth had been premature. [When I became pregnant again,] I told my doctor that I was very worried about prematurity because my child had been only four pounds twelve ounces. He poo-pooed it. The baby was born six weeks early and died.
>
> That thing about not being believed as a woman, that you don't know anything about your own body....And then friends were starting a rape crisis and domestic violence center ...It felt to me that it was all part of the same thing.
>
> Laura seemed to have a vision about where this could go. When I was involved with *off our backs*, I watched the women's health movement emerge in Washington, DC. I watched the women I knew create an underground abortion network. One of the cofounders of *off our backs* was a nurse. We were all involved together in different issues, and we didn't see them as disconnected.

Just as Coletta began to develop a critical consciousness of her own experiences, she became aware of their dearth of capital at Diana Press. "We were existing within capitalism, but we had no capital," she said. "As working-class women, the only way that we knew how to get capital was to exploit our own labor." Laura's thought, that women's businesses could use the system to make money for the movement, inspired her. With more capital, they could publish more feminist books, not to mention pay themselves. Coletta and others who cofounded FEN understood that women's liberation was an *economic* struggle.

From the moment Laura floated the idea for FEN, many people were resistant to it, including all the other FWHCs. Critics asked, why would feminist businesses want to participate in capitalism? But, Coletta pointed out, they were already inside of capitalism. In her mind, the idea that feminists could run businesses without also participating in capitalism was a fantasy.

I encountered a companion volume to *Valuenergy*, also published by Diana Press, in Coletta's personal collection when I visited her in summer 2021. Authored by Joanne Parrent, a white feminist and cofounder of the Feminist Federal Credit Union, *Sowing the Seeds of Feminist Economic Revolution* gave an overview of FEN's "herstory," founders, aims, and governance philosophy.

"We needed an organization that would take financial leadership and provide for the further development of our now infant feminist economy," Joanne wrote. "Self help, the sharing of our resources and experiences, is the foundation of all these institutions and is the foundation of the Feminist Economic Network."[15]

After FEN was formed in 1976, its founders bought a building. Not just any building: they bought the historic, brick, six-story Women's City Club building in downtown Detroit on Park Avenue. They renamed it the *Feminist* Women's City Club. It was to be FEN headquarters. The Feminist Women's City Club opened in April 1976.[16] Inside was a women's clinic led by Black feminists from Detroit and a Diana Press–affiliated printshop, along with a lounge, dining room, hotel, and indoor swimming pool. FEN leased space to shops and groups such as NOW, the Women Lawyers Association, and the Society of Women Accountants.[17] City Club members got perks, such as reduced rates on facility rentals and escort service to their car, bus, or taxi. The "escort" was an armed security guard; Coletta explained, "One of us went to security guard school and got a permit to carry a gun."

By providing escorts to ensure people's safety as they came and went from the building, FEN modeled a practice of community self-defense—an approach abortion defenders would continue to develop as they faced the increasing harassment and violence of anti-abortion extremists in the 1980s and 1990s. In *Sowing the Seeds*, there's a photo of the City Club "opening ceremonies." Taken in low light, it has a dreamlike quality. Dozens of people, necks craning to look up, down, all around, cram the building's foyer, both white women and women of color. That night Gloria Steinem gave opening remarks.

When I interviewed Barbara, she showed me a black three-ring binder, which contained a FEN organizational manual. The yellowed pages of the nearly fifty-year-old manual detailed FEN's story and structure. It explained that Laura, Joanne, and Casey were the board of directors. Barbara was personnel director, Coletta continued in her role as editor of Diana Press. FEN issued stock at $3 per share and invited feminists from around the country to become stakeholders.[18]

After FEN bought the building with loans from the Feminist Federal Credit Union, the cofounders moved to Detroit. "It was heady to take on such a grand experiment in individual and group self-determination," Barbara told me. It was a lot of work to keep a large building running, with limited resources and steep learning curves. "We were burgled over and over. We were threatened and certainly surveilled. We never had enough money."

Also in *Sowing the Seeds* is a photo of Joanne and Laura at the City Club. On the left is Joanne in profile, her posture relaxed and cool. Thick-rimmed glasses low over her nose. On the right is Laura, in a collared work shirt. Thumbs in the belt loops of her trousers, elbows out.

"FEN was ahead of its time in attempting to make feminism inclusive of all women by dealing honestly with economic realities," Barbara told me. "To create feminist, antiracist, antipatriarchal institutions and financial security for women and children is to strike the patriarchy with weapons it cannot so easily take from us."

AND THEN EVERYTHING came crashing down. In her memoir, Judy Grahn writes, "I don't think anything could have prepared the FEN women for the reaction they received."[19]

After FEN was incorporated, the Chico FWHC, with endorsements from Los Angeles, Tallahassee, Orange County, and Detroit FWHCs, circulated a statement saying that "Oakland's politics and structure have moved so far from the rest of ours that we feel the necessity to publicly disassociate from them."[20] The statement's authors claimed that OFWHC "took money, time and energy directly from the local women's community [in Oakland] . . . and sold it for profit making" and that "they are trying to build a 'Feminist Empire.'" Feminist newspapers ran op-eds about the "FEN scandal."[21] A feminist named Martha Shelley unleashed a "report" alleging the "fascist" politics of FEN's leadership structure.[22] LAFWHC released its own statement in February 1977, titled "Why FEN Must Be Opposed." It acknowledged that Martha's diatribe constituted "trashing" but maintained that FEN was "capitalistic, therefore necessarily anti-feminist" and a "tragic waste of women's strength and energy."[23]

After the City Club's opening night, Coletta told me, some Ann Arbor feminists held a protest right outside. "That protest was one of the ugliest things I've ever seen," she said. Amid escalating tensions, several people at the protest were assaulted. "Such a public denunciation and violence at the building itself drove the women of Detroit away from it. They didn't want to be involved in something so controversial."

In response to Martha's allegation that FEN was "capitalistic," Coletta said: "The idea that there's something better about you if you volunteer. . . . That's a class- and race-exclusionary idea. Working-class women and women of color have to be paid to live. They don't have the privilege of volunteering."

Jennifer Woodul, a Fury at one point, too, wrote a statement on behalf of Olivia Records, a Bay Area feminist record label. According to Jennifer, Olivia "developed respect for the idea of feminists sharing resources and developing them for women." She described Martha's claim that FEN was "fascist" to be a "vapid conclusion—a well-worn substitute for responsible analysis." In another piece, she argued, "It's ironic that women who claim to be anti-capitalist are using capitalist strategies as a road to liberation. . . . But it's also terribly creative."[24]

The campaign conflagrated by the other FWHCs, the Ann Arbor feminists, Martha, and others contributed to FEN's collapse. Later that summer, FEN didn't have the cash to cover the mortgage.[25] Upon its dissolution at the end of August 1976, Kathleen Barry asserted, "Part of the brilliance of the FEN concept was the taking of resources available to us in this patriarchy and using them to make women stronger . . . rather than joining forces with the patriarchy of socialism to fight the patriarchy of capitalism."[26] Years later, Judy would write, "As activists FEN put their economic plan into practice before anyone had time to absorb the theoretical basis of it. . . . In my opinion, the FEN women were grassroots activists who were seriously misinterpreted."[27]

At one point in *Sowing the Seeds*, Joanne writes that feminist organizations that employ a coalitional structure spend their time "political in-fighting and backstabbing." She argues that democracy is a patriarchal concept and that "the real issue is whether the representatives, or leadership, agree on goals and values and whether they 'represent' the skills, experiences and energy of the whole group." Joanne explains that anyone can self-select to be a director, so long as they are "willing to commit a large percentage of [their] time and energy implementing the goals of FEN."[28]

There are problems with FEN's theory of self-selection as a feminist alternative to election. There are many reasons why one might not be able to get along with a group (in this case, a group of mostly working-class white women), including one's different experience of race, class, or gender. There are also many reasons why one might not be able to "commit a large percentage of [their] time and energy" to a project: other activist commitments, waged-work obligations, caregiving responsibilities, and chronic illness or disability, to name just a handful.

All of that said, when we look beyond the sometimes corporate-sounding language of *Sowing the Seeds*, the vision we are left with of autonomous, committed participants is basically a description of a political group of friends. The model is portable. Any group of activists can self-select to collaborate on a project they care about. FEN took core principles of self-help and ran with them. However imperfectly, FEN centered skill sharing, relationship building, and taking advantage of existing structures (whether the clinic or the corporation) to improve and transform how people live.

The FEN controversy exposed theoretical questions that divided the women's movement and continue to divide the Left. Is horizontal organizing necessarily radical, let alone always feasible? What are limitations to affinity-group work? What do we mean when we invoke democracy, and what values are we upholding when we do? Is it possible to work through an oppressive structure while advocating for the abolition of that structure? Can a building that you bought be a bunker or a sanctuary, or is it just private property that makes you a capitalist? What structure of oppression underpins all others? What, after all, is the self-help clinic for?

ALICE ECHOLS TALKS about FEN at the end of her 1989 book *Daring to Be Bad*. In it she reinscribes Martha Shelley's and the feminist media's critiques of FEN.[29] Echols concludes, "The founders of FEN maintained that women could embrace capitalism and eschew democracy precisely because they were women and had common interests." She quotes Debi Law saying that a principle of feminism is the belief that there is commonality among all women. With reference to Debi, she concludes, "Here we see the convergence of cultural with liberal feminism. In arguing that one woman's power empowers all women, cultural feminists were echoing what liberal feminists had been saying all along. . . . The struggle for liberation became a question of individual will and determination, rather than collective struggle." For Echols, FEN marked a turning point in the movement when radical feminism gave way to a liberal cultural feminism.[30]

It's hard for me to understand how FEN could have

ultimately epitomized liberal cultural feminism when what went on inside the building was collective skill building among working-class people. It was at the City Club that Coletta and others (Coletta told me) first learned menstrual extraction. That Echols overlooked that FEN was undergirded by abortion self-help reveals the subversive nature of the self-help movement. Laura, Joanne, Barbara, Coletta, and others knew that FEN was a "reformist institution." That was the point: to build a temporary container, inside of which they could build a mechanism for deinstitutionalization.

To change the world order

The collapse of FEN shattered many relationships: Barbara cut ties with OFWHC / Women's Choice. She left women's health care and went on to work in real estate to help women, lesbians, and people of color buy houses. (Barbara comes roaring back into this story later, though —stay tuned.)

Judy Grahn, who ran Oakland's Women's Press Collective with Wendy Cadden, recalls visiting some of the FEN women in Baltimore shortly after FEN's demise. "I found a clutch of depressed radicals huddled in a dark house," she writes. "They were all wounded-looking, haunted, exhausted, decimated by their losses in Detroit and disappointed that they had not pressed the movement forward." Impressed by the FEN women's management skills, Judy and Wendy invited Coletta and Casey to move to Oakland and merge Diana Press with Women's Press Collective.[31] Coletta recalled how much they admired Women's Press Collective and respected Judy as a poet. The opportunity excited Coletta, so she and Casey agreed to the merger. The new project would simply go under the name Diana Press.

Then Laura proposed merging the new Diana Press with OFWHC / Women's Choice. Laura, enthusiastic about having her hands in both projects, became publisher of Diana in addition to being a director at the health center. Health center meeting notes, likely authored by Laura, stated: "There are two important factors that make the [OFWHC / Women's Choice] alliance with Diana Press both financially and politically feasible and logical. . . . Diana Press is a good financial investment. They can and will make money with the injection of capital necessary to expand rapidly. . . . Politically there is not a group in the world that we are as close to as Diana Press. . . . The larger and stronger we are the more the real the possibility of victory for us all."[32] By investing in Diana in the short run, the health center could use revenues from the press to help fortify itself for the long run.

I was working in the Diana Press Records at University of California, Los Angeles, poring over Laura's detailed notes when I learned of "the alliance." I wanted to get the story on Diana Press to write an article about it, and I was also working on what I thought would be an article about OFWHC / Women's Choice. That Diana and the health center were the same organization for a time was news to me.

After working at the press during the day, Coletta told me, people from Diana would go over to McClure Street and work abortion clinics in the evening. They were paid by the clinic as contract workers. They were subsidized by the clinic, she explained, because Diana didn't yet have the cash flow to pay them. In this way, press workers learned about abortion work, and abortion workers, in turn, learned about printing and binding.

It occurred to me that their work, all of it, was about creating the material conditions for empowerment. Reproductive autonomy, predicated on birth control and abortion access, and a radical education, predicated on access to books and other media, were fundamental to liberation. Of course, one could argue that the very nature of labor under capitalism is to alienate and enslave people and that the feminists were misguided in thinking that running small businesses could help them and others get free. But that conclusion strikes me (as it did the FEN women) as idealistic, foregone, and largely out of touch with what they were actually making happen on the ground. It's true that the feminists worked double shifts and were underpaid. And, at the same time, their work helped other women get abortions and encounter the paradigms of working-class feminism and Black radicalism.

As I read through hundreds of pages of Diana Press–OFWHC notes, memos, and financial reports, I learned that, despite their goal of achieving economic stability, the Diana and health center women were mostly destitute. To make ends meet, they lived together and shared food, clothing, and other expenses. In spite of their poverty, they were productive. With the help of abortion- and gynecology-clinic revenues, by 1977 Judy's poetry collection *She Who* was in production, and Black lesbian feminist Pat Parker's poetry collection *Womanslaughter* was next up.

The Diana Press–OFWHC group kept meticulous records of "woman hours" worked and dollars spent. They tracked numbers of abortions performed alongside costs to maintain publishing, platemaking, collating, and binding equipment. Schedules for book printing and distribution appear alongside notes about menstrual extraction kits, and names of newly hired typesetters alongside those of new nurse practitioners.[33] In seeming contradiction, through their work, Diana Press–OFWHC feminists learned firsthand what it took to create the material conditions for a more liberated existence.

Then, on October 25, 1977, everything came to a screeching halt when vandals broke into Diana Press. They damaged or destroyed thousands of dollars in books and equipment. Judy explains: "The damage had been very calculated. Chemicals and abrasive powders were poured into the delicate rubber rollers and other movable parts of our presses; sticky ink, just short of the consistency of tar, had been poured over the desks and over big pallets of finished books waiting to be shipped. . . . Particular attention had been paid in the photographic section, where large sheets of film layout pages, representing several books in process, were piled into a calf-high clutter of debris. The pages, expensive to create and crucial to the process of making plates for printing, had been torn, crushed, and drenched in ink."[34]

The vandalism was devastating, and, as Judy suggests, targeted. Who would do something like that? The Christian Right? The FBI or an FBI-infiltrated group within the movement? Enemies within the women's movement? They agonized over the question, but there was no way to know.[35] It's crushing to read

Judy's speculations at the end of her memoir. She knew that what they had made—the press, the health center, all of it—was revolutionary.

After the vandalism, Judy was ill for months on end. Laura and Pat turned their full attention to the health center. Coletta continued the work of Diana through 1978, after which the project folded. There would be other women's presses, Judy points out, but "none . . . as avidly ambitious as Diana Press."[36]

At one point, I came across some words the Diana staff wrote, which summed up why they were willing to risk so much for their feminist institution-building project, and that, to me, also captured the spirit of gynecological and abortion self-help. They wrote, "We work on the premise that if women are serious about changing the world order, we must learn to produce what we need. Otherwise our revolution would be based on forcing others to do what we cannot, or will not, do for ourselves."[37]

Chapter 4

Why Would You Not Want to Know What's Up in There?

In October 1977, twenty-seven-year-old Rosie Jiménez died from the complications of an illegal abortion. Rosie was Mexican American from Texas, the daughter of migrant farmers, and mother of a five-year-old. When she became pregnant, she was studying to become a teacher.

Rosie faced a choice: spend her scholarship money on tuition or on an out-of-pocket legal abortion. She didn't have the option of using her Medicaid insurance to cover the procedure, due to a new law called the Hyde Amendment that prohibited federal funding for abortion. She chose to spend the money on tuition so she could finish school and to have an illegal abortion, which was less expensive. Afterward, she started to run a fever. She was hospitalized and, a week later, died of septic shock. Rosie is the first person known to have died from an unsafe illegal abortion after the Hyde Amendment went into effect.[1]

Let me tell you more about the Hyde Amendment. In the years after the *Roe v. Wade* ruling, abortion opponents began to target public funding for abortion. In doing so, they attacked poor women. By the late 1970s, American attitudes about welfare programs were already hostile and racist.[2] These attitudes grew out of post-slavery-era ideas that African American women were not able to responsibly reproduce and out of the eugenics ideas that poor women's children were "illegitimate" and that they should be discouraged from having them.[3] Also by the late 1970s, Republicans were more fiscally conservative and pro-life. So in 1976, Illinois Republican congressman Henry Hyde was able to attach a provision to a Department of Health, Education, and Welfare funding bill banning Medicaid reimbursements for abortion except in the cases of rape, incest, or when a pregnant woman's life was endangered.[4] Passage of the Hyde Amendment left it to individual states to decide whether they would use their own funds to cover abortion care for low-income women on state insurance. Before the Hyde Amendment, Medicaid funded nearly a quarter of all abortions.[5] The Republican (and sometimes also Democrat) opposition was that taxpayers should not have to fund a procedure they opposed. Republicans argued, moreover, that it wasn't bans on funding but rather poverty that made it difficult for poor women to get abortions, a neoliberal mindset that it's the responsibility of individuals to pull themselves up by their bootstraps.[6]

Rosie's story exemplifies how the Hyde Amendment punishes poor women of color. As reproductive rights activist Sabrae Jenkins put it in 1990, "For Rosie and for millions of women of color in this country and around the world, oppression is the absence of choices."[7] Poor women on Medicaid may require more time to gather money to pay for abortions out of pocket, and the longer they are forced to remain pregnant, the riskier and more expensive the procedure becomes.[8] Being forced to carry a pregnancy to term is even riskier, not to mention degrading and dehumanizing.[9] Moreover, when legal abortion is not accessible, poor women may experience more coercion around sterilization, even today with more conditions for eligibility required by Medicaid, and also around long-acting reversible contraceptives (IUDs and implants).[10]

The Hyde Amendment hits Indigenous women especially hard. For health care, Indigenous people often rely on the Indian Health Service (IHS), a federal program that, under Hyde, does not provide or cover the cost of abortion in most cases. To make matters worse, settler colonialism perpetuates conditions in which Indigenous women are at higher risk of being sexually assaulted or becoming pregnant as teenagers.[11] They're at higher risk because non-Indigenous perpetrators, who are the offenders in most cases, cannot be prosecuted under tribal law, and the US government mostly does not prosecute them either, authorizing continued sexual violence against Indigenous women.[12] As a result of the Hyde Amendment, Indigenous women are almost entirely denied reproductive rights; one study found that between 1981 and 2001, IHS provided only twenty-five abortions.[13]

Just as the Right began wielding funding bans in the 1970s to punish poor women of color, women of color rose to leadership at Oakland Feminist Women's Health Center / Women's Choice. And these women, in turn, would serve many patients on Medi-Cal, California's state insurance program, which did and still does cover abortion care. They charted what would be the clinic's course for nearly thirty more years, shaping self-help philosophy and culture, the look and feel of abortion counseling and abortion work, and clinic attitudes about reproductive care labor.

We ran the clinic

I met Alicia Jones on a rainy November day in 2019 at a café in downtown Oakland. We sat at the end of the long community table, hands cupped over steaming mugs of tea. I asked Alicia, who was in her early seventies at the time, how she found her way to Women's Choice, where she worked for more than twenty years.

Born in Arkansas and raised in the Chicago projects, Alicia moved to Oakland from Chicago with her young son in 1972. Before joining the health center, she worked at the Alameda County Welfare Department, first helping families get approved for Aid to Families with Dependent Children, and later in the welfare fraud unit, where she became, in her words, an expert in tracking fraud overpayments. It was a good job, but she was a Black woman working in a very white male unit. "No matter how good my work was, some of them let their racism show," she said. "I didn't go to work to put up a battle against racism, so I left."

In 1977, Alicia saw an ad for job openings at the health center. "Since I'm adventurous," she said, "I wondered what that was all about." When she attended a health center open house, she found it refreshing to learn that she could be a part of something run by women. When she interviewed for the job, Laura Brown, in her frank way, asked if Alicia was a lesbian. "I said no," Alicia remembered. "And Laura said, 'Do you have any problem with [lesbians]?' I'm sure I said, 'No, absolutely not.'" Alicia wasn't an out lesbian yet. Within a few years, she would be.

When Alicia started working on McClure Street, she didn't know anything about self-help. "I had never done self-exam before," she said. "A year later, I was a model for a self-exam handout that the health center produced." She told me that she modeled for the breast and cervical self-exam handout because she wanted to reach women of color, whom she felt hadn't been empowered to ask what's inside of their own bodies. "It's *your* body," she said. "Why would you *not* want to know what's up in there?"

Right away, Alicia started working abortion clinics. "You needed people to be with the women from the moment they came in until the moment they walked out," she said. "I learned how to be an advocate [counselor]. It involved explaining everything to the women, going through all the paperwork, making sure they understood everything, getting urine samples to confirm pregnancy, and doing bloodwork." She remembered how even during procedures, health workers used the doctors' first names: Bud, Richard, Melanie. Alicia continued, "It's kind of mind-blowing to me that we called them by their first names. No one called them doctor, except maybe some of the patients who were afraid or timid about calling a physician by their first name. The doctors had medical degrees, but they were not over us. . . . We respected their medical expertise and the fact that they were abortion specialists, because not every doctor [at that time] wanted to do abortions. But we ran the clinic. They respected us and how we ran our clinic."

Alicia had been motivated by her experience advocating for her own medical care, especially when she was pregnant. "Being involved in my health care was always important to me," she said. "A lot of young Black women didn't ask a lot of questions of their doctor and maybe even didn't want to know a lot of things. But I always wanted to know a lot." She continued, "I would tell doctors, 'Look, it's my body. You have the degree, but you don't do *anything* that I don't understand or know about ahead of time!' I will always be involved in my health care. Back then, doctors were like, '*What?* Who the hell is she? Just a Black woman, don't know anything about medicine . . . ' Well, I know about *my body*."

The café was warm, crowded, and loud as people came in from the rain. Alicia had an inward gaze, deep in her memories. She never missed a prenatal appointment, she told me. She talked to her mother and grandmother and read books about pregnancy to learn everything she could.

As an advocate during procedures, Alicia explained to patients what was happening and "[held] their hands and [kept] them calm." Being an advocate meant sometimes needing to "tell a woman with authority, 'I need you to hold still, I need you to breathe deeply with me,'" Alicia said, "Since I had been my own advocate, being a patient advocate was ideal for me."

In Colerra Reid's personal collection, I came across a photo taken at the 1978 Bay Area Pride march. In it, a group of women hold up a Diana Press banner, and among them is a petite Black woman in oversized aviator sunglasses and an Oakland Feminist Women's Health Center t-shirt. The woman looked a lot like Alicia to me, so I texted her the photo. "Is this you?" I asked. "I remember that year!" she replied. "That was my first Pride. I hadn't come out yet." She would, in January 1979.

Not long after joining OFWHC / Women's Choice, Alicia moved into a leadership role. After learning about and trying out different jobs, she decided she liked bookkeeping, so she became the finance director. Even after she stepped down as director, she stayed involved and worked abortion clinics into the 2000s.

In the company of survivors

In the 1970s, Black feminists launched a self-help health movement that advocated birth control and abortion access along with a holistic approach to care. This movement grew partly out of and developed alongside gynecological and abortion self-help.

The story begins with Black feminist health activist Byllye Avery, cofounder of the Women's Health Center in Gainesville, Florida, in 1974. In her papers at Smith College, old photos printed with news stories show a young, confident Byllye with close-cropped hair, smiling widely into the camera. You wouldn't guess that just a few years beforehand, her life had been upended by a shattering loss.

In 1970, Byllye's thirty-three-year-old husband, Wesley, had died suddenly of a heart attack. Byllye, also thirty-three at the time, was left to raise their two young children. The loss of her husband revealed to her how structural barriers to Black family and community health were entrenched and connected. In her words, "[Wesley's] death, I think, politicized me more than any-thing. . . . It was truly a radicalizing experience for me. Here we were, two young black people, already got our college degrees, already got the two kids. We were really ready to take on the world. . . . And that was taken away from us. And I realized it doesn't really matter how much formal education you have. If you don't know how to take care of yourself, you're still basically in a state of ignorance."[14]

In 1971, Byllye joined a consciousness-raising group and with other feminists started giving presentations about reproductive rights.[15] They also did referral work. Abortion was still illegal in Florida, so she and her friends connected people with the estab-lished referral organization Clergy Consultation Service in New York, where abortion was legal. In the process, she learned about the obstacles that women faced even with a referral.[16]

This is how, with her feminist friends Joan Edelman, Judy Levy, and Margaret Parrish, Byllye came to found the Gainesville Women's Health Center in 1974. At that point, they'd met Carol Downer and Lorraine Rothman and learned about the Federa-tion of Feminist Women's Health Centers when the Los Angeles feminists visited Gainesville, and they adapted the FWHC model for their own clinic. Even though *Roe* had made abortion legal nationwide, the political climate in Florida remained unfriendly toward abortion, so Byllye and her collaborators had to be strategic. First, they hired a medical director. Then they found a building owned by an established psychiatrist and went to work setting up an abortion clinic.[17]

Once the clinic was up and running, they started offering gynecology clinics in the evening. They also offered "body sex workshops" that gave participants an opportunity to explore their bodies together. "We just really sort of gave ourselves permission to learn who we are, to explore who we are to our fullest," Byllye recalled. "And it gave us such a sense of pride, who we are."[18] Then, in 1978, the health center opened an alternative birthing center called Birthplace, which encouraged people to think about pregnancy, birth, and parenting within the framework of reproductive rights—a central tenet of what would become the reproductive justice movement.[19]

By 1980, Byllye had turned her attention to Black women's health concerns. She'd read that young Black women who had *not* been diagnosed with mental illnesses reported greater amounts of psychological distress than white women of the same age who *had* been diagnosed with mental illnesses, and she'd seen how Black women's silence around health issues inhibited their self-empowerment.[20] High blood pressure, heart disease, and diabetes in Black women were social problems, she started to see. The cause of these conditions was the "heart pain" of being used up by a society that sent Black women to work in toxic environments and then expected them to go home and care for children and households on top of it all. Over the course of their lives, many Black women experienced battery and sexual abuse, too.[21]

Byllye began to imagine a network of discussion groups that could "break the conspiracy of silence that kept [Black women] apart" by centering Black women's health concerns.[22] With the support of the National Women's Health Network, she developed the Black Women's Health Initiative with the aim of helping Black women "control and direct their lives." In her prospectus, she wrote:

Through a critical analysis of personal experiences, black women are beginning to realize that the individual has, to some degree, control over factors promoting health, such as diet, lifestyle, and approach to problem solving. For the black woman, health status, ethnic-economics, and her role in American Society should be viewed simultaneously. . . . This model of self help activism has been successfully used by the Women's Health Movement in its continuing quest to empower women to make health care decisions and heighten their awareness of reproductive health issues. It is essential that this course of action be conceived, directed and controlled by black women in an effort to reduce the disparity of inequality in American life.[23]

Drawing directly on her experience in the self-help movement as a clinic director, Byllye took the abortion self-help model and redeployed it through a Black feminist holistic health activist lens.

Not long after, Byllye moved to Atlanta, where she met the feminist Lillie Allen, who shared her interest in developing workshops for Black women. With health activist Eleanor Hinton-Hoytt and a number of other women, Byllye and Lillie organized the First National Conference on Black Women's Health Issues, held in summer 1983 at Spelman College in Atlanta. Nearly two thousand people attended, including women already involved in self-help projects: Faye Williams, Linda Leaks, and Ajowa Ifateyo from Gainesville, for example, had formed the Black Women's Self-help Collective to learn and practice gynecological self-help.[24]

In her keynote, a psychiatrist named June Jackson Christmas discussed the "troubling interrelationships [that] exist between racism, poverty, health care, and health status" for African Americans, especially Black women. She linked high infant mortality rates, chronic disease, and high levels of stress among women to a discriminatory and exploitative health care system.[25] The goal of the conference was to demand better health care for and thus improve the health of Black women and "heal a sick [medical] system."[26] A workshop Lillie developed called "Black and Female:

What Is the Reality?" facilitated participant storytelling and was the centerpiece of the conference.

After the conference, Lillie continued improving her workshop concept: she drew from group therapy models to develop a self-help talking process.[27] Her idea was that, in small groups, participants could confront health issues affecting Black women and also explore their emotions around those issues. She named the process "psychological self-help."[28] Together Lillie and Byllye went on to organize groups around the country, and in 1984 the National Black Women's Health Project (NBWHP) was officially established, with Lillie and Byllye as codirectors.[29] A blue clapboard house on a hill in Atlanta served as headquarters.[30] "We made a mother house. We made a place to say to black women, This is where you come. This is your house," Byllye recalled.[31]

Another household of self-helpers, I thought.

NBWHP supported women in establishing and facilitating self-help groups. They started groups in public housing communities, shelters, and rural communities, and for youth.[32] In the *Self-Help Developers Manual*, the Project wrote, "The mutual self-help model is a self-healing community developmental series of processes and activities. Leadership is democratic and shared. No one person is the expert. It is a relationship between peers/ equals. All the members of the group use the expertise gained from their lives to help self and each other. . . . No one pays or gets paid. No medical tools are used. The experiences may lead to a recognition of necessary changes within the individual and within the society and to a commitment to make both kinds of changes. . . . The goal is wellness—not elimination of symptoms!"[33]

In her introduction to NBWHP's first published book, *Body and Soul*, Linda Villarosa tells the story of her first time participating in Black feminist self-help. She recalls being unprepared for the stories of rape, medical abuse, and violence that people shared and the emotional pain that they carried. "Yet when I left that room," she wrote, "rather than feeling sad, I felt empowered, proud to be in the company of survivors."[34]

What did Black feminist self-help look like? According to the Project, "We cry, laugh, nurture, joke, scream, dream, hold, hug, touch, dance, sing, play, write poems, songs, stories, plays, clown, draw pictures, make movies, build houses, start businesses. We support each other's growth—not our mutual destruction. We bring our children so that they can participate in building the new communities."[35] Since some women in Black feminist self-help groups around the country had also studied gynecological and abortion self-help, the groups sometimes also integrated those self-help practices.[36] However, the emphasis was on talking processes.

NBWHP built on the futurism of earlier Black feminists—recall Toni Cade Bambara's call to "prepare yourself" for the revolution. The Project argued, "Health, for the [NBWHP], is not merely the absence of illness, but the active promotion of emotional, mental and physical wellness of this and future generations."[37]

In the late 1980s, reproductive rights activist Loretta Ross came on board as a director. In 1994, Loretta was among twelve Black women who, at an Illinois Pro-Choice Alliance and Ms. Foundation for Women conference in Chicago, began to imagine the reproductive justice framework, building on two decades of Black feminist self-help. The group called themselves the Women of African Descent for Reproductive Justice. They emphasized story sharing as a form of collective empowerment and advocated better health care, education, childcare, and other social benefits and resources for poor women of color to enable them to raise children in healthy environments. Reproductive justice also named structural barriers to the health of families of color, such as environmental degradation and incarceration. In 1997, Loretta cofounded SisterSong Women of Color Reproductive Justice Collective, a human rights advocacy organization. In Loretta's own words: "Reproductive justice was a breathtaking and innovative theoretical breakthrough that changed the way that mainstream and grassroots groups in the United States and abroad thought about reproductive politics."[38]

In 2002, NBWHP, renamed the Black Women's Health Imperative, shifted its focus away from self-help and toward health policy work.

The question is whether or not we have control of our bodies

Black feminist ideas were at the foundation of abortion self-help philosophy, and one Black feminist shaping force at OFWHC / Women's Choice was Pat Parker.

In the fall of 1977, Pat arrived at the health center. She was thirty-three at the time and a well-known lesbian poet. Pat was good friends with Judy Grahn and, through Judy, had met Laura Brown.[39] The two hit it off and, not long after, became lovers.

Alicia recalled how she helped Pat get her bearings. "I was her big sister," she told me. "Even though she was older than me, she would come to me and say, 'Okay, Big Sis.' After that she would call me Jones." Alicia and Pat (Jones and Parker) became close friends.

I wish I could have had the chance to sit down with Pat and ask her questions about her work at the health center. I imagine she would have dressed sharp, making her seem younger than someone in her late seventies. Charcoal vest. Cowboy boots. A handsome smile. Had it not been for Pat, I never would have come to the story of Women's Choice. As I was learning about her, I came to the fact that she had worked at the health center for a decade. Oakland had a feminist women's health center, I thought. How interesting. *I wonder what that was all about?*

Like a lot of Black women of her generation, Pat developed breast cancer. She died in June 1989. While I don't have access to whatever oral history she would have provided, I—we—do have access to her poems. And it was through her poems that Pat told the truth about the world around her.

PAT GREW UP poor and working class in the Houston area. When she was in her late teens, she moved to California. In her first decade in the Bay Area, Pat was radicalized by the Black Power movement and became a Black Panther. She also became a poet: in 1971, she published her first book, *Child of Myself*, with Shameless Hussy Press. Judy and Wendy Cadden's Women Press

Collective (before it merged with Diana Press) reprinted the book in 1972.

When she joined the health center in 1977, at the encouragement of Laura, Pat had never done health work before, but she was eager to learn. Her own experiences of structural violence against Black girls and women had prepared her. As a child she survived rape, and as a teenager she became pregnant and gave birth (she chose adoption for her baby).[40] Then, in 1971, her older sister, Shirley, was murdered by her ex-husband, who was only charged with manslaughter.[41] Pat would go on to write about race, gender violence, and Shirley's story in her long poem "Womanslaughter" (1978). In it, she reflects on how "[Black] men cannot murder their wives," because, according to the law, Black women are not murderable. She concludes by affirming her commitment to defending all women against misogynistic violence:

> I have gained many sisters.
> And if one is beaten,
> or raped, or killed,
> I will not come in mourning black.
> I will not pick the right flowers.
> I will not celebrate her death
> & it will matter not
> if she's Black or white—
> if she loves women or men.
> I will come with my many sisters
> and decorate the streets
> with the innards of those
> brothers in womenslaughter.
> ....
> I will come to my sisters,
> not dutiful,
> I will come strong.[42]

Pat imagines countering patriarchal violence by turning it back on male oppressors. On the one hand, she seems to call on other

Black women to lead the revolt against patriarchy, suggesting that they might enlist white women accomplices who share their experience of gender oppression. On the other, she speaks to the broader women's movement and expresses a view that Byllye and Lillie would in their work on NBWHP: if you want to abolish misogyny, you must also end racial violence, which is the structural root cause of illness and early death in Black women.

In September 1979, Pat wrote in her journal, "Am becoming quite the gyn worker. Still a tremendous amt. to learn, but I'm getting good at it."[43] At the health center, she promoted a Black radical politics. Like other Black women of her generation, she rejected the masculinism of the Black Power movement.[44] Her handwritten bio for a Diana Press author questionnaire states, "[Pat Parker] was a member of the Black Panther Party for a short time but found the sexist attitude of the men intolerable. Women did the office work and were, for the most part not involved in policy decisions." She also noted that, after coming out in 1968, her "attitude toward her work changed."[45] Pat refocused her energy on doing antiracism education within the women's movement. She often confronted racism through her poetry: "SISTER! your foot's smaller, / but it's still on my neck."[46]

In a speech she gave called "Revolution: It's Not Neat or Pretty or Quick," which she delivered at the 1980 BASTA Women's Conference on Imperialism and Third World War in Oakland, Pat elaborated her Black radical feminist commitment. She spoke on behalf of the Black Women's Revolutionary Council, the Eleventh Hour Battalion, and OFWHC / Women's Choice. In it she argued, "[An] illusion that we suffer under in this country is that a single facet of the population can make revolution. Black people alone cannot make a revolution in this country. Native American people alone cannot make revolution in this country. Chicanos alone cannot make revolution in this country. Asians alone cannot make revolution in this country. Women alone cannot make revolution in this country. Gay people alone cannot make revolution in this country. And anyone who tries it will not be successful."[47] Pat's revolutionary theory advocates a coalitional approach. Her words reflect the politics of the Combahee River

Collective, which argued, in 1977, that separatism is "not a viable political analysis or strategy."[48]

Pat grounded her revolutionary politics through her health work. She was a health educator and defender both at the health center and in the community. For example, she led a workshop at the First Black Lesbian Conference, held at the Women's Building in San Francisco in 1980. The workshop was titled "Health Issues and Black Lesbians," with a focus on the injustice of "institutionalized experimentation," referring to the experimental birth control and sterilization campaigns forced on women of color.[49]

Pat was involved at every level of clinic work and eventually assumed a director role. As the internal medical director, she was responsible for everything from writing clinic protocols to ordering supplies. In a health center audio memo dated August 7, 1985, she analyzed a series of proposals to reduce medical supply expenses. At first, it was indecipherable to me as a layperson. I'd heard recordings of Pat reading her poetry before, but the memo was a different thing entirely. She sounded . . . like an ordinary person: "August 7, 1985. . . . I think the idea of sterilizing [gauze] 4x4s in the sets is a good one. . . . As to putting chux [pads] under women for abortions, this wasn't very clear to me: Did you mean, using chux [pads] in lieu of sterile barrier towels during abortion procedures? If this is the intent, I would not advise it."[50]

Confused, I ran the memo by Linci. She explained that Pat was considering the question of how best to set up kits for abortions. Each procedure needed sterile gauze: "If you wrap the gauze in your sterile pack and sterilize it with the instruments, then it just comes in the pack. And it's cheaper to buy a giant thing of non-sterile gauze [and sterilize squares along with the rest of the equipment]," she explained. "The chux is just a barrier cloth. So if you only use a chux, it means that you have a non-sterile field. It's not a good plan."

Whether she was asking the question of how to abolish capitalism as a feminist poet revolutionary or thinking through how to assemble abortion kits both economically and safely as a health worker, Pat held the minutiae together with the whole, understanding praxis through theory, and theory through praxis.

If there were ever a definition of self-help, I thought, that would be it.

Pat left us with so many kernels of insight. Here's one from her 1980 speech on the relationship between reproductive freedom and power in the social realm: "The nuclear family is the basic unit of capitalism and in order for us to move to revolution it has to be destroyed. . . . The male left has duped too many women with cries of genocide into believing it is revolutionary to be bound to babies. As to the question of abortion. . . . The question is whether or not we have control of our bodies which in turn means control of our community and its growth."[51] Pat suggests that Black nationalism's heterocentric pronatalism is misguided because *all* ideologies of the nuclear family are ideologies of capitalism, in that they reinscribe the idea that the primary role of women in society is to have children and reproduce labor power. She argues that for women to be free from this capitalist exploitation and, moreover, have power in their communities, they must have access to reproductive autonomy; therefore, abortion access is integral to the freedom of women. And until Black women are free (that is to say, until Black women have real access to abortion), no one can be free.[52]

"I'VE ALWAYS TRIED to follow in the footsteps of Pat," Linci once told me. "She taught me to speak. And to trust rhythm. Fuck everybody. Say it how you wanna say it. Say it loud. Don't say anything you aren't willing to eat."

TEN YEARS INTO her job at OFWHC / Women's Choice, in November of 1987, Pat received a metastatic breast cancer diagnosis.[53] She continued to work at the health center and defend reproductive freedom, while also being a partner and a parent, until her death. When Pat and Laura were together, they adopted a daughter. Even after they split up, they continued co-parenting. Pat and Martha Dunham, Pat's partner from 1981 until the end of her life, adopted and raised a daughter together, too: Anastasia Dunham-Parker-Brady.

Pat died of breast cancer on June 17, 1989, two weeks before the Supreme Court's ruling on *Webster v. Reproductive Health Services*—the decision that would pave the way for the gutting of abortion access. In the last interview she ever gave, which she did on the topic of abortion that March, Pat told the *Bay Guardian*, "One of the things that's real clear is that if abortion is lost, women of color are going to die. . . . *Roe v. Wade* is in deep trouble, and people need to understand that."[54]

We will get through this together

Alicia introduced me to Arline Hernández, another feminist who worked at Women's Choice for two decades. In fall 1979, twenty-four-year-old Arline moved to the Bay Area. From a large working-class Puerto Rican family in Connecticut, she had been living with her grandmother in Puerto Rico. Not long after arriving in Oakland, she joined the health center. Arline had never worked in health care before, but her cousin had been working at the clinic, so in 1980 she got a part-time job there, too.

When Arline started, she already identified as a lesbian but wasn't out yet. And having grown up working-class conservative Catholic, she was still mostly anti-abortion. She remembered her sacrament of Confirmation, a lesson about gender. "You knelt in front of the bishop," she recalled. "You kissed his fucking ring. And then he slapped you, gave you the sign of the cross, and you were confirmed."

Finding her way to feminist community empowered Arline, like Alicia, to come out. (In fact, for years, the two were a couple.) Arline's views on abortion shifted, too. "It was a big deal to come into this group of women that was so powerful and strong in their convictions about giving health care to women and letting women decide what they wanted to do with their bodies," she said. "I changed my mind because of what they taught me."

At the clinic, Arline started working as an abortion advocate. She explained, "We didn't get into [the patients'] decision-making process. That wasn't our business. We believed that women had choices. They came, we took care of them. We told them how to take care of themselves after the procedure—what to do, what not to do. We talked about birth control, how to avoid pregnancy in the future. Which I loved to do, because the women really needed somebody to be an advocate for them. A lot of women were coming in, and their husbands or boyfriends or whoever didn't know. Some women had been abused or raped."

As Arline learned more about obstacles to abortion and birth control access, she became more committed to abortion work. "I knew that for a lot of women who came through, it was hard to make that decision," she said—a comment that registered the evolution of her own thinking about why and how people choose abortion.

Arline knew about the history of sterilization abuse in Puerto Rico and saw connections with the reproductive health injustices in the continental United Sates. "I saw the disparity. You know, nobody cared," she said. "'It was a bunch of people of color. Who cares?'"

Patients sometimes traveled to the clinic from small towns in other parts of California because they didn't want to get abortions near their homes. They came from varied ethnic and economic backgrounds, and some were scared when they came in. Because she was fluent in Spanish, Arline was able to offer translation. "I think the Latina women felt more comfortable and trusting when someone was speaking to them in Spanish," she told me. "Knowing that someone there could talk with them in their native tongue was important to them." She continued, "Mostly when you go to the doctor, they don't explain anything. The doctor knows everything, kind of like a priest. The doctor's education, title, position—all of those things give off a superior vibe to working-class people. But we were explaining things. We were teaching women to ask questions. To be their own advocates and speak up for themselves."

Arline also recalled explaining cervical self-exam to Spanish-speaking patients in the late 1970s: "I remember talking to women in Spanish, telling them it's okay. For Latina women, it was a taboo to be naked in front of other women, to show your vagina. So I would try to empower them and tell them, this is okay, you've got to know what your body is. You have to know how it looks, how you want to feel. You have power. You can do whatever you want. Take it. Just be with it."

Arline, like Alicia, similarly remembered how health workers ran the clinic, not the doctors, who would perform the procedures but who didn't say much and came and went quickly. Arline and the other health workers also assisted during procedures, handing instruments to the doctors.

In winter 2022, I talked to Alicia on the phone while she was snowed in in Chicago, and she told me more stories about her abortion work. She recalled, "The doctor would say, 'Give me a [cannula size] six. Give me an eight.' If the patient was farther along, 'Give me a ten.'" One time, a doctor invited Alicia to hold the cannula for a minute while he held and directed her hand. It was the only time she ever held the cannula, but it stands out in her mind.

According to Arline, abortion clinics "ran like well-oiled machines." The doctor would go back and forth between two exam rooms, each with just enough space for a table and a patient, doctor, doctor's assistant, and advocate. The advocate would hold the patient's hand and explain every step of the procedure: We're going to touch you now. The cannula is going in. You're going to feel some cramping.

Afterward, a health worker would take what are known as products of conception to the lab to evaluate them and make sure the abortion was complete. They also sterilized the equipment.

From the late 1980s to the mid-1990s, Women's Choice offered second-trimester abortion care. Alicia explained to me, "If the patient was early, you had to sift through the tissue to make sure there was [chorionic] villi, which is a product of conception." She continued, "If the woman was a little farther along, you had to count parts. It's gruesome to a lot of people. But that was the job. And if we didn't have all the parts, the doctor had to go back in and finish. You can't leave anything up in there."

Arline shared, "It was hard [examining the tissue] when women had later procedures. I can't say it wasn't. We had to do it to make sure nothing was retained [in the uterus] so that the person wouldn't get an infection. That was the goal: to make sure there was nothing wrong after a woman left our clinic."[55]

While tissue evaluation was happening, the doctor would walk across the hallway to the other exam room and do the next procedure. "We kept the flow going," Arline said. "We had it down. Everybody had a job, everybody knew their job, and we rotated. We all helped each other, and then we'd have a debrief meeting at the end to talk about what happened that day."

In the aftercare room, a health worker would sit with patients while they rested for a little while. "If they needed a blanket, you'd give them a blanket," Alicia said. "If they needed a ride, we'd call them a cab. We'd make sure they didn't have to leave by themselves if they didn't want to." She continued, "We weren't therapists; we couldn't do everything. But we wanted to make sure that when patients walked out the door, they were both physically and emotionally safe."

Arline could still see the clinic in her mind. The homey aftercare room with its fabric-covered bench and throw pillows. The walls painted a soft lavender gray. People in the waiting room talking with each other about their situations. I got raped. My boyfriend can't know I'm here. You want a ride? Are you okay?

SOMETIMES, ALICIA REMEMBERED, a patient would get upset during their abortion and be unable to calm down, jeopardizing the doctor's ability to complete the procedure. One of Alicia's superpowers was being able to take control of the room. In these cases, Bud Gore, the doctor, would tell the assistant, "Go get Alicia." She explained, "Bud knew I could help the patient get to the safety zone."

When we talked on the phone, Alicia described her work in a way that brought me right there into the exam room with her:

> I would explain to the woman, "I am your advocate. I am here to let you know what's going on and what's about to happen every step of the way. I'll hold your hand. I'll

breathe with you. I'll help keep you calm, and we will get through this together."

When I had to, I would get right down into the woman's face. I would make sure she opened her eyes, to help make a connection between us and to make sure she wasn't feeling faint, and I would say, "Look, I really . . . need you . . . to calm . . . down. I need you . . . to not . . . move. We need to make sure that you are not hurting yourself. I know you're uncomfortable. But we'll be done in a matter of seconds."

"Slow down your breathing. I'm gonna breathe with you. We're gonna breathe together. Breathe in through your nose. And out through your mouth." I used a firm voice of authority. "This is important," I would say. "We have started the procedure. *We have to finish*. We have to. You can squeeze my hand as much as you want, but we have to finish this procedure."

Somebody had to get that room calmed down so the doctor could manage. And I knew I could do that. You're right down there in their face, and they're looking at you, their eyes are getting big, and you have to convince this person, "We have to take control of this room—me and you, *together*."

Occasionally Alicia would hold her hand up to Bud to signal that he should stop for a minute, if she thought that it would calm the patient down, help them get the room back together, and keep the patient safe. Alicia felt that Bud, despite being the doctor in the room, respected her authority in those situations. "He wanted me to do it," she told me.

"If you're on the exam table and you're twelve years old—and that *has* happened—you don't want to listen to 'Don't move.' But once you have the cannula in the cervix, the procedure needs to be completed. Or you're going to be calling an ambulance and sending the girl or woman to the hospital. You can't leave it undone." It was a women's clinic, Alicia said, so it had to be the women who took responsibility for what happened.

After abortion clinics—"Once every last woman was gone, down to the last woman who was stable and ambulatory and could walk on out on her own," as Alicia put it—the health workers had their debrief meeting, then cleaned. During the meeting, they talked about the events of that day or night, and new advocates had the chance to ask questions. "Most nights, the doctors bought pizza for the staff," Alicia said. "There were years when I was, like, I don't want to see another damn pizza!"

From sweeping the floors to emptying garbage cans, everyone participated in cleanup, except the health worker who assisted during procedures—that person stayed in the lab to package tissue, sterilize instruments, and sterilize the area.

What was it like, I asked Alicia at one point, to be able to do all the different jobs? "When you go to your doctor, you're not in control of anything," she replied. "You're just there. But at Women's Choice, I learned that doctors are just technicians with medical degrees. For me, being able to do all of the jobs was freeing."

We raised children together

Pat, Alicia, and Laura were clinic directors. They were also parents. In addition to being a feminist clinic, OFWHC / Women's Choice was a place where health workers could share the labor of parenting.

Of Black women's parenting experiences, Pat wrote in her poem "Movement in Black":

I'm the woman who
Raised white babies &
Taught my kids to
Raise themselves.[56]

Pat points toward how, historically, Black women have been alienated from parenting roles by capitalism. First, by chattel slavery, and later, by an economy that continued to exploit Black women's (reproductive) labor power.

As Patricia Hill Collins points out, American gender and family ideologies grow out of the market-imposed binary between "public" paid labor and "private" unpaid housework.[57] And the devaluation of the latter is a product of modern capitalism, as Angela Davis argues.[58] Because Black women's work has straddled the public-private binary since slavery—because they have long "carried the double burden of wage labor and housework"[59]— Black women's labor and intimate relationships have been, as Collins puts it, "deemed deficient."[60]

As opposed to allowing capitalism to define and oppress them through their waged work, the women of OFWHC / Women's Choice, both the women of color and white women, tried to define their work for themselves. At the clinic, both women of color and white women resisted the racist economic imperative for women of color to leave their children behind while they worked outside of the home. All the women brought children to work and supported each other as parents both at and outside of the clinic.

Alicia had a son, whom she'd brought with her when she moved to California. She recalled how her friends supported her as a single parent and how her son connected with Pat. "She was an auntie to him," Alicia said. "Pat was the one who talked me into letting him get them damn white mice! They started off as two and multiplied." If Alicia had to work a Friday night clinic, she knew she could ask Pat to take her son to his baseball game. "She was there for him," Alicia said. "And he appreciated that."

Arline, too, recalled what it was like to be a part of a parenting community. "We were friends, and we raised children together," she told me. "I knew those babies."

In a poem titled "maybe i should have been a teacher," Pat writes about the seemingly impossible task of negotiating a writing career with a job, housework, and caregiving responsibilities. The poem begins, "The next person who asks / 'Have you written anything new?' / just might get hit." She also wrote of finally getting a vacation from the health center only to have to deal with a sick dog and a sick kid.

call Alicia
'What do you do
for fever?'
aspirins, liquids,
no drafts.⁶¹

When I asked her about the poem, Alicia told me the story
behind it:

> [Pat's daughter] had a fever. She had given her baby aspi-
> rin and didn't know what else to do. So I said, "Warm up
> the bathroom. Fill the tub with tepid water. Warm enough
> that when you put your wrist in, it's not cold but not hot.
> Get some alcohol. Sit her in that tub, and make sure the
> bathroom is warm, because you're going to open up all of
> her pores. Soak the towel over her with the alcohol and
> hold her up. Don't let her lay back or go to sleep. Rub her
> body down with the alcohol cloth and water. Put a towel
> in the dryer and have it nice and warm. When you take her
> out, get her all dry in the bathroom where it's still warm,
> and get her bed ready, and then put her in her pajamas
> and tuck her in real good. And that fever's going to break.
> Make sure you have extra pajamas for her because with the
> heat flashes the bed will be totally wet."
>
> I called her first thing the next morning, and Pat goes,
> "Girl, you were right. That fever broke. She was wet like
> she was in the tub."

IN FEBRUARY 1986, Pat gave a reading with Audre Lorde at the
Women's Building in San Francisco. The first poem she read was
"maybe i should have been a teacher." She prefaced it by saying
that there were a couple references that she should "clear up":
"There's an area of the poem where I talk about a woman being
pregnant in her stomach. And after reading this poem several
times, I found out that many of us still believe that women get

pregnant in their stomachs, from the days when our mothers said, 'There's a baby in my tummy.' We don't get pregnant in our stomachs if we can help it." The audience laughed, and then Pat added, in all seriousness, "That's why we have uteri."[62] In the poem, she referred to a case that she saw at the health center of an extrauterine pregnancy, when the embryo or fetus grows outside of the uterus and attaches to a fallopian tube or, in some rare cases, bowel or other organ.

> At work
> start on
> the new protocols
> go to director's meeting
> write a speech for a rally
> on the weekend
> lab work returns
> no products of conception
> call the woman
> get a sonogram
> she's pregnant—but
> in her stomach.[63]

Pat gets at the way clinic work was always more than just a job—it was activist work. It meant being available to respond to emergency situations like an ectopic pregnancy, even on the weekend. It also meant showing up as a feminist health educator in many different contexts, including at a poetry reading. You could say, to use Collins's formulation, that Pat was "constrained but empowered" by her job.[64]

Pat's poem registers a contradiction of "feminist health work": While *all* work under racial capitalism is exploitative, of racialized workers especially, making it the antithesis of "health," feminist health work was also figured *by feminists* as critical to women's survival and liberation. The self-help clinic was a place where people literally seized the mode or means of reproduction.[65]

On this point, I think of the Feminist Economic Network and the Diana Press–OFWHC alliance—how the women involved saw their brick-and-mortar institution-building work as fundamental to their material liberation.

In another poem, titled "love isn't," first drafted in 1982, Pat writes,[66]

> I wish I could be
> the lover you want
> come joyful
> bear brightness
> like summer sun
>
> Instead
> I come cloudy
> bring pregnant women
> with no money
> bring angry comrades
> with no shelter

Pat contrasts the unattainable ideal of a bright and sunny, highly available lover with what she can offer as someone always busy with her activist work. Then, at the end of the poem, she writes,

> All I can give
> is my love.
>
> I care for you
> I care for our world
> if I stop
> caring about one
> it would be only
> a matter of time
> before I stop
> loving
> the other.[67]

Here again Pat writes of being "constrained but empowered" by her work. For her, the caring labor of intimate relationships—

with lovers, friends, children—is inseparable from community care labor and liberation struggles.

In defiance of the nuclear family household, OFWHC / Women's Choice health workers brought family into work and activist spaces. They also treated community spaces as family spaces. As Pat said: "The nuclear family is the basic unit of capitalism and in order for us to move to revolution it has to be destroyed." The practice of intimacy is never *not* political. And political work is never *not* personal.

IN 1982, TO help support health workers who were also parenting, OFWHC / Women's Choice hired a childcare worker. José Alfresco, then twenty-two years old, was seeking a fieldwork opportunity to meet a requirement for an early childhood development class he was taking. When he saw an ad for the job at the clinic, he applied right away.

Health center workers with kids were mostly lesbian identified, and one reason they decided to hire José was so that their kids would have a male caregiver in their lives. When José started at the health center, he told me when we met up, he didn't know anything about lesbian culture, let alone abortion self-help.

"Pat Parker sat me down and broke it down in such a beautiful way," he said. "Pat was the first person at the health center to embrace me. I'm not sure if she embraced me because I'm Black, or because I'm from Houston like her, but she embraced me."

In summer 2019, José and I met at LuckyDuck Bicycle Café in Oakland, his favorite spot—he had his commuter bike in tow. In his sixties, his hair had only started to go gray. José was charismatic and funny, and I couldn't help but imagine him at twenty-two. When he introduced himself, he explained that his chosen last name, Alfresco, meant "one with nature . . . a fresh start."

José grew up in Oakland. The men of his family were among the thousands of African Americans who migrated from Texas to Oakland during and after World War II for shipyard jobs as longshoremen. Estranged from his father, José was raised by women.

Maybe it's not surprising that he went to work at a feminist-run health center.

As the childcare worker, José looked after five not-yet-school-aged children—two of whom were toddlers and one an infant. Years later, Laura would describe José as "grand master of the health center childcare program where he taught our babies post-revolutionary values."[68] One kid called him "Joe Baby," and the nickname stuck. He told me Linci still calls him Joe Baby when she sees him around town.

José grew invested in the health center's work and began taking on additional roles. He counseled men who came with their partners for abortions. He also started a men's group to educate patients about abortion and birth control. "I had the key to the birth control locker," he recalled. "I was the condom king." Eventually he started working at the clinic's sperm bank (more on that in chapter five).

"When you really believe in something, you put your heart and your neck on the line for it," José said. He worked at the health center until 1997, a total of fifteen years. Today, he has adult daughters. "I'm proud," he said, "because now I can tell my daughters: This is what I did. This is how I stood up."

Working at the Intersections

By the late 1970s, only a few years after its opening, OFWHC / Women's Choice was already a political and cultural institution. Maybe it was its proximity to arts organizations like Diana Press, and certainly because it had Pat in a director role, the health center had Black feminist artist star power and connections. Singer-songwriter Linda "Tui" Tillery worked at the clinic, too. Alicia recalled how patients would call and ask specifically for appointments with Pat or Tui.

Alicia and Arline would join Pat for readings of "Movement in Black," her choral poem about Black women's historical survival and power. Its refrain goes like this:

Movement in Black
Movement in Black
Can't keep em back
Movement in Black[69]

When I visited Pat's papers at the Schlesinger Library, I viewed drafts of "Movement in Black." On one typed version, perhaps for a performance, she had written the names of people who could or would read parts. At the top of the page in blue ink: Alicia Jones and Arline Hernández.[70]

The health center also invited the evolving queer community, which produced both tensions and alliances. Working-class Black feminist Lisa Moore joined OFWHC / Women's Choice in 1982 after graduating from University of California, Berkeley, where she studied public health. Now a professor of health education at San Francisco State University, Lisa remembered how her "version of queerdom wasn't the 'normal' one for 1982." She never identified as a lesbian or bisexual. "I slept with gay guys. I had male as well as female partners," she told me. "I was protoqueer, since 'queer' wasn't a thing yet, but the party line at the health center was very lesbian." Lisa recalled wearing her gay friend's leather cock ring as a bracelet to work "just to rile up the girls." She continued, "I never knew how to take that reified gender stuff seriously. Having a sexual orientation was, to me, like . . . what's the big deal?"

Even though she felt a little like an outsider as a non-lesbian-identified queer person, Lisa credited the health center for its inclusivity and for not privileging one anti-oppression struggle over another. "Other spaces were maybe feminist but super-white. Or a people-of-color space but not feminist or queer. At the health center, the liberation of working-class people was important. The liberation of people of color was important." Lisa added, "It was never a question of having to choose."

maybe i should have been a teacher

The next person who asks
'Have you written anything new?'
just might get hit
or at least snarled at
or cursed out.
I got a week's vacation
from work
the first
in at least two years.
The first day of vacation
I cleaned my house
scrubbed walls and floors
prepared it and me
to write.
The second day of vacation
I bought two reams of paper
a new ribbon for my typewriter
groceries to last the week.
The third day of vacation
the dog comes home
from his nocturnal run
he doesn't eat
his nose is dry
off to the vet
parvovirus

he'll die, no doubt,
but I doubt
been my dog
for twelve years
and I'm not ready
for him to die
so antibiotics
and broth every
two hours

and maybe he'll live.

Pick up the kid
teacher says
'she's been quiet today'
my kid is many things
at different times
what she's not
is quiet
take the kid home
temperature 100 degrees
call Alicia
'What do you do
for fever?'
aspirin, liquids,
no drafts.

So the routine begins.
Give the dog
his medicine
give the kid
her medicine
try and get
his stool for the vet
try and get
her to stay in bed
three days later
the dog is fine
the kid is fine
I'm exhausted
and it's time to
go back to work.
At work
start work on
the new protocols
go to director's meeting
write a speech for a rally

on the weekend
lab work returns
no products of conception
call the woman
get a sonogram
she's pregnant—but
in her stomach

somebody forgot
to turn on the alarm
that we got
after being ripped
off four times
letter comes from
the IRS
I'm being audited
for 1978
they want more money
a friend calls
she's broken up
with her lover
and is afraid to get
her clothes
could I please
go with her?
she doesn't want
to call the police
I decide to go
to the bar and drink
woman decides
I'm flirting with
the bartender
who she's been
flirting with
all night

now I'm in a fight

now I'm in another fight
outside the bar
and cop cars are
coming from everywhere
and I remember
my mother telling me
I should be a teacher
and me saying
but I want to write
paint pictures
with words
read poems for people
and I get a call
from a sister
who wants me
to come read
for her college
they only have
money for advertising

and I see me
giving Ma Bell
a poster
for my January phone bill
which is huge
since I called
my friend in New York
to say I think
I'm going mad here
cause my lover
who isn't my lover
because we haven't
defined the relationship
as such
thinks we're getting
too close
seen each other

five days in a row
after the fight
we had two weeks ago
because
I had not shown
enough caring
or commitment

decides maybe
we should be
good friends
who fuck
at least
we do
that very well
and why deprive
our bodies
even if we can't
get our heads
in synch
and I think
maybe
the next person
who asks
'Have you
written anything
new?'
Just might get hit.

—Pat Parker

Chapter 5

Become a Community Scientist

Gynecological and abortion self-helpers were community scientists who developed innovative approaches to teaching and research. They worked with their hands, masturbating to orgasm to understand the anatomy of their pleasure and examining the consistency of their cervical mucus to track their fertility. They worked with graphite on paper, detailing female sex organs from new angles and with greater precision than anyone ever had before. They worked with microscopes, analyzing cultures they had grown themselves and counting sperm.

Self-helpers' community-science projects, which I explore in this chapter, undermined conventional top-down research methods and instead centered nonhierarchical, participatory, hands-on approaches. In the process, they charted new objectives for community science, contributed knowledge to anatomy and sexuality studies as well as to the study of HIV/AIDS, and asked philosophical questions about what research could be and do. When research is participatory, they asked, what types of new relationships become possible? In addition to hard science, self-help community science was always also relationship science.

In the 1970s, the movement introduced the participatory clinic model. Self-helpers also offered a redefinition of the clitoris. In the 1980s, Oakland Feminist Women's Health Center/Women's Choice created a donor-insemination program and sperm bank, the first to serve single women and lesbians. Additionally, starting in the late 1980s, self-helpers at Women's Choice and elsewhere helped develop research advocacy platforms, education models, and health care protocols to fight HIV/AIDS.

As historian Sarah Schulman points out, a significant number of influential lesbian members of the HIV/AIDS direct-action organization AIDS Coalition to Unlock Power (ACT UP) came out of 1960s and 1970s feminist movements. These women, Schulman writes, "were highly effective at conveying ideologies and values from feminism that were grassroots in theory and approach."[1] Their theories and approaches fed directly into their research methods for both self-help and HIV/AIDS activism.

It's important to note that self-help community science was emotional. Camaraderie, curiosity, stimulation, presence, absorption, desperation, grief, and empowerment were some of the emotions that self-helpers described having. Self-help community science was emotional because it was political. "We didn't start out as researchers," Linci explained to me. "But the status quo of the medical industry was denying women's sexuality, down to the microscopic level. We were individuals who needed questions answered. The answers had been denied to us by the world."

In her study of ACT UP, sociologist Deborah Gould writes, "The *movement* in 'social movements' gestures toward the realm of affect; bodily intensities; emotions, feelings, and passions; and toward uprising."[2] While self-help community science aimed to (and did) achieve research goals in the study of anatomy, sexuality, and HIV/AIDS, this community science, like the citizen science central to ACT UP, also emphasized the importance of relationships, attachments, and, perhaps most fundamentally, overcoming fear and shame as part of a process of collective liberation.

A whole complex organ

Abortion self-help asked many different research questions, and one of them led a Los Angeles group of self-helpers to perform a breakthrough study of the clitoris for a book the Federation of Feminist Women's Health Centers was working on. In the process, they honed a research method that emphasized sustained researcher participation.

In 1981, the federation published *A New View of a Woman's Body: A Fully Illustrated Guide*, which would become a primary text for underground self-help groups in the Bay Area. The book contains chapters on birth control, menstrual extraction, abortion, and health problems of women and, importantly, chronicles the methods and findings of self-helpers. In a chapter titled "The Clitoris: A Feminist Perspective," the authors assert, "Using self-examination, personal observation and meticulous analysis, we arrived at *a new view of the clitoris*." Inspired by the lacking or incorrect information about female reproductive anatomy in published medical textbooks, self-helpers sought to redefine the clitoris. They argue in *New View* that the clitoris is a "whole complex organ" with tissue, muscles, nerves, and blood vessels that go beyond the external glans, hood, and shaft often talked about as the extent of it.[3]

Self-helpers named their method: a synthesis of self-examination, personal observation, and analysis. "We . . . observed the changes that occur during the sexual-response cycle when some of the study participants masturbated to orgasm. Then we compared our life experiences to the textbook version," they write. In this way, their method emphasizes researcher participation. Through it, the authors produced detailed description and analysis of the relationship between the anatomy of the clitoris and the stages of orgasm. The chapter also includes original anatomical illustrations by a self-helper named Suzann Gage that depict the clitoris—both external and internal views from various angles—as having greater reach and complexity than previously thought. The authors explain that the illustrations are based on "painstaking comparisons" of existing research to their own personal observations.[4]

These methods are an implicit critique of the idea of scientific objectivity. Instead, they advocate or require trusting one's own experience. Michelle Murphy describes self-help methods as "an attempt to practice research as a political project that could tell better truths." Self-exam was not so much a turn away from objectivity as it was a "reassembled status of the subject in objectivity," she writes. That is to say, the personal is political. Self-helpers relied on their experience not to de-objectify research but rather to imagine a "better . . . route to objectivity."[5] I would add that, for self-helpers, this "better objectivity" could only be realized through active practice over time, as they suggest through their emphasis on the repetition of practices, and the presentation of their findings in *New View* is an invitation for readers, too, to participate as "subjects in objectivity."

The chapter on the clitoris models a gradual, hands-on process of producing and transmitting knowledge. Tissue, muscles, nerves, blood vessels, glands, skin, and more that make up the clitoris are described and analyzed in detail. Upon finding that not all parts were named in the existing medical literature, self-helpers named those parts themselves: "Another spongy body extends inward along the ceiling of the vagina. This pad of soft tissue can be easily located by inserting your finger into the vagina and pressing forward toward the pubic bone; it surrounds the urethra, undoubtedly protecting it from direct pressure during sexual activity. This structure was not named in the textbooks so we called it the 'urethral sponge.'" They also identified and named the "perineal sponge," erectile tissue between the vagina and anus. "This redefinition of the clitoris is no mere semantic quibble," the authors argue. They understood that having an accurate and precise language for anatomy is a precondition for changing scientific and social narratives about how people with clitorises orgasm and ultimately for liberating them sexually. A better framework is also essential for understanding the consequences of medical procedures such as episiotomy, the cut that is sometimes made to the posterior vaginal wall, or the skin between the vagina and the anus, during birth: "When it is realized . . . that if the perineum is part of our sex organ, an episiotomy is more than a surgical incision. It becomes a mutilation of the clitoris."[6]

The community scientists who wrote *New View* drive home a key insight of abortion self-help: that for people to practice body sovereignty, they first have to learn how to be *in* their bodies and how to think and act self-consciously from that material place of the body.

In 2022, sexual health specialist Rachel Rubin told science writer Rachel Gross for the *New York Times* that "[The clitoris is] completely ignored by pretty much everyone. . . . There is no medical community that has taken ownership in the research, in the management, in the diagnosis of vulva-related conditions."[7] It is astonishing that this could still be true forty years after the publication of *New View*. But to be clear, a medical community *did* take initial ownership in and lay groundwork for future research—that movement was abortion self-help.

Our conditions for ourselves

"The Feminist Women's Health Center Presents: The Participatory Clinic," announces a Federation of Feminist Women's Health Centers trifold brochure from the late 1970s. The brochure explains, "The Feminist Women's Health Center has developed a NEW milieu for gynecological examinations!. . . . Together: The six to eight women participating meet with three lay health workers and a female practitioner in a relaxed, woman-controlled atmosphere."[8]

One trajectory of the self-help movement was directed toward underground self-help, or gynecology and abortion practiced outside of a licensed clinic. Another trajectory—the one I'm going to tell you about here—was directed toward the aboveground participatory clinic, what health workers sometimes referred to as "self-help classes." Historian Hannah Dudley-Shotwell writes, "Inside clinic walls, the self-help group became the 'participatory' group where women practiced 'well-woman' care."[9]

For many women, the participatory clinic was their first encounter with self-help. Directly undermining the individual doctor-patient exam model, which the FWHCs argued often left women with more questions than before their appointment, the participatory clinic instituted a horizontal power structure.[10]

Sexual health became a nonhierarchical, shared undertaking. I thought of Arline Hernández's words, which sum up the paradigm: *You* have power. *Take it.* Just be with it.

In participatory clinics in the 1970s and 1980s, patients had the chance to spend time (in some cases, hours) with a group of other laypeople and lay health workers. They learned how to perform breast and cervical self-exams and underwent physical examinations, pap smears, pregnancy tests, and lab work together. STI screening, fertility awareness, birth control, infertility, and abortion were some of the reproductive health topics covered by participatory clinics. Some catered to specific groups: lesbians or menopausal women, for example.[11]

At OFWHC / Women's Choice, lay health workers, most of whom were working class and some of whom were women of color, facilitated these clinics. By practicing self-help with and on each other, they became capable of teaching and, in the process, led a movement to educate other working-class women and women of color who, as the clinic director Alicia Jones put it, often "hadn't been empowered to ask what's inside their own bodies."

According to the brochure, participatory clinics aimed to spread the idea that "various gynecological conditions we periodically have during our lives are not 'abnormal' or 'diseased.'" The brochure went on, "Together.... We share self-examination... so that we have seen, and know, our conditions for ourselves."[12] I am struck by the depth of this claim. It is possible to know your material body, and in doing so, you begin to know what, how, and who it is that you *are*. I thought of what Linci said: "I'd never considered the knowledge that the tools of my *being* could give me." Byllye Avery's comment on the clinics offered by the Gainesville Women's Health Center rang in my ear, too: "We ... gave ourselves permission to ... explore *who we are* to our fullest." What's normal, they had begun to argue, is taking time to really *know* yourself.

Linci facilitated myriad clinics in the 1970s and 1980s. She wanted very much for me to understand what an important part of abortion self-help the participatory clinic was. "In the participatory clinic, you realize that you're all the same and you're all different," she said. From avoiding or achieving pregnancy to giving birth and then understanding and living in a postpartum body, participatory clinics addressed health and sexuality issues that came up at different points in a person's life. She explained, "Some of the women who had had children had lost the ability to pull their cervixes back and feel the opening of that space. They were searching for what had happened. They had very real questions about sexuality after birth. We were about people's real questions. And people participated in their health care." In the process, participants came to "really know what they were about," in Linci's words. The participatory clinic was an essential learning center.

In addition, the participatory clinic was a site for teaching and research innovation. The participatory clinic model emerged with the abortion self-help movement and, starting in the 1980s, became helpful to health workers and patients as they navigated the hyper-medicalization of clinic relationships and space during the chaotic and frightening HIV / AIDS crisis. The participatory clinic empowered people to actively and methodically participate in knowledge production during a time that many experienced as profoundly disempowering and disorienting.

One of the participatory clinics that OFWHC / Women's Choice offered focused on teaching the fertility awareness method (FAM). This same participatory clinic eventually led to innovations in donor insemination and the establishment of a sperm bank. The story begins in the late 1970s, when a health worker named Barb Raboy started questioning how fertility tracking could be used.

From pregnancy prevention to achievement

If ever there was a community scientist, it's Barb Raboy. In 2022, we sat outside a café in Oakland on a sunny winter day to have a conversation about sperm.

For a decade and a half, Barb ran the OFWHC sperm bank, later renamed the Sperm Bank of California—the first sperm bank to serve lesbians and single women and the only non-profit sperm bank in the United States. When it was first established, the sperm bank was an arm of OFWHC. From 1982 to 1988, its liquid nitrogen tanks stocked with vials of donor sperm were stored on the lower level of the McClure Street office. OFWHC's donor-insemination (DI) program and sperm bank exemplified the health center's belief that body sovereignty was not only about the right to choose abortion but also the right to choose pregnancy. Radical feminism supported people in either choice.

Barb wouldn't have guessed that DI would become her life's work. It was by chance that she came to OFWHC / Women's Choice in 1977 (the year Linci, Alicia, and Pat all came to the health center, too), before there was a DI program or sperm bank. She remembered scanning the classified ads for part-time jobs, running her finger down the newsprint page and stopping suddenly at "Part-Time Biller. Women's Clinic."

Barb was newish to California and in her mid-twenties. A few years prior, she'd followed her brother to the Bay Area from New York City, where they'd grown up in a working-class Jewish family. "I wasn't progressive or a feminist at the time," she told me. "I was pretty naive." But when she got the job, everything changed.

Barb started out doing Medi-Cal billing and then became interested in the abortion clinics, so she started training in those roles as well. Assisting doctors during procedures, packaging products of conception for laboratory analysis, and sterilizing instruments were some of the jobs Barb learned how to do. She learned how to be an advocate, too. Along the way, she developed an understanding of her own sexuality and politics, became a feminist, and came out as a lesbian. And one thing that became especially clear to her was that she wanted to work in health care for the rest of her life.

Like almost everyone else who came to work at the health center, Barb got interested in teaching self-help and soon started facilitating participatory clinics focused on cervical self-exam. She'd bring in a roll of exam-table paper, and participants would tear off a sheet and find a place on the carpeted floor.

As she researched to develop her curriculum, Barb came across articles about FAM for birth control—how some people were opting to track their cycles instead of taking hormonal birth control or using cervical caps. Eager to learn more, Barb enrolled in FAM training and became a certified instructor. Then, she developed a new participatory clinic focused on FAM. "We framed it as a natural birth control method," she explained. "You don't have to put anything in your body. All you have to do is identify those few days before, during, and after ovulation: your fertile period."

In 1980, after she'd been teaching the class for a year or so, Barb fielded a question that changed her perspective about FAM. "Can you talk to us about using FAM for pregnancy achievement?" a participant asked. Of course, Barb realized, FAM could be used not only for birth control but also for getting pregnant. It was around that time that she learned about insemination, when she attended a session on insemination for lesbians at a women's health conference at San Francisco State University. Barb hoped to become pregnant, so her interest was personal.

Until that time, the FWHCs and the broader women's health movement had prioritized helping people access birth control and abortion. "Feminist reproductive health care was about finding a birth control method you were comfortable with and having access to supportive abortion services," Barb said. At that point, abortion workers didn't really do "options counseling." She reflected, "We didn't talk with people about what to consider if they were thinking about having kids."

To learn about the services they offered, Barb reached out to some infertility practices in the Bay Area. She remembered talking with one doctor who had a successful practice in San Francisco, asking him if he took lesbians or single women as patients. He told her his practice was focused on married couples dealing with male infertility. When she asked the same question of another infertility practice, the married couple who ran it refused to speak with her at all. "They were horrified that I would even ask that question over the phone," Barb recalled.

A few years earlier, in the late 1970s, self-helpers Francie Hornstein, Ellen Peskin, and Suzann Gage had started experimenting with DI at LAFWHC. Francie used a friend's fresh sperm along with a syringe and cannula to get pregnant. They researched other methods, too—putting sperm inside a diaphragm or cervical cap and then inserting it, for example—and then started buying sperm from a nearby sperm bank and selling it to women who wanted to attempt DI (they would help them with the process, if the women wanted).[13]

Barb went to Los Angeles to meet with Francie, Ellen, and Suzann, and Suzann explained the protocols: first, participants who wanted to become pregnant took a FAM class to learn how to identify when they were the most fertile, and then they had some lab work done and met with a health worker to discuss the process. Finally, they signed an insemination contract and selected a donor from California Cryobank, where the health center bought sperm. Suzann took Barb to Cryobank so she could see how it was set up, and Barb was surprised to learn how uncomplicated sperm banking was. The director, Stephen Broder, told Barb he'd be happy to sell her sperm if she were to establish a DI program in Oakland.

On the flight home, Barb's mind raced. She was eager to adapt the DI program that LAFWHC had developed for OFWHC. But, she thought, what if OFWHC didn't have to buy sperm from Cryobank? All you needed was a storage tank that could hold one thousand vials of sperm at -196° Celsius. You needed liquid nitrogen, too. What if they got their own equipment and set up their *own* sperm bank on McClure Street?

The business of sperm

In 1982, when Barb had her great idea, the sperm business was still young. In fact, sperm banking branched from developments in the dairy and cattle industries. In the 1930s, farmers started artificially inseminating dairy cows with sperm from champion bulls. The idea was to improve the health of the gene pool and therefore the milk production of the cows.[14] In the 1950s, cattle farmers began using cryopreservation, or the use of low temperatures to preserve cells and tissue, to store bull sperm.[15] Over the following decades, farmers produced millions of animals with frozen-thawed sperm.[16]

In 1952, in the middle of farm country, a University of Iowa researcher borrowed these farming techniques and figured out how to freeze, thaw, and then use human sperm for successful insemination. A graduate student at the time of his research, Jerome Sherman learned that British scientists had successfully used glycerol, a sugary chemical, to preserve the vitality of animal sperm during freezing. He started freezing his own sperm and investigating which protocols produced the most viable sperm upon thawing.[17]

With the help of his senior colleague Raymond Bunge, Sherman took his experiments from the university lab to a fertility clinic. Armed with the finding that the slow freezing of sperm treated with glycerol was the most effective way to ensure "post-thaw motility," Sherman and Bunge established the country's first sperm bank in Iowa City. By the middle of 1953, three people who had been inseminated with frozen thawed sperm from their sperm bank were pregnant.[18] In December, the *New York Times* reported on the most advanced of the three pregnancies: "The first child ever conceived by insemination with deep frozen male sperm cells should be delivered in less than three months. X-rays of the unidentified mother show that the foetal skeleton is developing normally and the child is expected to be normal in every way."[19]

Like that, the business of sperm banking was born. Not three decades later, it would be Barb counting sperm under a microscope.

IN 1988, LAURA Brown would declare bankruptcy and put OFWHC / Women's Choice up for sale, prompting Linci and some others to buy and rename it. Barb and Laura would stop being friends around this time, but during the heyday of the clinic, Laura and Barb were the two "semen brokers," thick as thieves. Together they confronted anti-feminist, homophobic responses to their project.

Media would ask pointed questions like, "Is [insemination] anti-male?" "Since we've opened the sperm center," Lisa Radcliffe, marketing director at OFWHC / Women's Choice in this period, replied, "our respect for the other half of the world has increased tremendously."[20]

Barb squinted into the brightening sky. She exhaled through her smile, raised her dark eyebrows, and told me the story of launching the sperm bank.

The policy will be open-door

On October 5, 1982, the OFWHC sperm bank's opening day, the health center held a press conference. The health center had hired someone with experience working in adoption placement to direct the sperm bank, and he was scheduled to talk to the media. Barb was set to speak, too, about the specifics of the DI program.

The morning of the press conference, Barb brewed a fresh pot of coffee and arranged an autumn bouquet in a vase next to the podium. Laura, Linci, and others busily prepared for the press to arrive, too. For opening day, they had transformed the insemination clinic and sperm bank into a warm and welcoming place: potted plants and wall posters in the lobby, floral-print cushions in the pastel-painted exam rooms.[21]

"Hey," said Linci to the newly hired sperm bank director—a "hey" that harbored the mild irritation she brought to most interactions with professional men. "Can you take out that last bag of trash?" He was seated in a chair next to a waste bin reviewing his notes for the press conference. Apparently startled, he looked up and replied awkwardly, "Um, I don't . . . take out garbage." Linci stared at him icily. She bent, removed the liner from the small bin, knotted the flaps, and marched the bag down the stairs and out the door herself.

Fifteen minutes before the press conference was scheduled to begin, Laura pulled the young director aside discreetly and asked him to leave and not to bother coming back. "You're the sperm bank director now," Laura told Barb. "You're in charge."

During the press conference, Laura spoke about how the OFWHC's sperm bank was the first sperm bank run by women. "It's very threatening to some people," she said. "Women are not only going to control their bodies and reproduction through abortions, but they will also be able to control when they have children." Laura and Barb told the media that they anticipated critics would say the sperm bank was a conspiracy against men and that it would contribute to the breakdown of the family. But, as they put it, "We don't see it that way. It is simply an answer for the thousands of infertile couples, single women and lesbians who want children."[22]

The insemination program and sperm bank would offer services on a sliding scale. They would require that donors complete a thorough medical history, provide a sample for screening, and waive custody rights. Each sperm donor would then be limited to fifteen pregnancies. Meanwhile, women preparing to receive inseminations would be required to participate in FAM training and undergo a health exam and lab work prior to choosing their donor from a catalog, which would describe the donor's height, weight, race, and blood type and include a personal and family health history. Theirs was an open-door policy; anyone in good health could donate or inseminate, and donors from all ethnic, social, economic, and academic backgrounds were welcomed.[23]

With reference to their open-door policy—subverting what scholars Cynthia Daniels and Janet Golden have called the dominant "populist eugenics" paradigm typical of the industry[24]—Laura announced, "We absolutely don't believe in the natural superiority of one race or type of person over another. Biology is not destiny. Social conditioning is."[25] Even so, health workers would ask potential donors why they wanted to give sperm. If their reason was something self-aggrandizing like "servicing womankind" by "scattering their sperm," Barb told me, the sperm bank would refuse them.

Barb recalled how in the months leading up to their opening day, she and other OFWHC health workers practiced freezing, thawing, and doing semen analysis on samples provided by male doctors who worked at the health center. "As part of the analysis, you count the sperm using a microscope," Barb said. They also practiced handling and refilling the tank with liquid nitrogen.

In the months after the sperm bank's opening, the media fueled controversy around it by quoting critics who suggested that conceiving with donor sperm was a "quick fix" and "utterly irresponsible," revealing how inextricable the dominant ideology of compulsory motherhood was (and is) from the ideology of compulsory heterosexuality.[26] Barb confronted this conservative ideology by speaking frankly about the fact that they were offering a feminist approach to insemination. Sometimes health workers did the inseminations. A patient could bring their partner and have their partner do it, if they wanted. Another option was for a woman to self-inseminate. Here's the syringe, here's how you do it, Barb recalled telling patients.

Idant Laboratories, a sperm bank company in New York, proclaimed to the media that the OFWHC sperm bank "advocates certain techniques that are generally not acceptable by the general medical community." They added that calling it a feminist bank sperm "puts you in a very strong anti-male position." Jerome Sherman, by that time chair of the reproductive council of the American Association of Tissue Banks, supported these positions. In a question that reflected its deeply antiqueer agenda, the San Francisco Archdiocese asked, "Do we really want to separate entirely baby-making from love-making, as if the two had no connection? Do we want to transfer procreation out of a human bond of intimacy? (Linci laughed when she read this and said, "We were adding it!") "These are very significant moral questions," the Archdiocese continued.[27]

To such questions, Barb simply answered, "I think the main factor in these children's lives is that they have loving and supportive environments. Not whether they have a traditional Ozzie-and-Harriet . . . beginning." The February 1984 news story that featured this comment included a photo of short-haired, deep-dimpled Barb holding her toddler, who had been conceived through insemination. Both are smiling widely. A happy single lesbian mother with her happy child.[28]

Simply by *being* a single parent with a child conceived by DI, Barb exposed the Archdiocese's insinuation that the relationship between parent and child achieved through insemination was somehow outside the "human bond of intimacy" as ludicrous and out of touch. For years, she and other women had been realizing their own politics and ethics of insemination by building an infrastructure to support their freedom to choose pregnancy. They were reaching their own conclusions: that lesbians and single women who wanted to be parents deserved access to that experience—and that any children they might have would be lucky to have them as parents.

THE SPERM BANK'S open-door policy contrasted with the industry norm at the time, which was, once again, as Daniels and Golden put it, a "populist eugenics" one—the idea that desirable human traits can be bought through discerning donor selection.[29]

In the nineteenth and early twentieth centuries, doctors first experimented with DI as a therapy for married couples in which the husband was infertile. In the 1930s, the physician Frances Seymour, head of the National Research Foundation for the Eugenic Alleviation of Sterility, described DI as "eugenics in practice" and argued that it could help create offspring "as near as humanly perfect as our scientific knowledge can produce."[30]

By the mid-twentieth century, physician-controlled DI was thought of as both a therapy for infertility and a means of producing "superior offspring."[31] Leading sperm-preservation researcher Raymond Bunge himself wrote to a colleague, "The spermatozoa of great men can be preserved for long periods of time and perhaps a race of superior individuals can be ultimately expected."[32] As the industry became consumer-driven in the 1970s, sperm banks let recipients choose between various donor characteristics. As Daniels and Golden write of consumers, "Decisions about what kind of sperm to buy meshed personal concerns, populist eugenic beliefs and scientific findings that together constructed the quest for a better baby than nature could create."[33] From 1980 to 1999, consumers could buy "genius" sperm of Nobel Prize winners at the California Repository for Germinal Choice.[34]

By maintaining publicly and in practice that no one type of person was superior to any other and that "biology is not destiny," the OFWHC sperm bank challenged the dominant mentality of the industry. They also advocated the pursuit of new types of relationships that DI technology could make available to recipients, donors, and their donor-conceived offspring.

WHEN BARB DEVELOPED her vision for the insemination program and sperm bank, there were no tissue banking regulations at all in California—the technology was barely three decades old. Ironically, while the OFWHC sperm bank received harsh criticism for its unorthodox practices, it also helped establish standards of care that the industry would adopt. At the outset, the Oakland sperm bank formed a medical advisory committee that included infectious disease experts, a geneticist, and public health professionals.

When screening potential donors, a health worker would conduct an extensive medical history in the context of a formal interview. If a donor was cooperative and thorough, and if his physical exam and bloodwork came back okay, then the sperm bank would move forward with his application. Along with the medical director, Barb would give everything—lab and exam results, semen analysis, health history, contract, ID—one final look before approving the donor by signing and stamping the donor's paperwork with their approval.

In January 1983, the insemination program and sperm bank achieved their first pregnancy, with more soon after. It was a heady time. To Barb's surprise, in the months that followed, some recipients started to ask if they could meet their donors. Barb asked them why they wanted to. Recipients said they wanted to be open and honest with their children and give them the option of knowing more about or even eventually meeting their donor. Compelled, Barb asked their attorney to review civil codes and public policies and figure out if there were any legal restrictions on whether they could develop an alternative to the anonymous donor model. Barb recalled how, for the life of her, their attorney couldn't find a thing.

The sperm bank soon started inviting "identity-release donors." If a donor consented, his offspring could request an "identity release" of information about him when they turned eighteen. At the time, no other sperm banks in the country offered such a program. But in subsequent years, other sperm banks would follow suit. The innovation of identity release was that, as Linci once commented, it involved nothing more than simply telling the truth in a health care setting.

As the sperm bank continued to make news, people started reaching out from all over. People wanted to know if sperm could be mailed to them, so Barb developed a shipping operation. Dry ice arrived at the doorstep of McClure Street every morning for packing the frozen vials. The health center also offered clients the option of having sperm shipped in liquid nitrogen vapor tanks, where it could stay frozen for up to two weeks. To receive sperm by mail, clients had to meet with a licensed practitioner locally, in their state or country, learn about FAM, undergo an exam, and have the provider sign off on their sperm order.

Additionally, the sperm bank offered the option of private storage. If someone were to receive a cancer diagnosis, for example, and wanted to set aside sperm before undergoing chemotherapy or radiation, storage at the bank was an option. Men undergoing vasectomies were also eligible.

One protocol that the sperm bank helped establish was the quarantine period for donated sperm. In the late-1980s, when the antibody test for HIV/AIDS became available, the sperm bank established the protocol of screening donors for HIV at the time of initial donation and then again after six months.[35] In consultation with its advisory committee, the sperm bank determined that six months was the period needed to fully screen a donor and rule out disease. Six months became the federal mandate for sperm quarantining.

Because the OFWHC sperm bank was the first to offer open-identity donation, the people conceived with sperm from identity-release donors were among the first adults to have access to their donors.[36] The fact that no such program had previously existed meant that the social and psychological experiences the offspring had in the process of accessing their donors were completely unprecedented. Psychologist Joanna Scheib saw a research area ripe for investigation. To this day, the sperm bank has collaborated with Scheib to produce research on open-identity sperm donation. She and her colleagues have investigated the experiences of recipients, donor-conceived people, and donors. In her words, the research tells a story about "the outcome of releasing donor identities to donor-conceived adults" and thus can also help guide policy.[37]

Instead of reproducing a biological determinist view by uncritically propping up the industry-dominant populist eugenics paradigm, the OFWHC sperm bank emphasized autonomy and self-determination through programs such as identity release. For people conceived with donor sperm from the sperm bank, the question presented by the possibility of identity release was not what donor traits (whether heritable or not) have perhaps made you what you are, but rather, what types of available relationships do you want to pursue with your life and, thus, what type of person will you choose to become?

When OFWHC / Women's Choice declared bankruptcy in 1988, Barb established the sperm bank as its own nonprofit—the Sperm Bank of California—and moved it to a different Oakland location and then, in 1995, to Berkeley. She directed the sperm bank until 1998, and it continues to operate in Berkeley today.

We treated what happened

Above all, self-help community science was political: it was motivated by physical need, by feeling and emotion, and by the desire for liberation. This fact becomes especially apparent when you study abortion self-help in the context of the HIV/AIDS crisis.

In June 1981, the Centers for Disease Control and Prevention reported that five gay men in Los Angeles had developed a type of pneumonia found in immunosuppressed people. A year later, scientists started calling the condition Gay-Related Immunodeficiency Disease and, shortly after, renamed it Acquired Immune Deficiency Syndrome (AIDS).[38] The epidemic ripped through gay men's communities, and the state largely ignored it—except when advocating laws that would mandate HIV-testing or quarantine.[39] The reality hit hard and fast, Linci told me. She lost thirty-four friends to AIDS between 1983 and 1984, before anyone really knew what was going on.

In 1987, New York City activists launched ACT UP and started organizing protests and other actions to demand recognition of and a response to HIV/AIDS. Other cities such as Chicago and San Francisco formed ACT UP chapters, too. But ACT UP members weren't the first HIV/AIDS activists. Deborah Gould points out that, not long after the epidemic was announced, LGBTQ communities began fundraising, organizing support services, and doing education and advocacy work, and lesbians were involved from the start, some of whom brought lessons from their participation in the abortion self-help movement.[40]

Over the years, self-helpers played critical roles in fighting HIV/AIDS. Both movements understood that they shared a common enemy: the Christian Right, which *was* the conservative political establishment and wanted to police the bodies of women and queers. Case in point, the Catholic Church was supporting anti-abortion extremist groups such as Operation Rescue at the same time as it was thwarting the distribution of condoms and clean needles for HIV prevention.[41] Additionally, self-helpers and HIV/AIDS activists grasped that they shared the same fundamental principle: self-empowerment.[42]

The HIV/AIDS crisis transformed health workers' lives by demanding a tremendous amount of compassion and high levels of endurance. In January 2020, two months before the COVID-19 outbreak, which would transform health workers' lives yet again, I asked Linci what it was like to work in medicine during HIV/AIDS. We were sharing her living room couch, a light wool blanket over our legs.

In the 1980s at Women's Choice, health workers noticed that women were coming in with unusual health issues: weight loss from chronic diarrhea, systemic candidiasis, skin deterioration. These were AIDS-related conditions, health workers eventually learned. At that time, there was little scientific understanding of how women got HIV or of what AIDS looked like in women, as the Centers for Disease Control and Prevention's definition of both exposure risks and the presentation of the disease itself were based on infections observed in men.[43] When the blood test for detecting HIV became available, the clinic started offering it. With regard to their experience of the epidemic, Linci recalled,

> Seeing unusual things made us more aware, and we did more testing. I think we swabbed more orifices than most providers did. We treated what happened. We were dealing with the aftermath of women not being looked at seriously in the disease process. The standardization of men in the research process is a failure of science and an example of the ill effects of patriarchy. We created standards of care and protocols to address this issue. If you had a weird thing on your back, for example, we tested you for herpes. Our care changed to meet people's needs. We dealt with what was *real*.

Linci paused for a moment, then said, "When someone got a positive test, health workers would come and get me." Her voice broke as she went on: "For that face-to-face moment, they came and got me."

In 1989, women in ACT UP New York who had been involved in abortion self-help led a teach-in for their ACT UP comrades, discussing political strategies such as centering the needs of people with AIDS in the process of articulating a platform. Some ACT UP members formed an abortion rights group called Women's Health Action and Mobilization (WHAM!). They worked at the intersection of feminist and HIV/AIDS activism and eventually produced a book: *Women, AIDS and Activism*.[44] Marion Banzhaf, Tracy Morgan, and Karen Ramspacher from the group articulated how HIV/AIDS activism *was* reproductive rights activism, in that reproductive rights "include[d] ... the right to sex without risk of illness, including HIV infection."[45]

In 1990, abortion self-helpers and other feminists in ACT UP New York put pressure on the National Institutes of Health to hold a conference on women and AIDS (which it did that December), and on the Centers for Disease Control and Prevention to change the definition of AIDS, or its diagnostic criteria, to account for ways it presented in women. Marion Banzhaf, a self-helper who had been a director at the Tallahassee Feminist Women's Health Center, explained, "ACT UP's position was that we had to add cervical cancer, pelvic inflammatory disease, bacterial pneumonia, endocarditis, and two hundred T cells or less [to the definition]." At the second National Women and AIDS Conference in 1993, activists won the inclusion of these infections (with the exception of pelvic inflammatory disease), dramatically increasing the number of women with AIDS who could apply for social benefits and could access medications.[46]

Community science was a major component of HIV/AIDS activism. As sociologist Steven Epstein discusses, ACT UP activists and lay scientists became experts in virology, immunology, and epidemiology. They confronted research biases against the gay community, ran their own underground drug trials, and much more. Epstein credits the work that feminist health activists and self-helpers did a decade before the AIDS outbreak as "perhaps the most consequential for the cultural redefinition of relations between medical experts and lay consumers." Unlike ACT UP activists, though, he suggests, neither self-help groups nor the broader women's health movement "had much success in extending [their] critique of medical *practice* into an engagement with the methodologies of biomedical *research*."[47]

But as self-helpers' 1970s redefinition of the clitoris and 1970s and 1980s research-intensive participatory clinics and DI programs show—not to mention their research, education, and advocacy work in the 1980s and 1990s around HIV/AIDS—abortion self-helpers were always community scientists engaged in research innovation. Self-helpers' innovations were, in fact, adopted by the medical establishment, and the OFWHC sperm bank's quarantining and identity-release protocols, along with the advent of "participatory medicine" later in the 2000s, are primary examples.[48]

COMMUNITY HEALTH WORKERS in the 1980s and 1990s were dealing with compounding public health crises and doing their best to treat patients whose needs were increasingly complex. Linci explained to me that, during this period, HIV/AIDS, along with a breast cancer epidemic (producing what Audre Lorde described early on, in 1980, as an unwilling-to-remain-silenced "army of one-breasted women"), hit people Women's Choice served hardest: LGBTQ and poor people.[49] This is because the Ronald Reagan and George H. Bush administrations ignored and invisibilized structural contributors to both diseases.[50] For example, the federal government's inaction on the problem of widespread pollutants and carcinogens in the environment—most heavily concentrated in poor communities and communities of color due to environmental racism that permitted this contamination—likely contributed to the breast cancer crisis.[51]

Prompted by HIV/AIDS, health workers entered a period when they were forced to rethink their relationships to their physical work environments and their patients. The monetary cost of safety protocols in a health care setting is immense, Linci explained, and safety creates a lot of waste. By the late 1980s, all blood was considered suspect. The medical establishment "made blood illegal trash," she said. "I think of what we have to do with blood products in a clinic setting to dispose of them. It's ridiculous." Blood is not hazardous in and of itself, unless it contains pathogens, but with the HIV/AIDS crisis, all blood became biohazardous waste.[52]

Today the protocol and culture of personal protection remains the status quo in health care. Over time, it has changed the nature of the provider-patient relationship. "When you protect yourself with PPE [personal protection equipment], then every one of your patients becomes diseased. You start to think of people as communicable," Linci said. "We were taught that we were protecting ourselves. But in truth we were protecting our patients from *us*. We were the potential vectors."

New safety protocols changed the clinic atmosphere, too. Up until that point, medical staff at Women's Choice dressed up for their patients. They wore professional clothes, not scrubs, and visibly rejected the ideology of the white coat, the authority and exclusionary licensing process that it signified. But the HIV/AIDS era changed all of that. "We had no choice but to become more medical," Linci said of how they were forced to adopt more PPE. "We didn't want anyone to feel that we were undertaking risks in the name of feminism."

The HIV/AIDS crisis required health workers to become HIV-informed safe-sex educators. Linci recalled how challenging this work could be in a time of so much confusion. People often thought they were being safe by only having oral sex, but with more oral sex came more oral gonorrhea, which made people more susceptible to contracting HIV.[53] Being there and supporting patients as they processed these difficult realities was part of being a sex educator at the time.

"We dealt with what was real," Linci reiterated. "Was that research? Absolutely. It was developing an understanding of needs and of the changes people were going through, whether HIV positive or not, and not denying them care if they were."

The crisis touched the lives of health workers both in and outside of work. "You were high-risk," Linci said simply. "You worked in blood." As a high-risk person, suddenly you had a personal responsibility to use protection in your sexual life. And sometimes the safe-sex stuff threw people off. Linci remembered arguing with one partner about microwavable saran wrap. It's got little holes in it, she tried to tell her partner. It won't work.

Many health workers were lesbian or queer-identified, and they brought insights from their personal lives into their health education work. Linci explained: "Stepping back from the joyous hedonism of queer culture traumatized us and changed a kernel of who we were. Our lives were about our pleasure. And we owned that. There was such power in it. During HIV / AIDS, there were mental health issues. Some people never left their houses. There was so much fear. 'How am I going to navigate my relationships?' people wanted to know. As clinic workers, we talked people through it and tried to give them solutions."

Self-helpers taught each other, their patients, and themselves not to be afraid. "We taught about the importance of touch. When to wear gloves and when not to. Not to fear people," Linci said. "We were not going to let Western medicine use HIV/AIDS to create a disease state."

Responding to material needs, helping patients take care of themselves under exacting circumstances, and saying no to punitive state solutions were what self-help community science was all about. To recall Linci: this community science *treated what happened*, inside of people's relationships and lives. And the practice of this science, Linci asserted, was the practice of engendering revolutionary safe space.

Chapter 6

Your First Line of Defense Is Self-Defense

"The ultimate goal of the religious Right is to
replace democracy with theocracy."
—BAY AREA COALITION AGAINST OPERATION RESCUE

Everything changed for Oakland Feminist Women's Health Center / Women's Choice in 1985. It was the year one of its sibling clinics was firebombed.

By 1985, OFWHC ran a network of FWHCs: Oakland, Pleasant Hill, Santa Rosa, Orange County, and Los Angeles. (I'll call the Oakland health center "OFWHC / Women's Choice" and the Oakland led five-clinic network the "OFWHC network.") OFWHC / Women's Choice alone offered self-help classes, vasectomies, an infertility clinic, a DI program, and a sperm bank, in addition to gynecological and abortion care.[1] A decade after it opened, OFWHC / Women's Choice was a full-spectrum reproductive health services provider. Linci explained that, in the early 1980s, a team would go on the road for a few months at a time and work at the different locations: "You had a rotation of administrators, which helped us establish the same protocols at every site," she said.

Nationally, abortion infrastructure was strong. By 1985, almost 90 percent of abortions were performed at stand-alone clinics. But it was getting harder to be a feminist women's health center.[2] The Right that elected Ronald Reagan president in 1981 had worked throughout the 1970s to recruit and fold free-market conservatives and white Christians into a single, powerful base. By the 1980s, the Right was set to fuel a terroristic anti-abortion campaign. Violence hit OFWHC/Women's Choice close to home in 1985 when arsonists firebombed LAFWHC, an OFWHC network clinic.

How did the anti-abortion movement become such a leviathan? In the late-nineteenth and early-twentieth centuries, the movement mainly included white supremacists who, with regard to declining white birth rates, believed legalized abortion would mean "race suicide" for white Protestants.[3] Later, in the 1960s, leading up to the ruling on *Roe v. Wade*, the movement became a Catholic one, too.[4] After *Roe*, the Church intensified its crusade against abortion, and other conservative groups joined in interpreting the ruling as a rejection of traditional values; newly galvanized, these other religious and interest groups joined the movement.[5]

Starting in the 1970s, the anti-abortion movement began to push for laws that prohibited public funding for abortions. At the same time, Republican politicians were advocating that the government divest from families by slashing public benefits (welfare), further racializing poverty.[6] The anti-abortion movement and Republicans came together to pass the Hyde Amendment, which in 1977 banned Medicaid reimbursements for abortion.[7] The Republican anti-welfare campaign—which, as historian Laura Briggs argues, "more than any other single thing . . . ushered in the neoliberal moment"[8]—had come to imply an anti-abortion stance.

To be anti-welfare was to be anti-abortion, and vice versa. This ideology was reflected in the words of politicians themselves. Senator Jesse Helms of North Carolina, a Hyde Amendment cosponsor, declared that Congress should never "compel the taxpayer to finance a form of killing."[9] The implied equation of welfare and abortion—and the imperative to reject both—would animate the Right for decades to come.[10]

In 1978, an ex-monk and anti-abortion extremist named Joseph Scheidler began showing up in front of Fort Wayne

Women's Health Organization in Indiana and yelling into a bullhorn at patients. Scheidler and fellow anti-abortion harassers photographed patients, grabbed them, and blocked them from the clinic entrance. The clinic, along with a local feminist group, tried to thwart him and others by forming defense lines. Two years later, Scheidler formally founded the advocacy organization Pro-Life Action Network, vowing to stop abortion "by any means necessary." In response, NOW began training "clinic escorts"—volunteers who would accompany patients as they passed anti-abortion protesters—in different towns and cities.[11]

By 1981, "right-to-lifers" had started picketing in front of Santa Rosa FWHC, an OFWHC network clinic, harassing patients and health workers. In response, clinic allies developed tactics such as forming a human chain in front of the entrance and recruiting clinic escorts.[12] These were the early days of clinic escorting and defense.

By late 1983, there had been twenty-plus bombings and arsons of clinics by anti-abortion terrorists nationwide.[13] Moreover, Pro-Life Action Network and other extremists had started instituting "sidewalk counseling." Jeannie Hill, director of the Colorado organization Sidewalk Counselors for Life, Inc., published a "Sidewalk Counseling Workbook" in 1986, which stated that it was the sidewalk counselor's job to "rescue those persons imminently involved in an abortion decision" and to "cancel a baby's appointment for execution." The workbook describes clinic escorts as "abortuary staff" and advises sidewalk counselors to "remind [the client] that a new life is a miracle and that *you* can help her make it the happy occasion it should be," aggrandizing the role of sidewalk counselors and casting them as righteous activist heroes.[14] In 1986, the extremist group Operation Rescue would systematize the traumatic assault at clinic doors of women seeking abortion care.

Years of anti-abortion aggression did not stop the OFWHC network from providing services, but on the morning of April 8, 1985, arsonists attacked LAFWHC.[15] No one was ever convicted, and the Los Angeles Fire Department never declared the fire to be arson, even though the health center had received threats.[16]

"It broke us," Linci recalled simply. "The Los Angeles clinic was the original feminist women's health center. All of the FWHC history, all of the educational and community materials, it was all housed there. We had supplies there. Hundreds of cervical caps. Everything was melted and destroyed. We worked hard to build the clinics. The firebombing was the pinnacle of destruction of the strength of our network. It ended the stability of the financial web that we had created to support our clinics."

The morning after the arson, Linci packed a bag, jumped into a car with Laura Brown, and took the I-5 down to Los Angeles. The Central Valley, with its endless orchards, was a blossomy blur on the periphery of their vision. They arrived in Los Angeles six hours later to find the clinic charred and unrecognizable. "When you walked inside, it was just a giant hole," Linci said.

Carol remembered getting a call from the fire department on April 8—*the clinic was on fire*. At that point, she no longer worked at LAFWHC; she was in law school. Oakland was in charge. There wasn't anything Carol could have done anyway. The next day, she, too, walked through the rubble, dumbstruck.

"We lost the log Lorraine and I made of our self-help Greyhound bus tour," Carol told me. "Most things were destroyed. We were able to save a photograph of Margaret Sanger, but most things were ashes." She continued, "The fire department said the fire was probably from the restaurant downstairs. I didn't believe it. I never believed it."

Shortly before the arson, at the 1985 National Abortion Federation (NAF) annual meeting, Carol received a threat. At that time, anti-abortion protesters ("antis") were still allowed to attend NAF meetings. "People thought that the way to deal with protesters was to invite them to have coffee and donuts," Carol explained. The inclusion policy was controversial, and in 1985, a group of members came together with a plan to keep antis out. They took turns guarding the double doors of the hotel conference room.

While Carol was working security, a man came careening around the corner down the hallway—Joseph Scheidler. By then a major figure in the anti-abortion movement, Scheidler had just published *Closed: 99 Ways to Stop Abortion*, which outlined clinic harassment tactics.[17] "He was this massive guy," Carol said. "He literally ran toward me at full tilt. He stopped just short of me and yelled in my face. He said, 'Lady, your clinic is *gone.*'" Carol had no way of knowing whether Scheidler had anything to do with the arson, but the incident made clear to her that the antis were feeling increasingly emboldened.

Laura and Linci rented an RV and parked it across the street from the burned-out shell of the former clinic. From it, health workers provided pregnancy tests and abortion referrals.[18] "We're over here, we're open," Linci recalled saying to patients who showed up at Hollywood and Vine looking around for the clinic that was no longer there.

Within weeks, prominent pro-choice activist Bill Baird and a few other allies of LAFWHC set up a defense network to "coordinate information about anti-abortion terrorism and harassment, as well as [give] the public and abortion providers effective strategies to combat this threat." As Bill and Carol wrote on behalf of their new advocacy group in a fundraising letter, allies and activists "recognize[d] the need for a grass roots network to discuss [the] mounting terrorism." They described the LAFWHC fire as exemplary of a national trend: "Two weeks ago the Los Angeles Feminist Women's Health Center was destroyed by fire. The Bureau of Alcohol, Tobacco and Firearms will not investigate nor will the fire department release a report giving the details of this. We feel they are dragging their feet and this is a practice not uncommon in other areas of the nation."[19] Not long after, LAFWHC moved to a new location in a secure high rise on Wilshire Boulevard.[20]

The Los Angeles arson was a harbinger; in the years that followed, other clinics started to struggle with encroaching violence. Linci explained, "When you have people yelling at patients as they're going in the door, they're not going to keep coming to the door. Clinics were constantly being spraypainted. People were having crap done to their cars. There were nasty, threatening letters. Those were the active terrorism years of the anti-abortion movement, the war years." The anti-abortion movement created a climate so hostile for providers that many were forced to stop doing procedures or to close their clinics. Over the course of the 1980s, the United States lost almost 20 percent of abortion providers: in 1982 there were 2,908 facilities that provided abortions. A decade later, there were 2,380. The number of total providers would continue to decrease.[21]

In Linci's words, the attacks were spearheaded by "very angry men." "This was a fight about male superiority. And the worst of the Right wing came out to join that struggle. Not only were they women haters, but they were queer haters. It was a Christian militia."[22]

In 1988, as the clinics struggled to stay open in the hostile climate, Laura filed for bankruptcy and sold the five clinics in the OFWHC network. Because they didn't want to lose what they had worked so hard to build, Linci and a few other OFWHC/Women's Choice health workers, including Debbie Gregg and Yvonne Ramos, marshaled resources and bought the Oakland clinic for five thousand dollars cash. They changed the name of the container nonprofit from OFWHC to West Coast Feminist Health Project, and for the abortion clinic itself they kept the name Women's Choice.

"The bankruptcy was very difficult for those of us who stayed," Linci said.

To grasp what a feat it was for the Oakland clinic to survive the war years, which started in the 1980s and escalated in the 1990s, you have to look at the lengths self-helpers were willing to go to defend their clinics.

IN JANUARY 1985, three months before the LAFWHC firebombing, Pat Parker suggested to her comrades that they get serious about self-defense. She started a group to talk about how they should respond to the anti-abortion attacks on patients, health workers, and clinics that they were seeing in the Bay Area and elsewhere. The attacks had ranged from verbal and physical harassment of individuals to bombings of facilities.[23]

Pat, Debbie, and others weren't thinking of an advocacy

organization, like the one Bill and Carol would initiate just months later. Nor were they thinking exclusively in terms of clinic escorting, the historical precedent. Rather, they were imagining standing up directly to anti-abortion harassment and violence. They named their group the Clinic Defense Committee (CDC).

That spring, the OFWHC network opened a new FWHC in Richmond, just north of Oakland. Right away, antis started picketing in front. CDC mobilized to help build community support for the clinic and to beat back harassment. The San Francisco chapter of the Freedom Socialist Party–affiliated group Radical Women, which had done abortion rights work for years, joined CDC to help organize.

That August, after the LAFWHC firebombing, the growing CDC held a rally in Richmond and called for a "broad range of forward-thinking groups to participate." They wanted to catalyze a "Bay Area-wide, broad-based coalition of support for reproductive rights."[24] Women Against Imperialism, a feminist collective that grew out of the political group Prairie Fire, and the Revolutionary Workers League, a Trotskyist party, were just two of more than twenty other local groups that endorsed the rally.[25] CDC's announcement flyer called for the defense of Richmond FWHC, the safeguarding of state funding for abortion, and an end to the forced sterilization of women of color and poor women. Pat spoke at the rally, as did the poet Merle Woo. The assembly marked the first official action of a new Bay Area–based clinic defense coalition.

In May 1986, on the one year anniversary of Richmond FWHC, CDC and the OFWHC network threw a party and all-night vigil. "The last several months at Women's Choice Clinic of Richmond have been virtually free of anti-abortion harassment," wrote Debbie in the OFWHC network newsletter in June 1986, crediting CDC for the relative quiet.[26]

The article was accompanied by a photo of Linci and another CDC member, Terry Lake, standing on guard outside the clinic in daylight. Linci has her thumbs in her pockets, elbows out. Terry stands with legs slightly spread, militarily at ease. They look like people you wouldn't want to fuck with.

I thought of the Black Panther Party and the Bay Area's history of community self-defense. I thought of the Feminist Economic Network with its armed guard at its Detroit building doors, ready to escort people in and out. I realized that the CDC, cofounded by a Black Panther turned radical Black lesbian feminist, assumed a community self-defense ethos from its inception.

We can take stands

I met Nancy Reiko Kato in the Outer Richmond in the fall of 2020. When I wrote to National Radical Women, Nancy replied to me directly. Linci had told me that Radical Women had been an important member of the organization that CDC grew into in 1988: the Bay Area Coalition Against Operation Rescue, or BACAOR, which would, a few years later, be redubbed the Bay Area Coalition for Our Reproductive Rights, or BACORR.

At a table in front of a café on Clement Street, Nancy, a BACAOR cofounder, launched into a description of the coalition:

> BACAOR / BACORR represented a wing of the feminist movement that was talking about more than just abortion rights. We were talking about reproductive justice before "reproductive justice" became a catchall term. We understood that we're not just talking about women's bodies. We're talking about understanding that our bodies and our lives are interconnected. When you say that, things that maybe weren't considered reproductive rights are included. Economic rights. The connections with women of color and immigrant women.
>
> Now we're holding onto a legal decision, which is basically an illusion about a reality that doesn't exist for most women. You don't have the right to an abortion if you can't afford it, if there are no doctors, etc. BACORR understood that very deeply. It wasn't just about going out and saying "*Roe*," because *Roe* didn't work for most of us.

Nancy had a matter-of-fact communication style. A long-time organizer and skilled spokesperson, she was a student when she joined the Freedom Socialist Party and Radical Women (FSP / RW) in 1980, a group that promoted working-class women of color leadership. In 1977, FSP / RW called for resistance to the "Rightwing forces across the nation [that] have launched an all-out attack on everything feminists have fought for."[27]

Nancy was raised in a union family. "I got into union organizing because of my father," she said. "The only meetings he ever went to were church meetings and union meetings." Her parents were Japanese American, and during World War II they were forcibly relocated to internment camps. Deeply affected by their experience of incarceration, Nancy explained, her parents and others in their Japanese American community made a culture where people stood up for each other. "I learned from them that we can take stands," she said.

At University of California, Hastings, where she worked as a class scheduler for many years, Nancy became a labor organizer for her union. A number of labor organizers, like Nancy, and trade unionists joined BACAOR and participated in clinic defense.[28]

In 1986, Mary Ann Curtis from the Los Angeles chapter of Radical Women called for a "militant, multi-issue" abortion defense campaign that would put defenders in front of clinics and pressure city governments and police to do something about the bombings.[29] Attacks had increased around the country, and clinic defenders in some places were maintaining clinic defense lines in response. They were extending the clinic escorting and defense that activists had started doing in the late 1970s as they tried to fend off extremists like Joseph Scheidler and in the early 1980s as they stood on guard outside clinics such as Richmond and Santa Rosa FWHCs.

When the militant organization Operation Rescue (OR) came on the scene, defenders were forced to reimagine clinic defense. Nancy recalled the time she first learned about OR: "There was this woman who had traveled to Kansas to attend a meeting of a group that was trying to deal with Operation Rescue's attacks. I remember her coming back and telling us about it and thinking to myself, 'This is a whole new level of Right-wing activism that is really going to impact us.'" In anticipation of Operation Rescue's arrival, Bay Area clinic defense took off. And in the years that followed, it would spread its theory and tactics all around the country.

Operation Rescue

In 1987, a young born-again Christian named Randall Terry officially launched OR. As described by *Rolling Stone* writer Francis Wilkinson in 1989, "A former vendor of Big Macs, ice-cream cones, gasoline, tires and—yes—used cars, Terry . . . is the spearhead of Operation Rescue, a militant anti-abortion organization that fuses Christian fervor with 1960s-style civil disobedience to blockade and temporarily shut down abortion clinics across the nation."[30] Operation Rescue, incorporated as a for-profit enterprise, promoted the leadership of white Christian men. "Most people . . . are more comfortable following men into a highly volatile situation," claimed Terry. "It's just human nature." He would also repeat the mantra, "If you think abortion is murder, then act like it's murder."[31]

OR would organize abortion clinic "hits" (as clinic defenders called them) in which hundreds of OR members would mob a single abortion clinic, intimidating and harassing patients, blocking clinic entrances, and sometimes forcing the clinic to close for the day. OR sold members a story in which they were courageous saviors standing up to anti-natalists and referred to legal abortion as "America's holocaust."[32] Clinic defenders and abortion health workers were "pro-aborts," and fetuses were "pre-born children."[33]

OR extended the project of political organizations like Moral Majority, which was founded by televangelist Jerry Falwell in 1979. Moral Majority called on evangelical Christians to vote against abortion, gay rights, and welfare funding—in short, to vote Republican—and helped produce the structural behemoth that was the New Right.[34] Like the Moral Majority, OR conscripted white Christians to do the Republican Party's bidding, and both groups did so by instrumentalizing cult of personality types like Jerry Falwell and Randall Terry.

As Mary Ziegler argues, the marriage of the Republican Party to the Christian Right would gut American democratic processes through the deregulation of elections (that is to say, campaign finance laws) and, ultimately, the reconstitution of the Supreme Court.[35]

Abortion defenders mobilized rapidly to respond to OR. In late 1987 in Detroit, in anticipation of blockades around the time of the pope's visit, National Abortion Rights Action League (NARAL) worked with the Michigan Organization for Human Rights and local activists to train clinic escorts on how to shield patients from OR. In the summer of 1988, when OR launched the "Siege of Atlanta" during the Democratic National Convention, local clinics worked together to coordinate escorts.[36]

When OR arrived in the Bay Area shortly after, abortion defenders banded together to execute an unprecedented and militant street response, a response that would reflect their understanding that abortion access was a condition for everyone's freedom and autonomy and that clinic defense was community self-defense.

You do not depend on the police

One of the people Nancy organized with in the early years of the Bay Area Coalition Against Operation Rescue was Kass McMahon. In the mid-1980s, Kass migrated to California from her home state of Wisconsin and eventually landed in San Francisco.

Kass had previous experience with reproductive rights activism. As a student in the late 1970s, she had co-organized an event protesting the Hyde Amendment. She gave her first political speech to a room of eighty people (an impressive turnout for a small apolitical commuter campus, she told me) about the injustice of the government's withholding of public funding for abortion.

In San Francisco, a friend of Kass's invited her to a FSP / RW meeting about doing "clinic watch." Because she liked FSP / RW's politics, Kass kept going to their meetings.

When I visited her in Albuquerque in summer 2021, I spent a week rummaging through her plastic bins full of BACAOR / BACORR records and ephemera. As I thumbed through her notebooks, I learned that Kass took copious notes over the years. Her cursive was meticulous. She was a trained journalist, she explained to me, with a facility for documenting.

Kass learned one of her first big political activist lessons when she and two other clinic defenders found themselves facing charges in fall 1988, just as BACAOR was getting started. "We were BACAOR's first arrests," she told me. In defiance of their arrests, they decided to take on the San Francisco Police Department (SFPD).

But let me back up: Operation Rescue had come to the Bay Area, and September 17, 1988 was set to be their first big hit. As they looked ahead to OR's arrival, CDC members renamed their group Bay Area Coalition Against Operation Rescue. At that point, BACAOR was still what Kass described to me as a "counter demonstration force," having not yet developed the proactive tactics that would become known as clinic defense.

Early that September morning, fifty or so BACAOR members arrived at Pregnancy Consultation Center in San Francisco to find hundreds of OR demonstrators blocking the doors. Arriving in vans, the antis had descended upon the clinic well before sunrise and, in no time at all, blockaded the entrance to the mission-style medical building. Some of the men wore suits and carried walkie-talkies, clearly out to intimidate.[37]

BACAOR members arrived early that morning, too, but they were outnumbered. Antis crowded the entrance, several rows thick. "They were fanned out in front of the door in layers," Kass recalled. "The cops were there, too. They weren't going to let us get anywhere near OR. And they weren't going to help get OR out of the way, either." She continued, "There were police in OR.

That was documented. Our people would go to OR's meetings and see local cops there."

But BACAOR wasn't about to concede—they used bull-horns to lead a noisy counter demonstration and distracted OR with theatrics. A street theater group called "Ladies Against Women" arrived dressed in conservative garb and held up signs that read "Every Sperm Is Sacred!" while singing the Monty Python hymn.

"One of the things that made us successful was our use of visual activism to pierce the hypocrisy of OR," Kass explained. In the months and years that followed, Bay Area clinic defenders would continue to bring street theater to rallies, marches, demos, and occasionally defenses. They would incorporate costumes, props, puppets, skits, songs, and more, using humor, camp, and satire to antagonize OR and expose their theocratic agenda.

"What OR was doing was more than hypocrisy," Kass contin-ued, in explanation of BACAOR's tactical use of irony. "It was gaslighting. They were not peaceful church people. They were training to beat us up and implement fascism."

Despite BACAOR's efforts, OR was indefatigable in their plan to shut down Pregnancy Consultation Center. Antis swarmed women who tried to approach the clinic. "Please, we can give you money . . . please don't go in there," said one anti to a sobbing patient who approached the police line.[38] It was hours later when police finally started carrying away and some-times arresting antis who were lying or sitting limply on the ground in front of the doors. Many who had been physically removed immediately rejoined the blockade as soon as they were released.[39]

Then police ordered the crowd to disperse. Exhausted, Kass, Kathy, and their friend Roanne Hindin began walking away from the clinic. But as they did, several cops grabbed them and told them they were under arrest for failing to disperse. "I got singled out a lot by the cops," Kass said. "I was noisy. I was strong, ath-letic, and fierce. I'm sure they picked us up because they thought we were organizers." She continued,

They put us in cuffs. One cop grabbed me by the arm and said, "Those are big muscles for a woman." He totally knew I was a dyke. I was the dykiest one there. When the photographer was supposed to take my mugshot, that cop who had me by the arm leaned in on top of me. He invaded my space and put his cheek up next to mine and said something like, "Let's pretend this is our wedding picture." Because queers couldn't get married, right? That was the message I got. You're a dyke. It was insulting. They put us in the back of a van. It was stiflingly hot.

What happened at Pregnancy Consultation Center reinforced a core principle of BACAOR: you do not depend on the police.

The next day, BACAOR launched a media campaign. Outraged, they asked: How could SFPD stand by for hours as OR denied women of their right to abortion and then turn around and arrest BACAOR demonstrators just as they were *complying* with the dispersal order? "The anti-abortionists were given five hours to disperse; we were given five seconds," Roanne was quoted saying in a news release.[40] They also cited an incident that happened just days before, when SFPD had assaulted and horrifically injured United Farm Workers cofounder Dolores Huerta at an anti-Bush rally in the city, breaking her ribs and rupturing her spleen.[41] They argued that "the police are on a crusade to smash social protest."[42]

BACAOR called the media (Nancy took the lead), sent letters to editors, collected signatures from around the country for a petition, asked supporters to file complaints with the district attorney's office, and lawyered up.[43] The *SF Bay Guardian* published an editorial that read, "The San Francisco Police are out of control. The department's response to demonstrations and the press at recent protests indicates a complete absence of professionalism, a visible lack of consistent crowd-control policies and an alarming propensity for violence."[44]

The September 17 hit infuriated and inspired clinic defenders to ramp up their response to OR. "We are going to keep following them around wherever they go and we will show up as a counterforce," Roanne told the *Oakland Tribune*.[45]

A few weeks later, the district attorney chose not to press the charges against Kass, Kathy, and Roanne that had been brought by the police. BACAOR used the win to call for people to help organize in advance of OR's plan to hit clinics around the country on a single weekend in late October 1988.[46]

"BACAOR grew like a Jack-and-the-beanstalk after that," Kass said. Dozens more people came to the next organizing meeting. "The next time OR hit, we were ready. We had our tactics. We had a plan. This was no longer clinic watch. This was clinic defense."

They will not stay nonviolent for long

When Operation Rescue announced its plan for October 28 and 29, 1988, a "nationally coordinated action to shut down women's clinics," BACAOR got to work.[47] Right away they set up an "emergency response network" (phone tree) that people could join by calling them and asking to be added.

At that point, Kass, Nancy, and Debbie, among others, were deep into organizing clinic defense. More people quickly joined them: people in political parties, Berkeley students, local anarchists.

Marianne Jensen from the Revolutionary Workers League (RWL) had started coming to meetings. Marianne had mostly grown up in Knoxville, Tennessee, with white activist parents who were involved with the Unitarians, one of the few integrated spiritual communities in the early 1960s involved in the civil rights movement. By high school, she was participating in civil rights and anti-Vietnam war demos. She came to the Bay Area in 1985 when she was in her early thirties to build up RWL.

In college at the University of Michigan, Marianne grew tired of the male-dominated Left, so she moved to Denmark to study at a communist folk school. With classmates, she traveled to South America to support labor activists in Bolivia, Argentina, and Peru. Witnessing state violence against revolutionaries transformed Marianne's politics: "I realized social change isn't about debating debaters' points in a forum. . . . When you're an organizer, you have to meet people where they are." Back in Michigan again, and already a member of RWL, Marianne and some other clerical labor organizers helped form the first United Auto Workers (UAW) chapter made up of mostly women clerical workers at the University of Michigan. Eventually they broke off and formed their own independent union when UAW decertified them because of their insistence on membership control. All of which is to say: by the time Marianne arrived in the Bay Area, she was a seasoned organizer.

With the October hit looming, BACAOR launched into tactical planning. Pages and pages of Kass's cursive capture their process, which unfolded over a series of meetings that month. They were meeting sometimes twice weekly at FSP headquarters in San Francisco or at the Long Haul Infoshop, a new anarchist community center in Berkeley.

A few excerpts from Kass's notebook:

10/11/88
Do we "escort" clients in? Do we put ourselves in the middle of OR?
  We want to emphasize our own self-defense.
  We can link arms, stand foot to foot, encircle.
  [OR] will try to provoke us.
  They will not stay nonviolent for long.
  We need <u>security</u> for our own grp. Protect others against loose cannons.

10/12/88
As of now there are ten clinics performing abortions on Oct. 29 we'll need to cover.
  Someone fm. BACAOR must go to ea. clinic as a captain.

Contact clinic in advance.

- What door is most defendable
- Where is nearest payphone

What to do if you lose the door: Vigorous counter demo. Don't get isolated; neutralize them; steal their media; block them off; place yourself between them; keep more OR fm. joining the others. Sing.[48]

That October 12, Laura Weide attended her first BACAOR meeting at the Long Haul. She remembered how she walked into the space and found a roomful of people, many queer, intensely engaged in conversation. Some sat cross-legged on the floor in a semicircle, others on a rickety wooden staircase. She found a folding chair in a corner and quietly sat down.

Laura was a grad student at University of California, Berkeley at the time. She had grown up in a middle-class Jewish family in Southern California and, in the early 1980s, moved to New York for college, where she got involved in anti-apartheid activism. Through her work, she met other feminists, and together they began looking at the Right's intensifying commitment to controlling women's bodies. Anti-abortion groups had started picketing in front of clinics in the city and had set up a fake clinic—an anti-abortion center that tried to trick women into believing that it was an abortion provider but in fact existed only to frighten and shame them away from having abortions, a tactic still used today.[49] With several others, Laura snuck into the fake clinic and posted flyers with information about abortion. It was her first political action in the reproductive rights movement.

Laura explained to me when we first met that by then, only a decade into a *Roe*-era America, the Right had figured out how to dog-whistle their racism and build their forces around abortion in a way that enabled their followers to feel moral.[50] To make it seem as if they were fighting for other people, she added, and not just for their own ugly racism.

Laura was fascinated by how the media covered both the anti- and pro-abortion movements. After she joined BACAOR, it wasn't long before she stepped into a media relations role. "The anti-abortion forces were creating sympathy around themselves that was so damaging for our human rights," she said. "I felt motivated to push back. We wanted to lay bare the reality of who the antis were and communicate about the power of women and queers to fight for ourselves. And find reporters who could capture that story."

In addition to working to shape the narrative, BACAOR started making art. Joe and Agnes Sampson*, a white couple in their thirties, were both artistically inclined, and they joined BACAOR early on, too. Joe was an anarchist who was trained as a graphic artist, photographer, and videographer. Agnes was a radical feminist. In the 1970s when she was in college, inspired by the "barefoot doctors" of China who brought health care to rural villages, she helped found a feminist women's health center—one that would eventually become a member of the Federation of FWHCs.

Joe started documenting defenses and actions with his VHS camcorder. Given how unpredictable OR was, coupled with the hostility of the police toward BACAOR, he figured having video of defenses could help them if any legal problems arose. At one point, when a defender was charged with assaulting an officer, BACAOR was able to furnish video to disprove it, and the person was acquitted, Joe told me. With their footage, Joe and Agnes also made training videos and documentaries to track OR tactics and help the coalition develop and hone its own.

Joe and Agnes's first artistic contribution was a poster denouncing OR and inviting people to join the emergency response network leading up to the planned attacks in October 1988. When I interviewed them in late 2021, I got to see an original. I met them in their Berkeley backyard garden—a lush, leafy maze of raised beds and foliage-covered trellises. They sat side-by-side beneath a wooden gazebo in wide-brimmed sun hats, in their seventies at that point. Joe poured me a cup of nettle tea.

"I'd found this old graphic," Agnes explained. The poster, which they displayed on an easel, features an intricate ink-drawn image of a woman in eighteenth-century dress, engaged with someone or something outside of the frame. Stalking her are two truly terrifying figures. The first is a corpse with the skin and muscle rotted away from its skeleton, holding a skull in one hand, over the woman's head, and a cross in the other. The second is a mythical creature with long quills protruding from its head, back, and tail and sharp talons curling out from its feet. ("What always appealed to me was that there is a sense of self-containment about the woman," Laura said of the poster. "She is being stalked by the creepy assholes, but she's engaging with something else. They aren't getting her goat.") The macabre image is accompanied by alarming orange text: "Stop Operation Rescue. . . . Be part of the clinic watch or the emergency response network."

The poster's association of OR with the archaic grim reaper forces the connection to histories of violent religious warfare against women. Through its death imagery, the poster could also insinuate a link between OR's anti-abortion crusade and the Right's simultaneous weaponization of HIV / AIDS against queer people.

The disturbing posters were hard to miss against the colorful backdrops of the Mission and Castro neighborhoods and the college campuses where Joe and Agnes strategically placed them in early October 1988. And they worked. Dozens more people came out for the next BACAOR organizing meeting.

By the last weekend of October, BACAOR had a plan. They had rehearsed their tactics for holding the space in front of the door. They had strategized about how to deal with police and with the possibility of their people getting arrested. And they had assigned people to show up first thing at each of the Bay Area clinics that were likely to get hit by OR.

On the morning of Saturday, October 29, OR hit Family Planning Alternatives in Sunnyvale. Before sunrise, OR mobbed the clinic. "Fifteen or twenty of us watched as hundreds of ORs slowly emerged from the gray, pre-dawn darkness and came across the parking lot toward the clinic," Kass remembered. "I started telling people what positions to take. I asked if anybody wasn't up for it and said they should step out of the defense line before anything happened. Most stayed to try to hold the line."

"Stop Operation Rescue" poster, October 1988, by Joe and Agnes Sampson. From Joe and Agnes Sampson's personal collection.

BACAOR used its emergency response network to direct people from other locations to Sunnyvale, and soon more defenders arrived.[51] But then, journalist Christina Smith recalled, a crew of OR thugs moved in on clinic defenders, punching, shoving, elbowing, and kicking them.[52] BACAOR tried to hold the line, but they were overwhelmed by OR's violent tactics.

Laura was on the front line that day. "I was at the door," she remembered. "It was the first time I'd ever been in a crush of bodies like that and had the experience of trying to squeeze people in and push other people out. I remember the push of our collective will to create and hold space."

Next, ORs lay down on the ground, making it impossible for patients to get through to the clinic.[53] They harassed patients as they approached, saying disturbing things like, "Go away from these killing fields."[54] Of the hit, Debbie told the *San Francisco Examiner*, "This is not civil disobedience. They're waging a holy war."[55]

Several hours later, police in riot gear made their first arrest: per OR's request, they arrested Jeff White, OR "tactical director" and leader of the West Coast chapter.[56] Approximately 250 ORs were arrested in Sunnyvale that day. Some were disappointed when they learned that police had stopped making arrests and would not be hauling them all away. Nationwide, that weekend 2,200 ORs were arrested in various cities and towns.[57]

OR outnumbered BACAOR. It was that simple fact that ensured BACAOR's defeat in Sunnyvale. In the months that followed, BACAOR kept recruiting. They developed their strategies and grew their numbers by holding clinic defense trainings in Dolores Park, at the San Francisco Women's Building, at San Francisco State University, and at UC Berkeley. By spring 1989, BACAOR started to win. On the morning of May 13, when OR arrived at Women's Choice Medical Clinic in Redwood City, just south of San Francisco, BACAOR was already in defense-line formation by the door, with reinforcements on the way.[58] Five clinic defenders were arrested that day, among many more ORs, and charged with attempting to block the clinic entrance, but clinic defenders challenged the charges, with legal support from the National Lawyers Guild, and the charges were dropped.[59]

"We had camaraderie and success," Nancy said, "and when you have success, you're more likely to continue doing something. Because whatever you're putting in, you're also getting back."

Organizers traveled around the area and eventually helped launch two sibling clinic defense coalitions: one in the South Bay and one in Sacramento. Kass described them as "powerhouse clinic defense organizations in their own right."

When an OR hit was planned, BACAOR would station people at potential target clinics. To determine which clinics might be hit, they called the clinics to see which ones planned to be open. "Some clinics didn't welcome us," Kass told me. "A lot of them were like, 'We don't want you here.' We would say, 'Well, we get that. But the antis are bringing the fight to you. We're coming to help. This is what our tactics will be, et cetera.' Unlike the antis, we never showed up unannounced." Nancy added, "We wanted to have the clinics' approval, but sometimes we had to tell them that we were coming anyway, because it was about defending people's rights, not private property."

Marianne was a key liaison between the clinics and BACAOR. "I would talk to the directors and say, 'Hey, we've got info. We'd like to collaborate with you and help get your patients in,'" she explained. "In the early days, they would try to swat us away. There were times when they were mad as heck at us. But then they began to see that we were effective."

On the day of a defense action, someone would be stationed at a central "office," or land line. When OR showed up at a clinic, a BACAOR member would find a payphone and call the office to report it. Defenders waiting at other clinics would call the office for updates and then get instructions on where to go. ("One of the things we always had to remember was to bring calling dimes," Kass told me.)

Because BACAOR members could find themselves mixed up with OR members during a chaotic scene at a clinic's doors, they developed a way to identify each other in a crowd: screen-printed BACAOR bandanas. On squares of white cloth, Joe and Agnes printed BACAOR's logo— a Venus gender pictogram inside of a triangle of triangles—in vibrant purple and pink inks. BACAOR members arrived at clinic defenses with the bandanas tied around their heads, necks, and arms.

For Kass, her BACAOR bandana became a daily accessory.

In her stack of plastic bins, I didn't come across a single photo of her without it.

This clinic is open

It was hot in Albuquerque in June. A standing fan purred on me as I rummaged around in Kass's BACAOR / BACORR archive. I picked up a VHS tape in a hot pink slipcase. Black cover text in a punky font read, "We don't write letters. We're BACAOR" (a slogan that BACAOR's South Bay sibling defense coalition had come up with). I had the tape digitized the next day so Kass and I could watch it together.

An original Agnes and Joe Sampson production, released in 1989, the training video opens with Tracy Chapman's "Talkin' 'bout a Revolution." BACAOR's logo flashes onto the screen in grainy purple, and Marianne's husky voice provides the voice-over: "The Bay Area Coalition Against Operation Rescue is a coalition of women and men committed to defense of our reproductive rights. We defend local abortion clinics against attempted blockades and harassment by Operation Rescue. This video shows techniques for escorting clients past OR pickets and methods for successful clinic defense." BACAOR would distribute the video (and others) to activists around the Bay Area and in other cities, too—Boston, New York, Milwaukee. "The training videos were an important tool for spreading radical clinic defense. At that time, we were the primary organized clinic defense force," Kass explained.

The video cuts to footage of a defense at Pregnancy Consultation Center. The camera zooms in close to capture the faces of antis: mostly white men. Marianne explains, "OR comes to clinics to harass women. We put ourselves between women and OR sidewalk counselors. Part of escorting includes verbal and sometimes physical confrontation with OR and also more subtle and creative techniques for diverting their attention from clients."

The next shot shows Kass, in an orange vest with a BACAOR bandana tied around her head, diverting an anti's attention. She raises her voice and shakes her finger at the anti: "Women are responsible beings who make decisions based on things in *their* life that *you* have nothing to do with!"

Then the video cuts to a young white woman sitting in the grass in front of PCC on the cold early morning of the defense, explaining clinic escorting and clinic defense to a group of new escorts and defenders. She's extremely well-spoken. She looks directly at her audience and often nods and smiles warmly during pauses for emphasis. Her mullet resembles Kass's, and she wears her BACAOR bandana around her neck. Her name is Brenda Cummings.

Brenda runs it down for the group:

In general, what we expect is picketing. There may be as many as twenty picketers here today. Some will stay on Bush Street with signs, and many of you will spend much of the morning on Bush Street with signs. That doesn't mean you're not being useful. You're counter demonstrators. You'll get a lot of positive reinforcement from the cars driving by. More importantly, you are the backup force. If anything were to happen, if more people were harassing people up here on Octavia Street, we'd pull people from counter demonstrating to help out. The reason we don't have everybody up there to start, where most of the conflict happens, is that we don't want to intimidate the clients. Okay? Also, by being down here, you are the first people who can get to that door where they're blockading.

The other roles: There will be someone at the door checking people in. There are people at each stairway in orange vests, being [escorts] with the clinic in an official way . . . people who will help counter OR, or who will go up to a client and say, "People with the orange vests are with the clinic, we can help you into the clinic."

The other two roles are client escorting and OR dogging. We don't want everybody going onto a client at once. We just want to have one person explaining who we are, helping the client and whoever is with her to identify that there are people here who can help them and that they don't have to be scared. OR doggers: Some of the picketers will walk along Octavia Street. They are focused on directly going up to clients and harassing them. Our job as doggers is to try to keep the ORs focused on us and not on the clients as much as possible. As OR doggers, you'll for the most part be walking around all morning with an OR. We try to put two doggers on one OR. If an OR tries to attack a client, your job will be to put yourself physically in between the client and the OR.

Counter demonstrators. Greeters. Escorts. Doggers.

The video then takes us to an organizing meeting. "One of the things we're trying to do is establish that *we* control the situation," Brenda tells the group. "I work as an escort at PCC. Now we no longer have to get into shoving matches with OR because they've learned the boundaries. They know that we will have us around each of them and that we're not going to let them go up to clients. So, we very rarely get into a situation where we have to shove them. We're defining the situation. In some sense, we might be risking arrest. We have to decide for ourselves and as a group whether it's worth it. I think controlling the situation is the most important thing."

The video explains that BACAOR makes a specific plan in advance for each clinic on a hit day. They identify which entrances are most defendable and where defenders should be placed to hold the doors.

"The key to a successful clinic defense is getting there first," Brenda adds. Behind her is Kass, leaning in with her forearms on her knees. "Keeping the door and corridor open is critical." If there isn't a corridor through the crowd, Brenda says, defenders can force one using a wedge formation.

The video cuts to footage from a defense where police are trying to stop both antis and defenders from getting near a clinic's door. "Together we pushed past police and OR to get clients into the clinic safely," Marianne explains in voice-over. Defenders and clients suddenly break into a run for the door. "Run, run!" Brenda yells, waving for people to follow her. There is a tangle of defenders, ORs, and police, with police grabbing and yanking people away from the doors.

The video then shows and explains "clinic defense boards," which are flat 2' x 4' plywood panels, like wooden shields, that can be tied together in various ways to create a blockade or to bolster defense lines. Kass demonstrates for the camera how you can tie simple knots to create hand and foot loops.

Marianne adds, "Several defenders can safely lift and remove an individual OR from behind defense lines. Control the action and momentum and do the bulk of clearing an area before enough police arrive to intervene. This helps ensure the clinic can be open with the least risk of arrest to defenders. . . .When we have stabilized the balance of power in our favor, confrontation ceases, and the clinic stays successfully open. Now we have an OR-free zone and clients can easily enter."

I came across simple instructions for making clinic defense boards in Kass's archive, with helpful illustrations of the knots and loops.

By early 1989, BACAOR could count on as many as a thousand clinic defenders to show up when they put out a call. They published a monthly newsletter and sent out mailings to help keep people engaged. Marianne explains in the training video, "BACAOR is a multi-issue organization and has worked in coalition with others to link up the issues between struggles for reproductive rights, lesbian and gay liberation, and an end to racism. We see the attack on abortion rights as only one part of the Far Right wing's agenda."

The video shows BACAOR on the offensive, too, marching in the streets or in front of churches with creative props. In one scene, defenders carry a giant skeleton puppet wearing a pope's hat. They march while holding up boards that, side-by-side, read "Clinic Defense: BACAOR."

The training video begins to wrap up with a shot of defenders burning a paper-wrapped wire hanger and chanting, "Never again!" Then Lucinda Williams's upbeat "Passionate Kisses" comes on. The last eight or so minutes of the tape contain B-roll overlaid with Public Enemy's "Fight the Power." At one point, the camera captures defenders marching defiantly down a street in the direction of a clinic with a giant sign that reads: "THIS CLINIC IS OPEN." And people cheer.

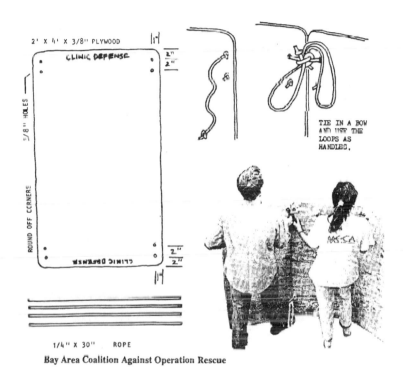

Bay Area Coalition Against Operation Rescue

"Clinic Defense Boards Instructions," July 1989, by BACAOR. From Kass McMahon's personal collection.

I did not understand what being a girl was

Brenda Cummings grew up in rural Maine, and that's where she was when we chatted online in fall 2021. As a kid, she would attend town hall meetings with her father, who was a journalist and later a town selectman. Her mother was the town treasurer. Smart and creative, Brenda received a National Merit Scholarship to attend Antioch College. Then she became pregnant. She explained,

> I graduated from high school about four months pregnant, having gone through an extraordinarily public process about my decision about whether to have an abortion. Being young and naive, I somehow felt like I could continue the pregnancy. So I did. I considered adoption after Jon was born in 1981 but decided against it. I went to a Catholic Charities unwed mothers home. I was in-between in my life. I didn't know what I was going to do next. There was a lot of pressure on me. I was expected to do well. I did not understand what being a girl was until I got pregnant.

Brenda *did* go to Antioch College, taking Jon with her, but right before she went, she became pregnant again, and then again after she arrived. In those cases, Brenda chose abortion. "All it took was me getting near a penis and I would get pregnant," she said. "I wasn't experienced with how to say no. I wasn't experienced with contraception. I grew up in rural Maine. I was supposed to be looking at Harvard. Instead, I was getting pregnant."

At Antioch, Brenda fell in with a very queer crowd and had her first relationship with a woman. Her new friends helped her take care of Jon, babysitting for free while she went to class or worked on the college newspaper. "In some ways I was just like all the other young twenty-something-year-olds," Brenda said, "but with a completely different set of responsibilities than everybody else."

Shortly before finishing her degree, Brenda decided to move to San Francisco with her son and her friends. Her new housemate, Jade, was already established in the city and had gotten involved with Prairie Fire, a political group that had developed out of the Weather Underground.[60] "At Antioch, I developed a political analysis and a feminist analysis. But I was certainly not a radical activist," Brenda told me. "But then my housemate invited me to shut down the Golden Gate Bridge with Stop AIDS Now or Else."

On January 31, 1989, Stop AIDS Now or Else blocked the Golden Gate Bridge during the morning commute. They held up a massive banner that cut across all six lanes of traffic. It read: "AIDS = GENOCIDE / SILENCE = DEATH / FIGHT BACK." The group's organizers were from AIDS Action Pledge, which would eventually become ACT UP San Francisco.[61]

"There I am at the end of the line of people getting arrested on the bridge, and I'm worried about whether I'm going to be out of jail in time to pick Jon up from daycare," Brenda recalled.

The organizers of the action were mostly women, and some were or would become clinic defenders. By 1989, HIV/AIDS and reproductive rights activism were sibling movements. It was through Stop AIDS Now or Else that Brenda met Marianne, who introduced her to BACAOR.

The next thing Brenda knew, she was at the center of an explosive movement to keep clinic doors clear and, more broadly, to stand up against Christian fascism and the police.

One penis under God

On a spring afternoon, Agnes and Joe had me over for a screening in the garden. They'd been going through their BACAOR/BACORR tapes and digitizing them, and they'd found the notorious July 1989 "wedding scene," an example of BACAOR on the offensive. I'd heard about the wedding, that it was a classic.

Joe hit play on his laptop, and the still image of a group of BACAOR protesters erupted to life. Young people of all genders marched in a tight circle in front of First Orthodox Presbyterian Church in San Francisco chanting, "Racist, fascist, anti-gay! Born-again bigots, go away!"

Demonstrating in front of churches that hosted Operation Rescue was one of BACAOR's new tactics, and Agnes had the idea that they could stage a mock wedding at this one. She and Joe had made some props and costumes, and to their delight, the group ran with it all. "BACAOR attracted creative types," Agnes said. "They just made it up right there."

In front of the church, people got acquainted with their props and into their roles; a young blond woman zipped herself into the ratty old wedding dress Agnes had just found at a thrift store. It was crusted with dried red paint, especially in the crotch. Wedding attendees circled the bride and started pushing, pulling, and taunting her. They dangled red-painted wire coat hangers in front of her, some of which were strung with naked plastic babies. Some hooked the hangers onto the bride's dress, others pulled at her dress, tearing it away from her body. The bride moaned, "*Nooo!*" One wedding attendee led the group in a prayer:

> I pledge obedience
> To the men
> Of Operation Rescue
> And to the repression
> For which they stand
> One penis
> Under God
> With slavery and repression
> For all women

Everyone cheered.

When it was time for the ceremony, a man in a thrifted suit-coat stood next to the disheveled bride. Someone assumed the role of minister and began: "We are here today to join this couple." Wedding guests threw bloody hangers at the bride while she screamed. One flamboyant guest interjected, "Get over it, honey! You'll get used to it. Use a little KY! It won't hurt so bad."

The minister then commanded, "Take this woman, your lawful wedded wife . . . and baby-making machine! I pronounce you man and property. You may impregnate the bride." A member of the wedding party stepped forward and presented a red velvet pillow, on which there was a pair of handcuffs. The groom cuffed one of the bride's wrists, and then one of his own.

Then wedding guests moved in on the bride and shoved her to her knees in front of the groom. "Do your duty! Do your duty," they chanted. "Breed! Breed! Breed!" With a look of disgust, the bride started bobbing her head in what appeared to be a mock blowjob. (Had this mock wedding really turned into a mock rape? Yes, it had.) Everyone was yelling and screaming. Guests continued to pelt her with bloody hangers and plastic babies. Some started spanking the babies. The bride crawled around miserably.

"Not the church, not the state, we don't want to procreate!" a BACAOR member started chanting, calling everyone back to center and ending the scene. Others joined in. "We won't go back! We won't go back! We won't go back!"

IN 1989, BACAOR was made up of lots of lesbians and queer folks. Inspired in part by the performative tactics of ACT UP, BACAOR embraced visuals and words that confronted and exposed the hypocrisy of their enemies. When they were on the offense, demonstrating at Christian churches or in the streets, they used humor, camp, and satire. BACAOR's mock wedding action took place six months before "Stop the Church," an ACT UP NY action that would receive global media attention.[62]

What struck me most about BACAOR's mock wedding was that it did not hold back in its representation of violence directed at the bride. "We were unruly," Laura Weide said of the scene. It was too much. And in the "too much" lies the exposure. This is how the satire packed its punch: the moment when the mock wedding, which was bold and bawdy, escalated into a mock rape outside of a church—when the satire becomes contemptuous, devastating, and total—was the moment of truth.

It's difficult to go to these types of places and tell the truth: that the Christian Right did (and does) subject women to violence by forcing marriage, heterosexual procreative sex, pregnancy, birth, and parenthood on them; and that this violence can be emotional, physical, sexual, or all three.

In our discussion of the scene, Agnes pointed out that the wedding captures what it might feel like to be a woman who becomes pregnant and doesn't want to be—as if the whole world is pelting you with dangerous objects, *including* men and babies.

"It felt great," she said of pulling off the scene. "There we were in front of a church, the center of the oppression. And we were able to make just total vicious fun of them and their whole woman-hating thing. It felt good to say what it was really all about, which was women being stomped into the dirt."

As Agnes's comments suggest, the scene registers how personal the movement was for clinic defenders. BACAOR had a political analysis, and they also had lived experience. They were women who had had unplanned pregnancies themselves and who had experienced discrimination and policing by the medical institution, churches, and the state. They were lesbians, gays, queers, and gender-nonconforming people who had been the target of homophobic and transphobic speech and violence. Their street theater reflected the emotional pain, exasperation, and outrage they harbored toward institutions that seemed hellbent on pacifying, controlling, immiserating, and erasing them. As they wrote around the time of the mock wedding, "The attack on reproductive rights is also an attack on sexual freedom, particularly for women, youth, and lesbians and gay men."[63]

"The only political statement I've ever heard that has more layers to it than 'the personal is political,'" Kass said to me, "is 'silence equals death'"—the message central to ACT UP's campaign.[64] BACAOR members were not afraid to allow their politics to be informed by their deepest, rawest wounds. And they were unwilling to stay silent.

The wedding was satirical improv street theater, but when you start to think about what women and queer and trans people were up against—especially with the *Webster v. Reproductive Health Services* decision coming down at that same time and marking the beginning of the end of *Roe*—the irony starts to crumble. BACAOR did its work at the edge of this sinkhole.

They had to be countered

Just as BACAOR worked to develop tactics to fight antis at clinic doors, it also started developing its intelligence arm. Back in December 1988, reflecting on an unsuccessful defense, Agnes wrote, "I'd like to throw out the idea of forming a 'think tank' of trusted and proven people including those who have an intimate knowledge of OR tactics. This group would carefully study OR maneuvers to figure out if there is a possible weak link."[65] In the months that followed, BACAOR members started embedding themselves in OR to do opposition research.

A BACAOR member named Connie infiltrated OR. She and another clinic defender started going to OR pre-hit rallies in the South Bay. According to Connie, fiery sermons at the rallies often focused on how "problems in this country (from drugs to the deficit) [were] happening because god is angry at the US for legalizing abortion." OR members were required to pledge that they would obey the male OR marshals during the "rescue" itself. Then members were given a meeting place for the next morning (they were not told which clinic they would hit). After the rallies, Connie would deliver as much information as she could back to BACAOR so that BACAOR could try to deduce where OR was likely to hit.[66]

A BACAOR member named Vanessa* told me about a time she infiltrated OR. Vanessa's aim wasn't to get intel about OR's plans, but rather to shut down their meeting altogether so that they couldn't announce the next day's meeting spot. Her goal was to create confusion so that OR members wouldn't know where to go and wouldn't be able to proceed with their attack. Here's the story she told me:

Vanessa was an out lesbian and anarchist punk from New York who had recently relocated to the Bay Area. She was very engaged with abortion defense. The attempted shutdown happened on a Friday night in fall 1989—a turbulent time. Abortion activism had been intense in the Bay Area. Earlier that year in March, at a BACAOR counter rally at St. Dominic's Church, San Francisco police pepper-sprayed a group of protesters. Horribly, one cop grabbed a BACAOR member from behind, pushed her to the ground, and beat her on the head and legs. She was hospitalized for a head injury and severe reaction to the pepper spray and was disabled for more than a month afterward.[67] In April, leading up to the Supreme Court's *Webster* decision, tens of thousands of choice supporters took to the streets in San Francisco alone.[68] Meanwhile, OR continued to escalate its attacks on clinics all around the Bay Area. The stakes felt high.

That Friday night, OR's pre-hit rally was being held at a conservative church in Fremont. Vanessa and two other BACAOR members, Willow* and Suki*, arrived at the church in ankle-length skirts. Vanessa had tucked her spiky blue mohawk beneath a wig of thick long hair. She wore a loose-fitting cardigan. She looked like a Christian white woman, or a slightly frumpy secretary.

Vanessa, Willow, and Suki smiled as steadily and widely as they could as ORs warmly welcomed them to the event and ushered them into the church. The rally opened with speeches by OR leaders. There was some singing, and then it was time for a skit. Out onto the raised altar came a flamboyant OR member dressed in a slim-fitting red costume with pointy horns and a red staff. "He started saying that he liked killing babies," Vanessa recalled. "He kind of swished around on the stage. He was this gay pro-abortion devil. It was clear he loved getting to act gay. Obviously, he was gay."

Next, OR started to "rile up the troops about babies." They screened a slideshow of fake images of mutilated fetuses while the crowd whispered and moaned. Clearly OR was getting ready to announce the approximate location of the next day's hit. That was Vanessa and her friends' cue.

The three took turns leaving their pew, staggering their exits so as not to draw too much attention. Long heat vents ran all along the bases of the church's two side walls. Toward the back, Vanessa pulled a vial out of her sweater pocket and deposited a few drops into the vent. "We had access to some chemicals," she explained. "Nothing that would hurt anyone. It basically just created a powerful stink-bomb."

The stink-bomb was fast acting. Soon everyone was screaming and rushing out the doors. Just as Vanessa crossed the door's threshold to the outside, a beefy security guard grabbed the back of her cardigan. "Somehow I managed to wriggle out of that sweater and kept running," she recalled.

Outside the church, BACAOR was holding a counter rally. Vanessa and Willow tried to take cover with friends, but perhaps their secretary garb gave them away, because three cops soon approached and cuffed Vanessa, Willow, and another BACAOR member (not Suki, who had taken off on foot).

The cops had Vanessa, Willow, and the third person stand in the glaring floodlights. ORs swarmed them, eager to identify the perpetrators. "Is this your sweater?" one cop asked Vanessa. "Nope," she replied. "I've never seen that sweater before in my life."

They were taken to the police station, and the third woman was soon released. But Vanessa and Willow were shipped off to Santa Rita Jail, where they would spend the next five days.

"We were banned from the entire city of Fremont for two years," Vanessa told me after finishing the story. "And every time I would go to a defense, ORs would recognize me."

"What do you think about the action now?" I asked her. Planting a stink-bomb at an OR church rally was, after all, one of the riskier offensive actions that BACAOR members took. Vanessa said, "The tactics that OR employed were dangerous to women: threats, screaming in women's faces, sending in their thugs to beat up clinic defenders. . . . It took a real toll on a huge range of people—clients, clinic staff, activists, concerned people. I'd like to believe that some of the things we did to counteract those tactics helped convince OR that they had to change, that going to clinics and beating up on people was a bad idea. They had to be countered." In Vanessa's mind, she was giving OR a taste of their own terroristic campaign in the form of an inconvenience, or maybe a scare. Moreover, she pointed out, employing tactics that stood a chance of stopping OR from executing a hit was necessary and in alignment with BACAOR's goals.

By that same fall, BACAOR had articulated its goals clearly in its printed materials: "We fight for abortion rights in the context of our demands for full reproductive freedom—to be educated about our reproductive options, to be free from forced or coerced sterilization or population control, and to be able to choose to have and to care for our children." Their numbers had climbed to more than two thousand people.

BACAOR was explicitly antifascist—certainly they were a leading antifascist movement of their generation. Theirs was a philosophy of autonomous action: "We understand that we must rely on ourselves, not our elected officials, to defend and expand our freedoms." In other words, as they wrote, echoing the community self-defense philosophy of the Black Panther Party: "Our first line of defense is self-defense."[69]

Later in 1990, BACAOR began to see OR numbers abate in the Bay Area, so they started sharing strategies with clinic defense groups cropping up around the region and country. Some BACAOR members worked with RWL to organize a national clinic defense conference in March 1990 in Detroit. The outcome of the conference was the formation of a new national group: the National Women's Rights Organizing Coalition (NWROC). Back in the Bay Area, BACAOR changed its name to the Bay Area Coalition for Our Reproductive Rights (BACORR), partly because it had largely driven OR out of the Bay Area, and also to reflect its "broader reproductive rights agenda."[70]

The fact that OR mass blockades were dwindling in the Bay Area, at least for the time being, was a win for clinic defenders. But instead of mobbing clinic doors, OR members and other anti-abortion extremists who did show up to harass people at clinics tended to be the "more fanatical bands, mostly of men, who picket[ed] with overt hostility and direct physical combativeness aimed at escorts."[71] Their enemy was evolving.

BACAOR bandana, c. 1990. From Kass McMahon's personal collection.

Chapter 7

No One Person Has the Power

It wasn't until two years into my research that gynecological and abortion self-helpers started to tell me stories about their underground work.

Maybe the story abortion self-helpers told about how menstrual extraction was fundamentally different from abortion stopped me from asking whether it might, at the same time, not necessarily be different. What I had yet to grasp was that while menstrual extraction was not abortion, menstrual extraction was also definitively abortion.

I'll try to explain what I mean in the following sections, which explore the development of a cluster of Bay Area underground self-help groups and the work they did to learn how to perform abortions themselves and then provide them to people in their communities.

By the late 1980s, after a decade-and-a-half-long anti-abortion campaign against *Roe* along with Reagan's nomination of the anti-abortion conservatives Antonin Scalia and Anthony Kennedy to the Supreme Court, abortion rights groups believed it was likely that the Court would soon overturn *Roe v. Wade*.[1] The Court had the opportunity to do so in the case of *Webster v. Reproductive Health Services* in 1989. The case concerned the constitutionality of a Missouri law that said life began at conception and that "unborn children have protectable interests." The law also said that a doctor could not perform an abortion after twenty weeks if the fetus was "viable" and, moreover, that public funding, employees, and facilities could not be used for providing abortions or abortion counseling. Lower courts had ruled that the Missouri law violated the *Roe* ruling, but in July 1989 a Supreme Court majority voted to uphold the law.[2]

In the *Webster* ruling, the Supreme Court argued that notions of "trimesters and viability" were not in the Constitution. Thus, "there is . . . no reason why the State's compelling interest in protecting potential human life should not extend throughout pregnancy."[3] *Webster* all but struck down *Roe*, creating a pathway for individual states to further restrict abortion. It exposed what abortion defenders already knew: the state was invested in "fetal life" before all else, before the lives of women, especially poor women, their children, and their communities.

The win with *Webster* fueled the anti-abortion movement, and it prompted Bay Area underground self-helpers to start building out their network. As they always had, self-help groups relied on the human and other resources of clinics—in particular, Women's Choice. The clinic supported underground abortion self-help groups by facilitating the transfer of restricted knowledge and supplies.

By that point, Women's Choice had a new container nonprofit: West Coast Feminist Health Project. This is the name that Linci, Debbie Gregg, and a couple of others gave the organization after they bought the clinic in 1988, when former director Laura Brown declared bankruptcy. (I'll refer to West Coast Feminist Health Project / Women's Choice as WCFHP / Women's Choice.)

In terms of race, the three arms of Bay Area radical abortion defense—first, abortion care and abortion self-help at Women's Choice; second, clinic defense; and third, underground self-help— fell on a spectrum, with the last being the whitest. Women's Choice was staffed by a number of working-class women of color, many of whom were also parenting. Clinic defense attracted a lot of young people who were coming from different experiences of race and class and who had diverse politics. Self-help groups were made up of mostly white women, both working- and middle-class, and many were anarchists, the people I interviewed conveyed to me. Of course, I don't know if this tells the whole story about who was doing self-help.

Something's going to happen here that's just us

Cindy*, a twenty-seven-year-old lesbian with bleached hair and
a spray of freckles across her nose, was fascinated by lay health
care movements. A committed activist, she was eager to get
involved in the Bay Area collective scene that she had heard so
much about, so in 1988, she moved up the coast from Southern
California.

When Cindy arrived in the Bay Area, she moved into a communal house and signed up to volunteer at the Berkeley Free
Clinic, a radical health collective that was started in 1969. There
she quickly plugged into a diverse group of lay health workers
and activists. Through her new community, Cindy met Britt* and
Jo*, a lesbian couple she liked a lot, who shared with her that they
were in a self-help group. "We talked with the group," Britt told
Cindy, "and they're willing to meet you."

Cindy already knew a little about self-help because an older
activist in Southern California had shared the history with her a
couple years earlier. "She took me for a walk. She just knew I was
hungry, probably," Cindy told me. "She was like, I've got something to tell you about."

When her older friend offered to visit the women's health
group Cindy and her friends had started and teach them cervical
self-exam, Cindy remembered being excited and a little shocked.
When the elder visited, she fitted everyone with cervical caps,
too. So in early 1989, already clear about her desire to learn about
lay gynecology, when asked to join Britt and Jo's self-help group,
Cindy did.

When Cindy started practicing with the group, two people
who both worked at WCFHP / Women's Choice were doing most
of the teaching. Their names were Ann* and Linci.

LINCI AND ANN had weathered a tumultuous year—the collapse
of Oakland's network of FWHCs, the OFWHC / Women's
Choice bankruptcy, the break with the sperm bank. The new
WCFHP / Women's Choice was still on McClure Street, and it

had been the target of some arsons. Nationally, violence against abortion providers was on the rise.[4]

Cindy met me under the persimmon tree outside my Berkeley shack one afternoon in spring 2021. She arrived on bicycle, in tan palazzo pants. She seemed to float in, with wispy strands of hair framing her face.

"In self-help, no one person has the power," Cindy told me. "It was always three people who did everything. If we were practicing pelvic exams, it was always three people who sized the uterus. That's how we always did it. And that's how we passed on how to do it." The purpose of having multiple group members do each practice was to make sure nobody missed anything. It was a safety check, in the interest of the person receiving care. One effect, Cindy pointed out, was that groups were nonhierarchical.

"We were so into each other," she remembered. "We'd just climb on top of each other! We were so close. We were up for anything."

Cindy moved into a small cottage behind Linci and Ann's house. Linci remembered helping drag Cindy's piano around to the back and the light pinging of Cindy's hands flitting up and down the keys. "She had these four-wheel skates," Linci said of Cindy. "She flew fast. That's how I think of her. Balance and speed. And music."

"We were always in each other's beds," Linci continued. "The intimacy that we shared was closer for many of us than our relationships with our lovers. If we had something going on with our body, we went to our self-help group."

A couple of years later, conflicts broke up the group, one of which was the collapse of Linci and Ann's relationship. After the group dispersed, Cindy went on to start her own. She would stay in the movement for another decade.

CINDY TOLD ME about some of her experiences practicing in self-help groups over the years. In Oakland near the DMV, there was a medical supply store where she would use her clinic credentials to buy speculums, gloves, gauze, chux pads, syringes,

cannulas, and other supplies. Eventually she acquired an autoclave, which enabled her and other group members to sterilize
equipment at home, as opposed to having to use the autoclave at
WCFHP / Women's Choice.

If a friend outside of the group became pregnant and wanted
to have a menstrual extraction, Cindy said, the group would meet
with her first. During this initial interview, the group would perform an exam to make sure the person was within the window of
time for an extraction, up to about eight weeks. Then they would
explain the procedure, along with the risks. Finally, they would
emphasize that it would be a group process and that multiple
group members would repeat each of the practices to make sure
nobody missed anything. That's how they made sure it was as safe
as possible.

Cindy told me about the atmosphere of the room and the
roles that group members held:

> It was a lot of silence, frankly. We wouldn't go if we didn't
> have enough people to do everything. There'd always be
> one support person on each side of the person who was
> having the ME. One would help them breathe. If that was
> your role for the night, then you'd sit by her side, hold
> her hand, look in her eyes, help her breathe. You'd tell
> her she's going to get through it and that it's okay. There
> would be somebody who would handle the sterile stuff.
> And then there'd be three people who would do the pro-
> cedure. We would meet first and talk about who was going
> to do what that night.

They would do whatever they could to make the extraction feel
soothing, she explained. "Sometimes the woman would have
somebody there with her but usually not. It felt like a ritual. A
warm, loving ritual that was also kind of intense. We would stay
afterward to be supportive. The willingness of people to hold
intensity and to listen—that felt powerful to me."

Cindy commented further on the intimacy and intensity of
self-help. "You're not just coming into a room to have a cup of

coffee," she said. "You're coming into a room ready to be exploring something together. You feel it. You feel the energy in the air. There are certain things that we would always do to create that safe space, which added to the feeling of . . . something's going to happen here that's just us. This is a protected bubble that we're all inside of. You're ready for something very intimate to happen, together, and you don't know how it's going to unfold, but you're there, and you're ready to be really, really open."

WITH TWELVE YEARS of experience working at the clinic, Linci was skilled at teaching abortion self-help. So, that spring of 1989, in a political climate that was increasingly hostile toward abortion, she decided it was time to step up the outreach. With other self-helpers, Linci started recruiting people—at pro-choice events, communal houses, and, in August, at the women's gathering at the Anarchist Conference and Festival.

Cindy remembered Linci reporting back to the group about her recruiting activities. "I branched out, you guys," she said. "Don't be mad. But . . . there might be a lot of interest."

Remember, 1989: the year West Coast Feminist Health Project launched. The year, Linci told me, that she launched into her fucking *life*.

No going back

Linci wasn't the only one who felt it was time to start branching out. In 1989, leading up to the Supreme Court's ruling on *Webster*, the Federation of FWHCs released a film titled *No Going Back: A Pro-Choice Perspective*. The film introduced viewers to abortion self-help and featured "historic footage" of a menstrual extraction.[5]

"We want you to understand the facts and to be able to clarify them for others," says a young Black woman narrator at the beginning of the film.[6] The film cuts to an interview with a silver-haired Lorraine, at that point in her late fifties. Lorraine explains self-help and emphasizes the importance of groupwork to ensure safety. She notes, "Of course the most popular reason [people practice menstrual extraction] is the fact that menstrual extraction can be used to remove a fertilized egg if a woman should suspect that she became impregnated." Self-help groups are all over, Lorraine adds, suggesting that the movement was widespread, robust, and prepared.

Then *No Going Back* brings viewers into a room with a self-help group. First the group's facilitator, a Latina woman named Selina, demonstrates cervical self-exam. Then she presents and explains a Del-Em, which appears center frame. To the left appears a sleeping infant, in the arms of a group member. Moments earlier, this group member had explained that she had used self-exam to track her fertility and that's how she was able to achieve pregnancy.

The film cuts to footage of a menstrual extraction, followed by video of a clinic abortion, contrasting the "gentler" former technique with the more efficient latter. Back again in the room with the self-help group, a member says, "I've felt so helpless about the possibility of abortion becoming illegal. And now I feel like I've learned a skill, or at least heard about it, that I can use or my friends can use when and if it happens."

The federation sold hundreds of these VHS tapes to individuals, clinics, and organizations. They also sent them to major media outlets. "The purpose was to shout from the rooftops that women were arming themselves with the weapons needed to go underground if abortion became illegal," writes Hannah Dudley-Shotwell.[7]

Of course, self-helpers were already working underground. They had been consistently from the start. You could read the film as suggesting as much—recall Lorraine: *self-help groups are all over.*

First you do the basic training

I was in Max's* bedroom, where I'd helped her pull a box of files out of storage. The folders' contents were splayed out on her bed:

news clippings, pamphlets and zines, photocopied chapters from medical textbooks, outlines for workshops, handwritten notes. Max offered me a sparkling water from her stash in the closet— where her teenager won't find it, she told me. She leaned back against a stack of pillows. I was at the foot of the bed, trying to orient myself in her history.

When she was nineteen and in college on the East Coast, far away from where she'd grown up, Max became pregnant. "It was probably one of the first times that I'd had sex," she said. "I was appalled, horrified. I felt horrible being in my own body. It felt like there was a parasite in me." Max continued, "It felt so completely different when I became pregnant later, when I *wanted* to be. I wanted a different word for a pregnancy that was not welcome."

Max went to student health services to get an abortion. She remembered how the doctor, an older man, made rude comments about the size of her vulva. "It felt wounding," she said. "But at the time, I didn't have the wherewithal to name it and call it out and challenge the system that would allow somebody who has the power of a doctor to make rude comments, who instead of approaching a female patient with the utmost respect, just talks in such a gross way. . . . My personal experience created a space for a critique of the system."

After college, Max moved to the Bay Area and joined her first self-help group. She would be active in one or more groups throughout the 1990s. Over the decade, Max participated in self-help groups, started new groups, taught workshops for people new to self-help, and recruited more people to the movement. She was, in her own words, "a groupie." Across the groups she was a part of, Max estimated, they must have performed at least a hundred menstrual extractions, many of which were for people who were pregnant, or what Max called "pregnant MEs," and many for pregnant people outside of their groups.

Pregnant MEs. I thought of the story earlier self-helpers told, that abortion was not an aim but a corollary to a self-affirming and radical action that one could take: "Pregnant ME" was not that story. A pregnant menstrual extraction was an abortion procedure, or a procedure to help a person who's pregnant, and doesn't want to be, to be not pregnant.

WHEN SHE ARRIVED in the Bay Area, Max had already heard of menstrual extraction and wanted to learn more. So in 1989, when she heard about a meeting in Berkeley on laywomen's health care, she had a pretty good idea that it was what she was looking for.

The night of the meeting, Max followed a narrow staircase into the musty basement of a Berkeley communal house. She staked out a chair and checked out the room. The others, maybe twenty in total, were a little younger, probably students. Cute, punky girls with a lot of ripped denim, vegan leather, and scuffed combat boots.

Two queer-looking women, probably in their thirties, convened the meeting, and the room's nervous chatter quickly subsided. "Tonight we're going to show you how to do cervical self-exam," one explained. She wore her hair in a medium-length shag, but she still managed to look androgenous, the sleeves of her untucked button-up rolled up to her elbows. When she spoke, her turquoise eyes shone. "And if you want to do your own self-exam tonight, you can do that, too."

The two presenters told a history of the gynecological self-help movement—how it began in a house in Venice in 1971, nearly two decades in the past. They passed out smudgy photocopies of a chart for tracking one's cycle. "Come by Women's Choice, and we'll get you a free basal thermometer," one of them told the group. Then, the androgynous facilitator stripped off her trousers and laid down on a blanket on the floor to show everyone how to insert a speculum and look at one's own cervix with a mirror and flashlight. "If you're interested," she said afterward, upright again, "get a group of your friends together or find some people in this room to do the basic training with. We have some speculums for sale."

People reached into patch- and safety-pin-covered backpacks to retrieve wallets or loose dollars. They swarmed the two presenters, eager to take plastic speculums home with them. Max exhaled and stood up, her head buzzing. She was ready to find some others to start a group with.

Just a handful of years later, it would be Max giving the self-help presentation at the front of the room.

IN SUMMER 1989, Vanessa, the frumpy secretary from the church stink-bomb action, traveled to the Bay Area from New York to help plan the Anarchist Conference and Festival. Excited to have a few overstuffed weeks with Bay Area anarchists and queers, she also helped organize a "women's gathering," to take place the week after the main conference in an East Oakland warehouse.

Held in San Francisco's Mission neighborhood, the main conference was a weeklong feast of workshops and discussions covering everything from anti-imperialist struggles to monogamy alternatives and sex work. Anarchists organized a Day of Action, too, and worked with San Francisco Food Not Bombs to plan a picnic for and with unhoused people across from city hall in protest of the city's arrest of people for serving free food in the park the week before.[8] ("Don't forget to mention the Coke truck!" self-helpers laughingly reminded me, in reference to a now-legendary carjacking that occurred on the Day of Action.)

After a nonstop week, young people at the women's gathering piled onto a couple of worn-out couches. A few others sat cross-legged on a thin carpet, talking intently. The ground-floor commons area swirled with ebullient energy. It had been an intense week of conversation, and people were hyped up.

Vanessa found a spot on the carpet in front of a platform where the presentations were being held. "This is Linci Comy, the director of Women's Choice Clinic," one of the organizers announced. "She's going to talk to us about self-help."

Linci stood up from where she'd been sitting on the ground. She had on loose-fitting blue jeans and an untucked plain t-shirt—a contrast to the metal, leather, and black all around her. Fifteen years older than most of them, Linci was all business. She talked about the Right's militant attack on reproductive freedom.

She held up a speculum and explained cervical self-exam. Then she held up a jar, tubing, and syringe and explained menstrual extraction.

Vanessa recalled how the frenetic room was transformed. Suddenly everyone zeroed in on Linci. Some people who had been half-listening from the balcony made their way into the commons area, seeking an open space to sit on the floor. The room went silent.

"I'd never heard anyone speak who was so good at bringing together theory, concept, and action," Vanessa told me. "Linci was talking about something *real*. We were all so young. What experience did we have? And here was Linci. We were spellbound."

Learning the thing she had to teach was a way to contribute to community knowledge, Linci explained. But before a person could contribute, *they had to learn the thing*.

After narrating her history in the self-help movement, Linci invited everyone to find a partner and give cervical self-exam a try. "You can learn this stuff," Linci assured them at the end of the meeting. "But you'll need to form a group. Who wants to get involved?"

Pretty much everyone did. Vanessa remembered that three new groups formed out of that women's gathering conversation. She hadn't planned to stay in town long after the conference; she liked New York. But too many interesting things were happening in the Bay Area. She wouldn't be leaving anytime soon.

"IF SOMEONE WAS interested in doing a self-help group and had a group of friends who were interested, too, we'd work with them," Linci explained to me. "And turn them into radical revolutionaries. Usually within a few months."

CHLOE* GULPED HER lukewarm coffee, still not fully awake. It was Sunday afternoon, and she was at the community table in the kitchen of her big Berkeley communal house. Down the hall, someone had the Clash in their tape deck. Rosie* slid onto the bench across from Chloe, running a hand over her close-shaved head. Chloe leaned forward, "Have you talked to Simone* yet?"

Chloe and Rosie were both from white families in the South. After arriving in Berkeley, both started going West Coast punk: various degrees of shaved head and ratty oversized flannels from free boxes on the street.

Simone came into the kitchen and joined her friends at the table. She was from a middle-class immigrant family on the East Coast—a biology major, studious and soft spoken. But everyone who knew her knew she was a badass. She was a vegan with a nose ring and streaks of purple in her hair. "It's about being prepared," Simone explained. "Someone will teach us. But first we have to get a group together."

By that point in 1989, Simone, Chloe, and Rosie were already active in the reproductive rights movement. They had bonded while participating in a few clinic defenses. On campus, there had been meetings about how the Supreme Court could overturn *Roe*. They had read *Our Bodies, Ourselves*. They'd met Linci at some presentations she'd given on reproductive freedom. Rosie, poster-maker extraordinaire, with her eyes closed could paint a wire hanger in a circle crossed out.

None of them was yet twenty years old.

Chloe nodded. She was awake now, and her heart was pounding. "I definitely want to learn. We need to be ready," she said.

Rosie's eyes sparkled as she looked at Chloe and then at Simone. The Bay Area was a constant swirl, and she loved her wonderful, wild, freethinking friends.

IZABEL* CAUGHT UP with Fuchsia* on Sproul Plaza. Throngs of students milled about, some leafleting for clubs, causes, and upcoming demos, while others walked by briskly, late to class. Fuchsia was with Max—they were lovers at the time.

"So, tell me about the group!" exclaimed Izabel, breathless from navigating the plaza hubbub on a warm day. Izabel had met Max through Fuchsia, and they had become friends, too. It was fall 1989.

"It's a group of women that meets regularly to learn lay health care," Max said, one arm around Fuchsia's waist. "It's called self-help," she added. "Do you want to do it?"

Izabel and Fuchsia had both chosen to go to University of California, Berkeley, to get a political education. Born and raised in white middle-class families in California, the two quickly found each other on campus and became friends. Through communal living and political organizing, they had connected with other student and community radicals: anti-apartheid, Third World Strike, queer liberation, and ACT UP activists. Another friend of Izabel's who was always inviting her to "opportunities to go underground in a political way" had mentioned self-help to her—secret meetings, invitation only.

Fuchsia had had an abortion herself and had started to get involved in reproductive rights activism. But neither she nor Izabel knew about self-help or what to expect when Fuchsia agreed to host a meeting at her North Oakland communal house.

The night of the meeting, twenty-some people, mostly students, crowded into Fuchsia's small living room—in chairs, on the couch, on throw pillows on the floor. When the meeting started, the two facilitators explained that they were convening a new self-help group. Their names were Linci and Vanessa. "We want to teach you things like how to insert a speculum and find your own cervix," Linci said. "Eventually we can teach you how to perform exams on each other."

That same night, leaning against a couch and with the help of a mirror and flashlight, Izabel and Fuchsia inserted plastic speculums into their own vaginas and glimpsed their cervixes for the first time. "I definitely knew people who were freaked out and who were like, 'You want me to do *what?*'" Izabel told me. "But I was comfortable with it right away."

Some of that night's attendees decided not to join the next meeting a couple of weeks later, but not Izabel and Fuchsia. They showed up. And they would keep showing up for ten more years.

Conquering heroines

In spring 1990, after the release of *No Going Back*, federation self-helpers went on a Midwest tour to screen the film and talk about menstrual extraction.[9] Women's clinics, student groups, and radical collectives were among their hosts.[10] The film and tour received a fair amount of media attention that registered a range of ambivalent responses. As Dudley-Shotwell notes, the pro-choice medical establishment didn't hesitate to express its disapproval.[11]

American Medical News wrote of the "controversial abortion approach," reporting that "self-help menstrual extraction stirs legal, public health concerns." A vice president at Planned Parenthood is quoted saying, "These people don't know what they're feeling and, worse, they don't know what they don't know." But then, too, the article quotes a Utah clinic director who points out that manual-suction technology was used all over the world where abortion wasn't legal.[12] The director here was referring to the manual vacuum aspiration device manufactured by Ipas—the same menstrual regulation device from which 1970s self-helpers wanted to differentiate their Del-Em, alleging that the former was a misuse of the technology for population control.

In Health magazine ran a feature in November 1991 about the federation's 1990 self-help tour. Journalist Ann Japenga asks, "Is the plastic speculum really the symbol of a viable pro-choice alternative? Or is it just a shiny pacifier for women who have long felt powerless over their reproductive destinies?" She tells the story of a menstrual extraction demonstration in Toledo, and her final anecdote depicts participants at a restaurant after the demonstration: "They entered the restaurant with the swaggering attitude of a pack of middle-aged men who had just won a football game. Conquering heroines. They were joking and rowdy—obnoxious, the waitress might have said."[13]

News coverage of the tour created buzz around the abortion issue and ultimately introduced the notion of lay gynecology as a form of resistance to a broad readership. Although patronizing,

propping up stereotypes about progressive women as naively earnest, even infantile, this media coverage still had the potential to
serve the movement's aims by piquing the interest of some while
flying under the radar of others. It could simultaneously signal
to radicals that there was an underground in the process of marshaling resources, to liberals that they were right to be concerned
about the future of legal abortion, and to conservatives that they
probably did not need to worry about such laughable cells of conquering heroines.

ON THE HEELS of *No Going Back*, post-*Webster* decision, came *A
Woman's Book of Choices: Abortion, Menstrual Extraction, RU-486*,
published in 1992 by the Federation of FWHCs and authored
by Rebecca Chalker and Carol Downer. The book echoed a key
takeaway of *No Going Back*: that menstrual extraction was a safe
alternative to clinic abortion.

Barbara Ehrenreich, already well known for her books *Witches,
Midwives and Nurses* and *Complaints and Disorders*, about sexism
and the medical institution, states in her introduction to *A Woman's Book of Choices*, "This is bound to be an extremely controversial book—not only because it is about abortion, but because it
is about women's direct, physical empowerment. There will be
efforts to ban [it], to intimidate booksellers who carry it, to discredit all that it says." The book begins with sections about the
procedure itself and testimonies by people who had had clinic
abortions. Then it features sections about menstrual extraction;
the "friendship groups" in which the procedure is learned;
detailed accounts of two procedures; and legal questions and
concerns. The book concludes with a section on RU-486, or the
abortion pill mifepristone, which wouldn't be legalized in the
United States until the year 2000.[14]

Some book reviewers asked whether it was irresponsible of
the authors to have included so much detailed information about
menstrual extraction. The *Village Voice* raised this question but
then wrote, "The idea of withholding information, professing
to know better than a female populace who'd tend to misuse it,

is an equally distressing paternalistic argument."[15] Similar to *No Going Back*, the new book created buzz by risking disseminating more detail about what self-help groups were really doing than the movement ever had before.

The book was released just months after the Supreme Court issued its decision on *Planned Parenthood of Southeastern Pennsylvania v. Casey* in June 1992, a case that challenged a Pennsylvania statue that imposed multiple restrictions on abortion access and that many people (again) thought the Court would use to overturn *Roe*.[16] The Court did not reverse *Roe*, maintaining that "overruling *Roe*'s central holding would not only reach an unjustifiable result under *stare decisis* [legal precedent] principles, but would seriously weaken the Court's capacity to exercise the judicial power and to function as the Supreme Court of a Nation dedicated to the rule of law."[17] But through *Casey*, having laid the groundwork to do so with the *Webster* decision, the Court eliminated *Roe*'s trimester framework, creating the opportunity for states to restrict early abortions, and adopted an "undue burden" standard.[18]

The Court defined an undue burden as one that creates "substantial obstacles" for people seeking abortions prior to "viability." It added, "To promote the State's interest in potential life throughout pregnancy, the State may take measures to ensure that the woman's choice is informed. Measures designed to advance this interest should not be invalidated if their purpose is to persuade the woman to choose childbirth over abortion. These measures must not be an undue burden on the right."[19] In other words, states could now pass laws requiring providers to take measures to discourage people from having abortions.

Like *Webster*, the *Casey* decision reiterated that the state had an interest in protecting fetal life. And, as Ziegler points out, the decision also ushered in an era in which the Right would increasingly try to argue that abortion was harmful to women's health.

The tools of abortion

In winter 2021, I met Izabel and Fuchsia at Aquatic Park in Berkeley. I'd interviewed each of them individually before, and now we were getting together to see what memories and insights a triangle might produce. The two recalled how their initially large group quickly split into a couple of smaller ones, made up of about eight people each. They couldn't remember if they were always (or ever really) in the same group, but over the years their work overlapped.

Linci taught their groups. "There was a curriculum," Fuchsia recalled. "It was a progression. We learned how to do a pelvic exam and how to size the uterus. We learned sterile technique. At some point they introduced the jar and tubing and syringe, and we learned menstrual extraction. Oh gosh, we learned, a person could be pregnant, and we could still remove the menstrual cycle."

Izabel described what the aha moment was like: "We realized we were practicing so that we would be able to end early-term pregnancies. And that really lit me up. I was like, Oh *yeah* we are, because this world is not safe for women."

Then, Fuchsia told me, the groups got cooking. Group members would rotate hosting at their various communal houses. Meetings were once a week or every two weeks. As they arrived, people would chat a little as friends. But then, Izabel remembered clearly, someone would announce what they were going to study that day. Each meeting started the same way: "First we would practice doing speculum exams or pelvics," she said. "Like doing scales, you'd do them over and over and over again."

Group members would pair off and find a sunny corner. Each person would do an exam on their partner. "Where are the ovaries? People would describe it as a flitter across your fingers," Izabel recalled. "I did it for years before I felt any flutter."

Fuchsia remembered doing pelvic exams at most meetings and was still able to describe the exam in detail.

Doing an exam—it's so cool! First you find the cervix.
You insert your fingers. You basically stabilize the cervix from underneath. On top, you press on the uterus.
You're scooping; the non-pregnant uterus is the size of a
walnut. You're holding the cervix underneath, and you're
pressing on the belly. You're trying to capture the walnut
between your hands. And you're getting a sense of the
distance between the fundus and the cervix. The fundus is the top of the uterus. You might be scooping and
nothing's moving. That means you're not on the uterus;
you're just pressing on the belly. But then you go here,
and all of a sudden it moves. Okay. That means you're
pressing on it. And then you go to the side—here's the
edge. At first, it's totally vague. But then you do a few
more, and you're like, oh, okay. Textbook is straight,
but the uterus could be folded over. So at every meeting, you would try to do several pelvic exams. Because
you're going to feel different things. And then one day
you might be like, oh, it's not a walnut . . . it's a plum.
Or oh, it's a mandarin. Or oh, it's an orange. The pregnant uterus gets bigger. At first, it's just getting an idea
of what you're feeling between your two hands. You're
translating what you feel to a mental image of the uterus.
And then a pregnant uterus. You compare your theoretical how-big-it-should-be to the dates the person reports
around the pregnancy.

Fuchsia remembered unpacking the idea that a retroflexed or
retroverted uterus was somehow retrograde. "That problematic
language women often hear from gynecologists: 'Oh, your uterus
is tipped or tilted.' There's nothing wrong with that! The uterus
can be in different positions and that doesn't mean that it's wrong
or bad or retrograde. There's just natural variation."

Then the group would come back together and circle up
to study the topic of the day. One topic was sterile technique.
Another study topic was lidocaine injections. Group members
practiced drawing up lidocaine with a syringe and sticking a piece

of soft fruit, like a plum. Then they practiced injecting it into each other's cervixes.

At first, I didn't understand why you would need to numb the cervix to do a menstrual extraction. Everything I'd looked at said that on or close to the first day of your period, the os is open enough to allow for a thin plastic cannula to pass through. It occurred to me that Izabel and Fuchsia weren't learning that type of menstrual extraction. As they would explain to me, they were learning how to administer local anesthetic and how to sound the uterus and dilate the cervix. They were learning how to do tissue evaluation. Their group was learning something much closer to the clinical procedure for abortion.

"THE OAKLAND GROUPS used extra instruments," Linci explained. "We just utilized the abortion procedure." She continued:

> We did do sounding. We used the sound for distance and direction, as a way of knowing the angle and confirming our pelvic exam. If the sounding didn't correlate with what we felt on the pelvic exam, we'd confer. If we felt that it was a retroflexed uterus, that it was tipped back, then the sound should be tipped back. If we felt that it was in a forward-flex position, then we should feel that with the sound, and it should follow that curve.
>
> We felt that in terms of determining how to move forward in a blind situation, using the instruments gave us a better scope of care. Because everything should match. The sounding should match the size of the pregnancy. It should match the position of the uterus. We felt that it gave us a lot of strength in scientific intervention.
>
> It was more intervention than in traditional self-help groups. We really did model our menstrual extractions after the abortion procedure in a more technical way. Right from the beginning, we taught abortion. We spoke about it carefully. We did use the tools of menstrual extraction. But we also used the tools of abortion.

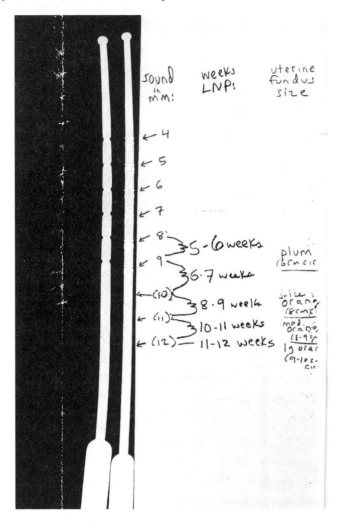

A self-help group handout (undated) showing two uterine sounds marked with the distance in millimeters from external os to fundus. Next to these are a conversion of the depth measurements into number of weeks pregnant (from last menstrual period, or LMP), as well as notes about how the size of the uterus changes over the first twelve weeks, ranging from plum to large orange. From Izabel's personal collection.

IN 1989, SIMONE, Chloe, and Rosie also started practicing in a self-help group, mostly with people they had met previously.

Two WCFHP / Women's Choice health workers came on board as their teachers. At the early meetings, the group learned about female reproductive anatomy and how to do cervical self-exam, put on sterile gloves, and do speculum exams on each other.

"We thought it was an empowering political action," Simone said to me as we sat in her backyard. "We didn't need to be radicalized. We knew ME was the point of the self-help group." She wore her hair (now sans purple streaks) in a low ponytail at the nape of her neck. It was six months into the pandemic, and Simone had on a blue medical mask—it hit me that she had, after all, become a gynecologist. It struck me that this is how she looks to her patients.

What did you think learning self-help was for, I asked Simone. "We wanted to be ready for the revolution," she responded right away. "We didn't know what was going to happen, and we wanted to have the knowledge and the power to do abortions."

They started meeting weekly. Simone would show up to group meetings on her motorcycle with speculums and other supplies in a bag strapped to the back of the seat. The group progressed quickly: They practiced cervical exams. They learned how to sterilize steel instruments using a pressure cooker. They learned menstrual extraction and practiced on group members who were about to bleed. Before injecting lidocaine into each other, they first practiced with a syringe into a grapefruit.

"Women's Choice provided some peel-pack sterile equipment, like plastic uterine sounds," Chloe told me. "We learned different ways to make suction." Chloe had become a doctor, too—a surgeon. It took time to learn all of the steps, she explained. Even just to find the cervix, to do a pelvic exam. It's a technical skill—no thumb on the clit! Even so, within months group members were practicing menstrual extraction on each other. "One of us would call and say, 'I'm going to have a red balloon party.' And then everybody would call everybody else."

I remembered a news story I'd seen in the archives, published in 1992, a few years after Chloe, Simone, and Rosie started learning abortion self-help. The article opens, "Caroline, a sophomore at Berkeley, reads this note scribbled down by her roommate:

'Full Balloon party tonight, 7 p.m., Sylvia's apartment.' College pranksters planning fun? Guess again . . . the cryptic message indicates these young women are involved in the growing underground self-help movement, and 'full balloon party' is actually a meeting to perform an early abortion technique called menstrual extraction." The article goes on to quote Linci saying, "The *Webster* case was a real turning point. Significantly more young women started to join . . . the average age I see now is about 23 instead of 30."[20]

I asked Chloe to describe the procedures they would do. She thinks and talks fast, I thought. I could hardly keep up with her as she gave this account:

> We would take a medical history. We would do a pelvic exam to make sure the uterus wasn't too large, that they really were early in their pregnancy. You needed to put on sterile gloves. I think you could use the glove packet partially as a sterile field. I remember you needed to create a sterile field for your equipment. We used a metal speculum that was sterilized. And then we swabbed out the vagina with betadine. Then we'd sound the uterus. You'd sound and get the depth on the sound. Then you'd know your cannula depth and that you couldn't go any deeper than that. I feel like we might have had metal dilators. You couldn't just shove the cannula right in. I think you had to dilate at least twice. And then you could cannulate. If you were the sterile person, you couldn't do the suction. Someone else had to do the suction because that part wasn't sterile. If you were the sterile person, you just did the cannula. You were waiting until it felt kind of gritty. It felt like little ridges or something, like grit, grit, grit. And because we were trying to learn, usually someone else would also have sterile gloves. It wouldn't be like, 'Here I am, savior on a white horse, here to do your abortion, all me.' There would always be someone else with sterile gloves who was also doing it. I might have dilated twice, and then another person would dilate, so that they could practice, too. And then I might've felt for

the ridgy-ness, and then another person would have felt for the ridgy-ness, too, because we were both learning how it should feel. And that's it. You take out the speculum. Say, 'How are you feeling? Take some Tylenol.'

IZABEL AND FUCHSIA explained to me when we met in the park that if someone was going to have a procedure, group members would have communicated by phone about it beforehand using a secret code—Fuchsia was pretty sure that it was "spaghetti dinner with red sauce." They would have shown up ready to get to work, since the procedure takes time.

Picture this, Fuchsia said. You're in someone's bedroom. The person receiving a procedure is propped up by pillows, comfy as can be. They're only undressed from the waist down. They're cozy and wearing socks. There's a circle around them. Someone's holding the flashlight. ("Flashlight holding" is an important job in and of itself, Izabel explained, because you're keeping an eye on the big picture, holding the space, and watching to make sure no one breaks sterility.) The person receiving the extraction is wearing sunglasses so the flashlight doesn't get in their eyes. There's a support person or two, breathing with them, maybe doing acupressure points. There are a couple of tech people passing the instruments. And there's someone doing the suctioning itself.

It wasn't until she'd been practicing for almost three years that Izabel took on the role of inserting the cannula and doing the suctioning. Many times, she'd practiced inserting a cannula just barely into an os. But in the case of an actual menstrual extraction, you have to apply pressure to get the cannula through. "That feeling of pushing and actually being inside. . . . You have to have a mental image of how big the uterus is so you can know how far you can go." Izabel said it was the scariest part for her. "You have to push hard enough to get to the place you're going, but if you push too hard, you could perforate." Inserting the cannula all the way was thrilling to her. She would think, Oh my god, I did it! Now, whenever she has the experience of jiggling a key in a sticky lock, she thinks of getting through the os.

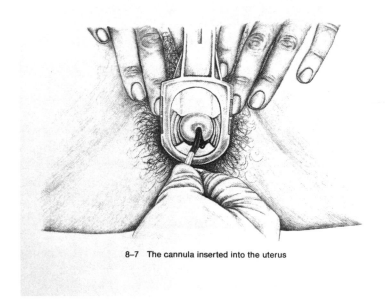

8–7   The cannula inserted into the uterus

"The cannula inserted into the uterus," by Suzann Gage. FFWHCs, *New View of a Woman's Body*, 126.

The suctioning itself Izabel described as a "moving and vac-uuming." She continued, "You're trying to get a sense of a grating kind of feeling that tells you that you've emptied everything out that needs to get emptied out."

After the extraction, it was someone's job to evaluate the tis-sue collected in the jar. Someone with clinic access would then take the steel instruments in and autoclave (sterilize) them.

"I love how everybody knew all of the jobs," Izabel said. "I love the team-ness of it. And that any one of us could have filled any of those positions at any time, and that we trusted each other in all of the positions. We really trusted each other. We let each other do this on our *bodies*. It was a trust that was hella earned, through very intimate work."

An epiphany about us

Max remembered the first time she received a menstrual extraction. She'd been learning self-help for about six months by then. Her group had gotten close, meeting weekly.

They, too, learned how to track their cycles and do cervical exams on each other. They learned to recognize each person's "normal" versus when something was off kilter, a yeast infection or an STI. "Is there discharge? Itching? Some discomfort that somebody might go to a doctor to get diagnosed that we could actually take care of in the group?" Max asked. "A whole host of things can happen if your pH is off balance." She added, "The first principle is: we're going to learn this stuff. And we're going to take care of each other. You don't learn menstrual extraction without first learning what I would call 'cunt self-care.'"

After learning basic cunt self-care, the group moved on to pelvic exams and menstrual extraction. Max recalled,

I remember being on a futon and volunteering to be someone who people could practice doing pelvics on. I'm sitting back. I have my head on a pillow. My legs are spread. People are feeling my uterus. Then I remember putting the speculum in and having this row of faces around me. This was my first menstrual extraction. After I put the speculum in, a friend put a cannula in, and I just had this epiphany about how I thought about my body. Everything underneath my skin had been a mystery that I'd thought only somebody who had a tremendous amount of education, only somebody who'd been to medical school and a residency and who had dedicated a serious portion of their lives to learning about medicine, could possibly understand or relate to. But holding the jar and seeing the blood of my period coming into the jar, I had this epiphany about my insides and my outsides. In that moment, one of those incredible aha moments, the curtain lifted. My eyes got a little bit bigger. There was more light. I thought, my uterus! It's not heart surgery.

I can relate to this part of my body. And it was such a happy moment.

I did a painting of my knees, of my feet on my bed, and the happy faces of beloved people I had relationships with, friends who were in the group with me, who I felt very warmly about. And everybody looking in with curiosity, warmth, and engagement. With minds that were just interested in learning. It was an epiphany about me, but it was also an epiphany about us.

At the time, Max felt it was vital to learn menstrual extraction in case abortion were to become illegal. In the years that followed, she and her group members performed numerous menstrual extractions, both not pregnant and pregnant, on people inside of the group, and also on people outside of the group. Max described how she thought about performing pregnant menstrual extractions on people from outside: "I didn't really think about it as a service. It was more of an exchange that was very horizontal—an opportunity to learn and share information. It was more like a match. We would do MEs for people outside the group who were in our networks. We kept it fairly close. We wanted to keep people medically safe and also politically safe. It was a mutual relationship; we were working and collaborating together to do a thing that would help somebody not be pregnant at the end of it."

WHEN I MET with Chloe, she told me, "It felt extra important and special if we were doing a real abortion, because that's what we really needed to learn how to do." She recalled, "[When you're pregnant] the uterus is a little bigger and softer, so the risk of perforation goes up. Looking for the products of conception and making sure you did a complete abortion, it was important. You really had to not fuck up."

One of the pregnant people they performed a menstrual extraction for was Chloe's mother. "My mother is the world's worst contraceptor," Chloe told me in her expressive way. At that time, Chloe was living in Oakland, and on the day of the procedure, the group met at her house. Chloe's mom was in her forties then. "I don't know if my mom had health insurance. She had had a lot of negative experiences with abortions. She'd had multiple illegal ones." Chloe cleaned her room and made her bed for her mom. During the procedure, she leaned in to support her mom and hold her hand as she laid on her back, undressed from the waist down. Other group members applied local anesthetic, stabilized the cervix with a forceps, dilated the cervix, and inserted the cannula.

The groups knew that what they were doing was illegal. Often they didn't know a lot about what was going on in other self-help groups, even when those groups included their own friends. "The secrecy about what went on in each group was on purpose," Chloe said. "We felt we needed a decentralized system so that if somebody got busted, it wasn't going to get everybody sent to jail. We were in separate pods, making sure not to expose each other."

According to Chloe, the number of pregnant extractions her group did for people outside the group was relatively limited, and, like other groups, they mostly limited their services to friends or friends of friends. "We wanted to be more useful," Chloe recalled. "But the fact was that abortion was legal. So people weren't like, 'Oh, let's go have an abortion with these guys!' You don't exactly hold up a sign that says, 'Hi, would you like to have an abortion done by amateurs? We're good. Really.'"

"We did my mom's abortion in my bedroom," Chloe explained, "because it's more comfortable for the person having an abortion to be on a bed."

I USED THE encrypted messaging app Signal to dial Rosie. She was hesitant to talk to me. At the time, she was doing health work in the South, where she's from. It was only after I assured her that I would anonymize her for this book that she agreed to a voice call.

"I was a virgin when I arrived in California," Rosie recalled. "I grew up in the Reagan eighties. I appreciated my parents and the way they raised me, but the larger culture was so anti-sex." She remembered how the sexuality of girls was such a big deal socially. When she was a kid, topics like the question of a girl's virginity would get brought up in casual conversations among adult men.

Despite the sexism and misogyny, women were talking about owning their own bodies and sexuality. "I was attracted to this discussion," Rosie said. "I felt empowered by it. It was just intuitive to me that other women and I should be able to make our own choices." She realized that the clinic defense and abortion self-help movements were the first contexts in which she was asked by other women what she wanted to do with her life. "The reproductive rights movement was an environment where it mattered what I thought," she said.

Rosie remembered what it was like to first learn about reproductive anatomy in her self-help group. "I wasn't ashamed to learn. You know when a kid is learning something new and they're not judging it, they're just absorbing it? That was me." She added, "I had faith in my skills, and I didn't know enough to be scared."

Then Rosie became pregnant. "It was a broken condom. With sexuality, I was very immature. I remember the guy saying, 'What are the odds?' Well, the odds were not in my favor." Her group had never done a menstrual extraction on a pregnant person before, and she would be their first.

By that point, it was 1990. On the evening of her extraction, Rosie arranged pillows on her bed and lit candles and incense. As she heated water for tea, group members started to arrive. "These were people I intuitively trusted," she said. "We spoke with each other in a way that I think is rare in society. Empowered women speaking to empowered women is rare."

During meetings, Rosie's group spent a lot of time practicing gentle, nonviolent language and touch. She gave me examples: "If you're going to touch someone's inner thigh, tell them before you actually touch them. If you're going to do something, let them know what you're going to do before you do it. And then do it slowly."

As the recipient of an extraction, Rosie said, you had ownership over the procedure and how it took place. You got to tell your group when to go slower, when to stop. She recalled that having her cervix dilated was painful, so at her request, her group took lots of breaks. The procedure took time, but there were no complications.

Not long after her extraction, Rosie had a conflict with another group member about confidentiality. That group member chose to share information about Rosie's abortion outside of the group. Rosie still experienced feelings of betrayal, and she wanted me to understand that group trust relations were fragile and that the dynamics were imperfect.

Her disclosure made me think about how ambitious the interpersonal and political work of self-helpers was, and also about how young so many were. When they started practicing, many self-helpers were teenagers coming to adult friendships, community relations, sex, and intimacy for the first time. The self-help movement was a youth movement, and for many I interviewed, their self-help stories are coming-of-age stories.

Overall, Rosie recalled, in the process of receiving an extraction, her agency and sense of purpose were empowered. Afterward she felt relieved and calm. After all, she had just had an abortion in her own bed, on her own terms, performed by people she trusted. "Throughout, people were cooperative and attentive," she recalled. "They were themselves."

I THOUGHT OF Chloe's comment about how her group wanted to be more useful but the reality was that legal abortion was accessible in California. In fact, though, people *did* choose to have their self-helper friends and friends of friends end their pregnancies. I asked Max once, why do you think people not in self-help groups chose menstrual extraction for pregnancy termination?

Multiple reasons, she replied. Some people had had alienating experiences with doctors and wanted to feel that the experience was in their control and that they were participants. They wanted to feel engaged and embodied and that there was space for them to do what they needed to do. If somebody wanted to smoke pot first, they could do that. If they wanted to have their partner be a part of the process, they could have that.

There are *many* benefits of receiving attentive, quality health care outside of the medical establishment, Max maintained.

I thought of the story Rosie told about her extraction: *you have ownership over the procedure.*

AFTER LINCI, ANN, and Cindy's group dissolved, Cindy started her own. In her new group, she met Cecilia*. Cecilia had been raised by activist parents in the Bay Area. Not long after getting her bachelor's degree, she started volunteering at the Berkeley Free Clinic and getting interested in gynecology. There she studied and then started teaching about contraception, STIs, pap smears, colposcopy, cervical cancer, and more. She and Cindy became friends.

When I first met Cecilia, she reminded me of Cindy. Warm and open. Mussed bleach-blond hair. By the end of our interview, I'd learned that Cecilia loved music—just like Cindy, with her piano. The two were in the same group for almost a decade.

Cecilia invited me to disclose that on her left breast, she has a tattoo of an ovary and fallopian tube, which she got when she first started working in women's health. The ovary has an egg with yellow musical notes inside of it, and the fallopian tube has purple notes. She designed it herself as a metaphor for perception, she told me, with the complementary colors representing how perception is different for everyone.

Before participating in her first menstrual extraction, Cecilia studied self-help with her group for a year. Her group always wanted to make sure it was an informed process for the person receiving the extraction. "There were some people who would have a preliminary interview with us and ultimately decide that it wasn't what they wanted to do," she said. "We didn't take it personally. We were just like, this is what we do."

The community-building aspect of the self-help group was important to Cecilia. "Self-help is about love," she told me. "And health care for me is about love. It's about love for people and community and humanity."

Once, Cecilia and her group went up north together to spend a weekend on some land with only a single trailer. She still has the photos—group members with legs spread wide for the camera, speculums in place. Farther in the background are their sun-hatted heads with faces scrunched and squinting into the bright day.

"There was always the component of, 'This is really important work.' But there was also a really playful component of trust and relationship building," Cecilia said. I thought of what Cindy said. *We were so into each other.... We were so close. We were up for anything.*

CECILIA TOLD ME about a complication that another group close to her had. Someone outside of that group who received a procedure had later gone to the hospital with an incomplete abortion. Not long after, someone brought a message to the self-help community: *You guys shouldn't be doing this. This is practicing medicine without a license. Who are you working with?*

Between the interpersonal intensity and the risks they took together, it was a lot to hold. "It hit me that bad stuff can happen," Cecilia said. "Even though it usually didn't. Because we knew what we were doing and feeling. We talked about it. And we did it collectively. That's why we had a second check. Because it shouldn't be up to any one person. We did it together."

Sometimes people came to them who didn't really have a choice, Cecilia told me. It was a hostile time for people seeking abortion care. Many people were afraid of the health care system. In some cases, they were undocumented. Members of Cecilia's group spoke Spanish and worked with immigrant communities, so they were able to connect with undocumented people seeking care. But people who had more options and choice also came to them. Some were from the home-birth movement, for example. On one occasion, Cecilia's group did a pregnant extraction for her college friend Mimi*.

Cecilia had experience working as a mechanic on diesel engines, and it occurred to her within a couple years of joining the movement that she might be able to swap out the syringe and valve components of the Del-Em with a piece of equipment that could be found in almost any mechanic's garage. She started talking with some other self-helpers: Could they create one-way suction with a brake bleeder?

"You need negative pressure to extract. You can use a big syringe, or you can use some other kind of gentle pressure in a closed system. When you bleed brakes, you get the air out," Cecilia explained. "As a mechanic, I really understood the hydraulic nature of it. And I knew where to get brake bleeders. And where to get the right hoses. Previously we'd been getting stuff from the aquarium store." So Cecilia's group replaced the syringe and valve on their Del-Ems with a brake bleeder. Other groups quickly followed suit. It was a game changer. The brake bleeder created more suction than the syringe and, thus, more efficient procedures.

Cecilia didn't think of what she and her group members did as "practicing medicine." That is, she didn't feel that she ever had the kind of authority over a person's body that Western medicine asserts. She went on to practice medicine as a nurse practitioner. Today, she told me, she values and prefers practicing health care with other people. "I am somebody who likes to work on teams. As a health care provider, I'd rather work in a collaborative setting than on my own," she said. "I think it has almost everything to do with the way I learned how to be a provider. I learned through my work at the free clinic and through self-help."

Chapter 8

You Only Need to See the Front Line of Musclebound White Male Thugs to Know What This Struggle Is Really About

A group of a dozen comrades, new and old, convened in San Francisco's Mission District, and Raven* leaned in close.[1] They crowded around the row of tables they'd formed, surrounded by posters and framed photographs of their heroes and sheroes on the walls of Café Macondo. Some of them were students, some were not. Some had gotten political educations in old-school study groups. Several were communists, a few were anarchists, and some identified themselves more culturally than politically.

In her late twenties, Raven had been exposed to Left organizations in the past, but she wasn't in one. The group had convened to imagine a new formation that would center their anti-imperialist politics and direct-action orientation. They were internationalists who saw wars abroad and at home as inextricably linked. Their question at the café that day was what to call themselves.

Days before, the group had attended a talk by Tahan K. Jones, a young Black man from Oakland. Tahan was a marine reservist who had filed for conscientious objector status and then, in fall 1990, when he refused to report for duty, was charged by the state with desertion.[2] He spoke passionately about the racism of the state—its use of young, mostly poor people and people of color to fight its wars—and expressed his frustration over racism in the antiwar movement. Despite serious charges, Tahan's case wasn't high-profile like some other white conscientious objectors' cases were, and it was difficult for him to relate to the white and middle-class character of the antiwar

207

movement. Raven recalled, "He spoke for all of us that day, and that led us to Café Macondo."

After brainstorming all the obvious words to describe who and what they were, the group landed on the word "Roots" along with the phrase "Against War"—RAW for short. As they talked, one comrade, Spie, drew intently, then slid a napkin into the center of the table. "RAW" appeared in bold graffiti style, springing up from a tract of earth where bodies labored in rows in fields, suggesting the stripes of the American flag. The word RAW was breaking through the chain links and barbed wire that ran across the horizon line, and a map of the Middle East spread down and into the foreground. In the distance, hovering across the top of the graphic, was a silhouette of raised fists and hands gripping guns and other tools—symbols of liberation struggles worldwide.

I interviewed Raven at her rent-controlled apartment in Oakland, where corporate landlords were known for harassing tenants and letting properties fall into disrepair so that tenants would move out and landlords would be free to raise rents as much as they wanted. (Raven was involved in organizing Oakland renters to resist these unethical practices.) She showed me her binder of RAW materials, and in it was the napkin.

Soon after, Raven told me, RAW would add clinic defense to its repertoire of resistance actions, and they would play a significant role whenever they showed up. "RAW could say things about the intersection of race, gender, and class and show up in a way that no one else really was at the time," she said. In 1992, RAW wrote, "As young, angry, conscious people of color, Roots Against War carries on a proud history of resistance against imperialism," invoking earlier militant movements of the 1960s, like the Black Panthers, Young Lords, and American Indian Movement at home, while also linking themselves to contemporary struggles in places like South Africa and Palestine.[3]

For their first action, RAW organized a "Night of Resistance" in San Francisco for January 15, 1991, the date the United Nations had set as the deadline for Iraq to leave Kuwait or be targeted by the US military machine. Their flyer read,

Sisters and Brothers, Homeboys and Homegirls, let's be straight up! This country has never done shit for us! except put us up against the wall, put us in jail or juvenile hall— Now they want to put us in a uniform with a red, white and blue flag on it to kill and die for them. They call this the "land of opportunity" but the only choices we have are between a McDonald's job and the military, a check on the 1st and 15th, or dealing <u>their</u> dope to <u>our</u> people. Now it's up to you and me. Let's get together and show some unity. Resist the war!⁴

Original Roots Against War napkin drawing, by Spie, fall 1990. From Raven's personal collection.

In their materials, RAW linked anti-imperialist struggles to prison abolition and fights against anti-Arab policies and xenophobia at home. And because women's liberation and leadership were central to their analysis and vision, they also made connections between war and reproductive rights: "The courts are taking away women's right to an abortion, yet they encourage women to join the military to kill for them—50% of women in the army are Black."[5] They analyzed patriarchy, underscoring how it punished women of color by criminalizing them for seeking abortions and by denying them social benefits.

In the leadup to the war, RAW did outreach on the radio and on college campuses and street corners, with an emphasis on the Mission and the Fillmore neighborhoods. "We just had a different vibe. Our outreach was an event in and of itself," Raven explained, scratching her dog behind the ears. She was dressed in all black, her long black hair piled on top of her head in a knot.

> We brought a boombox and banners and a table full of sharp and irreverent materials, like a sticker with George H. Bush getting his head kicked off by a high-top basketball shoe. Our soundtrack was Paris's "Break the Grip of Shame," Public Enemy's "Fight the Power," "The Coup" by the Coup, and Queen Latifah's "U.N.I.T.Y." We had impromptu speak-outs with the rhythm of congas. We knew our audience because it was us. If you experienced our outreach, you knew our events would be raw and unapologetic. It would not be a bunch of old white folks on a permitted Saturday stroll, singing "Give Peace a Chance," ringed by people in orange vests.

On January 15, people began taking to the streets before dawn, stopping business as usual on both sides of the bay. By 5:30 p.m., protesters were answering RAW's call for a "Night of Resistance," gradually filling the intersection of 24th and Mission until it was completely shut down. "The night before, we figured three to five hundred people would be cool. About fifteen thousand showed up," Raven remembered. "Our purpose was always to inspire and unleash people, not to control them," she said, chuckling, "but we did have to hustle to get to the front of the march that we had called."

In the months that followed, RAW grew exponentially. In their literature, signs, and chants, RAW named the ways the war on women was bigger than the attacks on abortion access: it was also about fascism, homophobia, normalizing sexual violence, and exploiting women's unpaid reproductive labor amid welfare cutbacks. In characteristic RAW style, their March 8 International Women's Day event was called "Yo Mama Wears Combat Boots!," and participants literally and figuratively took a sledge-hammer to TVs and scales and burned fashion magazines and other symbols of women's oppression. "These issues are about control of our lives and we've gotta fight back, women and men together," RAW wrote.[6]

Another RAW member, a revolutionary communist named Dani-Rose*, came from a family of Black civil rights activists. Dani-Rose had gotten involved in anti-apartheid, antiwar, and reproductive rights activism as a student at UC Berkeley.

"We were inspired by liberation movements in Africa, Asia, and Latin America, and organizations in the United States like the Black Panther Party," Dani-Rose told me when I interviewed them at their house. "We were trying to emulate what we were seeing from the resistance around the world."

The early days and months of RAW were a swirl of resistance, Dani-Rose remembered. "A hundred things were happening. 'What are you going to do? Where are you going to go? Raven, come pick me up.' It was this constant motion of things."

Raven remembered encountering BACORR out and about amid the constant motion. "Radicals are always assessing the scene and are on the lookout for each other. We saw BACORR's banners, literature, and speakers, and saw them in action. They were more white and kinda punk rock, but it was instant recognition. We were definitely gonna fuck with BACORR," she said. "RAW was especially important because Operation Rescue was increasingly mobilizing people of color and claiming that abortion was 'Black genocide.' While most people were afraid to call them out or burn an effigy of [Black Supreme Court justice] Clarence Thomas for fear of being called racist, we were not."

Dani-Rose's connection to reproductive rights was personal. In their second year of college, they had an abortion at the campus hospital. What they remembered was that the abortion was free and that a volunteer supported them through the procedure, holding their hand and rubbing their forehead. "It was free abortion on demand," they said, referencing how all health insurers in California, including state-funded Medi-Cal, were (and still are) required to cover abortion care. It was a provision that stood in stark contrast to many other states; "Learning that people were being prevented from getting that in some places was horrific," Dani-Rose added.

RAW soon became the newest member of BACORR. "We wanted to stop antis," Dani-Rose said. "It was all hands on deck." The timing couldn't have been better. Because clinic defenders were about to face some of the most intense opposition of their generation.

These wombs were made to be free

In summer 1991, Operation Rescue descended upon Wichita, Kansas, in the thousands to terrorize the city's abortion clinics. A doctor named George Tiller worked at one of the clinics. He was one of a few doctors in the country who provided abortions later in pregnancy. In 2009, Tiller would be murdered at his own church by an anti-abortion extremist.[7]

That summer 1991, Wichita clinics agreed to close for a week in exchange for a commitment from police that they would ensure access to clinic doors after the week was over. But the clinic closures only fueled OR's fire—OR saw an opportunity and called in reinforcements, and more antis flocked to Wichita. A couple weeks into the siege, a federal judge sent US Marshals to the city.[8] By the time it all ended, six weeks in, twenty-five thousand antis had invaded Wichita; twenty-seven hundred were arrested.[9]

"When we heard about Wichita, a bunch of us were like, whoa, wait, *what*?" Raven remembered. So, less than a year later, when OR announced that they would hit Buffalo starting the week of April 20, 1992—the same week that the Supreme Court would hear arguments in *Planned Parenthood of Southeastern Pennsylvania v. Casey*, a case antis hoped the Court would use to overturn *Roe*—BACORR mobilized. They put out a call: anybody who wanted to go to Buffalo could come with them. They collected donations to help cover people's travel expenses.

A Buffalo coalition, Buffalo United for Choice (BUC), started organizing in advance of the hit. They coordinated with clinic directors and invited pro-choice supporters from around the country to Buffalo.[10] BACORR stepped up to provide tactical support.

In 1990, BACAOR had developed a clinic defense training manual. An updated 1992 "second edition"—with the new name of Bay Area Coalition for Our Reproductive Rights (BACORR) on the cover—includes an opening statement titled "National Clinic Defense Strategy." In it, they advocate a "national organizing strategy" to help ensure "No More Wichitas!" and argue that good tactical leadership is cooperative and unassuming: "The operational modalities employed by BACORR in the SF Bay Area are based on the ability of clinic defenders to work through untoward events collectively and democratically, by means of on-site analysis of the various elements which come into play. The analytical model we employ is situational, not static. We assume nothing." They add, "Clinic defense is a dynamic, open-ended system. . . . We in BACORR are . . . militant fighters who have painstakingly analyzed over and over, both our failures as well as our successes in waging war against Operation 'Rescue,'" suggesting the power of clinic defense when executed by capable and experienced activists. They conclude that, given their experience fighting OR, BACORR should make up part of a tactical committee in Buffalo that should also include BUC; NWROC, an arm of RWL; the political group Refuse and Resist; and Women's Health Action and Mobilization (WHAM!), the reproductive rights activist group within ACT UP.[11]

BACORR (including RAW) and NWROC sent twenty-five clinic defenders to Buffalo, Raven among them. On the plane, Raven settled into her seat and turned to the person sitting next to her. "Are you with BACORR?" she asked. "I am," the woman replied. "I'm Linci." The conversation that followed would be the first in what would become a decades-long friendship between the two. Dani-Rose, the artist couple Agnes and Joe Sampson, and Kass McMahon and Marianne Jensen, by that time close friends, were all also on that plane to Buffalo.

When Bay Area clinic defenders arrived, they were greeted by freezing rain. In the days that followed, BACORR members learned lessons about the challenges of organizing with Left groups from different places and with different political cultures and approaches. The conflicts largely played out between self-identified militants and liberals whose politics were more conservative. Despite their conflicts, clinic defenders had the numbers and the will to keep OR at bay. No Buffalo clinics were forced to close during the week and a half that OR harassed them.

DURING MY VISIT to Albuquerque, I came across a tape in Kass's VHS collection called *Boot'em Out of Buffalo!* The film was a collaboration between Agnes and Joe and their friend Bob Koonz. Excited to view it, I had the tape digitized right away. The documentary opens with the following text on screen: "In April of 1992, dark forces threatened to close abortion clinics in Buffalo, NY. This was the pro-choice response."

The film takes us to a clinic in downtown Buffalo predawn, where clinic defenders are practicing techniques for holding the space in front of the door. They stand with arms linked and legs spread. I spot Agnes in the defense line, her BACORR bandana tied loosely around her neck. The clinic defenders are in good spirits, talking and laughing—the inevitable feeling of camaraderie when your limbs are entwined with others' for hours on end as they are in a clinic defense line. The soundtrack of Siouxsie and the Banshees's "Spellbound" begins to drum frantically. The activists chant, "O-R, we say no! Boot 'em out of Buffalo!"

The documentary cuts to a group of defenders holding up signs and taking turns at the mic. Standing in front is Kass in a hot pink baseball cap. Next to her is Raven, who speaks into the mic: "This is some challenging-ass shit that we're doing out here! We're goin' up against something that we have not faced . . . the threat to the *fuckin' right to abortion*. This is something that's totally new to us." She continues, "Yeah, we're gonna make some mistakes," likely referring to in-fighting among clinic defenders. "But we're gonna fuckin' *win*." The group cheers.

Twenty years earlier, there had been no constitutional right to abortion. And here were Gen-Xers, who had mostly had access to legal abortion for their entire adult lives, facing down a fanatical Christian militia, the manifestation of two decades of conservative backlash.

"You're not going to talk to *anybody*. Just stay back behind the line," Kass yells at one point, with characteristic authority, into the face of an OR named "Reverend" Robert Schenck. That week, Schenck had gained notoriety for parading around with a preserved twenty-plus-week-old stillborn fetus that he falsely claimed was aborted and that antis had named Baby Tia. "Want to touch her?" Schenck would creepily ask people outside one of the city's embattled clinics, located on High Street.[12]

"Abortions are performed safely and legally inside this *open* clinic," shouts Dani-Rose at an anti in the next shot, shaking their finger. "You want to close the clinic so we'll *have* to use coat hangers and back alleys," they continue. "Legal abortion is one of the safest fuckin' things that you can do to a woman! You wanna take us back to the Dark Ages, but we're not gonna fuckin' regress!"

Clinic defenders secured their win in Buffalo within days of the siege's beginning. On the rainy morning of April 21, 1992, defenders—both out-of-towners and locals—worked together to form a multilayered semicircle around the door of the High Street clinic. They also readied a "mobile squad," reinforcements, and escort teams to assist arriving patients. The defenders held the door even after police ordered them to move. When riot cops arrived and issued a second order to disperse, clinic defenders moved from their position and instead lined up should-to-shoulder on the sidewalk all the way down the street, making it still impossible for OR to get by them.[13]

In the final emotional scene of the documentary, the cameraperson pans the defense line extending down the street. The shot is set to Everything But the Girl's acoustic cover of "Time after Time." Clinic defenders in dripping ponchos sing and laugh as they huddle under umbrellas. A flamboyant troupe of men in drag, the Church Ladies for Choice, an ACT UP NY affinity group, sing a "hymn":[14]

> This womb is my womb
> Your womb is your womb
> And there is no womb
> For Randall Terry
> . . .
> These wombs were made
> to-oo be free

The film's last shot is of a young woman chanting, "Hey hey, ho ho, boot 'em out of Buffalo!" She lets out an exuberant "woo hoo!" and grins widely, and the film cuts to credits.

"Faced with impenetrable walls of clinic defenders outnumbering them at every Buffalo clinic, OR was forced to concede defeat and 'suspend' their clinic attacks in that city on April 29, just 10 days after beginning," wrote Kass in a BACORR news release after the action.[15] Their success in Buffalo marked a turning point: their approach to clinic defense had gone national. And BACORR was in it to win.

Do not go anywhere alone

By the time of the June 1992 Supreme Court ruling on *Casey*, OR had announced that they would hit clinics in New Orleans and Baton Rouge that July. Some BACORR members traveled to southern Louisiana early to help train local people in clinic defense. They had had success in Buffalo, and this time they wanted to start building relationships with locals sooner in hopes of further strengthening their defense lines.

"Baton Rouge was wild!" Raven told me. There's no way BACORR could have guessed what was waiting for them in Louisiana. Over the course of the week, they faced brutally violent antis, police who were complicit with OR's assaults on clinics, and a political meltdown among clinic defenders themselves.

The New Orleans-based Coalition to Reclaim Our Abortion and Reproductive Rights (C-ROARR)—which included BACORR, ACT UP New Orleans, the Industrial Workers of the World, Refuse and Resist, and other local organizers with deep activism experience and community relationships—started organizing well before the hit.[16] Like BACORR, C-ROARR argued that clinic defenders should not rely on police protection and should assume police would help OR.[17]

Laura Weide was among the BACORR members who went to southern Louisiana early to help locals organize the coalition. "The people I knew in Louisiana were in the early stages of building something like BACORR," she recalled. "They were a lot of queer people who were already organizers and had connections to the women's health community. We had meetings and communicated and built an organization that was true to the people who were there."

C-ROARR developed processes for making decisions together, given the "diversity of tactical and political perspectives within the Coalition."[18] In preparation for the siege, they organized lodging for out-of-towners, childcare, meals, and rest sites. They also outlined roles for defense days (for example, "office"; police liaison; clinic, communications, escort, and legal team coordinators) and devised a security plan to help keep clinic defenders safe.[19]

"To date, C-ROARR has trained hundreds of Louisianians in clinic defense techniques," wrote Laura in a letter to supporters.[20] She remembered how much work it was. C-ROARR did outreach to other community organizations and held multiple clinic defense trainings for trainers, who would then go out and train more people. They also had members infiltrate OR meetings to get intel.

In Louisiana, people hadn't experienced OR-style attacks before. Prior to the hit, C-ROARR organizers were invited to attend a meeting with local clinic directors and police. Police told C-ROARR that their plan was to allow OR to sit in front of the clinic and then, eventually, if they refused to move, lift them onto stretchers and take them away.

"Absolutely not," Laura remembered thinking. "No way were we going to allow OR to portray themselves as harmless victims who were so vulnerable that they needed to be carried away on stretchers." For the police, Laura explained, the focus was on taking care of OR. "They were Right-wing religious cops who were anti-abortion. Probably many of them had Klan or white supremacist affiliations, whether themselves or in their families."

BACORR knew their people weren't necessarily safe in Louisiana. Raven traveled to Louisiana early to help organize, too, and she helped develop a security plan to protect clinic defenders from police and OR surveillance and violence. According to the plan, everyone had to have a buddy, and under no circumstances could buddies split up. "We are not in California or Buffalo—do not go anywhere alone," Raven and her team wrote. Clinic defenders were to leave demos and rallies as a group. They were not to carry people's names and phone numbers in their packs or pockets or written on their bodies. They were not to talk to cops. They were to keep each other safe, to the extent that they were able. "We are entering Klan territory," wrote the team. "Keep an extra eye out for our sisters and brothers of color. They will be at greater risk."[21]

Dani-Rose was in Louisiana that July. I asked them what it was like to be a Black nonbinary person on the front lines facing off with the antis. "I was afraid of being lynched," they said matter-of-factly.

BACORR (ABOUT TWENTY members) and other out-of-town defenders started arriving in southern Louisiana over that Fourth of July weekend in 1992. Hundreds of local people showed up for C-ROARR's Sunday night kickoff meeting.

At the meeting, feelings of solidarity and bravery that Laura, Raven, and all of C-ROARR had worked to cultivate for months were put to the test. That night, people were both hypervigilant and depleted from stress and anticipation. They still had so much to do, and OR could start hitting clinics any day; defenders planned to be ready outside of clinics the next morning. C-ROARR meeting facilitators called for people in the packed room to find seats so they could get started.

Suddenly some RWL / NWROC members stood up and announced that they wanted to take a vote on which member groups should be in leadership for the week. Some people in the room were confused, others angry. Some accused RWL / NWROC of stacking the vote.[22] "More and more people started getting up and leaving," Laura remembered. "It's like there was a hurricane, and we were in the middle of making survival kits, and then someone comes in and says, 'Let's vote on who should be president!'"

BACORR members noted in their log, "Much screaming and yelling ensued, later nearly fistfights. . . . NWROC tried to bum rush the facilitator; the mt. ended."[23]

Laura reflected on the effects of the incident on the political relationships of clinic defenders in Louisiana: "When you're about to do something risky, you want to feel like you can trust the people around you. NWROC chiseled a web of cracks in that room. They destroyed the sense that we had each other's backs. They undermined the leadership that existed in the local community. They saw it as an opportunity for their organization to grow. They used extremely unprincipled tactics to promote themselves."

Marianne coauthored a response on behalf of RWL/NWROC to the "false charges," arguing that, "The 'purge NWROC and the RWL' tendency [of BACORR] claims that NWROC and the RWL are undermining BACORR by politically criticizing it. On the contrary, political discussion, debate and criticism strengthen BACORR." RWL / NWROC wanted "discussion of political questions, ending in a democratic vote"—that is to say, they wanted an ideological commitment from the room. It wasn't a secret: "The

united front, which permits the political independence of participating groups and individuals as well as the required discipline for
unity in action, is the arena in which all organizations and individuals may raise their program in front of clinic defenders and struggle
to win them over. This is how political consciousness is raised."[24]

The clinic defenders I interviewed who were there found
RWL/NWROC's Trotskyism bullying and paradigmatically mis-
matched to the moment. Laura's comments about feeling like they
were readying for a hurricane register with what some defenders
thought of as the potentially serious consequences of what they
were doing. That week in Louisiana during an OR hit, a clinic
defender would be attacked by an anti with a Kryptonite lock.
A client would be assaulted by an anti and have her glasses broken.[25] Defenders would be harassed, grabbed, punched, kicked,
and arrested. Dani-Rose would be one of three defenders to be
attacked by police at a counter demo at a prayer rally. Another
was a young African American man, a member of RAW, and he
was not only beaten but also arrested and jailed for days for not
having his ID on him.[26] *Do not go anywhere alone*. The personal
risk of clinic defense could not have been more real. And as they
faced all of this, C-ROARR members argued, RWL/NWROC
"created an adversarial relationship and fostered an atmosphere
of distrust."[27]

When I asked Marianne about what happened, she stood by
RWL/NWROC's call for a vote: "I do think that in a coalition
an open discussion of what each organization stands for should
be stated up front and that actual leadership [should] be openly
elected by all the activists present."

Despite the turbulent start, clinic defenders in southern Louisiana managed to prepare themselves for OR to hit. The next day,
Monday, it was eerily quiet, so defenders practiced forming and
holding defense lines. But then the Baton Rouge Delta Clinic
became ground zero for OR.[28] Thursday was the first day of the
week that Delta was scheduled to perform abortions. Operation
Rescue started showing up two days early, on Tuesday.[29] And by
Thursday everything blew up.

AFTER THE PRESENCE of OR for two consecutive days at Delta, clinic defenders arrived at the clinic on the third day, Thursday, before sunrise. The Delta Clinic was in a quiet subdivision of Baton Rouge with strip malls, big-box stores, and empty lots. The clinic itself was exposed, with two large vacant lots, both overgrown browning lawns, next to it and across the street. In anticipation of the standoff, police had erected tall fences to create a large perimeter around the clinic and had installed floodlights as well.

When defenders arrived that morning, all was quiet. Delta Clinic staff had made advance arrangements to meet patients offsite and drive them to the clinic doors that day. To get to the doors, escorts and patients had to pass in cars through a gated opening in the temporary fencing. "Our goal was to keep the gate clear so that when patients arrived, they could get through," Laura explained.

What Laura remembered about that morning was the velvety southern air and heavy summer sky. "Even in the dark, it was already hot," Raven recalled.

Hundreds of clinic defenders showed up that morning. Among them was nineteen-year-old Jennifer Whitney, an anarchist and writer who had grown up in Baton Rouge. She'd been living in New Orleans, and when she saw the call for people to come to Delta, she drove north. It was her first clinic defense.

As Laura, Raven, Dani-Rose, other C-ROARR members, and local activists like Jennifer started lining up, a mysterious glowing apparition appeared down the road. Laura squinted to try to make it out. She couldn't believe what she was seeing. Coming their way was a parade—a massive throng of marching antis, appearing larger with every moment of their approach. Soon, Laura could make out some details. The women were dressed in white gowns and wore pointy white hats. "Their faces weren't covered, but it was very Klan-like," she recalled. "They were long flowing Victorian dresses with high collars," Raven remembered. According to Jennifer, it was a procession in which the women were dressed very formally.

The antis carried tall lit pillar candles whose individual flames, from a distance, blurred together into larger flames. Like torches.

Big burly men and also some women led the procession. In the middle of the bizarre scene was a truck, and some of the women in long dresses rode in the truck's bed. Laura's jaw dropped.

The antis' invocation of Klan imagery and tactics through their formation and dress recalls a local history of overlap between the early anti-abortion movement and eugenics and segregationist movements. Sarah Churchwell explains, "When the resurgent Ku Klux Klan paraded in Louisiana in 1922, they bore banners that read 'White Supremacy,' 'America First,' 'One Hundred Per Cent American,' 'Race Purity' and 'Abortionists, Beware!' People are sometimes confused by the Klan's animus against abortionists, or impute it to generalized patriarchal authoritarianism, but it was much more specifically about 'race purity': white domination can only be maintained by white reproduction."[30] OR was not only an anti-abortion extremist group. They were, through their own symbolic admission, a white supremacist militia.[31]

"Somehow, the cops formed a line behind us," Raven said. "And then these *Handmaid's Tale* people were in front of us." What happened next was surreal, Laura told me. They were significantly outnumbered by OR. Hearts thumping, clinic defenders did the only thing they could: they locked arms and stood tall with legs spread, as they had practiced.

"The men surged forward at us," Laura recalled. "It was a pitched physical battle. They kicked and shoved us. And we kicked back. I remember gripping onto other people. My arms were shaking. I was sweating. The cops just stood there."

The lunging, kicking, and shoving went on for what seemed to the clinic defenders like a very long time. As the sun climbed higher in the sky, they began to swelter. Raven remembered how at a certain point, the police broke their defense line and started pulling antis through. "Betrayal by the police was not a surprise to us," she said. "But, still, it was infuriating." Clinic defenders regrouped and held their line once again.

Eventually, Raven said, OR sent a "battalion of zombies" running across the field toward them to break their line, rushing at them like in the children's game. Jennifer gave a similar account: "They just charged us, Red Rover style." She remembered how the antis yelled at them, telling them they looked like trash, that they were dirty.

The underground self-helper Chloe was at the Delta Clinic that morning, as well. Once Chloe had described clinic defense to me as "almost like a sport." Remembering the zombie battalion, she said, "My friend had taught me how to tackle. I remember, I ran and tackled this guy to the ground. And that was it. I did it! He got up and walked away."

"I was a little bit of a bruiser," Chloe admitted. "I wanted to get in there. All of the shit that comes down on you as a girl? I wanted to physically fight back. It was real to me. It was black and white: we wanted to keep the clinic open. I was like, *fuck* these motherfuckers."

Jennifer, who has hypermobile joints, remembered how standing on the defense line with arms linked started to hurt her body, so she changed roles and instead began walking up and down the line between antis and defenders, misting defenders' heads, faces, and armpits with a spray bottle of water and sharing sunscreen and snacks with them. In the process, something clicked for her. This was where she wanted to be—on the front line, but in a support and diversion role. She would continue to fill this role at political actions for years to come.[32]

Raven sighed as she told me the story of the Delta defense. OR would return to the clinic the next day, and also the next.[33] Her ambivalence about Baton Rouge was evident: "Those battles, you don't always have to win them. Baton Rouge called national attention to clinic defense. It brought forces together. The experience advanced the politics of the groups who were involved." I learned later that clinic defenders did indeed keep Delta open that day.

In a C-ROARR statement after the hit, Laura wrote: "You only needed to see the front line of musclebound, white male thugs in a frenzy from physically assaulting women seeking health care to know what this struggle is really about. Any sign of women controlling their own lives makes these people crazy. I heard some OR's chanting 'KKK anti-gay' against us when we were chanting 'Racist, sexist, anti-gay, born-again bigots, go away,' which again affirms that these people violently oppose everyone's civil rights."[34]

Unlike after the Buffalo siege, the feelings defenders were left with after their days-long defense of Delta were more mixed. OR retreated that Saturday afternoon and, according to a local newspaper, all patients seeking access to Delta that week got in.[35] In terms of protecting access, clinic defenders were successful, but Baton Rouge also marked a turning point for BACORR. In Louisiana, the difficulty of coalition work became apparent. It signaled the end of BACORR's political work with RWL / NWROC, with BACORR voting to separate from them.

As I was researching the Delta defense, I searched the Delta Clinic address on Google Maps. The brown building wasn't an abortion clinic anymore. As of 2021, the building was the site of an "American Holocaust Memorial: Formerly Delta Abortion Clinic of Baton Rouge, Louisiana," run by Christian Patriots for Life. At their website, a virtual tour of the "memorial" showed exam rooms with surgical instruments strewn about and suspicious stains on the floors. Plastered all over the walls were large, obviously fake images of aborted fetuses. Crucifixes, tabernacles, bibles, and other Christian iconography covered countertops and tables.[36]

Baton Rouge provided Bay Area clinic defenders with yet another firsthand experience of the anti-abortion movement's violence. As Baton Rouge made painfully clear, OR wasn't just a moment in the history of the Right; rather, it was part of a culmination of more than a century of segregationist campaigning and terrorism that sought to subjugate, exploit, and harm people of color, especially women. This reality came into sharp relief for clinic defenders the moment OR decided to don white gowns and hats and move in ritualistic, threatening, mob-like formation toward a place where women, many poor and of color, accessed health care.

A climate of psychological terror

On March 10, 1993—not two months after the inauguration of President Bill Clinton—Michael Griffin, an anti-abortion extremist, stepped out of a throng of protesters in front of Pensacola Women's Medical Services clinic and opened fire on a doctor named David Gunn, who died in surgery shortly afterward.[37] Gunn was forty-seven years old. That day, Griffin and other antis had shown up for a protest organized by John Burt, a regional director for the anti-abortion group Rescue America and a former member of the Klan.[38]

This was the climate in which Operation Rescue announced its plans in May 1993 to deploy troops to clinics and doctors' homes all around San Jose, California, and in five other midsize cities across the country, in July.[39] OR called the campaign "Cities of Refuge," their "biggest pro-life offensive in five years."[40]

Right away, BACORR members started collaborating with other reproductive rights groups, including their sibling clinic defense coalitions in the South Bay and Sacramento, and formed a large container organization, the Abortion Rights Defense Coalition. At that point, their defense line and escorting tactics were tried and true, so they organized defense trainings all around the Bay Area. A training outline explained, "If you are swamped by too many antis, fall into a formation fitting to the level of attack" and featured sketches of two escorting approaches for getting a patient to and through a clinic door: a wedge and a bubble.[41]

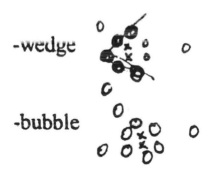

Wedge and bubble formations, "Clinic Defense Training Outline," 1993. From Laura Weide's personal collection.

BACORR held press conferences at WCFHP / Women's Choice on McClure Street and phone banks to spread the word. "We have come . . . to face the front lines of a combat zone," Linci said at one press conference, calling OR a "paramilitary force."[42]

By the first big day of the siege, Saturday, July 10, BACORR and others were ready to cover all San Jose area clinics and prevent OR blockades. For that Saturday, they got the Berkeley City Council to sponsor a bus to transport clinic defenders to the South Bay.[43] In her notes, Kass estimated that one thousand clinic defenders from all over the Bay Area and Sacramento, too, showed up to defend San Jose that day.[44] For the next full week, and even on some days after, BACORR and its allies covered area clinics starting predawn. On several occasions, they sent defenders to the homes of local abortion providers where OR members were picketing and harassing them. Prior to the siege, OR had mailed threatening letters to doctors, saying "You have been identified as an abortionist" and ordering them to stop performing abortions or face consequences, and they had encouraged their members to show up at doctors' houses to "expose evil."[45]

"'Cities of Refuge' was ten days of grueling organizing uncertainty with no sleep," Kass recollected as she paged through a stack of call logs and clinic maps from her "office" folder from that week. When they did sleep, it was in vans in the driveways of friends. In the end, years of clinic defense organizing in the Bay Area and beyond had taught Kass and other BACORR members important lessons that they were able to integrate by the time OR arrived in San Jose. The weeklong defense was a win for BACORR and for the reproductive rights movement more broadly in which "historic cooperation took place." By Sunday, July 18, OR had retreated from the area; clinic defenders had successfully ensured that no clinics were forced to close.[46]

While the week was a win for BACORR, it was also a time for reckoning with where OR was heading ideologically. Early one morning of the siege, when Kass was working the office (a windowless storage unit they had rented), Raven, Dani-Rose, and a handful of other BACORR members jumped into Raven's pickup truck to follow OR from a church to their planned hit.

Using two-way radios that they had rented, Raven and Dani-Rose put in repeated calls to the office to get intel from Kass. With Digable Planets's "La Femme Fetal" playing through the truck speakers, Raven took a windy road up a hill through suburban San Jose. At that point, they had deduced where the antis were headed. "When you're in an OR follow car, first you're hanging back, but then when you figure out what's going on and where they're headed, you gotta be in front," she explained. "Because you want to get there before they do."

But when Raven turned into the cul-de-sac where the doctor lived, she realized that OR had beaten them to their destination—at the end of the road was a mob of antis. To make matters worse, Raven and Dani-Rose's crew was the only group of clinic defenders on site. "There were a shit ton of those fuckers, including Jeff White," Raven remembered. Then, two Chevy Camaros pulled up behind Raven's truck—were they antis? Cops? She couldn't tell. That they'd driven directly into the lion's den was all they knew.

What happened next was crazy, and both Raven and Dani-Rose remembered it the same way: the antis came running at the truck. When Raven turned the car around to get the hell out of there, the antis, at first on foot and then in cars, along with the two Camaros, started chasing them and filming them with camcorders. Raven and Dani-Rose tried to call the office, but the radios weren't getting a signal in the hills. "We were about to throw down with these yahoos in the suburbs, and we had no radio contact," Raven said. At one point during the chase, they found themselves on a narrow dead-end street, which required Raven to sharply turn around and head back the way they came in, with antis and Camaros right on their tail. During the chaotic turnaround, one of the Camaros crunched into an anti's car, creating just enough leeway for Raven to make her escape and get the crew down the hill.

Once they were down, one of the Camaros pulled up alongside Raven, and the driver, a white dude with a mullet, flashed a badge. Raven pulled over. "Dani-Rose and I started arguing about whether he was a real cop," she remembered—OR had been known to try to confuse and derail clinic defenders by pretending to be cops. "He was like, 'You're doing some dangerous driving here,' and I was like, '*Do you know who these people are?*' They're terrorists!"

Raven and Dani-Rose were not arrested that day, but, over the week, about a dozen clinic defenders would be. Approximately one hundred antis would be arrested, too, amid the isolated chaos: on July 12, antis blocked a San Jose Planned Parenthood, and a group of teenagers attending a youth contraceptive clinic were trapped inside.[47] On July 17, antis would drive through a police line outside of Pregnancy Consultation Center.[48]

Afterward, a BACORR member named Tom Burghardt wrote that "future provider harassment" on the part of the anti-abortion movement would likely include "clandestine attacks, creating a climate of psychological terror." He cited examples of previous harassment, including OR "wanted" posters, stalking, sabotage, and death threats against providers and their families. Tom continued, "It is here precisely, at the political and tactical level, that analogies between OR and the Klan can be made. While it is important to expose OR's ties to the Far-Right and neo-Nazi groups and individuals, it is even more critical that we reveal that the tactical modalities employed . . . are linked to a methodology of terror classically employed by the far-right world-wide."[49]

I found a place of ferocity

After San Jose, Operation Rescue would mostly steer clear of the Bay Area, and BACORR would lie low and then rally again in rowdy resistance whenever there was a surge of anti-abortion harassment or violence. The following year, BACORR traveled around the state to build relationships with and defend clinics. And they would mobilize in protest when the Right would try to legislate obstacles into existence. Or in support when comrades would propose creative solutions to structural barriers to access.

Remember the well-spoken clinic escorting and defense trainer Brenda Cummings? In 1993, she and another clinic defender founded a practical support network and program to make rides and lodging available to people trying to get abortions in the Bay Area. They named their organization ACCESS. Later it was renamed ACCESS Women's Health Justice, and today it is the community-of-color-led nonprofit organization ACCESS Reproductive Justice, the only statewide abortion fund and practical support network in California, serving the Bay Area, Central Valley, Los Angeles, and San Diego.

OVER A PILE of garlic fries at a pub in Oakland, Laura and I talked about how the anti-abortion movement was and is about subjugating women and queer people. She told me that from the time she started fighting antis when she was in college, she realized how urgent it was to expose them for the lies they told.

> It was such a kick in the head to see what the antis were doing, how they would be frothing at the mouth around women, especially queer women, who were exercising independence. To see their hatefulness, and the contrast between that and how they talked about themselves as fighting for the civil rights of the unborn, innocents protecting innocents, how they co-opted the language of the civil rights movement—that contradiction moved me. Saying the opposite of what is true, denying your violence, and saying that what you are doing is protecting women and children, that what you're doing is *good*.... That is the tactic of abusers everywhere. It's the epitome of patriarchy.
>
> I had never been beat up before I did clinic defense. The antis would just come barreling at us and punching and kicking us. They clearly enjoyed hitting women. That's what they wanted to do. They wanted to hit women. I wanted to oppose that with every fiber of my body. I found a place of ferocity in me and in my comrades. I learned about what it means to defend not only myself but to defend other people.

There is so much in what Laura said. What strikes me is her argument that what the Christian Right did was create a moral justification to themselves for their violence against women. *The tactic of abusers everywhere.* As part of their work to achieve their goal of reproducing their own power, the Right—the reign of Christian white men—through the imposition of the *idea* of the child, the infant, outwardly condoned and rehearsed, even advocated, the abuse of women. It was the intolerability of this fact that drove Laura to the front line of the war.

For Laura, clinic defense was radicalizing. She reflected, "There you were, holding a clinic defense board or shoving an anti away from a door or helping carry a woman over the heads of people into the clinic. All the different things that people did pulled something forth from them." She continued, "Doing clinic defense led me to be an anarchist, not the other way around—it was seeing that I was part of building an autonomous community that was not dependent on the existing power structures and building power from within."

WHEN I MET with Dani-Rose, they told me about how clinic defense was radicalizing for them, too. It led them to be a communist, not an anarchist as it led Laura to become, but their primary lesson dovetails with Laura's: clinic defense taught them that "what's required of you in this moment is to take responsibility and get out there and be part of leading [the resistance]." They continued, "We're *all* leading this."

Dani-Rose recalled what they learned from their experience in Baton Rouge: "I feel like I'm always afraid. . . . But when you're on a line like that, with people so fierce and determined and honorable, you feel a level of safety and righteousness." BACORR allowed for political differences, fought to maintain collective processes, and made space for political evolution within its membership in the interest of achieving a coalition that was big enough and strong enough to stand up to the threat they were facing.

Dani-Rose remembered making eye contact with patients at the Delta Clinic who'd made it past the shouting antis—they looked upset, hurt, and tired. Dani-Rose reflected, "For me, to make it so that the women could get an abortion. . . . You know how you talk about what you want your life to be about, what you want to live for? Well. It was a privilege to have been there."

Chapter 9

Rage Is Your Bitter Fuel

Let me take you back, for a moment, to 1982.

That year, a French biochemist and endocrinologist named Étienne-Émile Baulieu announced a discovery. Two years prior, he and some other researchers had synthesized a steroid. What they found was that when taken for four days, starting two days before the date of a person's expected period, the steroid would block progesterone receptors in the cells of the uterus. If the person were pregnant, the steroid would make the uterus less hospitable to the implantation and growth of the pregnancy. After taking the drug, they would experience the bleeding of an early abortion. If they weren't pregnant, it would simply bring on a normal period.[1]

Like a pharmaceutical version of a menstrual extraction, you might be thinking.

The anti-progesterone steroid came after years of research.[2] In the 1940s, American scientist Russell Marker and Austrian scientist Carl Djerassi figured out how to synthesize sex hormones from steroids derived from Mexican yams. This was the scientific development that would set off the medical and social transformations of synthetic sex hormones, including oral contraceptives, hormone replacement therapy, and gender-affirming care. Marker and Djerassi set up shop in Mexico City under the company name Syntex, which would be the main supplier of steroids for oral contraceptive manufacturers through the mid-1970s.[3]

In 1970, Baulieu began to focus his research on progesterone receptors and became an exclusive consultant to the French pharmaceutical company Roussel Uclaf.[4] A group of Roussel Uclaf researchers were also investigating steroids and receptors; under the consultancy of Baulieu, the company developed the anti-progesterone.[5]

A "menses regulator" was how Baulieu initially described it. The drug could offer flexibility that oral contraceptives did not as it could be taken on an as-needed basis. If someone didn't have unprotected sex with the risk of pregnancy in a given month, they could forgo taking the steroid, he reasoned. And taking the drug meant being exposed to pharmaceutical intervention for only four days as opposed to three weeks. More testing was needed, Baulieu admitted, but he was optimistic. Roussel Uclaf labeled the compound RU-486.[6]

In 1982, the company began testing the drug in humans, and after six years of testing in France and across Europe and South Asia, France approved RU-486—or the generic drug mifepristone, what's known as "the abortion pill"—for pregnancy termination. When 600 mg was taken with a prostaglandin (misoprostol), which would cause uterine contractions, the success rate of the regimen was 96 percent.[7] Baulieu described the effect of the pill as "contragestion" because, as he put it, it counteracted gestation.[8]

Due to the political situation in the United States, in the 1990s, RU-486 was only available there through clinical trials. It would be another decade before the drug would be approved by the FDA and the mifepristone / misoprostol regimen would become widely available to people seeking abortions in the United States.

All of which is to say: it's not possible to historicize abortion defense in the 1990s without centering the fact that the 1990s were the first years of abortion with pills.

IT'S ALSO NOT possible to historicize abortion defense in the 1990s without centering how brutal the decade was for providers. The decade saw horrific acts of anti-abortion violence in which *seven* health workers—doctors, clinic staff, an escort, and

a security guard—were murdered by anti-abortion domestic terrorists in the United States.[9] During this time, it was more expensive to be an abortion provider than ever before, due in part to
rising insurance costs for clinics. As a result, West Coast Feminist
Health Project / Women's Choice, like many other clinics, was
forced to make do with less. Even so, under Linci's directorship,
the clinic continued to provide abortions as well as other essential
services, including HIV / AIDS and breast cancer screenings.

The clinic institutionalized feminist health care during the
1970s and 1980s, and throughout the brutality of the 1990s continued its process of knowledge deinstitutionalization and dispersal while also maintaining and operating a licensed institution.
Clinic workers continued to share human and other resources
with underground self-help groups. WCFHP / Women's Choice
also formalized a Feminist Health Educator internship, providing laypeople with a structured education in all aspects of
gynecology.

The consolidation and dispersal of feminist health care
knowledge into the community is not a story of growth and
decline. Rather, it's a story of radical institution building that was
always at the same time a form of institution breaking; the clinic
was revolutionary because, from the beginning, it knew its power
needed to be given away. The dispersal of clinic knowledge is also
a story about "life under occupation," as Linci described it. That
is to say, what you have to do to survive a fight against not one
but two enemies—the Christian Right (from casual misogynists
to domestic terrorists) and liberal democracy (from hostile legislation to police intervention).

In the 1990s, WCFHP / Women's Choice got creatively serious (and seriously creative) with abortion advocacy: the clinic
helped bring mifepristone to the United States. Mifepristone
wasn't approved by the FDA until 2000, and prior to approval,
the clinic helped precipitate a Supreme Court case focused on the
drug. Also, the clinic was among a number of providers nationwide that ran abortion pill clinical trials.

WCFHP / Women's Choice worked on the front line to make
the abortion pill—a pharmaceutical commodity—available. It did

this advocacy at a time when it was also doubling down on its commitment to supporting underground self-help groups. This was the clinic's dialectic. It became a professional abortion care institution to achieve the opposite: to demystify, deinstitutionalize, and disseminate abortion care.

Another contradiction of abortion work and defense was that, under the liberal Clinton administration, health workers and activists were forced to fight the state while also working with it. In 1994, the federal government intervened with the passage of the Freedom of Access to Clinic Entrances (FACE) Act. The FACE Act was passed to protect doctors, clinic staff, and patients and to make it more difficult for anti-abortion extremists to attack clinics. The law made it a federal crime to block a clinic's entrance. In addition to passing the FACE Act, the federal government intervened by putting cops—local police, federal marshals, and FBI agents—in and around clinics, requiring health workers to cooperate with them.

Breaking through the stranglehold

Melissa Moffitt tugged open the door of the Women's Building on 18th Street in San Francisco. In the foyer, dozens of young people zipped around, and voices ricocheted off the walls, adding to the din. It was 1990, and a feminist group had organized a gathering. Eighteen-year-old Melissa was there to check it out. A San Francisco State University women's studies major at the time—and an ambitious one; she had started college at age fifteen—Melissa was eager to get involved in activism.

As she tracked all the presentations, Melissa's head swam. She was starting to feel tired but decided to stick around for one more session about an abortion clinic: WCFHP / Women's Choice. A presenter named Linci, probably in her late thirties, got up to speak. She shared that the clinic offered a Feminist Health Educator internship, a one-year volunteer commitment that offered training in all aspects of gynecology. Melissa thought: I could do this for credit.

She got the internship. As an intern, Melissa worked weekly abortion clinics and learned all the roles, as her predecessors had. She participated in self-help classes, which were taught by other lay health workers. Soon Melissa found herself circled up with the rest of the interns, legs spread and a plastic speculum locked into place. Mirror in one hand, flashlight in the other.

Teaching laypeople gynecology in a clinic setting was a central component of the health center from the beginning. Throughout the 1980s, health workers offered participatory clinics; but after the clinic declared bankruptcy in 1988 and Linci and few others bought it, they had to scale back and stopped offering the range of participatory clinics that they had earlier. Even so, health workers continued to teach each other self-help.

Under Linci's directorship in the 1990s, interns were trained in abortion counseling, phlebotomy, and as medical assistants. "They really learned gynecology," she told me. "Where else could you see hundreds of abortion specimens?" For the internship, the clinic recruited laypeople from the community. "Medicine is restricted knowledge," Linci said, echoing the sentiments of early 1970s abortion self-helpers. "We wanted to break through that stranglehold." In addition to spreading knowledge about abortion care to laypeople, the internship inspired some to become feminist providers who took what they learned at the clinic with them into more mainstream medical contexts. As Linci once put it, "We infused the system with feminist spies."

Melissa did the internship and then stayed on—she would work at WCFHP / Women's Choice as one of a handful of paid staff health workers for nearly a decade.

HEALTH WORKERS AT WCFHP / Women's Choice practiced harm reduction, Linci emphasized to me when we talked about the clinic in the 1990s. The local harm reduction movement took off in 1988, when Bay Area activists started a needle exchange program to help stop the spread of HIV / AIDS among people who injected drugs. They called themselves Prevention Point and provided people in the community with sterile syringes and other supplies in exchange for used ones. The goal was to discourage people from sharing needles and thus help them lower their risk of being exposed to or transmitting HIV.[10] In the early years of needle exchange programs, it was not legal for laypeople to give out sterile syringes, so activists had to work underground. They would push a stroller of supplies up and down the streets of neighborhoods like the Tenderloin in San Francisco where there were higher numbers of injection drug users.[11]

In the 1990s, the clinic began serving more Medi-Cal patients, and, as a result, its patient base increasingly intersected with the communities that harm reduction workers served. The clinic practiced harm reduction by helping patients, some of whom were sex workers, access anonymous HIV, Hepatitis C, and other STI screenings so that they could keep their status confidential, if they chose, and out of their records. They supported gay male sex workers by distributing female (internal) condoms. And they supported injection drug users by connecting them with needle exchange services.

Anybody can learn

Clinic culture in the 1990s was a product of the work that Pat Parker, Alicia Jones, Linci, and others did in the late 1970s, in the 1980s, and even into the 1990s. The elder health workers instilled the importance of learning how to do all the jobs, of really being *with* people, both during procedures and in post-clinic debriefs, and of actively learning through hands-on experience. The younger abortion workers of Melissa's generation and beyond developed and understood these principles through the more recent paradigms of harm reduction and trauma-informed care.

Early on, Melissa learned how to work with her hands. She told me about drawing blood and plating out gonorrhea and chlamydia tests: "These days, when you do gonorrhea and chlamydia tests, you do a Q-tip swab, and it goes to a lab. But at Women's Choice, we took the swab and put it on an agar plate. If you can remember back to biology in high school, you'd have these little plates, and they'd be filled with a substance. We would grow the cultures ourselves. It was pretty self-helpy. We would do our own wet mounts with the microscope to look for yeast and trichomonas and that sort of thing."

Another intern in the early 1990s was Joanna Davis. She remembered in detail what it was like to work the abortion clinics. Some of her recollections were like those of Alicia Jones, with whom Joanna sometimes worked, which made me think of how important the transmission of protocols was for health workers at the clinic. Of being an advocate, she recalled, "You go into a room with your group and close the door. You explain the procedure and show the women the instruments and explain what they are for. You tell them how long each step of the procedure will take. 'The doctor will say this before they touch you,' you tell them. 'Somebody will be with you the whole time.' At the end of the clinic, we would have a meeting. We would debrief about how things went and eat garlic pizza. I remember the smell of the pizza; it was intoxicating."

Melissa commented on the post-clinic meetings, too, saying they were for "sharing how we felt about what had happened during the clinic. High points and low points." She added, "Sometimes there were hard things. Sometimes we would see little girls. Or people who didn't seem to be under their own power." The post-clinic meeting gave everyone a chance to process their experiences together.

At WCFHP/Women's Choice, Melissa learned that abortion is a simple procedure. "You could do it yourself," she said. "What's the big deal?" She started to feel this way about a lot of the work she did at the clinic. "Looking at blood tests or doing an ultrasound—these are procedures that you can learn and teach others easily. There doesn't need to be this big facade of professionalism around them." She continued, "Today, I practice medicine as a feminist. I remind the people I teach, who aren't just teenage girls anymore but other physicians, about the white coat and what it suggests about class and professionalism."

To make sure I was hearing her right, I asked Melissa directly: "Do you believe that abortion is so simple a procedure that you don't need to be a trained doctor to learn how to do it?" Melissa lived on the East Coast, so we were talking online. On screen, she wore a pink T-shirt and ruby red lipstick. She was now a gynecologic oncologist. Without hesitation, she replied: "Oh yeah. I think everybody believes that. I mean, everybody who knows anything about it. Abortion is basically the same as changing the brakes on your car. There's a series of steps you do. Anybody can learn them."

Would you tell me about the patients you served? I asked Melissa. "We had a lot of Spanish- and Vietnamese-speaking patients," she replied. "A lot of immigrant women. It was the local community." The clinic saw people coming from all kinds of different situations. "I remember a young girl who came in. She was in tears. She said she was still a virgin. How all they did was rub their bodies together and there was no penetration. How could this have happened to her? And then there was this woman who came in for like her sixth abortion, whose life was so hard. She didn't want to have kids, but she couldn't get it together to use a reliable birth control method because whatever was happening for her was so intense."

I asked Melissa whether she practiced menstrual extraction in a self-help group outside of the clinic. "There weren't, to my knowledge, people who were doing that," she answered. "The women who did things like menstrual extraction were the generation before me." She added, "I don't know what Linci was doing in the evenings, but the rest of us at the clinic were not doing that."

ALSO AMONG THE interns in the early 1990s was purple-hair-streaked Simone, who by that point had been in an underground self-help group for a few years. When Simone started the internship, she'd already decided that she wanted to go to medical school. "I had some knowledge from my self-help group, and I wanted to get more training in surgical abortion in a clinic setting," she told me.

Simone had practiced abortion self-help and done clinic defense, but where she felt most at home was at the clinic. "I thought, this is where I'm supposed to be," she said. No one in

Simone's family was a doctor. She found herself observing the doctors carefully as they did their jobs, curious about them. What kinds of people were they? How did they carry themselves as providers? How did they interact with Linci, who was not a doctor but who was their boss?

According to Simone, the doctors treated the patients with compassion and gave good care. She respected them. But they weren't very available to offer her mentorship. The person she did receive mentorship from, she told me, was Linci.

Like Joanna, Simone had vivid memories of doing group abortion counseling—explaining the procedure to a small group of people and passing around the instruments. "People signed their consent forms in a group setting, which was pretty revolutionary. That's not usually how you consent to a medical procedure," she said.

Today in her work as a gynecologist, when Simone counsels her patients before surgery, she meets with them one-on-one. A benefit of one-on-one counseling, she explained, is that patients may feel more of a connection with her as their doctor and therefore more comfortable asking questions. I asked her how patients at WCFHP/Women's Choice responded to the clinic's philosophy of group abortion care. "I don't think everybody liked it," she said. "Some people were nervous. But that's how it was done." She continued, "Some of us were anarchists and very antiestablishment. Group abortion care seemed like a feminist alternative. At the time, I thought, yeah, this is the way it should be."

In 2001, after finishing medical school and becoming a gynecologist, Simone returned to the Bay Area. "I called up Linci and was like, 'Linci, want me to come work for you?' And then I started doing abortions at Women's Choice."

Their whole life turned around, turned back right again

I asked Melissa what it was like to work at a stand-alone abortion clinic in the 1990s.

"Financially, the place was a mess," she told me. "Linci used to say, 'I'm a good feminist but not a good capitalist.'" She continued, "We were always late paying everything, including ourselves. It was a labor of love, you know?"

Melissa recalled how, when she started, there was a lot of fear among providers about safety. "Would we be bombed? Would people shoot us?" She remembered people doing clinic defense right outside the door. "We were hypervigilant. The antis were okay with the idea of killing people who were doing abortions. They also did things like publicize providers' [home] addresses. It was scary."

But then, in 1993, when Clinton lifted restrictions on abortion counseling at federally funded clinics, also known as the "gag rule," along with some other Reagan- and Bush-era restrictions, many pro-choice advocates no longer felt the need to be on the defensive.[12] Soon the government would pass the FACE Act, which would further signal progress to the liberal pro-choice movement. As a result, WCFHP/Women's Choice, like many other clinics, saw donations decline.

I asked Linci about the clinic's financial challenges in this era. To answer me, she first explained the relationship between public assistance and managed care under the expansion of managed care, which emerged in the 1970s. By the 1980s, amid rising health care costs, managed care—the use of containers like health maintenance organizations (HMOs) and preferred provider organizations (PPOs) to make health care more economical—had become the primary model in the United States.[13] By the 1990s, Medi-Cal worked with multiple managed-care PPOs. Each PPO worked with its own network of providers to control and mitigate costs.

Also in the 1990s, the clinic began serving more Medi-Cal and Medi-Cal-eligible patients. More low-income patients came to the clinic because it had increased its outreach and become better known for providing quality, trauma-informed care regardless of a patient's income. In the process, the clinic got savvy about navigating Medi-Cal along with managed care. Medi-Cal covered (and covers) abortion and all abortion-related services (for example, clinic visits, labs, and ultrasounds) with state funds, enabling the state to fill the gap that the Hyde Amendment created through its ban on the use of federal funds for abortion services. "Learning how to access Medi-Cal and state-supported provision of abortion funding and certifying people to access it became a route to being able to use that funding," Linci explained. In other words, as a PPO in-network provider, the clinic was eligible to obtain reimbursements for services provided to Medi-Cal patients.

But the reimbursements didn't cover costs. Medi-Cal didn't fully reimburse actual fees charged, and, because the clinic kept fees low, individual Medi-Cal reimbursements to the clinic were small. Also, the amount of labor required to obtain reimbursements grew over the 1990s as managed care expanded. Medi-Cal began to work with more managed-care models and plans, so, to get reimbursed, the clinic had to join more managed-care plan provider networks. "Because of the managed-care system, we worked a lot more with the insurance industry than we ever had before," Linci told me.

When WCFHP / Women's Choice would see uninsured low-income patients, they would enroll those patients in Medi-Cal. "If we could demonstrate that people were in need of emergency services, we could get them on the emergency Medi-Cal track so that they could get the care they needed," Linci said. "That became a full-time job." It was an important service to the community, and it also meant endless paperwork, endless billing, endless rejections.

In 1994, after more than twenty years on McClure Street, the clinic moved around the corner to 431 30th Street. From the outside, the new, smaller location looked like a house. "We were just right there, available to everyone," Melissa explained. "On McClure Street, there was a driveway. Through the windows, you could see everybody who was coming up the driveway. I felt protected by that." You couldn't just walk into the 30th Street clinic, though, she added. There was a locked door. You had to ring a bell, and then someone would come and let you in. Once inside, there was a reception window. After checking in, you'd walk through a door on the right of the window into the clinic.

Linci may not have been a good capitalist but, under the nonprofit container organization West Coast Feminist Health Project, she did oversee a successful fundraising campaign. In the mid-1990s, the clinic turned the basement of 30th Street into fundraising headquarters. They enlisted volunteers to do door-to-door canvassing and coordinate direct mailings. The fundraising team kept the clinic open for years longer than it otherwise would have been able to.

The generosity of a small group of donors who consistently came through for WCFHP / Women's Choice also helped keep the clinic open. Linci remembered Hannah, a steadfast supporter who taught her an important political lesson: always question the answers, because the answer in one moment may not be the answer in another. "Perspective and time affect judgment and solutions," Linci explained. "Rigidity is what makes things crumble and causes failure."

AFTER A DECADE working at WCFHP / Women's Choice, Melissa applied to medical school and got in. "I know Linci felt like I was leaving her," Melissa said. "I think she thought I would take over after her. It was hard for her when I left. But she was proud of me. Like, she made me be somebody who went to *medical school*." She continued, "Women's Choice served as a starting point for so many young women's careers. People would just show up there having no idea what they were doing in life and work there for six months or a year or a couple of years, and then suddenly they were going to be a nurse practitioner, or they were going to be a doctor. Or they were going to go do global health work. It amazes me when I think of all the people I used to work with and what they've gone on to do."

When you think of your time at the clinic, I asked, what words or thoughts most immediately come to mind for you? Melissa replied, "Mostly love. Love of my colleagues and all the women I worked with there. A love for easing the suffering of women. I know that most people don't think about it that way, but that's what abortion is. Women come in suffering. And with a safe, five-minute procedure, their whole life is turned around, turned back right again. I think of friendship. Deep bonds. Support. I'm still friends with many women from Women's Choice. If I need anything, they're right there. Like family."

Like a household, I thought.

I would absolutely do it again

As I said, it's impossible to tell the history of abortion defense in the 1990s without accounting for the introduction of medical abortion, which is most often referred to as medication abortion or abortion with pills. And the story of medication abortion is an important part of the story of Women's Choice.

In fall 1988, France approved RU-486, or mifepristone, for early abortions, and Roussel Uclaf contracted with the World Health Organization (WHO) to distribute mifepristone in developing countries. The anti-abortion movement in the United States responded by threatening that it would boycott any US pharmaceutical company that attempted to manufacture the drug.[14]

In the years that followed, a large study in France revealed that mifepristone was safe and effective when taken with the prostaglandin misoprostol (Cytotec).[15] But in 1990, despite international demand, Roussel Uclaf had only extended mifepristone to England, for fear of political backlash. The company's majority stakeholder was a German pharmaceutical company called Hoechst, which had billions in annual revenues in the United States, and Roussel Uclaf feared a US boycott. Also, the company had given the WHO the responsibility of approving mifepristone internationally, but as Baulieu had gone on record saying, the WHO would not approve it due to fears that if it did the United States would withhold funding.[16]

Pro-abortion activists were at an impasse. Then a Berkeley activist named Leona Benten became pregnant.

ON THE NIGHT before Leona Benten's scheduled abortion at WCFHP / Women's Choice, in July 1992, clinic defenders held an all-night watch. For days, the country had been following Leona's story. (BACORR members Laura Weide and Raven told me that they remembered watching the news coverage as they made flyers on the floor of the house they were crashing at in New Orleans, preparing for Operation Rescue to lay siege.)

"Frankly, we were worried somebody was going to bomb us," Linci told me.

Fortunately, that night and the next day, the clinic and Leona were left in peace. She was able to access the care she was seeking without interference or drama.

Before settling in to tell me the story of what happened, Leona passed me a container of homemade molasses cookies. We sat in camping chairs on a patch of sun-dappled grass in a Berkeley city park. It was March 2022—nearly thirty years had passed.

In 1992, Leona was in her late twenties. The weeks leading up to her abortion were unlike anything she'd experienced. "It was terrible," she told me. "And I do not regret doing it. I don't know if I can say both of those things about anything else I've done in my life."

On July 1 of that year, Leona was six weeks pregnant. That day, she tried to bring a dose of RU-486 into the United States from England, where it had been legal for a year. She had learned from friends who worked at WCFHP / Women's Choice that a group of abortion activists was looking for a test plaintiff to challenge the FDA's ban on imports of RU-486. Leona had already decided to have an abortion, so she volunteered to be that plaintiff.

Because Leona was an anarchist, actively engaging with and working to change the law were unusual forms of political action for her. In fact, she told me, "If politics is about representation, then I consider myself *anti*political, because I'm not about representation. I believe we are ourselves. Ideally, we'll work through the world as ourselves. Not as representations of other things." Yet, as the plaintiff in a class action lawsuit, it was Leona's job to represent other women. It was the first of a series of contradictions that she would have to embrace.

As the organizers laying the groundwork for the lawsuit anticipated, Leona's pills were seized at the airport upon her entry into the United States. By the time she got off the plane, the group leading the import attempt, Abortion Rights Mobilization, had already alerted US Customs—and they promptly confiscated the pills.

"It was about having a lawsuit so that we could take it to the Supreme Court," Leona said. "And we knew it would happen in a hurry because I was pregnant."

How did the clinic get involved with the people planning the lawsuit? I asked.

"I don't know," she replied. "I mean, if you were looking to connect with an activist women's clinic at that time, Women's Choice was it."

The person who orchestrated the lawsuit was Lawrence Lader, who became an abortion activist in the process of interviewing Margaret Sanger and writing her biography. He had been calling for the repeal of all abortion laws for more than two decades. In 1969, Lawrence cofounded NARAL, and by this point in 1992, he was president of Abortion Rights Mobilization.[17]

In the 1990s, Lawrence wanted to bring attention to the RU-486 import ban and see it overturned. As legal scholar Rachael Pine argued in 1992, the ban had come to represent the "zealous and ideologically-driven interjection of politics into science by the U.S. government where the lives and health of women are at issue." While the FDA prohibited the import of drugs that it had not approved, it did permit the import of many drugs for personal use on a discretionary basis. But in the late 1980s, the agency had banned the import of RU-486 entirely, declaring that border police should "automatically detain all shipments of unapproved abortifacient drugs." Pine pointed out that the ban helped ensure a hostile climate around the development of drugs related to reproductive health and choice more generally.[18]

Lawrence and Abortion Rights Mobilization initiated the RU-486 campaign first by working with lawyers to understand the "potential penalties" for importing the drug. In 1990, lawyers advised him against attempting any import: "The best I can suggest is that we try to figure out a way to accomplish your objectives through some other route. . . . [T]his alternative is far too risky," wrote the lawyers.[19] In 1992, Lawrence proceeded with a plan to import a single dose.

On her return flight to the United States, Leona looked over a script the team had asked her to memorize. She was exhausted. She and her team had arrived in England, obtained the pills from their contact, and departed the very next day. Leona remembered how they also asked her to wear a black miniskirt on her return so that she'd have more "media appeal." "Maybe they were concerned about whether I was going to be sympathetic enough?" Leona speculated. "I don't know what the skirt thing was about." In any case, she complied—in her words, "It was a costume." The team had also asked Leona to take a tranquilizer, so she wouldn't freak out in front of the media, they told her. Leona did not comply with that request.

Upon deplaning at JFK airport in New York City, a not-at-all-sedated Leona was swarmed by reporters. "The script included one really fucking stupid line that I did not read," she told me. "But I basically accepted the rest of it. Which continues to bug me today."

Do you remember the line? I asked.

"Yes, of course," she replied. "That one line. How many decades later? The line was, 'This is just a medical procedure like any other medical procedure.'"

I wondered why Leona took issue with "just a medical procedure." It seemed to me to resonate with the widely embraced principle that "abortion is health care," a claim made frequently by reproductive justice advocates. She replied,

> I get the political perspective. The idea that one way to address the drama and angst around abortion is to say, "It's not a person. It's an outgrowth of cells. Abortion is just a medical procedure." But the clump-of-cells argument only works for a limited amount of time, very early in a pregnancy. Also, my conception of how to address

the issue is the opposite. One of the reasons that I'm an anarchist is because I want us to take responsibility for our lives. I want us to feel the agency and recognize the power that we have. To say that these decisions we make are meaningless—to say "just a medical procedure" or "clump of cells"—goes in the opposite direction of taking that responsibility.

As I thought about it more, I began to see that "abortion is health care" and "abortion is just a medical procedure" are not the same claim. Abortion *is* health care, and it is, also, a procedure that *is* meaningful, not "just" anything, in that it embodies a choice not to participate in pregnancy and birthing with one's body at a particular moment in one's life. It is a choice not to engage with a very specific biological process, regardless of what story you tell about the development at the center of it, as either a fetal life or a clump of cells. Abortion, just like consensual pregnancy, is above all a powerful exercise of body sovereignty.

On this logic, deciding to undergo (or not) *any* medical procedure is highly meaningful because your decision regards a biological course in your body. I thought about all the people who have undergone procedures without their consent: those who have been coercively sterilized or who have been forced to remain pregnant and deliver. In these cases, the meaning of participating in those procedures—autonomy—is denied. The body sovereignty of those who would choose is denied.

I want us to take responsibility for our lives. It seemed so basic when I wrote it down, but it felt important: the condition of possibility for taking responsibility is having choice.

"THE THING I remember most is reading the script that I wasn't stoked about," Leona recalled about the day her pills were seized at the airport. "And then the doctor who was with us was nice to me, and I started crying. As soon as I started crying, the cameras all started going off. That pissed me off, even though it's totally predictable that the media would want the show of emotion."

Smiling, she added, "Nobody showed my miniskirt. That was funny to me."

In the days that followed, the media were unrelenting. To escape the deluge, Leona left town. In her absence, the media approached her neighbors and even asked her mail delivery person for a quote. She returned home to letters from anti-abortion advocates telling her she didn't need to have an abortion because they would adopt her child.

Within a week of her return to the country, Leona, Lawrence, and the New York Center for Reproductive Law and Policy sued FDA commissioner David Kessler in the US District Court of New York, demanding the return of her pills. Their team argued that the FDA had not allowed for public comment before implementing the import ban on RU-486 and that the ban was "arbitrary, capricious, [and] an abuse of discretion." They also argued that the ban interfered with Leona's constitutional right to abortion because it created a substantial obstacle. As Pine put it, "In substance, they argued that government action that contributes to depriving women of the choice to employ a drug-induced medical means of pregnancy termination has the purpose and effect of substantially reducing access to abortion services and of requiring a surgical form of treatment where surgery could have been avoided."[20]

The district court ruled in Leona's favor and ordered the return of the pills. In his opinion, the judge wrote, it seemed that "the decision to ban the drug was based not from any bonafide concern for the safety of users of the drug, but on political considerations having no place in FDA decisions on health and safety."[21]

But then the court of appeals issued a stay (halt) on the ruling, so Leona's team made an emergency application for the stay to be lifted by the Supreme Court.[22] By that point, the story had gotten big. The *Los Angeles Times* proclaimed, "An Unorthodox 'Everywoman': Leona Benten was supposed to engender sympathy in her role as banner-carrier for RU-486. But she proved to have a mind, and an agenda, of her own." The article described Leona as a "quintessentially Californian," tattooed Berkeley activist who "seized the chance to speak out as well against police harassment and welfare cuts, and for lesbians' rights to raise children." It pitted a caricatured version of Leona against Lawrence and his team, saying that she "refused invitations" to talk to the media about the case and that Lawrence had found her "difficult."[23]

Leona found the media and public's discussions of her to be superficial and alienating. "Who you are is taken away from you and reflected back, badly," she said of celebrity more generally. "The public gaze distances you from knowing who you actually are. I'm very anti-celebrity today."

The irony of it all struck me hard. Leona had been conscripted by progressive activists to help fight for the autonomy and privacy of women around abortion care. Yet, in the process, she was subjected by these same activists, along with the media they purported to be allied with, to surveillance and scrutiny of her personal life and choices. The media and public's sense of entitlement to access to her—to personal information about her body—revealed a lot about how the culture thought (and thinks) about women and feminized people: they are expected to furnish information about their lives and bodies on demand, to cooperate and comply.

On July 17, 1992, the Supreme Court decided not to lift the stay. The Court said Leona was not entitled to have her pills returned simply because the FDA hadn't allowed for public comment before issuing the import ban. The Court did not, however, issue an opinion on whether confiscation of the pills created "undue burden" and violated Leona's constitutional right to abortion.[24] Justices Harry Blackmun and John Paul Stevens, the former of whom authored the *Roe v. Wade* decision, dissented. In his dissent, Stevens addressed the question of constitutionality, arguing that while the government has an interest in the method by which a person terminates their pregnancy, it was "not sufficient to justify the burdensome consequence of this seizure."[25]

In her assessment of the case's outcome, Pine pointed out that it certainly registered the period's bleak abortion law landscape in the United States. But she also asserted, "The creation of this 'test case' by Leona and her companions reflects, equally, a new courage and commitment to struggle for change among pro-choice forces." WCFHP/Women's Choice, which introduced these groups to Leona in the first place, deserves much of the credit for this tactical achievement.

Leona did not get her pills back, and she did end up going to WCFHP/Women's Choice to obtain a surgical abortion. But, as Pine suggested, the case wasn't really a loss; rather, it registered a coming sea change. *Benten v. Kessler* put direct pressure on government and industry to legalize abortion with pills. After Clinton was elected—amid escalating anti-abortion violence, including the murder of David Gunn in Pensacola—Roussel Uclaf and Hoechst agreed to investigate possible manufacturers and distributors of mifepristone in the United States. Also, the FDA agreed to review any company's application for the drug's approval quickly. "The abortion pill could be available by summertime next year," heralded activists.[26]

In reality, it would be another eight years before the FDA would approve abortion with pills.

YET ANOTHER CONTRADICTION: when we talked in 2022, Leona didn't think the legalization of abortion with pills necessarily translated to a more liberated society. "I support us having access to abortion at any moment at any time. But the idea that we can just take pills to fix things is part of our reliance on things we don't have control over and our alienation from our bodies. Pills just continue the trajectory of us not knowing what's really going on."

Leona's point also contends with the pharmaceutical industrial complex. Not only do pills promote our passive understanding of and relationship to our bodies, but their availability has been and is facilitated by and predicated on global capitalist supply chains. Recall that the sex hormones used to make birth control pills and mifepristone initially came from Mexican wild-yam-derived steroids. To launch the hormone industry, American capitalism appealed to and incorporated Indigenous peasants who knew how to cultivate the yams, propping up the modernization project of the Mexican government.[27] Notably, the late 1990s, leading up to mifepristone's approval, were years when drug company profits were significantly higher than those of other industries, the result of unregulated price setting.[28]

Later, I asked Linci what she thought about medication abortion. She pointed out that abortion with pills allows people to have secrets. "Having secrets can bring us comfort and safety in a hostile world," she said. With pills, someone in a non-supportive or abusive relationship could simply say that they had a miscarriage. "The absolute win of it is women's safety."

Even so, Linci explained, surgical abortion remains the bottom line: if there is any retained tissue, or even just painful blood clots that a person is not able to tolerate passing, aspiration is then used to complete the abortion. "We're never going to eliminate the need for aspiration abortions with medication abortion," she said. "What we are going to do is allow women the dignity and privacy to terminate their pregnancies as they choose."

"I DID THIS thing," Leona said to me, thoughtful in the warm midday light. "It caused a lot of uproar. I had a lot of feelings about the thing. It was a terrible experience. But I had my abortion, and then I went on with my life. And I would do it again."

Being the test case plaintiff was not only physically and emotionally hard, Leona explained, but also meant engaging with institutions and corporations she loathed, with tactics she believed were short-sighted and contradictory. Yet, despite the problem of relying on pharmaceuticals, she felt that the availability of abortion with pills ultimately helped move society closer to what it was she was fighting for: agency, access, and choice. Leona reiterated: "It was terrible, and I would absolutely do it again."

Life under occupation, I thought.

IN JANUARY 1993, two days after he was inaugurated, Bill Clinton sent a memo to the Department of Health and Human Services. It's time to get serious about the testing and licensing of RU-486 in the United States, the memo said.[29] That May, Roussel Uclaf donated its patent rights to the nonprofit Population Council, which was tasked with conducting clinical trials, finding a company to manufacture the drug, and, finally, applying for FDA approval.[30]

Clinical trials enabled activists to provide mifepristone in the United States and played a key role in helping bring about the FDA's eventual approval of the drug. In August 1996, WCFHP / Women's Choice announced that medical director Bud Gore was launching a mifepristone / misoprostol trial as part of a nationwide study.[31] The purpose of the nationwide study was to determine the safety and efficacy of mifepristone, and whether a lower dose was as effective as a higher dose, in combination with self-administered vaginal misoprostol, in two thousand pregnant women.[32] That July, an FDA advisory committee had made a recommendation to the FDA that it should formally approve mifepristone.[33]

The nationwide mifepristone / misoprostol study that Bud was part of was sponsored by Lawrence Lader and Abortion Rights Mobilization and led by the doctor Eric Schaff from the University of Rochester. At a press conference in July 1996, following the FDA advisory committee's recommendation, Lawrence said, "For four years since we brought Leona Benten from London with RU-486 to challenge the ban against personal use . . . we have pledged to a campaign to bring RU-486 to American women as soon as possible. We promise we will not be stopped."[34] In a letter he drafted to the *New York Times* that December, Lawrence explained that the clinics participating in the study were located on the West Coast and East Coast and in the Mountain West and Midwest and that they "hope[d] to open other outlets in the South and South West soon so every woman [would] be in reasonable flying distance of treatment."[35]

Linci remembered how the trials created reams of new paperwork for health workers. It also meant lots of follow-up for patients. "If you chose medication-induced miscarriage, you had to come back," she said. "We followed you with blood tests and ultrasounds to make sure your hormones were dropping. We followed you to ensure the absolute termination of pregnancy.

Because what happened wasn't under our control. It was under *your* control. We really had to check to make sure everything was done because we weren't there. We didn't do tissue evaluation. We didn't do pathology. We didn't have that assurance [of a complete abortion] that we have in a surgical procedure. That's why you had to come back for so much follow-up. Because *you're* the one who passed that pregnancy."

In spring 1997, Schaff published some initial research findings from data gathered from July through November 1996 about the effectiveness of the drug combination when misoprostol was administered vaginally: 98 percent of study participants had had successful mifepristone / misoprostol abortions with the protocol.[36] In January 1999, Schaff published additional findings from trials run between November 1996 and October 1997 that involved a lower dose (200 mg) of mifepristone, which was found to be 97 percent effective—and Bud was a coauthor of this paper.[37]

Bud and WCFHP / Women's Choice continued to participate in clinical trials, helping to advance research and push the FDA toward approval of the drug.

It wasn't until September 2000 that the FDA ultimately approved mifepristone, ending a decade-long political battle. Mifepristone was to be manufactured by Danco Laboratories under the name Mifeprex.[38] "I'm not surprised it finally received U.S. approval," Leona told the *New York Post*. "Just that it took so long."[39]

We have medication abortion as an option in the United States today thanks to the political labor of activists like those at WCFHP / Women's Choice—Leona, Linci, Bud—and all of the abortion workers and study participants who made the trials possible.

The war was at your door

Once again, it's not possible to talk about abortion defense in the 1990s without confronting how brutal that decade was for abortion workers.

Standing in the parking lot at Ladies Center Clinic in Pensacola, Florida, in the early morning of July 29, 1994, a white anti-abortion extremist named Paul Hill watched a doctor named John Bayard Britton, then sixty-nine years old, arrive for work in a truck. Britton was being driven by his escort, abortion rights activist James Barrett, who was seventy-four, along with James's wife, June. James parked and started getting out of the truck when Hill lifted a twelve-gauge shotgun, took aim, and shot him in the head, killing him. Next, he shot June Barrett in the arm. Then Hill reloaded his shotgun and killed John Britton.[40]

Paul Hill had spent the previous year on the road with the group Defensive Action, proclaiming to churches and anyone who would listen that the murder of the doctor David Gunn, by Michael Griffin on March 10, 1993, was "justifiable homicide."[41] The murders of Barrett and Britton would be the first committed by a leader of an anti-abortion extremist group.[42]

During the first seven months of 1994, more than half of US abortion clinics experienced death threats, stalkings, bombings, invasions, arsons, and blockades. By the end of 1994, there had been four murders and eight attempted murders of abortion workers.[43]

The murders, combined with the flurry of bombings and other attacks, and not to mention the coordinated clinic blockades of previous summers, compelled the US government under Clinton to pass the FACE Act, which made injury, intimidation, or interference with people seeking or providing in-clinic reproductive health services federal crimes.

The law also criminalized injury, intimidation, or interference with people exercising their "First Amendment right of religious freedom at a place of religious worship," a line that made me do a double take when I first read it. The law insinuates that pro-abortion activists were likely to attack members of the anti-abortion Right *at their churches*.

Attorney General Janet Reno, who had tasked the Department of Justice and Congress with creating the law, gave this explanation in May 1993: "I emphasized that the legislation must secure the rights of women seeking reproductive health services and the individuals who provide those services, while respecting the First Amendment rights of those who oppose abortion to express that opposition in meaningful ways."[44] The act was signed into law a year later.

The FACE Act was effective in stopping anti-abortion extremists from blockading clinic entrances, but it didn't criminalize many forms of harassment that antis engaged in outside of clinics. In fact, as Lauren Rankin points out in her book *Bodies on the Line*, a 1998 congressional report revealed that clinics around the country experienced *more* anti-abortion protesting outside of their buildings after the FACE Act was passed, not less.[45]

The FACE Act was a conservative law from the start. So, arguably, in August 1994, when the FBI launched an inquiry (operation VAAPCON [Violence Against Abortion Providers Conspiracy]) into whether the violence was a mobilization of anti-abortion militants "that endeavor[ed] to achieve political or social change through activities that involve[ed] force or violence" (as abortion rights groups had argued it was), and the Department of Justice deployed US Marshals to clinics that had been sites of "violent demonstrations" around the country, they had already decided the answer to the question of their operation.[46] Americans were divided along ideological lines, the FACE Act implied. And while murder could not be tolerated in a liberal democracy, everyone in that democracy had a right to express their religious beliefs. In short, the state was unwilling to side definitively with women and others who could become pregnant.

Just a few months after launching the investigation, the FBI determined that it couldn't prove a conspiracy against abortion providers. After the investigation was officially closed in January 1996, one FBI source told the *Washington Post*, "We have been sort of reluctant workers in this. We have done our duties to the utmost. I guess the best you can say is that it was better to be safe than sorry"—a narrative that registers the state's unwillingness to take seriously systematic violence against women.[47]

TWO AND A half years later, in October 1998, a doctor named Barnett Slepian and his wife returned home from synagogue on a Friday night in suburban Buffalo. Slepian, fifty-two years old, walked into the kitchen, where a sniper's bullet shattered a window before entering his chest. Slepian died within two hours.[48] Anti-abortion extremist James Charles Kopp was later captured and convicted, in 2003, of second-degree murder and, additionally, in 2007, of violating the FACE Act.[49] This was the fifth sniper attack on an abortion worker in the Northeast since 1994. (Three took place in Canada and one in Rochester.)[50]

Two weeks later, the Department of Justice launched a Task Force on Violence Against Health Care Providers. In the months before Slepian's murder, clinics around the country had been attacked with butyric acid, arson, attempted bombings, and letters that claimed to contain anthrax.[51] The task force's job was to investigate and prosecute attacks on abortion providers, track national trends, make security recommendations, support local working groups, and train law enforcement.[52]

This new task force was about to come knocking on the door of WCFHP / Women's Choice.

IF YOU WERE in an underground self-help group, you understood that under no circumstance were you to talk to the police. But during the Clinton years, law enforcement and FBI agents were closer to WCFHP / Women's Choice than ever before. Linci had to get dispensation from her fellow self-helpers, because the reality was that she was about to start talking to the police, whether she liked it or not.

She told me the story as we sat in the sand at Ocean Beach, wrapped in blankets. We'd chosen a spot at the base of a dune so that we would have some protection from the whipping wind. Sea and sky were a similar winter ash gray. It was January 2021, a few days after a mob of more than two thousand Donald Trump supporters violently invaded the US Capitol.

"It's bitter fuel," Linci told me. "Rage. And when you're living under occupation, it's the only fuel you've got."

Linci emphasized to me that, in the 1990s, abortion clinics were under siege. She remembered the hate mail. The liability insurance premium hikes. She remembered being on the job and asking herself if today was the day she was going to have to climb out on the fire ladder. Or wondering, while she was driving around, if she should be wearing a bulletproof vest.

Starting in 1993, a high-profile doctor named Bruce Steir, who worked some shifts at WCFHP / Women's Choice, was accompanied by federal marshals to and from the Redding Feminist Women's Health Center, where he provided abortions once a week.[53] Bruce was well known among both abortion activists and antis because he was someone who traveled to multiple clinics around the state and was able to perform later procedures—he played a critical role in making later abortion care available in California.[54] He was assigned federal protection when he received a threatening letter at the Redding clinic from an anti-abortion extremist named Ron Walters. It read: "Dear Dr. Bruce. . . . Goodbye. Testify that he has cursed both God and the King. Then take him out and stone him to death."[55]

Linci told me that US Marshals accompanied Bruce when he worked at WCFHP / Women's Choice, too. How did the other health workers feel about having the federal officers *inside* of the clinic, I asked her. Did they feel that you needed to accept the support because you were at war?

"I think we had mixed feelings," Linci said. "One of the things we did to deal with that was to set the guy up in the hall so that he wasn't in anyone's personal space." She continued, "It was something that was put on us. The escort was for the doctor. I was glad that they had officers picking them up and taking them to clinics, though."

She was glad about it, Linci explained, because doctors were being shot at coming and going from work, and their cars were being bombed. One doctor at WCFHP / Women's Choice got himself a handheld mirror, which he used to check under his car to make sure nobody had cut his brakes or planted an explosive. In 1994, clinic health workers started wearing bulletproof vests to work.[56]

After the federal task force was established in 1998, Linci was asked to participate in a local working group that included staff from other clinics, the FBI, and local police and their intelligence department representatives. She told me that being in the working group was just something she had to do, in her words, to help "deal with weapons of mass destruction." Gunmen firing. Bombs. Chemical weapons.

Slepian's murder, along with news of a website that listed the names of abortion doctors—with Slepian's name and the names of three other murdered doctors crossed out—compelled them to ratchet up their security game. In early 1999, WCFHP / Women's Choice put out a call for donations to help cover the cost of bulletproof vests for escorts (the cost of a single vest was $500 to $1,000). Because of frequent protests, the clinic had stopped offering abortion clinics on the weekends.[57]

Linci told me about some of the ways she and other abortion workers were forced to change their lifestyles during the war years. "You had a different code about how you were supposed to live as an abortion provider. You weren't supposed to always drive the same way to the clinic, and you were supposed to check and see if there was a problem before you parked your car. You were not supposed to have your windows or curtains open. You were supposed to live in a state of seclusion under a state of occupation. The war was at your door."

She added, "Just trying to deal with that stuff on a day-to-day level really took its toll." A lot of people couldn't handle it and left. "It was really, really hard," Linci said. "For those who walked away, they were walking away from something really intense. And I think it's always okay to say, 'I have to leave the war.'"

She continued, "One of the things we tried to do was declare that the clinic was revolutionary space, and that when you walked in the door, you left the bullshit drama behind. We did the best we could with what we had to make the space as safe as we could. Every health worker gave their time and undivided attention to the women and their needs. We did it with the idea that women could teach each other, and reach each other, and make decisions. All they needed was for someone to tell them what the truth was.

That fueled our lives. But the burnout of doing reproductive care work was atrocious. The hatred took its toll."

Chapter 10

No Way to Learn Except to Do

"Whatever I choose to do with my body is my own business.
And no one has a right to say what I can or cannot share. If
I want to share my cervix with you, I get to do that. It is not
obscene behavior. It's health education."

—LINCI

In the 1990s, underground gynecological and abortion
self-helpers in the Bay Area dedicated themselves to practice.
They did so at a moment when radical queer feminists were challenging entrenched, degrading narratives about sexually active
women, about women's roles in sex, and about sex work by
unapologetically claiming the different kinds of sex, sexual roles,
and sex work they had or had performed in their lives. In doing
so, they modeled sex-positive feminism—what sexuality studies
scholar Lynn Comella describes as "a way of conceptualizing and
talking about sexuality that seeks to intervene in a culture over-
whelmingly shaped by the belief that sex is a dangerous, destructive, and negative force."[1]

Abortion self-helpers led this charge. For them, the fight
for reproductive freedom *was* sex-positive feminism—a mode
of resistance to the war on women that the Right was waging
with the anti-abortion movement and on queer and trans people through its ostracization and abandonment of people with
AIDS.

In the 1990s, self-help was certainly about learning how to do abortions, and, as self-helpers conveyed to me, it was also about learning how to feel safer and more comfortable and confident in your sexuality and sexual life.

So long as you keep it underground

During our conversation, Vanessa told me about the atmosphere and energy of underground abortion self-help. One thing she started to grasp through self-help was that some things require a lot of time and skill to learn. The anarchist politics she'd been involved in up until that point had moved a lot faster; self-help required that she slow down. "You can't just be like, okay, I'm interested in menstrual extraction, let's do one right now. It's more like, you're interested? Great. Now spend a year finding cervixes," she explained. "I think it was a year before I did anything more than put my hand on Linci's while she did an extraction. She'd let you hold onto her hand so you could get the feeling of when you had finished an area. It was an apprenticeship model."

In Vanessa's mind, self-help groups were like political affinity groups: they required you to trust and share with each other, understand the legal status of your activities, and keep secrets together. An important difference was that, unlike shorter-lived affinity groups, self-help required a long-term investment in collaborative skill building. Another difference had to do with the vibe. "The thing with affinity groups is that you're usually doing something intense. There's fear and adrenaline," she explained. "In our self-help groups, we were trying to achieve the opposite. We were trying to make things less fearful, more normalized. We tried to cut the adrenaline however we could."

Eventually Vanessa joined Max's group. She recalled how the framework felt different from her previous group, maybe partly because Max had gotten interested in sex education. Also, most group members were queer and had started to really come into their sexual selves. In Vanessa's words:

In my first group, the framework was, "We need to learn how to do this. We need these skills so that we can provide this service to women." We were more medical-procedure-oriented. The second group was more body- and sex-positive. People talked about how their bodies *felt*. What felt good, what didn't. We would create a nice space with candles and blankets. We made it into something enjoyable. Like, this is a special thing that we're going to do in a special space. It was an honoring-our-bodies kind of approach.

We would talk about how we responded to things sexually. Not in the context of sex, but in the context of just . . . talking it out. I'd felt sort of sexually repressed. The group helped normalize sexuality and sensuality. The medical model puts a sheet over you and divides you from your vagina. My group did a great job of reintegrating women's bodies and sexuality.

For Vanessa, self-help was an opportunity to develop awareness of bodily feeling and sexuality in an environment that was enjoyable but that was not itself sexualizing. It was a space where sexuality was considered normal, part of the whole.

I thought of a comment Max once made: "We were all curious about our bodies and had an open discourse with each other about our orgasms and how we got off. It was all integrated into our curiosity and sharing." Not only was sexuality normal, but it was the subject of curiosity and meaningful discussion.

When I talked to Izabel about the body sharing, she said, "There was something about having other humans know my body but not in a sexual context. . . . My cervix was always super easy to find. That was a feature of me. And to have that be communal knowledge. . . . It was delightful!" Self-help taught people that they could be seen as sexed and sexual beings, but without being sexualized in the moment of that recognition. In self-help, your sexual being was, again, part of your whole person.

A self-helper named Grace* was in Izabel's group. Grace was from a middle-class white family in Michigan. She had been going to school and waiting tables in the Bay Area when she got involved in self-help. When I asked her how the group felt, Grace described it as "spicy." "When you start keeping a secret with someone, there's extra power and extra intimacy. You're protecting the secret, and you're protecting each other," she said. "This was true of self-help. It was intimate, underground, and radical. At a rally, or in advocacy when you try to change the law, you don't necessarily have power over what happens. Whereas in self-help, so long as you keep it underground, you have a lot of agency and power."

Grace recalled having non-pregnant menstrual extractions. "I remember being nervous. There's something about having something go that deep into your body when it isn't actually necessary. . . . I wondered, am I crossing a line in my relationship to my body? At the same time, I wanted to be of service to this thing that felt very important."

What was "the thing"? Self-help meant asserting the right to say *yes* to sex while at the same time saying *no* to subjugation and policing by the state and medical institution. Self-helpers grasped how radical this yes-no was, in a country where being a woman meant being forced to submit to sexual and reproductive monitoring, governance, and non-sovereignty. In the process of saying both yes and no, some self-helpers, like Grace, came up against a line that was new to them. They chose to cross that line in the name of repudiating the medical police.[2]

My mind went back to what I think of as self-help's non-sexualized feminist body sharing. Maybe it was the slow progression and collaboration that self-help required that made both medical demystification and non-sexualized body sharing simultaneously possible. Self-help could be "spicy" but not sexualizing. It could be vulnerable but also safe and empowering.

Self-help wasn't conventional medical practice. And it wasn't sex. It took up a third space, in which there was the heat of affinity, political secrecy, and mutual protection. Of having pushed the envelope by saying both yes and no—of having gone deep into each other's bodies together and then having come out again, okay yet changed.

To go into sex totally and not be hurt by it

In 1990, HBO launched a documentary series called *Real Sex*, with each episode featuring short segments on human sexuality, sex work, and media representations of sex, internalizing a critique of the fact that it was itself a representation. Often, the series featured sex workers on sex in their own words. Episode four features a segment on the performance artist and sexual health educator Annie Sprinkle and her work in sex, including her roles in porn films. She tells the interviewer, "I'm teaching by example. [Viewers or audience members] get to see a person who has no shame or guilt about their own body or their genitals. They see that I've really explored my desires, that I've been very promiscuous, that I've gone into sex totally and not been hurt by it. And so it inspires them to explore their desires more."[3]

The segment cuts to a skit from a live performance of Annie's *Post Porn Modernist* one-woman show—her "Public Cervix Announcement."[4] She holds up a hyperbolically simple diagram of female sex organs and waves at it with her pointer. "Everybody, *vag-in-al canal*," she instructs the audience. "Okay. This is the *ut-er-us*." Then Annie holds up a metal speculum. "This is a standard gynecological speculum, just like they use in the doctor's office," she says before lying back. "And what we can do is, just insert the speculum, open it up, okay. . . . It's amazing how tight that pussy is after all these years! Why don't you all come and make a line. We aren't gonna have time for everybody, but step right up. Now, I think there are a few speculums left. Buy a speculum. You can show your friends. It's a great party trick." Audience members approach her, taking turns holding a flashlight and leaning in to look at her cervix.

Then the segment takes us back to the interview with Annie, who reflects, "I think in this time of AIDS, it's very important to expand our concept of what sex is. Traditionally, sex has been about fucking and sucking and bodies coming together, but we can start focusing more on sharing energy and intimacy and using our entire bodies as sex organs."

What most people in the audience wouldn't have known was that Annie's public cervix announcement built on two decades of cervical self-exam in the self-help movement—one that from its inception asked you to overcome guilt and shame about your body and talk openly about what you were doing and experiencing. *I think there are a few speculums left. Buy a speculum. You can show your friends.* In the 1990s, Annie lived in the Bay Area. She must have attended a self-help informational meeting, I speculated, because hers was not a common script.

Curious, I called her up. It turns out that Annie first performed a version of her public cervix announcement at a New York City festival called Smutfest in the early 1980s. She had heard of gynecological and abortion self-help but didn't think of herself as part of the movement. (Of course, she was making a major contribution to it.) Instead, she had been learning about sacred sex and sexuality and women's health at the Wise Woman Center just outside of New York City.[5] In 1988, she remembered, she attended an event about cervical self-exam in a public park in New York.

Inspired by everything she was learning, Annie took her public cervix announcement, at that point part of her *Post Porn Modernist* one-woman show, on the road. "I toured it for six years," she said, "from 1989 to 1995. I showed my cervix to tens of thousands of people in twenty countries." But, Annie said, "it was never about exhibitionism. I was never getting off by showing my pussy. It was innocent play." I thought of what Linci said: *It is not obscene behavior. It's health education.*

Annie articulated and performed a sex-positive feminism that built on gynecological and abortion self-help, especially the idea that your body was nothing to fear or be embarrassed about. Her work, along with that of other sex-positive feminists, would inform underground self-help's creative, intimate, and playful sexual health education focus in the 1990s and beyond.

But sex was just not what we were doing

In their groups, Izabel and Fuchsia performed numerous extractions on other members, some of whom were pregnant at the time. They also received multiple extractions. "To get the skill set outside of medical training, you have to practice a lot," Fuchsia explained. "Some people received a lot of MEs, and some people didn't. People with a high pain threshold like me were more likely to volunteer."

While on a road trip, Izabel accidentally became pregnant. Shit, she thought. I definitely can't do this. And how lucky I am, she also thought, to have my group. They'll get me through it.

Izabel and Fuchsia estimated that, in a decade, each of their groups probably did ten to fifteen procedures for pregnant people outside of their groups. Early on, they both participated in a procedure for an acquaintance in Berkeley. They told me about it in our triangle meeting at Aquatic Park. The procedure stood out in Fuchsia's mind because the recipient's boyfriend was there with her, which was unusual. This particular partner was "extra nice and supportive," Fuchsia said. "He had it all arranged and comfortable for her in her bedroom. He held and supported her the entire time."

Of boyfriends in general, Izabel said, "We didn't find them useful. We also didn't want another person to have seen us. We didn't want another security risk. And we were better at supporting the person than any male partner anyway." Fuchsia laughed. Izabel added, "We had our way, and they were just going to be in the way."

Regarding the work ethic of self-help, Grace recalled how strongly self-helpers believed in what they were doing. They were committed to providing care for people outside the group. She said, "It was like, okay, we're *doing* this. And it's on an edge that's not a thousand percent comfortable. There was always the question of, What's this going to lead to? Are we going to get in trouble? And yet this is important. It's essential for women to be able to choose their own futures. How far do we have to go to secure that?"

While wanting to be of service to their communities, self-helpers were nevertheless especially cautious when providing extractions for people outside their groups. They didn't use their real names with people they didn't know. Before doing a procedure, they would meet with the person to help them prepare, make an aftercare plan (in Izabel's words, "to make sure the super nurturing caring space we would make was going to continue on after we left"), and answer any questions they might have.

According to Izabel, they would also inform the recipient: We don't think this is going to happen, we use really low pressure, but if you need to go to the emergency room, you would say these words. This is how you would explain it. (What would you tell them to say at the hospital? I asked another self-helper. "That they're pregnant and they spontaneously started bleeding," she told me.)

On the day of the procedure, they would only send exactly the number of people needed, never more, for fear of too much exposure. "But you sure did want to go, didn't you?" Izabel asked Fuchsia, leaning in toward her friend. "I don't know if you had that feeling, but I always wanted to be able to go."

Neither Izabel nor Fuchsia recalled ever having any major complications during or after procedures their groups performed. "I have a lot of respect for all of us," Izabel told me. "We worked really hard and we were very committed to really learning our craft and not having anybody be harmed."

Fingering her braid, Izabel told me, "I have a body memory. . . . There's a way that it got so intimate." It was August 2020. We were sitting beneath a coast live oak cracking and rustling in the breeze. "There's a little bit of the experience that reminds me of sex. There's a thrill. An 'I can't believe I'm doing this' feeling that I've had also in sex. Because it's so physical. It's a place that brought out the absolute best part of me. The absolute best part of me is what was present, in whatever role I was in. And whatever role I was in, it was such an honor."

MAX AND I sat on her living room couch next to the heat vent. I sipped coffee from a mug that was covered in cartoon breasts, all different shapes, colors, and sizes. "You are perfect!" the mug exclaimed. It was a foggy winter day in early 2022. Max had fried us each an egg from one of her hens, who had just started laying. That day we talked more about "the third space" of self-help. Not clinical but having to do with medicine. Not sexual but having to do with sexuality. Something else. What was it?

When she and her group first started learning how to do pelvic exams, Max remembered, Linci and her co-teacher had taught them to be conscious of where their thumbs were. (I could hear Chloe: no thumb on the clit!) "It was pretty straightforward. If you feel somebody touching your clit, it creates a direct nervous response in your body and a more sexual feeling. But if you're doing a pelvic exam, your purpose is not sexual." One aspect of not inadvertently sexualizing a pelvic exam is learning about anatomy and how the body works so that you can interact with another person's body in mindful, non-stimulating ways.

Max suspected that the queer identification of many people in her groups helped make the third space possible.

> For queer women, putting a glove on and sliding a couple of fingers into somebody is a thing that you also do in sex. Somehow right away, though, we were comfortable with the idea that that didn't have to be sexual.
>
> And there was, at the same time, an understanding that you don't want it to feel bad for someone. You want to use lube. You're not trying to make it sexually pleasurable, but there might be a nice feeling. And just because you have a nice feeling doesn't mean it has to be a sexual feeling. It's about context and what you're doing. We were providing health care for ourselves and for each other.
>
> It's not that health and sex are a binary. Sex is healthy, too. I'm just trying to find the words to explain the clarity that I think we all had and the ease with which we jumped into doing pelvics. I think it was because it was

part of the process of learning how to size a uterus. And learning about how you can tell which side somebody's ovulating on.

And how amazing to be able to learn how to do those things, to feel them with your hands, I thought.

"Once, when someone was doing a pelvic on me, they identified that I had a cystic ovary. When you're doing a pelvic, your fingers come up along the side of the uterus to look for the ovary. And if you're pressing down from the top of the abdomen, the ovary feels like a little fish that's hard to hold onto. In my case, it was easy to feel. I could feel it, too, and it was uncomfortable. It was so great to have that identified through the process of someone doing a pelvic."

A thrilling aspect of doing a pelvic on someone, Max seemed to be saying, is that you can't know in advance precisely what you'll find when you insert your fingers into someone's body. But because of the knowledge that you've gained through practice, you know what to feel for and can detect variation and even pathology, such as a cyst. This intimate form of relating, in which one arrives at anatomical knowledge through direct and loving contact with the bodies of group members, who are willing subjects throughout the process, distinguishes self-help from clinical practice. And self-help's aim, of honing technical health care skills, distinguishes it from sexual practice.

Max remembered what it was like to be in a group with someone who was her lover. "There was a sexual familiarity," she said, "but sex was just not what we were doing."

She continued:

I think that we have so many misconceptions about sexuality, so many mythologies about the uncontrollability of sexual passion. Self-help challenges that. Through making those choices and making that distinction, I came to feel much more embodied myself and, through that embodiment, a better advocate for my own pleasure. Sharing my body, my vulva, vagina, uterus, ovaries, and pelvic floor, that whole part of my body, with my friends to learn skills helped me to be more comfortable with my sexuality.

I don't think we bring our minds into our cunts very much in this society. There is a rampant idea that there's something unsavory about vulvas. That they are fishy. That they look weird. Really negative ideas. But in self-help, we're just sitting there looking at each other's vulvas and we're learning about our health and our bodies. It allows for a positive re-creation, a positive frame, and a positive space to experience one's body without layers of negative ideas.

In group, "sex was just not what [they] were doing"; yet self-help still transformed the way some members of groups experienced their bodies and the bodies of others. Through that transformed experience, they came to have deeper relationships to their own pleasure and sexuality.

I asked Max, "How, in a self-help context, do you develop presence and awareness?"

"Okay," Max said. "Bring your consciousness into your hand, where you're holding your pen. Can you feel your fingertips? Put your mind into your fingertips. Are there parts of your hand that you feel more and parts of your hand where you feel less? Can you feel the air on the skin of your hand? Can you feel the more muscular part of your hand, where your muscle might be sore from writing? The fleshy part under your thumb? Can you feel your wrist? Now, take that kind of insight and think about your cunt. Bring your mind there. Can you feel the outer part of your vulva? Can you feel the inner part of your vagina? If you kind of squeeze, as if there were a flow of urine, can you feel those muscles? Can you maintain an awareness even after you relax? It's that kind of awareness that happens in self-help."

I wondered, how do we learn our bodies and come to know them as real? For women and feminized people especially, we're taught to receive recognition of our sexual body parts from doctors (in a clinic) and sexual partners (in sex) who touch and penetrate us. We are not encouraged to recognize our bodies through our own hands-on learning or to bring our minds into our bodies. In Western clinical and straight-sex contexts, one is often taught, better *not* to be mentally present when receiving these types of touch. But in the third space of self-help, it seemed to me, people practiced actively learning about and being in their bodies as a way of claiming body recognition, and thus more power, for themselves and each other.

Max continued,

> The idea of cunt consciousness that I'm playing with is different from an essentialist French feminism. I'm talking about bringing awareness into a part of the body. I'm not saying anything about what that awareness or consciousness inevitably is and therefore suggesting that there's something that's shared by all people with vaginas. That's not where I'm going with it.
>
> I developed a new view of my own body through these practices. An awareness of my cunt as being active and not passive. I went on to become a sex educator and was very comfortable talking about the anatomy of pleasure. It's not like we have a clinical body and a sexual body; it's just one body. That body is all in our experiences.

It's just one body. All of it. And in our one body, we are actors.

Max added,

> Be careful about where your thumb is. That one prompt says everything about our intention to be thoughtful. And if somebody forgot about their thumb, I think everybody was empowered enough to say, watch your thumb! Because we were always giving each other feedback. That was part of our learning and training. That if you were having something done to you, you would give feedback. Whether you were receiving a pelvic, or having vinegar put on your cervix to see if you had warts, or being helped with a yeast infection. Regardless of what we were doing, we were always empowered to give feedback.

Demedicalized, non-sexualized, feminist body sharing, I thought. Gradual. Intentional. Normalizing. Positive. Honest.

We are not incubators

Mimi* locked herself in a bathroom stall and started tearing open boxes of e.p.t tests. She pulled down her pantyhose, hiked up her skirt, and reached down between her thighs. She caught some pee on the tongue and recapped it. Then she did it again with another test. Then again.

At the bathroom sink, she lined up her tests in a row, five in total, like white fangs. Mimi tucked a chunk of straight black hair behind her ear and leaned in closer. Five little blue plus signs. Pregnant, pregnant, pregnant, pregnant, pregnant.

"You're pregnant," said a coworker, who had slipped into the bathroom without Mimi noticing. "Congratulations."

MIMI DID NOT intend to stay pregnant. In her early thirties at the time, her life was gaining momentum. She was single, working, independent, busy. She did not want children. When she confided in her old friend Cecilia, a health worker whom she trusted, Cecilia said that she was in a group that could do Mimi's abortion.

Mimi thought about it and not long after called Cecilia. I want to do it, she said. So Mimi, Cecilia, and Cindy met for an interview. Mimi remembered how, in addition to explaining the procedure, Cecilia and Cindy asked her questions that really made her think. Are you sure you don't imagine a child fitting into your life? Do you think you might want to have kids at some point? The conversation helped Mimi feel certain about her choice. She didn't plan to have kids. She didn't want anyone to know. She didn't want to be put under anesthesia at Planned Parenthood. She didn't want it. And this was how she was going to do it.

A few days later, Cecilia, Cindy, and a third person from their group went to Mimi's house to perform the extraction. Mimi had ordered pizzas, thinking they'd get hungry at some point. The group got situated on Mimi's king-sized mattress on the floor in the middle of the bedroom. Cecilia explained, "We can take as long as we want to do the procedure, depending on how you're doing with the pain."

When Cecilia started unpacking the equipment—mason jar, tubing, brake bleeder, sterile cannulas, instruments, gloves— Mimi thought, holy shit, this is pretty old-fashioned! She had thought it would be more complicated. She slipped out of her jeans, scooted down to the bottom of the mattress, leaned back, and opened her legs. In sterile gloves, Cecilia inserted two fingers into Mimi's vagina to feel her cervix and size her uterus. Mimi was eight weeks pregnant. The other two each took a turn feeling Mimi's cervix and uterus to confirm. Then it was time to start the extraction.

As they worked, group members described every step to Mimi. We're going to insert the speculum. We're going to go through the cervix into the uterus. You might feel pain. You might feel a lot of pressure. Do you feel pain? We're in now, and we're going to start the suction. How much pain do you feel?

"I remember feeling pressure, but I don't remember feeling that much pain," Mimi told me. "Maybe a little but nothing excruciating. You know the test they do for uterine cancer? That's way more painful. On a pain scale, the biopsy is a ten while the abortion was like a one." When I asked Mimi if she could describe the feeling, she said, "It was a downward pressure, almost like you're going to have a bowel movement. Some light cramping at the same time. I've had worse cramps going to the bathroom."

During the procedure, one person performed the suction, one person supported Mimi by sitting next to her and holding her hand, and one person oversaw the procedure to make sure they didn't break sterility. The three group members took turns rotating through each of the roles.

Mimi didn't remember the suction itself taking all that long, maybe thirty minutes. After they finished, Cecilia took the jar and tissue into the bathroom.

"Oh my god," Mimi heard her say.

"What's going on?" Mimi asked from the bed. Cecilia came back into the bedroom and sat down next to her. "There are two sacs," she said. Mimi exclaimed, "My grandmother was right! She always told me there were twins in the family and that I was going to have twins." Mimi added, "Just because I didn't want one doesn't mean I would have wanted two!"

Cecilia took Mimi into the bathroom to show her the tissue. Mimi leaned in to get a closer look. The sacs looked like two tiny dark marbles. "I thought, 'This just came out of my body? These little sacs of cells develop into eight-pound babies?' I was amazed. And I was so relieved. My nightmare was ending." She continued, "It was kind of out-of-body. This thing came out of me. It was a distant feeling. Intellectually, I got it. Emotionally, there was no connection. I had no emotion other than relief. There was a moment when I felt shame that I didn't have a connection. But then I thought, "What the fuck, I don't have to have a child if I don't want to!" And then I was fine. I realized that I shouldn't have to feel something that I didn't."

It occurred to Mimi that she was hungry. "Does anybody want pizza?" she asked the others. "I want pizza."

In the days that followed, Cecilia checked in with Mimi regularly. How's your bleeding? Heavier? Less heavy? A couple of weeks later, the group visited her for a follow-up checkup. Everything seemed to be fine.

"I think that if you could put the model of care that happened to me in a clinical setting, then that's the way it should be done," Mimi said. "The interview, the care . . . it all made me feel more strongly that women should be able to do what they want with their bodies."

In Mimi's case, the group—by that point, highly experienced—successfully completed the abortion. But since they didn't have imaging (ultrasound), they couldn't have known in advance that Mimi had two gestational sacs in her uterus. For this reason, Mimi's extraction was a riskier one. It's likely that an experienced self-helper would have been able to feel with the cannula that the uterus was not yet fully emptied. Even so, if they had inadvertently not completed the suctioning, upon evaluating the tissue post-procedure the group could have located a single sac and thought that the abortion was complete. But Mimi would still have been pregnant, and incomplete abortions can cause serious complications. At very least, it would have required a follow-up procedure in a clinic.

I asked Mimi what she would tell a younger generation of abortion defenders and reproductive justice activists. She said, "You need to own your body, and you need to send a clear message. You need to get back in the streets and cause a real uproar. Your sexual practices are yours and yours alone. Your life has meaning, and you get to determine what that is. We are talking about a lifetime decision. We are not incubators."

No way to learn except to do

Lori* and I had our interview beneath the Hachiya persimmon tree in my yard. The late-season fruits were ripe, every day dropping and splattering all over the picnic table and deck next to my shack. It was winter, wet and musky.

She arrived early and caught me by surprise, having found her way around the main house and into the garden. "You must be Lori," I said, interrupting her study of the roses and the clay art. She smiled widely.

Lori wasn't sure about doing an interview, and she talked with me just once. She was secretive about who she practiced with, careful not to betray her connections. Later it occurred to me that she may have worked with some of the other self-helpers I'd talked with; after all, she was active in the movement for fifteen years.

White and working class, Lori was raised by a single mom in Berkeley. She recalled being feminist- and anarchist-identified from a young age. She had done clinic defense, and at one point in the late 1980s another clinic defender invited her to a meeting about self-help.

I asked Lori what attracted her to lay gynecology. "I was interested in sex work," she told me. "I was also sexually active. I'd had an abortion when I was nineteen or twenty years old at a hospital. I did not like my hospital abortion." She continued, "I was excited to learn ME for abortion, but that doesn't mean that's how it was being presented to people. We were practicing on all kinds of people and on all states of bleeding. There was this desire to have this smokiness about what was going on. And then there were times when I was having sex with people when I was like, I'm okay with getting pregnant because I want us to be practicing."

To use menstrual extraction as a method of birth control was bold. It was to categorically refuse the state's definition of what birth control was and was not—it was to understand birth control as encompassing abortion. "I wanted us to know enough about our own bodies to know how to deal with unwanted pregnancies. And I wanted us to have friends that we trusted enough and who also knew how to deal with it," Lori said. Because self-help empowered people to do these things, it was, in her mind, the perfect anarchist action.

Because Lori did not feel like a particularly social person, learning how to work in a small group was both the challenge and the reward of self-help. "Groups of people are difficult. It's hard to pull people together who can actually deal with each other for a long period of time," she said. "The clearest consequence of being in a self-help group for me is that now I overemphasize the capacity of groups of people who know each other well. I totally believe in them."

Going to group was like going to class, Lori remembered. And she liked getting her hands dirty. "I liked the thing about taking your clothes off in front of strangers and learning not to give a fuck. And appreciating women's bodies. How they're different from each other and how they're the same. How some people are shy and how some people aren't."

Part of the mythology of self-help, Lori explained, was that self-helpers learned things that countered the Western understanding of female bodies. She added, "It was hands-on science, in a way. We were experimenting on our own bodies. I tend to be antiscience. It's a worldview I disagree with. But there's something about getting your hands into things that you normally wouldn't and testing things and then having to make decisions.... It's scientific, but I don't want to call it science."

Lori told me a story about a time she received a pregnant extraction that didn't go as it was supposed to. Blood and tissue were not coming through the cannula as expected, so Lori started deeply massaging her own belly, and the blood started flowing. "I was engaged with the process even as the recipient," she said. "People were pretty excited about that because it expressed something about intentionality and agency."

Performing a procedure on someone outside the group meant group members didn't know that person's body in the way they knew each other's, Lori told me, which posed additional risk. Yet a primary goal of the group was to get to a place, in terms of process and proficiency, where they could offer procedures to more people outside. Whether they knew it or not, group members were often at different places in terms of their individual capacity to deal with risk. Lori told me a story to illustrate her point. Once during a pregnant procedure she and her group were doing for someone outside, she worried she had perforated the uterus. She explained,

> I was doing the suctioning. I couldn't find the end of the uterus with the cannula before I started suctioning. At some point it was clear that the cannula had gone farther than it should have. There was no feeling for me that I had gone through the uterus, but people were concerned that it had because nobody could see how the cannula could still be in the uterus. We stopped, and the person went to the hospital. I still don't know what happened, whether I perforated. It was totally prophylactic to have her go to the hospital. But it had consequences for the group. Some people never did another procedure. It scared the fuck out of them.

Lori remembered being frustrated with the reactions of some of her group members. She felt they hadn't realized what it was they were actually doing.

People in this culture are so divorced from death and the real consequences of our behavior. I am just as much as anybody is. But I don't like it. I feel that it makes up part of our deep alienation from the world. Shit can happen. Doctors hurt people, too.

Let me back up. My take on abortion is that infanticide is a thing that women do. Women monitor and attend to when children make sense for a group and when they don't. ME was a way to get out of the entire "When is a baby valid? When is a baby viable?" Death is part of who we are. Sometimes it doesn't make sense to have children. Some times we don't have access to the capacity to *not* have children, and yet we can't have children. So you do what you have to do. Philosophically, I support our capacity to kill.

Death is part of our living. In Lori's words, "We are always killing things, whether we recognize it or not." Sometimes ending life is what we must do to take care of ourselves and each other. Sometimes ending life is part of care. Despite the state's mandate that only *it* may be the legitimate administrator of death, in the form of laws regulating abortion, laws sanctioning the executions of prisoners, laws with the implication that some illnesses will not be prevented or will be left untreated, laws condoning the murders of Black and Brown people by police and the spread of carcinogens in the environment.

I asked Lori if she believed that lay gynecology is one of the most powerful things that a group can do to resist the state. She replied, "I'm not going to say it's the most. There's also challenging how we eat. And how we are with partners. There are lots of ways to come at keeping the state out of our lives. And out of our hearts. What I mean is, yes. And no. Yes."

She continued,

I want ME to be something that we all know how to do. Partly because we need to know how to do it, but also because the process of learning how to do it is so significant. Putting your hands inside of somebody is a good thing to learn how to do. And allowing other people to put their hands inside of you is also a good thing to learn how to do. It demystifies our bodies. It encourages us to look at ourselves.

It's a relationship that you're not going to have in any other way. It's not about having friends; it's about having a particular kind of peer. It's building an affinity group in a different way. Frequently, affinity groups are about people who like each other, and that's awesome, but there's also a real limit to that. I'm curious about how we build affinity with each other that isn't simply about liking each other or being similar. I'm interested in affinity through practice.

In the end, Lori said, "Self-help is a way to interact with each other that is anomalous and fascinating. There's no way to learn self-help except to do it."

And then it was time for Lori to go.

LINCI ALSO TOLD me about a complication she encountered once, in one of her groups. They were doing an extraction for someone who was around twelve weeks pregnant. As they suctioned, the person's bleeding showed no sign of stopping, and their uterus was tipped backward, which made the suctioning that much more challenging. Linci recalled how the group filled a mason jar to the brim—it was a lot of blood. They began to ask each other whether they should take the person to the emergency room. They started to fill a second jar, and it was only after that jar was filled that blood stopped coming through the cannula and tubing. At that point, the abortion was complete.

CHLOE THOUGHT I might like talking to Theresa*, who, like Chloe, had also gone on to become a professional health worker. Chloe and Theresa weren't in the same self-help group, but they had traveled in some of the same scenes.

One night in January 2021, I met up with Theresa at her apartment. Sometime after midnight, she showed me the vintage cardboard suitcase she'd pulled out of her closet. The suitcase had been her grandmother's and bore her initials from before she was married. It was a beautiful antique. Theresa unlatched it, and inside was a bunch of plastic tubing, a couple of metal speculums, old lube (which she threw in the trash), plastic sounds, and a brake bleeder kit. She unrolled a fabric wrap to reveal a full set of steel cervical dilators.

We had already been talking for hours. Theresa wouldn't let me record her voice, so I scrawled furiously as she shared, trying to keep up. The first time we'd met, in a park, she'd asked that I turn off my phone before we start the interview. She knows a thing or two about security, I thought.

Born and raised in the Bay Area, Theresa came out as a lesbian when she was a teenager. She got radicalized early on by the local punk scene, and one of her early political projects was self help. In 1990, when she was nineteen, one of her housemates, Cindy, from her "dykey collective house," as she described it, invited her to join her group. Theresa stayed involved for the next decade and practiced with several different groups, including one she herself started.

"In that decade," I asked, "how many procedures do you think you helped do for people outside your group?" Theresa tucked a dark tendril behind her ear. "Maybe twenty? Twenty-five?" The group she started, she explained, was one that intended to risk offering their services to more people outside of it. They believed they were putting more options and more "choice" into the hands of more people.

In Theresa's opinion, "Nobody who actually knows about medicine would advocate ME." She was adamant. "As someone who works in medicine, I wouldn't advocate it today. I don't think it's a good option." She recalled that her group had some complications—an incomplete abortion, for example.

Theresa stopped practicing menstrual extraction in 2000, after going back to school to get her nursing license. "I didn't know what an emergency was the way I know now," she said. "If it were me today, I'd be going through a checklist in my head. I'd know how to run it down." She continued, "We didn't know what to do if [the procedure] wasn't rulebook. Evaluating a complication means understanding the body's systems and how they work. That's what I learned in school."

The self-helpers turned licensed practitioners I talked to held different views on lay gynecology and abortion care. The irony is that had it not been for their work in their self-help groups, they may never have become licensed practitioners at all.

TWO YEARS LATER, post-*Dobbs* ruling, I talked with Theresa again. Has the political situation changed your mind at all about whether people should practice menstrual extraction? I asked her.

"The thing with menstrual extraction is that we just don't know," she replied. "One thing that happened around the time I entered medicine was the shift to evidence-based medicine. Today you can't talk about research without talking about evidence-based medicine."

In 1996, a few years before Theresa went to nursing school, an American Canadian doctor named David Sackett proposed that "evidence-based medicine means integrating individual clinical expertise with the best available external clinical evidence from systematic research."[6] Today, evidence-based medicine says that information from randomized controlled trials should be used to create clinical practice guidelines to ensure the highest quality of care, and it has become the standard of care.[7]

Theresa pointed out that the protocols (practice guidelines) of menstrual extraction were developed before the advent of evidence-based medicine, through trial and error, observation, and extrapolation. She continued, "Early self-helpers didn't use the sorts of rigorous modalities of research that are now what we think of when we think of research, so it leaves a lot of question marks. There are critiques of evidence-based medicine that look at who has access to this kind of research and also all the ways people get excluded from these rigorous standards. Even so, I think by and large it's a good thing."

Her point troubles a fundamental assumption of abortion self-help: that there is inherent value to and justification for transmitting received feminist practices. If we're serious about keeping people safe, why would we transmit practices without looking at (the dearth of) external research findings about the safety and effectiveness of those practices?

Notably, a study published in 2011 asked, "Can [newly trained] nurses perform manual vacuum aspiration (MVA) as safely and effectively as physicians?" The study, which recruited 897 consenting women who were ten or fewer weeks pregnant, was conducted in India, where access to safe, legal abortion is limited, and where, as the authors write, "there is a need to explore the feasibility of expanding the [MVA] provider base to include nurses." The study found that failure and complication rates between the newly trained nurses and the physicians were about the same; and for both provider types, the procedures were 98 percent successful.[9]

The study prompts a follow-up research question: can newly trained laypeople perform MVA as safely and effectively as newly trained nurses?

And if the shit really does hit the proverbial fan?

By 1992, the antis were using the courts to chip away at abortion access across the country and winning. "We were aware that having just a few groups around wasn't enough," Max told me. "We knew we had to share and spread the skills if we wanted these practices to be helpful in the case that abortion were made inaccessible or illegal."

And so, around that time, despite the risk of potential infiltration by the police or the Right, Max's group began to do outreach. She and a couple of other underground self-helpers started giving introductory presentations and workshops at college campuses, women's centers, co-ops, and even house parties. Some traveled internationally to talk about self-help with reproductive freedom activists around the world.

In Max's papers, I came across a packet titled "Self Health Workshop Presenter Outline," along with a yellow legal pad filled with her notes. The workshop included several parts: according to the outline, in this instance Max was to give the self-help introduction and historical overview of lay abortion care in the late 1960s and early 1970s. The next presenters would introduce menstrual extraction and show the group a Del-Em, explaining the components. They would stress that menstrual extraction was "not inherently a revolutionary technology," with reference to how menstrual regulation had been brought by population planners to the global South, and that it was how it was used and in what social context that determined whether it was revolutionary.

Then self-helpers would discuss sterile technique and walk the audience through the process while drawing comparisons to the procedure a person would receive in a clinic setting. Finally, they would have the audience break into smaller groups for a "hands-on session."

I imagine a twenty-something Max with her nose pierced and head shaved on the sides, long thick mohawk in a messy high ponytail, standing in front of a dozen or so nineteen-year-olds. Max had scrawled notes to herself all over the presenter outline. With regard to a planned segment called "How [to] network information & support? How [to] spread information to women who want it," Max had written, "After, if time & if seems right."

I asked her, What if some workshop attendees were interested in starting a group? How would you have decided whether you were going to teach them menstrual extraction? It depended, Max replied. Was there a way to vet people? Did anyone know them through political organizing? Anyway, there was a lot a new self-helper could learn and practice before getting to the "phase-two stuff." Ultimately, different self-helpers made different decisions about how much personal risk they were willing to undertake, whether they were willing to work with a new group they didn't know very well. It just really, really varied, she said.

MAX TOLD ME about a complication one group had. "It goes back to the fact that we don't all have standard bodies," she told me. "People's bodies are different." In this complication, Max explained, the recipient of the extraction had a septate uterus, or a tissue membrane called a septum that divides the uterus into two sections. "They were pregnant, but the pregnancy was on the other side, so it was hard to reach," she said. If this person were to have gone to a clinic, an ultrasound would have revealed the condition and informed the approach to the procedure. Max explained that the group thought they had completed the extraction but in fact had only completed the suctioning on one side of the septum. The person continued to be pregnant and ended up having to go to a clinic to successfully terminate the pregnancy. "It's an example of a limitation of using very basic equipment," Max said.

"There are self-helpers who really feel that as long as abortion is legal, people should get their procedures at clinics, because you can have imaging." I thought of Mimi and her two sacs. "It's different when you don't have imaging," Max added.

THERESA PRESENTED ME with a stuffed manilla envelope. It contained a series of handouts, some made with what must have been an early-1990s dot matrix printer. "Menstrual Extraction Kit List of Parts." "Gestational Age, Uterine Size, and Fetal Dimensions." A stapled packet with a cover sheet detailing "Telephone Guidelines":

> Avoid names addresses and phone numbers if at all possible!

> Use stuff like "usual place" or "East Bay" or "SF"

> Don't mention days, dates, times etc. on phone machines or with roommates—Just say call me back

> Use the code!!!! and try to use it often enough to sound comfortable.

If it's really touchy use the pay phone or go see someone in person.

Don't make anything sound fishy particularly if it is.

Call at work if you can.

Don't use party

Page two contained the code:

PLEASE DON'T LEAVE THIS AROUND OR IN AN EASILY ACCESSIBLE SPOT.

The event is a pasta dinner with:

Red sauce = blood

White sauce = other

To figure out how many weeks ask how many cups of cream.

Theresa explained that if someone said they're hosting a "pasta dinner with red sauce," it meant someone in the group was going to have their period extracted. (Fuchsia's memory was right, I realized.) If someone said they're hosting a pasta dinner "with white sauce," it meant someone inside or outside of the group was going to receive a pregnant extraction.

The code continued: "Drink stirrers" were sounds. "Straws" were cannulas. "Salad tongs" meant stabilizer. "Lydia and her friend" meant lidocaine in injectable solution. The Italian dinner-themed list of terms continued on down the page.

The next page contained the "After Dinner" (post-procedure) code. "Lucretia has food poisoning," it stated. A list of questions followed: "Is what she ate still inside of her?" (Could it be an incomplete abortion?) "Is she allergic to Lydia's perfume?" (Is she having a reaction to the lidocaine injection?) "Is she throwing up?"

(Is she bleeding?) "Has she spent any money on medicine?" (Does she have clots? What size coin do they resemble?)

A handout titled "Security Protocol (or—what are we gonna do if the shit really does hit the proverbial fan)" followed. If "something big happens": self-helpers were to contact other groups; destroy written materials; contact friends, family, and housemates and tell them a cover story (for example, "every Tuesday we had a support group around health issues") so they're prepared; and stop meeting.

Finally, there was a thick packet secured with a binder clip about possible abortion complications: anaphylactic shock, cardiopulmonary arrest, fainting, hemorrhaging, hyperventilation, reaction to local anesthetic, vasovagal reaction, seizure, and perforation.

Being in a self-help group meant taking security seriously. Self-helpers knew they faced potential surveillance and legal action, not to mention the possibility of inadvertently hurting someone. What did it take to accept those risks and go forward? To push a cannula through an os into a uterus, to go inside of someone else's body? Knowing that it was a blind procedure without the guide of imaging? Knowing the risk of incomplete abortion and hemorrhaging or of perforation?

I remembered Rosie saying, "I had faith in my skills, and I didn't know enough to be scared." Then I thought about how licensed practitioners risk inadvertently hurting people's bodies, too. They have formal training, licenses, and immediately available clinic resources, including insurance, but these things don't eliminate the risks of procedures. It's a wager of the health worker, whether lay or licensed: if you have skills, and if someone has a need that you can meet with your skills, you use them.

And then I thought about what Izabel had said: "We really trusted each other. We let each other do this on our *bodies* . . . "

A fundamental question that abortion self-help posed was: If what you have to do to empower your community is let your community inside of your body, will you let your community inside of your body? And, in turn, will you enter your community's bodies? And then, what will you do when your letting-in exposes the constructedness of social and legal boundaries and limits regarding the body and medical practice? When your letting-in lays bare how the rules governing who is authorized to cross those boundaries ultimately exist to strengthen capitalism and the state, while diminishing the self-determination of many people? How will you allow your learning to change your life?

Chapter 11

Everyone Deserves a Place

In 2001, West Coast Feminist Health Project / Women's Choice moved from 30th Street, where it had been for seven years, to 570 14th Street, a yellow art deco building in the heart of downtown Oakland, a block from city hall and Oscar Grant Plaza. On 14th Street, from 2001 until 2009, when the clinic closed, a new generation of feminist health workers transformed the practice and meaning of gynecological and abortion self-help.

In this period, activists stepped up once again to shield patients from anti-abortion harassment and ensure clinic access. Importantly, abortion defenders working both inside and outside of the clinic health workers and clinic escorts—centered trauma-informed care. In the process, they made a safer space for, as one self-helper put it, "dignity inside of choice."

Having been influenced by Black feminist holistic self-help, which centered the relationship between emotional and physical health, abortion self-helpers at WCFHP / Women's Choice were already practitioners of trauma-informed care. They knew to consider the ways their patients' health issues were inextricably linked to their past adverse experiences. In the early 2000s, they acknowledged even more consciously the stress and trauma patients carried in their bodies and worked to mitigate the activation of that trauma.[1] They did so from a place of deep understanding: in the aftermath of the 1990s, marked by extreme anti-abortion violence and the devastating HIV / AIDS and breast cancer epidemics, self-helpers were traumatized themselves.

291

Moreover, those who were connected to the clinic were grieving. The decade ended in tragedy for the community in November 1998 when longtime clinic worker and defender Debbie Gregg was found shot behind her trailer in Morgan Hill, where she had planned to retire. Her neighbor, with whom she had had a property dispute and who had threatened her, witnesses testified, was charged with murdering her. He was later acquitted.[2]

Seven years later, in September 2005, another longtime WCFHP / Women's Choice health worker, Yvonne Ramos, was shot and killed in a targeted drive-by attack while gardening outside her house in Richmond, just north of Oakland. Yvonne had worked as a nurse at the clinic and was an influential activist in her community.[3]

Debbie's and Yvonne's murders were not random acts of violence. Though they were not murdered for being abortion workers, they were both bold, independent, political women, and they were punished for it. Their murders were acts of gruesome violence in a society where powerful older women are seen as disposable obstacles to the patriarchal order.

For self-helpers in and beyond the clinic community, the 2000s were a time of reckoning with the violence—whether direct or indirect, sudden or slow, discrete or accretive—that had been directed at girls, women, and other feminized people and their reproductive lives in the decades after *Roe v. Wade* was decided, a time when people's reproductive autonomy was ostensibly more enshrined in the law than it ever had been before.

We heard you'll teach us how to do things no one else will teach us

I met Annah Anti-Palindrome in summer 2019 at a café in the hot, dry city of Davis, halfway between Oakland and the Sierra foothills town where she lived at the time. Annah was a health worker and volunteer coordinator at WCFHP / Women's Choice from 2005 until the clinic closed. When we talked, she was working in the foothills at a shelter for youth experiencing homelessness. She was also a poet; I'd read her book *DNA Hymn*.

Annah grew up rural working class. As a teenager in the 1990s, with Bikini Kill shouting in her ears, she started to identify as a feminist. She joined a band, came out as a dyke, and sought out other feminists. She and her friends made zines and got involved in political organizing; "We had *endless* conversations about SmashingThePatriarchy," Annah remembered. "The more I learned about misogyny, the angrier I got. The angrier I got, the more important it felt to integrate feminist activism into my daily life."[4]

When Annah was in her twenties, her mom died of an overdose. It was then that she changed the spelling of her first name from "Anna" to "Annah" with an "h" so that it wouldn't be a palindrome (a word spelled the same way forward and backward). As she writes at the beginning of *DNA Hymn*,

/ ' palin, drōm/e-

noun

a word, number, sentence, verse, or double stranded sequence of DNA that reads the same backward & forward (anna, see bees, see bees, anna); term is derived from the Greek root "palin dromo," meaning "to run back again," "a recurrence," or "a revolving cycle."

If a palindrome embodied "running back again," or repeating a cycle, then her refusal of palindromes—specifically, the palindrome of her own name—was a way for Annah to imagine disrupting the toxic cycles and harmful narratives about poor women that had been administered to her over her lifetime. Resisting palindromes, she writes, "reminds me of the commitment I've made to myself, to consciously resist participating in the destructive patterns I've learned over time."[5]

Annah's book is about how girls and women collectively survive poverty and gender oppression. One poem in her book titled "middle c" imagines the mouths of "the women who raised us":

teeth exhausted from the work of being conduits
for sound to pass through
so relentlessly
for so long

Here, a woman's mouth is a metonym (one thing that stands in for another, typically of which it is part) for the "relentlessly" laboring woman's body. The caregiver's speech—words or other utterances of instruction, reprimand, praise, love—is labor, too, the poem suggests. Later in the series, she writes,

those women
always gripped our hands
left half moon shapes in our palms
from cheap acrylic press-on nails))))

& tenderly led us outside to play
anytime a man
said the word Bitch[6]

Here women defend children against gender violence and do the work of making safer spaces for children and girls. Unfair as it may be that women bear this extra labor burden, the work of making safer space is also critical survival work.

I thought of Pat Parker and her poem about all that she brings: "pregnant women / with no money / [. . .] angry comrades / with no shelter." Pat wrote, simply, "I care for you / I care for our world."[7] For Annah, perhaps, like for Pat, abortion work was an extension of the revolutionary care and defense work that women and other feminized people do for the people they love.

When she was in her late teens, before her mother died, Annah moved to Sacramento and started volunteering at the Sacramento FWHC as a clinic escort. Not long after, the clinic invited her to become a health worker. When she told them she didn't know anything about medicine, they said, "That's the point. That's why we hire laypeople." They told her they would train her to do everything that she was legally allowed to do.

When Annah told her coworkers that she wanted to move to the Bay Area, they told her that there was a FWHC there "run by a punk named Linci." So, in 2005, Annah up and moved to Oakland to work at the clinic, where she soon started managing the volunteers.

People contacted her from all over the country. "We heard you'll teach us how to do things no one else will teach us," some would write. In the 2000s, volunteer interns still received training in phlebotomy and also learned how to do ultrasounds, assist during procedures, be a patient advocate, and do tissue evaluation. And they could still learn about menstrual extraction.

One of Annah's goals, she told me, was to promote a culture that was shameless about abortion. "The moralizing and apologizing around abortion is very American," she told me. After WCFHP / Women's Choice closed in 2009 and Annah went to work at Planned Parenthood, she learned about the mainstream pro-choice movement firsthand. "It was a difficult culture shift," she said. "But it's how I put myself through college. I did it because I cared about reproductive justice."

What distinguished WCFHP / Women's Choice from other clinics, Annah explained, was how seriously it took informed consent. Health workers would sit down with patients, show them the instruments, and explain how and why they would be used and what they would feel like. Patients had the chance to handle the instruments and ask questions.

Just as they had for decades, I thought.

Annah emphasized that the clinic centered harm reduction, echoing Linci's claim about the harm reduction approach that began to define care in the 1990s. When Annah invoked harm reduction, she was referring to an approach informed by 1980s and 1990s HIV / AIDS prevention work. She was also referring more generally to approaches that helped people mitigate risks in their sexual lives, including the risk of pregnancy. If a patient decided after their abortion that they wanted to go on birth control, health workers would recommend methods that might best suit them to protect against pregnancy, explaining the benefits and risks. If a patient didn't want to take hormones, health workers would explain how they could track their cycle using the fertility awareness method.

As an abortion worker, Annah developed a feminist politics in which creating new narratives about abortion was empowering and healing. What she learned at WCFHP / Women's Choice enabled her to go out and be "an undercover subversive radical feminist in places that didn't actually make room for feminism," such as at her job at Planned Parenthood. I thought of what Linci said at one point when I asked her how she thought about the legacy of self-help. "We infused the system with feminist spies," she said.

Integral to trauma-informed care, Annah's narrative of her abortion work suggests, is helping people to think about their abortion choice as inextricable from taking care of themselves and their loved ones and as coming from a place of empowerment as opposed to shame.

The land of rainbows and choice

Cherie Harper's story starts in small-town Louisiana in the early 1990s. One day at cheerleading practice, sixteen-year-old Cherie thrust a pom into the air and then collapsed onto the gym floor. Cherie had never needed to think about the word abortion before, but by the time her mama came into her room that night to ask if she could be pregnant, the word had already flickered on in her mind like a neon sign.

"I ain't havin' no babies," Cherie remembered thinking. To get her abortion, she had to drive with her mom to Jackson, Mississippi, where the closest clinic was. It was an hour and a half away. After her procedure, she told me, she mainly felt hungry. And ready to get back to her life.

I had first seen Cherie at a party of Linci's. Across a patio, Linci pointed at me with her pinky finger and whispered something into the ear of a Black woman, about my age, who smiled. Later, Linci handed me Cherie's card. "Intuitive CMT Bodyworker," it read. "She worked at the clinic," Linci told me.

In spring 2022, Cherie and I sat in front of a café in Oakland. Next to us, Piedmont Avenue exhaled a cacophony of revving engines and beeping trucks. Despite the chaos of the street, Cherie seemed relaxed as she moved into storyteller mode. During her first year of college, in the mid-1990s, she became pregnant again, her third pregnancy. This time she would have her daughter. Her brother had moved to the Bay Area, and when Cherie was forty weeks pregnant, his girlfriend asked if Cherie wanted to move there. Let's go, Cherie responded.

Right away, Cherie fell in with her brother's Black nationalist set. "There was just a whole bunch of independent Black stuff happening," she told me. "We were doing study group. We had a home school. We were training." She remembered how she threw herself into it, her daughter in tow. She read the books and trained up. She cut off her perm.

Fast forward to the late 1990s when Cherie became pregnant again. Her choice felt more complicated that time, she explained, because she had a community that could support her, but in the end, she chose abortion. For her procedure, she went to WCFHP / Women's Choice on 30th Street.

"Being in such a vulnerable space with women who actually cared about you and treated you with dignity.... It felt so loving," Cherie remembered. "It was like you were with your friends." She remembered the living room-like vibe of the waiting room and being impressed by the Black woman doctor, Marjorie Gross, who performed her abortion. "I was like, 'I want to be a part of this,'" she said. When she saw the clinic was looking for a bookkeeper, she applied for the position and got it.

At that point, most of the clinic's patients were on Medi-Cal, so Cherie learned firsthand about the challenges of obtaining Medi-Cal reimbursements. Many relied on the clinic for other services, too, including pregnancy testing, pap smears, birth control, STI screening, and HIV / AIDS counseling and testing. Like so many people who worked at the clinic, Cherie soon developed new skill sets: in addition to being a bookkeeper, she trained to become a patient advocate and a medical assistant.

"There were a lot of patients who looked like me. A lot of Black and Brown women," Cherie said, and it was for this reason that she felt her work supporting patients in the exam room was especially important. Cherie had previously trained as a massage therapist, and she described what she learned about how she could support people both with and without touch: "When you touch someone and you can tell they don't want to be touched, you can remove yourself and still be present for them. Sometimes just being with somebody and not saying anything is enough. Or there's that thirteen-year-old baby girl who's going through this situation, and her mom is really disconnected from it, and you can be there and comfort her."

The clinic, she explained, "was your best friend, your sister, your mom. . . . It was women of all ages and on both sides of the table." Patients were able to "share parts of their lives in that moment and be heard, seen, and loved as human." She knew that sometimes the clinic provided love and sisterhood that patients weren't getting anywhere else.

"There were so many women who came through the clinic who were able to choose themselves inside of their life and whatever they were going through and be supported and loved. We provided love and care for women in vulnerable, traumatic situations where they were able to have dignity inside of their choice and walk away feeling whole and complete. That's major when there's so much shame and blame in the world."

We were doing something that is needed *now*, Cherie said simply. They were holding space for women to choose themselves inside of their lives. This is what Annah was talking about, too: trauma-informed care frames the patient's choice as holistic and empowered. *Dignity inside of choice*, I thought.

CHERIE RECALLED HOW she and the other clinic workers would just sit around and talk about their lives. I thought of a series of photos of the 14th Street office that Linci had shown me. One showed a poster: "100 Simple Things You Can Do to End the Patriarchy," it read. In another photo, an intern practiced a blood draw on another. In others, health workers paused mid-task to smile or make a face for the camera. It looked like they had a lot of fun together.

Being in the clinic around other radical women taught Cherie how to talk about bodies and sex in ways that were normalizing. She and other health workers accessed care at the clinic themselves, too. "I went to the clinic every year to get my pap, my birth control," she said. Her facility with sex talk and her grasp of the relationship between sex and health made it possible for her to better talk with her daughter about sex and to teach her that sex is something natural.

Clinic work wasn't without conflict. The health workers were powerful people who spoke their minds. Even so, the phrase that came to Cherie's mind when she thought about what the clinic was like was "Rainbowland"—an inclusive, loving place. (When she told me, we both laughed.)

Cherie was a homeschool teacher, too, so sometimes she would take her kids (of all genders) to do a clinic walkthrough. "There would be girls [receiving care at the clinic] who were their age," she recalled, grounding our conversation again with reference to what was often the difficult reality. WCFHP / Women's Choice, a place that served people, sometimes children, going through moments of acute trauma, was—needed to be—a place where there was always more love to go around.

I thought of Pat Parker's poem: "All I can give / is my love."

Cherie remembered a time her daughter called her just after she had gone to college in the South. She said, "Mama, thank you for talking to me about my body, for allowing me to be expressive with you, and for having conversations with me."

"What's going on?" Cherie asked her.

"I have so many girlfriends who don't have relationships with their moms, or whose moms won't talk to them about their bodies," her daughter replied.

"It was our duty to make sure other women didn't go through the not-knowing," Cherie explained to me with regard to health education. She left me with these words: "I'm telling you, it was the land of rainbows and choice. At the end of the rainbow, you got your pot of gold. Even though the clinic closed, we got so much from each other. So much love and understanding. You had to be accountable. I'm grateful for all the lessons, all the mama energy, all the wisdom. It gave me so much to be able to give to others. It made me who I am. We were doing some revolutionary work."

The ferocity of a lion

In the first decade of the 2000s, trauma-informed abortion care didn't only happen inside of the clinic. It happened just outside of the clinic, too. Necessarily so. The anti-abortion movement, under the new George W. Bush administration, which would appoint two conservative Supreme Court justices (John Roberts and Samuel Alito), began to adapt its 1990s tactics for the twenty-first century. Bay Area abortion defenders rose up, this time by developing a clinic escort training program, the goal of which was to minimize trauma to people who were in the process of accessing abortion care.

In the years after the FACE Act was passed, Lauren Rankin points out, antis shifted their approach, transitioning from large blockades to routine, banal harassment.[8] As a result, clinic defense and escorting, too, evolved into something more muted and normalized, with an emphasis on escorting.

IN THE EARLY 2000s, anti-abortion advocates forged ahead with their campaign to incrementally restrict abortion at both the federal and state levels. In 2003, Congress passed the Partial-Birth Abortion Ban Act, which criminalized nationally a safe later-abortion procedure called dilation and extraction. The phrase "partial-birth abortion" was introduced by the National Right to Life Committee, and the law unapologetically adopted this partisan language as opposed to medical language.[9] It was the first federal abortion ban since the *Roe* ruling.[10] In 2007, the Supreme Court voted to uphold the ban in *Gonzales v. Carhart*, establishing a model for how the anti-abortion movement could target later-abortion procedures.[11]

The procedure, once again, more neutrally known as dilation and extraction (intact D&E), was introduced as an alternative to dilation and evacuation (D&E) for pregnancies after twenty weeks, at which point a D&E requires cervical dilation and the use of surgical instruments inside of the uterus.[12] While it was well-established that D&E was a safe method for procedures after thirteen weeks,[13] dilation and extraction, some doctors argued, could help reduce risk after twenty weeks by dilating the cervix and then removing the fetus intact.[14] It was performed infrequently: in 2000, dilation and extraction was estimated to comprise .17 percent of all abortion procedures in the United States.[15]

In 2003, in California, residents saw a new parental involvement law make its way onto the ballot. If passed, Proposition 73 would have required people under eighteen to notify a parent or guardian before getting an abortion. This would have put the state among thirty-five others that required parental consent.[16] In a November 2005 KPFA radio interview leading up to the vote on Prop 73, Linci remarked, "Making laws that you have to communicate with your kids legally shows the dysfunction that we have within the family system." She also pointed out that by denying minors abortions, the state would create higher-risk pregnancies that would pose greater danger to young pregnant people than abortion procedures would.[17]

At the street level, antis started to deploy new strategies and campaigns, too. In 2004, a Catholic anti-abortion group called 40 Days for Life staged a round-the-clock "vigil" at a Planned Parenthood in Bryan, Texas. Soon the group would go national.[18] Taking its name from biblical events that lasted forty days, 40 Days for Life coordinated (and still coordinates) nonstop demonstrations over Lent in front of clinics across the country. Antis also escalated intimidation tactics such as videotaping patients as well as their cars and license plate numbers. Linci pointed out, "It's a hostile situation. . . . The only reason someone would be videotaping you or writing down your [license plate] is because they plan on pursuing you personally. If that was happening in a personal relationship, you'd be able to have a restraining order."[19]

It was in this context of harassment that veteran feminist Barbara Hoke—indeed, the same Barbara Hoke from Tampa who helped launch OFWHC / Women's Choice in the early 1970s—along with other local activists, developed a clinic escort training program. Barbara's program was one evolution of the movement that Bay Area Coalition for Our Reproductive Rights launched in the late 1980s and early 1990s.

Barbara remembered driving by WCFHP / Women's Choice in the mid-1990s and seeing a throng of protesters. She had been focusing her activism on real estate and housing equity and hadn't realized that local clinics were *still* under assault by antis. While BACORR was still active at that time and doing clinic defense, Barbara saw that even more clinic escorts were needed and that the community needed people to train them.

Into and throughout the 2000s, Barbara and her program trained hundreds of escorts who helped people access clinics all over the Bay Area, including WCFHP / Women's Choice. The escort program focused, in particular, on building a relationship with Family Planning Specialists in downtown Oakland, a clinic that provided later abortions.

At first, the director of Family Planning Specialists hesitated when Barbara and her co-organizers approached her about what they were doing, Barbara told me. In her words, in the 1980s and early 1990s (the most intense years for clinic defense), clinics had had to deal with "a whole bunch of people yelling." She saw a need for training that emphasized consistency. In a 2013 clinic escort training, she told participants, "Clinic defense requires independent thinking, thinking on your feet, and at the same time also acting as any other escort would act. Part of our working together is really getting to know each other. It's about trust."[20] By showing up and supporting patients with consistency, she felt, she and the other escorts earned the trust of staff at Family Planning Specialists.

Clinic escorting went much like it had for decades. There were two escorts per clinic shift. First, a clinic escort would approach a patient outside the clinic and ask her for her permission to walk with her by the antis. Then the escort would put their body between the patient and the antis, walking the patient all the way to the clinic door. One person would do the actual escorting, and then the second person, positioned close to the door, would be a spotter. The spotter would keep an eye on the whole scene and make sure the security guard unlocked the door at exactly the moment the patient was approaching.[21]

Barbara thought of clinic escorting as distinctly different from clinic defense. (BACORR did, too, Laura Weide pointed out to me.) She explained that the clinic escort training program accounted for the fact that by the time some patients got to the clinic, they were exhausted. They had endured the harassment of the state in the form of "miserly Medi-Cal funding." There were women who came to the clinic with their children. "The last thing they wanted was to have to walk through a political demonstration," Barbara said. "When you have a complex problem like accessing abortion services, you have to consider everybody's protection in your process if you're going to make a difference in the long run."

Among the escorts was longtime abortion defender Pat Maginnis, at that point in her late seventies. "She was such a target—the antis hated her," Barbara remembered. "Once when she was escorting, a protester came up and threw a substance in her face. From that time on, Pat wore a bulletproof vest when she escorted. We passed the vest around at various times, depending on what was going on."

Abortion clinics at Family Planning Specialists started at 7:00 a.m. on the weekends, so escorts would arrive at 6:45 a.m. sharp. When they arrived, they would sign in and retrieve their yellow vests from the lobby. If no patients were there, they would sit in their cars and wait. If antis never showed, they would never get out. "The point was to protect the privacy and safety of the women going inside," Barbara said.

"They were masters of guilt," she remembered of the antis. "They would talk about how if [the woman] had the abortion, her fetus would come back to her and haunt her." She continued, "We would approach the patient and say, 'Do you want to continue talking to these people? If you don't, I'm an escort from the clinic, and I'm happy to help you get into the clinic.' The antis would sometimes touch us. Generally, they didn't."

Jane Kaplan was also part of the escort team. In her fifties, Jane had been practicing law in the Bay Area for many years. She had represented anti-apartheid activists and people trying to get out of the US military, among other political cases. She recalled how scenes in front of clinics were often chaotic, intimidating, and loud. Antis would sing hymns and hold up grotesque signs. They would take photographs of patients. In her experience, no one was violent, but there was always an undercurrent of potential violence, she told me when we met.

When Jane started escorting in the 1990s, some of the other escorts worked in city and county government and had connections to women in office. One escort, Vicki Laden, was a city attorney. Vicki worked with the director of Family Planning Specialists as well as with Barbara, Jane, and other escorts to develop a bubble ordinance in Oakland. The "bubble" was a designated perimeter around a clinic where harassment was prohibited. The process was long and painstaking, Barbara recalled. City councilmember Nancy Nadel authored the ordinance, and getting it passed took more than a decade. The team had started working on it in the mid-1990s, modeling it after one passed in Colorado in 1993.[22]

In December 2007, the Oakland City Council passed the bubble ordinance. It prohibited protesters from coming within eight feet of anyone attempting to enter an abortion clinic once they were within one hundred feet of the clinic. Almost immediately, however, antis challenged the bubble in court, arguing that it should apply to escorts, too. The court agreed, and the city adopted an amended ordinance in 2008, emphasizing that both antis and escorts must obtain a patient's consent before approaching them.[23]

The ordinance forced antis across the street, creating a substantial buffer zone around the clinic. Emboldened, antis mounted cameras on tripods and filmed both patients and escorts, further intimidating patients while hoping to catch escorts violating the law.

On one occasion in the late 2000s, three squad cars showed up at a clinic to arrest three escorts. "For us, it was like having the world turned upside down," Barbara recalled. "We were shocked. What do you mean we are in violation of the ordinance? We *instituted* the ordinance!"[24] Because the court had ruled that the ordinance applied to escorts, too, it became even more important for escorts to be consistent with how they presented themselves to patients and to always ask consent.

During the 2013 training, one of Barbara's comrades told the group, "There's a saying among escorts, that [we] have the gentleness of a lamb and the ferocity of a lion. That's what escorting looks like."

Clinic escorts kept showing up outside of Family Planning Specialists as anti-abortion harassment persisted throughout the 2010s, until the clinic's closure in 2018.

What we want to create is okay

In Linci's papers, I came across a flyer for the Feminist Health Educator internship. The flyer sought to recruit new West Coast Feminist Health Project interns for 2010, the year after the clinic's closure. It read: "Feminist Empowerment occurs thru real life experiences affecting mind, body, and spirit. We will address the stumbling blocks to success by forming our own action pack to roam our world with passion and healing intent. Our loss of our clinical site due to budget cuts has decimated the local health care system, [but] by doing outreach and prevention / harm reduction education we can have direct impact on our community's survival."

Linci's vision for the WCFHP action pack included self-help classes, street outreach, networking with other groups, and self-defense classes. I thought of her composing the flyer, squinting through wire frames at her monitor, long graying hair tied back in a half ponytail. I imagined the tangle of emotions she must have felt. The clinic had been preparing for this moment for almost forty years: the moment of deinstitutionalization and the time to take their work fully beyond the walls of the clinic.

As Laura Brown wrote so many years earlier, "Creating Feminist Institutions will not free us, but they can be the mechanism that we use to build the kind of global communication necessarily to bring about total and real changes." From the beginning, the self-help clinic was never one place. A physical clinic was only ever a means to an end—a rolling autonomous zone where "each person is a whole unto itself and a part of the larger whole."[25]

It was a revolutionary vision, to be sure. But when the clinic closed for good, it happened so fast.

During the 2008 financial crisis, the State of California froze Medi-Cal reimbursements. It was a death knell for the clinic. "We haven't been able to make our rent payments," Linci told the *Oakland Tribune* in April 2009. "We've been waiting for the checks from Medi-Cal and they're not forthcoming.... It all came down on us in March. Our landlord let us know we have to be out in a couple of weeks. We're looking at bankruptcy." The *Tribune* article praised the clinic for serving some two thousand patients a year, including uninsured and Medi-Cal patients, teens, and queer and trans people. "We will not be able to provide health services anymore, but we plan to continue to be a presence through community outreach and sex education projects," Linci said. "I'm just not yet sure how or where that will be."[26]

Of the clinic's closure in 2009, Linci told me, "We couldn't pay the rent. We couldn't continue to choose between buying supplies and getting paid. For years people waited on paychecks. They waited on life. The clinic became a single, isolated unit. We had the strength of our community, but we were too exposed. We became a lightning rod. The brightness of all those years of work, it really terrorized [the Right]. I think about the struggle of dealing with domestic terrorism for decades of my life. I wish caring about women's bodies and reproductive rights hadn't meant engaging in a thirty-year war."

The story of the closure of WCFHP / Women's Choice made me think of all the clinics around the country that were forced to close in the years that followed due to Targeted Regulation of Abortion Providers (TRAP) laws. Emerging in the early 2010s, TRAP laws have created obstacles for abortion providers by imposing costly, medically unnecessary requirements. They've been a primary tactic of the anti-abortion movement in the last decade, often making compliance so prohibitive for providers that they've been forced to stop doing abortions.[27] As of this writing, twenty-three states have TRAP laws on the books.[28]

One common iteration of these laws imposes facility obligations such as requiring clinics to be functioning ambulatory (same-day) surgical centers (ASCs), even though abortion is a low-risk procedure that uses lower levels of sedation (if any) than procedures typically done at such surgical centers.[29] ASC requirements include everything from specific hallway widths and exam room dimensions to the setups of janitor's closets.[30] As of this writing, seventeen states impose structural standards comparable to those of a surgical center.[31]

Another common type of TRAP law requires an abortion provider to have admitting privileges at a hospital within a certain distance of their clinic, even though fewer than .5 percent of abortions result in a complication that would require hospitalization. Admitting privileges allow a provider to admit a patient to a hospital without entering through the emergency department, a right typically restricted to doctors on staff at the hospital itself. The laws are misleading, because in fact federal law already requires that a patient be treated by any hospital in an emergency. Credentialing for admitting privileges is hard to obtain. Providers are often required to live near the hospital and admit a minimum number of patients a year—but because abortion is a safe procedure, it's unlikely that a provider would meet that minimum. Under these laws, providers and clinics located in rural places far from hospitals are also ineligible. Nine states require hospital admitting privileges or an alternative agreement.[32]

These TRAP laws have shuttered clinics. Between 2011 and 2017, the laws forced the closure of fifty clinics in the South and thirty-three in the Midwest.[33] As of this writing, post-*Dobbs* decision, abortion is now banned outright in fourteen states: Alabama,

Arkansas, Idaho, Kentucky, Louisiana, Mississippi, Missouri, North Dakota, Oklahoma, South Dakota, Tennessee, Texas, West Virginia, and Wisconsin.[34] When there are few or no providers in a region or state, people seeking abortions in that area or state are then often forced to travel. Having to make travel plans adds not only logistic complication but may mean added delay, pushing the abortion later into the pregnancy and making the procedure both riskier and more expensive. This is especially burdensome for people with preexisting health conditions or who are low-income.[35]

I DIDN'T WANT the story of the clinic to end. I wanted Linci to keep telling it, and I wanted to keep writing it. I talked to Linci about the difficulty I was having. We sat on her steps one hot bright day during that week after the *Dobbs* decision that overturned *Roe* and *Casey*. It was now the moment, if there ever was one, I remember thinking, to draw on the lessons that abortion self-help and clinic defense had to offer us.

That day, Linci and I started out talking about other things. She had been telling me about a project of hers. For a while, she'd been working with a couple other activists on creating a community center in West Oakland to support people, including veterans living with PTSD, with a message of positivity. "You're mission oriented," I said. "I've always been goal-oriented," she replied. "I want things to have a conclusion. Even when something's a long-term thing, I like to have a conclusion."

She told me about how when she was a kid, one summer she and her friends built a mini-golf course across three backyards. They sorted the garbage, burned it, and saved the large cans for their purpose. Getting cans and turning them into the golf course was tricky, but all the neighborhood kids helped. It took half the summer.

"We played that thing for like three years," Linci remembered. "We would change it. We'd add contours. We'd do all kinds of crazy things. It became a game that no one else had. The goal was for us to have our own unique experience."

Through an extended metaphor, what Linci was actually doing was telling me a story about abortion self-help. Here's where she went with it:

> We couldn't afford to play putt-putt
> But you know what
> We played putt-putt
>
> What I learned is
> You have to break through the idea
> Of the haves and have-nots
> And everywhere I go
> I try to make that space
> And hold that place
> Where we can do and be something different
> Where what we want to create
> Is okay
>
> At the clinic what we created
> Was a sacred healing space
> And all that we did
> Was in the name of health, concern, care
> Compassion, and education
>
> And the importance
> Of self-affirming knowledge
> If you could not affirm for yourself
> That you were making this decision
> Then we did not let you make that decision
> We held it as a sacred trust
>
> Because in our space
> In that revolutionary territory
> Individuals were respected
> And treated with dignity and as peers

That's how
The demystification process
Was done

That's my mission
To create a space
Where the world that I want to exist
Does exist
I'm not waiting for it to happen
I'm creating that energy
Through my force of will alone

That's what safe space is
It is territory that is declared
New

Being in that space
Is what engenders the healing
That allows people to pivot
Into their best selves
And take up the challenges
Of what they can do
With their lives

It's that nourishment
That feeling
Of cracking open
What they say
Is not for me

Because everyone
Deserves a place[36]

We are rising

"This society and this government are not about compassion—they're about oppression," Linci said during one of our last interviews for this book. It was an overcast day in early September 2022, a few months after the *Dobbs* decision. On this day, Linci's head was in a different place than when she told me the story of the clinic's closure. She was animated, once again envisioning an action pack of resistance. Connecting the past work of abortion self-helpers and clinic defenders—achieved over time and across very different social, political, and legal contexts—to the work that laid ahead, she spit this poem:

> We reached out to help everyone we could
> *Rise*
> To positive sexuality
> To understanding that orgasm
> Is your god-given right
> And that it's more important for you to get high
> Off your uterus
> Than it is to pop out a baby
>
> That reality of feminist thinking
> That it's the right of your body to experience joy
> That understanding changed us
> It helped us break through the ways we're told
> We cannot be
> And see
> Those are laws that need to be broken
>
> You cannot criminalize women for saying
> I don't want to have a baby
> You cannot criminalize women for saying
> I don't want to have bad sex
> And yet we do
> The hatred of women
> Is built into the economic, financial, and public structure

So we rise

And if it means we need to tear down
The so-called court that is supreme in my life right now
I say
You cannot make me a criminal
You are the criminal
And if you make this law
Then I will break this law
Because it is against nature itself

Women will always find a way
To keep the knowledge alive
Whether we do it underground or aboveground
In our minds, in our books, or in our hearts
We rise

The people in Kansas who stood up and said
You will not change the constitution
We insist on our right to body sovereignty
Kansas rose
We are rising

And those of us who have been all along saying
Do not trust the state
Do not trust that these laws we thought would always be
Will be
This cry has rung from our lips for decades

The truth is we have lost to theocracy
So don't act like we have democracy
Act like what it is

Arise and start to make a difference
Because it's now or never
And we won't leave anyone behind[37]

All Throughout Your Life You Learn

When the *Dobbs* decision was announced on June 24, 2022, a Friday, I took BART into downtown San Francisco. Bay brine crusted the air, and the mood in the streets was electric. It was Pride weekend, and when animated abortion rights protesters marched down Market Street, they intersected with the Trans March, and the two throngs became a single, vibrant, undulating sea of people with numbers in the thousands.

I thought of something Linci once said, probably a full two years earlier, that to me spoke to the sentiment of protesters on Market Street that night: "Self-help is about not getting too comfortable. Because if they give you something, at any moment they could take it away. But the one thing we are never giving back is our bodies. They can never have them back. That's one of the absolute things that a self-helper learns. They don't ever allow anyone to cross that line again."

This book begins and ends with the *Dobbs* decision. It also begins and ends with revolutionary calls to defiant action by some of the fiercest feminists and community health defenders out there.

In the service of something higher

Cindy, Vanessa, Chloe, Izabel, Fuchsia, and Max—all from what I think of as the Gen-X cohort of underground self-helpers— sat around a long patio table with me in Max's backyard for a group interview. It was June 2021, and the *Dobbs* decision, with its wide-ranging impacts, was still a thing of the future. People heaped banh mis, veggies, and hummus onto plates and chatted. The combat boots and shaved heads of decades past had been swapped for comfy activewear and long hair. Izabel, now an educator and facilitator, wore a black t-shirt with a message: "Octavia tried to tell us."

We'd planned the group interview to help tease out more memories and collectively analyze the political significance of underground abortion self-help.

"Even though we were only serving a small number of people, we were doing something tangible," commented self-helper and Operation Rescue infiltrator Vanessa, who had gone on to get her doctorate in education. "I cherish that. We were *doing* something."

Chloe, the self-helper and clinic defender who became a surgeon, added, "The tangibility made it very real. It's very affecting to do political work that's hands-on and has material results." She then made the seamless connection to clinic defense: "There were these real women, and they had their laminaria dilators [placed in their cervixes the day before in preparation for the procedure], and they were right there, and they were going to get pelvic sepsis if we didn't get them in the door so they could get their abortions. That made it really immediate."

"Part of what we did was driven by a feeling of incredible threat," Max recalled of underground self-help. In addition to becoming a sex educator, she had gone on to work in communications. "But we were also motivated to show people, look, we can do this *ourselves*. We don't have to rely on the state to do this stuff. It was electrifying."

"It was romantic and exciting," added Fuchsia, now a Chinese medicine practitioner. "We were underground. We had codes. We put in so much time and energy! You could say that we were so deep underground and paranoid that it kept us from doing something that could have been more effective. We were so secretive."

"You wanted to be like this underground Lefty hero—at least I did," Chloe confessed, agreeing with Fuchsia. "If *Roe* goes down, we're ready! But realistically, it's gone down by little degrees over decades for women in socioeconomically disadvantaged situations. We have to fight in different ways now."

Not so much in counterpoint as in observation, Max added, "When the state has all the power, what are the options for making change? There's fighting the structures by trying to use the tools of legislation, of electing more progressive politicians—those kinds of strategies. But there's also something very compelling that radical folks do, which is to try to help people who are the most affected by something fucked up by doing direct service." I knew from our previous interviews that Max believed there continued to be a need for underground abortion self-help.

I thought of Women's Choice, which served a diverse population, in contrast to the smaller, whiter populations that underground self-help groups tended to work with. The diversity of people any given self-help group served was predicated on the makeup of the group along with the networks, reach, and lived experiences of race, class, gender, and sexuality of the group's members. While a couple of groups were made up of mostly white college students, Cindy and Cecilia's group included community health workers and some fluent Spanish speakers, better enabling them to serve undocumented women.

I asked the group what self-help taught them about their bodies. Fuchsia observed: "I think working with pain and discomfort taught me key lessons. Maybe in other realms you learned about what was pleasurable. In self-help, you learned about what's uncomfortable and how to deal with it in the service of something higher. And how to coach other people through difficult things in the service of something higher. I think that's such an important political lesson. Also, so much of being in a body is just negotiating and learning to live with discomfort."

My mind went back to Grace's comment: "I wanted to be of service to this thing that felt very important." Once again, the right to a radical yes-no: a yes to sex, a no to medical policing.

Fuchsia's comment also made me think of the discomfort that can come with political learning. She was talking about learning to deal with the physical discomfort of menstrual extraction. But you could apply her insight as well to navigating the emotional pain that comes with recognizing that you've been conditioned to believe your body is not your own and that someone else has better authority to determine what should be done to you and what you get to learn and touch.

On "being in a body," Max, too, reflected,

> When I was in grad school doing a content analysis of health and sex education books, there was nothing about the clitoris. It was just not there. For me, my vagina was an area of absence. Something turned off. Something not in touch. Not embodied and not em*brained* either. There was a lack of connectivity.
>
> I remember my first ME, a *this is me* moment. I connected the dots. I can see inside of myself. I know what I'm feeling. I have this awareness now. Self-help intersected with my sex education work, which was the positive side of what we were fighting for—being embodied, sexually happy people. It was part of our fight against the antis and what they wanted the lives of women to look like. It was all interconnected to me. When people were like, the G-spot doesn't exist, I was like, what do you mean? I can feel it! We know some stuff in our bodies because we've felt it and seen it and experienced it.

As Max pointed out, political learning—the process of developing personal, social, and structural consciousness—can also be joyful. Abortion self-help was consciousness-raising practice, in the classic sense: drawing from lived experiences to cultivate greater social and political understanding. She added, "We have the earlier generation of feminists who started the movement to thank. We did some things that were different. But we were explicitly nonhierarchical, and that's what our received practice from them was."

WE TOOK A break. Chloe and Fuchsia had to take off, but Cindy, Vanessa, Izabel, Max, and I stuck around a little longer. We moved from the long table to some chairs around a firepit and into a discussion of lay gynecology as a form of political resistance.

"We're all supposed to believe that we can't understand this stuff. But there are things we *can* do," Cindy said. "Self-help was especially exciting because it's all the stuff that's not talked about."

"Self-help fueled my reactivity to authority," Izabel added. "To know-it-alls and to people who are gonna act like they know more about my body than I do and who talk to me in a way that doesn't actually help me know about my body."

"What's your message for abortion defenders today?" I asked.

"I'd want to talk with them about abortion pills before I talked about ME," said Max. "But I do think it's important to continue the knowledge of self-help, because it's conceivable that a fascist government could cut off the medication. A lot of people say, no, too many ports, too many places where the medication comes in. But I think it's a real threat. And there are places where people can't get it. We need to have multiple ways that women can have safe abortions. So, yeah, I think it's essential to keep the knowledge."

SIMONE, THE SELF-HELPER and clinic worker who became a gynecologist, wasn't part of our group interview in June 2021, but when I asked her later whether she thought laypeople should learn and practice menstrual extraction, she had this to say: "I would say [surgical] abortion should be done in a medical setting because that's the safest. But I would also say that birth should be done in a medical setting because that's the safest. I recognize that in the United States, people choose to have births outside of the hospital, and I respect patient autonomy. Abortion and birth outside of the hospital are not the same thing. But I also recognize that [surgical] abortion outside of a medical setting has had a historical role and may continue to have a role, depending on the political situation."

Simone's comments suggest that, while medical settings, complete with imaging and other technology, along with licensed professionals, help facilitate safe delivery and abortion procedures, there are reasons why patients might opt for alternative settings and, crucially, if medical settings are not available, people will still both give birth and terminate pregnancies. Therefore, the question of whether laypeople *should* learn how to do suction abortions is basically moot, because in reality people *will* simply learn how to do what they need to know how to do, even in the absence of supportive health care infrastructure.

LATER, MAX WOULD insistently tell me, "I want the readers of your book to know that *they can do this*, wherever they are. You can learn and study self-help with a group, practice with care and dedication, and build skills together. And if you need, menstrual extraction can be a tool your group has for the well-being of your community."

I thought of my conversation with Theresa and the findings of the 2011 India study: that the failure and complication rates in manual vacuum aspiration procedures—with the simple industrially manufactured Ipas MVA used all around the world—between newly trained nurses and physicians were the same, and that with both provider types, procedures were 98 percent successful.[1] I also thought of the gynecologic oncologist Melissa Moffitt's words: "Abortion is basically the same as changing the brakes on your car. There's a series of steps you do. Anybody can learn them." *For the well-being of your community.*

FOR THIS BOOK, I also interviewed four underground abortion self-helpers and an abortion doula of the generation after. These were people practicing in the 2000s and 2010s. Presenting and discussing their stories is beyond the scope of this book, but they taught me so much about how underground abortion self-help has traveled and continues to travel. Here's some of what they wanted to talk about: Learning how to use an Ipas MVA and then providing manual-suction abortions for friends. Helping people obtain medication abortions. Exploring the effects of trauma and white supremacy on the body and integrating this information

into their abortion self-help practice. Learning about the historical roles trans people have played in imagining the possible appli-
cations and meaning of self-help. Building knowledge of and
relationships with plants and herbal abortifacients to decolonize
one's relationship to medicine and, as the abortion doula put it,
"call in the whole ecology of abortion."[2] Practicing consent in the
context of gynecological and abortion care. Centering reciprocity.
Learning lessons about grace.

#AbortionSavedMyLife, #BodyAutonomyForAll

On a cold morning in Oakland, with the sun just starting to
creep up over the hills, Laura Weide, her partner, a friend of
theirs, and I grabbed fistfuls of a well-worn cotton sheet and
together lifted it over the top of the guardrail of a pedestrian
bridge. Facing the westbound traffic below, the block letters we
had painted on it read: "Abortion Saved My Life." We worked
quickly to cable tie the banner to the cold metal and then scram-
bled back to the car.

Banners decorated four consecutive overpasses on the I-580
that day, and a dozen other banners were dropped, too, by groups
all over the Bay Area. They all featured the message "Abortion
Saved My Life" and often included additional messages: Body
Autonomy for All. Reproductive Justice Is Racial Justice. No
Forced Sterilization. Stop Fascism. Free Abortion on Demand.
Christofash, Fuck Off! Health for All. End Gender Violence.
Repro Justice 4 All.

It was January 21, 2023—what would have been the weekend of the fiftieth anniversary of *Roe v. Wade*. It was also the day
of the Walk for Life West Coast (or, more accurately, "walk of
lies"), a massive annual "pro-life" march supported by various
anti-abortion groups and churches and held in downtown San
Francisco. This year's event promoted even more extremist positions, such as the argument that there should be no legal exemp-
tions to abortion bans even in the case of rape or incest, with
Rebecca Kiessling, a high-profile advocate of such no-exception

bans, as a speaker. Shawn Carney, cofounder of the clinic block-ade campaign 40 Days for Life, was a speaker, too.

Laura, a handful of other activists, and I had organized the coordinated banner-drops. Our phones dinged and vibrated as friends texted photos taken from their cars of the banners decorating overpasses. We felt that the message "Abortion Saved My Life" was a powerful refutation of the lie, propagated for decades by the Walk for Life and the broader anti-abortion movement, that "abortion hurts women."[3] No, the banners proclaimed, abortion does not hurt women; abortion saves women's lives.[4]

Back at Laura's, we threw the images up on social media with hashtags—#AbortionSavedMyLife, #BodyAutonomyForAll—hoping people would notice.

Afterward, I went into San Francisco for a Walk for Life counter demonstration. I arrived to find throngs of protesters of all ages and from different political groups forming a city-block-length force of lively pro-abortion and antifascist solidarity. Linci and the longtime BACORR clinic defenders Raven and Nancy Reiko Kato were there that day, too.

With the city's support, Walk for Life organizers bus in thousands of people from around the state—a tried-and-true tactic of the anti-abortion movement, one that Operation Rescue used to employ as well. On the day of the event, the city also provides a heavy police presence around the perimeter of Civic Center, a public plaza encircled by government buildings. We watched and raged as the walk of lies snaked around Civic Center and turned onto Market Street after their rally. They were on their way, and our side began to thin as counter demonstrators grew fatigued and left.

Then eight or so big white guys with their heads and faces covered by ski masks walked nonchalantly past the droopy police line and into our counter demo. They unfurled a large white banner with black lettering that read: "150K White Kids Per Year / Abortion Is Genocide." Counter protesters were caught off guard by the sudden appearance of these white supremacists, though some mobilized quickly, using their bodies to try to obscure the message. Some banded tightly together as the men began lunging at them. The breath went out of my chest; it all happened so fast. The thugs backed down when more comrades joined in pushing back.

I thought of the hundreds of Walk for Life participants, many with children in tow, all certain of their moral rightness and all, knowingly or not, participating in a rally where self-identified white supremacists brought up the rear and were okay with using their bodies to frighten and possibly hurt young people.

And I remembered what Laura said of OR: "They clearly enjoyed hitting women. That's what they wanted to do. They wanted to hit women." It was horrible, yet the self-helpers and clinic defenders I'd spent years talking with had taught me what I needed to know to be able to grasp how this seeming contradiction—men attacking women while purporting to care about them—was in fact not a contradiction at all.

All around the country, social justice defenders have started to recognize that the war on the body autonomy of women and queer and trans people is at the foundation of the Far Right's fascist agenda. I appreciate Mary Ziegler's work deeply, but I don't agree with her claim at the end of *Abortion and the Law* that "we have only begun to understand what makes the abortion conflict so intractable." We know what makes it so intractable: that getting to the root of "the conflict" means confronting and uprooting American fascism itself.[5]

The struggle against fascism continues. As of this writing, these same political forces of the Far Right are pressuring potential Republican presidential candidates to call for a national abortion ban. They demand that people in banned states who seek abortions, along with those who help them travel elsewhere for care or who mail them abortion pills, be prosecuted. They are the same forces suing to overturn the FDA's approval of mifepristone, which has been legal nationwide for almost two and a half decades.[6] They are also advocating laws that would grant the same legal rights and protections to fetuses as to people.[7] They are trying to exploit or change state constitutions.[8] The Right has signaled that it will try to restrict birth control access, too.[9] Moreover, they are introducing bills to restrict gender-affirming care for trans people and ban care, including puberty blockers and hormone therapy, for trans youth and also criminalize adults who support youth in obtaining care.[10]

Regarding abortion: restrictions and bans will not stop people from having abortions. But they will create obstacles that will ensure women and other pregnant people seeking abortions, especially rural and low-income people and people living in banned states, will be forced to illegally self-manage earlier medication abortions without the support of a physician or pursue riskier and more expensive later abortions, whether legal or illegal. Bans will force the closure of more clinics. By creating delays for patients, bans will endanger people with ectopic pregnancies or high-risk pregnancies. They will lead to the criminalization of poor women, especially poor women of color, along with more coerced sterilization. And the laws will mean that some women will be forced to remain pregnant and give birth, introducing physical and mental health risks and causing trauma to them, and even costing some their lives.

We accompany each other

"So," I said, meeting Linci's sharp eyes with my own. We were on the porch in the sun. It was back in August 2020. I'd been visiting Linci as often as possible, and finally she'd started talking to me for real. "Tell me again what you did?" I asked. She then told me the following story, which was so much of the story; though of course, I didn't know it yet.

"Abortion technology in the first trimester is straightforward," Linci said. "Simple and easily done in a confident, clean setting. It doesn't require intensive surgical training as, say, repairing a broken bone does because *nothing's broken*." She explained, "The body is meant for the placenta to fall away. With the hormones that the uterus gives us to be able to do the work of birth, regeneration, and menses, we have shedding. Abortion is going along with a process that is inherent to women's intimate cycles of life-and-*eggness*. In my lifetime, I have probably developed four hundred eggs and turned them into lifetime opportunities that I then shed joyously. That's an important difference between medical manipulation or surgery and the simple process of abortion. The underground self-help groups really understood that."

"These small groups, they hung together for years! Part of it was that they intimately gained an understanding of what was going on with their bodies. And as they aged, things changed." She continued,

When you're a young person, you're fucking a lot. Avoiding pregnancy is much more of an issue than trying to obtain pregnancy. But later, infertility issues come up. People say, "Yeah, I had chlamydia, I treated it." Yeah, you treated it, but that chlamydia crawled all up in there and caused some scarring of your tubes. Having chlamydia infections caused a lot of infertility issues. Once you've destroyed a tube, you can have extrauterine pregnancies, like the one Pat Parker wrote about.

What happens if that happens in a self-help group? Well, you send the person to the hospital. Because if you have a tubal pregnancy, you need surgery. There is no home remedy for a tubal pregnancy, if the pregnancy is not in the uterus, it is not within the normal framework of self-help. So if you can figure that out—if you know from doing pelvic exams that you can feel the difference between a swollen tube and a uterine sac, and you know what their ovaries feel like, or don't feel like, because you don't usually feel them, and you know what their uterus feels like, what position it's normally in, because you've been feeling it once a month for a year—you have a different relationship to health care and self-knowledge.

And in doing that, in practicing self-help, you really start to understand female sexuality. Deciding to have children, the wonder of being able to practice on uteruses that are getting bigger, that's *wonderful*. You get to learn, oh my god, this is what a twenty-week pregnancy feels like! It's a fucking watermelon, Japanese seedless style!

All throughout your life you learn. That is what the self-help group is about. How do we help each other? We accompany each other, and we share our influence and our knowledge, and that's self-help. And we do that within the medical system, within our community, within our family, and within our soul.

The deep care of self-help

In an op-ed published in January 2023, the *New York Times* editors situate the war on reproductive freedom within Republicans' larger agenda of suppressing the basic rights of Americans: "Make no mistake: [Republicans] are bent on stymieing . . . efforts to protect the constitutional rights of Americans that have been whittled away by the Supreme Court and Republican-led states. Among those rights is the freedom of reproductive choice and bodily autonomy for women."[11] The editors then note that in the most recent midterm election, people in conservative states who voted on abortion (for example, Kansas) voted for access, not bans. Therefore, they conclude, while reproductive rights advocates should push Congress to write abortion rights into federal law, in the time between now and when a federal law is won, their best bet is to push state-level ballot initiatives.

It's a difficult conclusion that points toward the painstaking, long-game institutional work that lies ahead for abortion rights advocates. But what abortion self-help and clinic defense teach us is that this work is not enough. The meaningful political work of abortion defense and reproductive justice necessarily extends to our personal relationships and lives.

Abortion self-help and clinic defense teach us that social and political transformation happen over time, through seemingly ordinary actions that we risk taking with each other every day, to show ourselves and each other that we can do and be something different. The building blocks for transformation are our relationships, and with these relationships we can form affinity groups, coalitions, and networks; create safer spaces, households, and even institutions in which to work and live; develop political analyses, strategies, and tactics; and share resources. Combined, these seemingly ordinary actions are the substance of both underground and on-the-ground work. As we face a Far Right as emboldened as ever, here are some possibilities for radical abortion defense that synthesize lessons from decades of abortion self-help and clinic defense—actions that ordinary people can readily take.

Make the referral

Histories of abortion and reproductive justice activism make clear that one key to safe abortion and good reproductive health care is the referral to knowledgeable, trustworthy care. For centuries, the referral has been a tool of underground abortion workers. Consider Pat Maginnis, Lana Clarke Phelan, and Rowena Gurner's mimeographed provider referral lists; Women's Choice Clinic's export of human resources, feminist knowledge, and medical supplies, resulting in a two-way referral pipeline of abortion care to the community and allies from the community to defend the clinic; and also today's practical support networks, from the established abortion funds that help cover the costs of procedures, travel, and lodging to the autonomous networks we're still building, along with abortion pill education campaigns like PlanCPills.org and fulfillment services like AidAccess.org. The referral has been and continues to be fundamental to ensuring safe, accessible abortion care, both legal and illegal, no matter the legal landscape.

How can we make the referral? First and foremost, identify the closest abortion clinic (use www.ineedana.com) to better understand local access issues. How far might someone local have to travel to get to a clinic? Then talk to people in the community and share information. Are there local doctors who are willing to provide abortion resources and care despite state-level bans or a lack of local, stand-alone abortion clinics? We can ask our own doctors and share what we learn with family and friends. Also, periodically ask around whether anyone needs help with a ride, a plane ticket, childcare, or lodging to obtain an abortion. We can make clear to others that we are willing to provide practical support in the case that someone in the community needs it.[12]

Additionally, we can learn about how all people, regardless of state laws, can obtain abortion pills by mail at PlanCPills.org and AidAccess.org. Spread this information widely, especially to young people, who in many states are required by law to involve a parent in their decision to pursue a legal abortion.[13] As of this writing, more than half of abortions in the United States are performed using combination pills: mifepristone and misoprostol. AidAccess.org, for example, founded by the Dutch physician Rebecca Gomperts, fills requests for combination pills regardless of the legal status of abortion in the recipient's state or country. If abortion is not legal where the recipient is located, a licensed doctor in Amsterdam will prescribe the medication, fill the prescription using a pharmacy in India, and have the pills sent to the recipient by mail. AidAccess.org also fills requests for "advance provision pills," which are prescribed to someone who is not currently pregnant for later use in case of an unwanted pregnancy.

If mifepristone is not available, misoprostol can be used alone to terminate a pregnancy. For instructions on how to do an abortion at home with mifepristone and misoprostol, or with misoprostol alone in the case that mifepristone is not available, visit www.howtouseabortionpill.org or www.womenonwaves.org.

We can keep advance provision abortion pills on hand in case we ourselves or a friend or family member needs them. This will help prevent situations in which people in our communities have to wait a long time for their abortion pills to arrive if the pills need to be mailed from outside of the country. To learn about more options, visit www.plancpills.org.

Making the referral has always meant potentially defying the law, which reflects how it has always also been one of the most powerful actions that abortion defenders can take.

Work with many hands

The most important lesson I've learned through studying Bay Area abortion self-help and clinic defense is that small groups of people working closely, securely, and dynamically together can make revolutionary change. Working with others can feel difficult and takes patience and practice, but when we do it successfully, we build community power from the inside. That's why learning how to work in small groups is one of the most important political lessons there is.

What can we do with our hands? Think about how many hands it takes, whether in an underground or licensed-clinic setting, to make sure just one person gets an abortion. Sometimes it takes a lot of hands just to get somebody from the street through the clinic door. It can take many hands to get so many things done (not just abortions), so we should offer our hands to each other when we can.

To start, we can build skills by working collaboratively in small groups. This could mean starting or joining an underground abortion self help group (remember what Lorraine Rothman said: *self-help groups are all over*) or getting trained in clinic defense or escorting, though these are not the only powerful ways that we can work together with our hands. A small group could start by organizing a demonstration or direct action to expose a fake clinic—making protest banners and signs, props, and art for political actions are all hands-on activities. To prepare, find fake clinics at reproaction.org/fakeclinicdatabase, research who or which groups are funding these fake clinics to expose their anti-abortion agendas, and learn about the unproven, unethical "abortion pill reversal" procedure that some fake clinics promote. Also, check out existing "Expose Fake Clinics" campaigns and toolkits: www.exposefakeclinics.com or reproaction.org/campaign/hold-fake-clinics-accountable, for example. Keep in mind that it's not necessary to work with an existing organization.

Remember what Max said: *I want the readers of your book to know that they can do this, wherever they are.*

Fight to keep clinics open

Women's Choice was a broad-spectrum sexual, reproductive, and abortion health care provider. It was a store of knowledge to its community, which included mostly low-income women, many of color, along with queer and trans people. As Linci put it, the clinic *treated what happened*; despite being under attack and occupation, it responded to community need. This was revolutionary.

The story of the Oakland clinic is just one among those of many other independent abortion clinics across the country. The Abortion Care Network explains that indies still provide the majority of abortion care, often offering both medication and surgical abortion. The ongoing presence of clinics is critical; abortion pills alone are not enough. In regions where surgical abortion is not available due to a lack of nearby clinics, those seeking later abortions are put in a difficult and costly position. Also, people who would have been able to end their pregnancies safely at a clinic may be compelled to terminate outside of a clinic where they are not safe due to an abusive relationship, being unhoused, or a lack of support. (That said, the opposite can also be true: for some, it might be less private and therefore less safe to terminate in a clinic setting.)

In fact, Planned Parenthood clinics provide fewer abortions nationwide than independent clinics do, and doctors' offices and hospitals even fewer still. Sixty-six percent of abortions provided after sixteen weeks are provided by indies, as are one hundred percent of abortions provided after twenty-six weeks.

While the number of telemedicine abortion services have increased, especially during the COVID-19 era, the number of brick-and-mortar independent clinics went down by 35 percent between 2012 and 2022, and in 2022, the year of *Dobbs*, forty-two independent clinics closed, in many cases as a direct result of *Dobbs*. With the loss of brick-and-mortar clinics comes the loss of later abortion care.[14]

What can we do to help keep clinics open? Defend the indies. Donate to a local indie clinic—find them at abortioncarenetwork. org/abortion-care-providers. Organize a fundraiser. Write and ask whether the clinic is seeking volunteers or escorts. If they provide other sexual and reproductive health care services, consider obtaining services from them as a patient. Send thank-you cards.

We can also study and practice community self-defense tactics such as clinic defense with trusted friends. Organize a training in a park. Make sure to communicate with clinic directors before showing up to do clinic defense.

Band together against the body cops

Abortion self-helpers and clinic defenders understood that the fight for reproductive freedom and justice was inextricable from the struggle against homophobia, queerphobia, and transphobia and, starting in the 1980s, the weaponization of HIV/AIDS. Early Bay Area abortion self-helpers were lesbians who knew that starting aboveground clinics and underground self-help groups was about creating safer spaces where they could be out together. Some self-helpers became organizers for ACT UP in the fight against HIV/AIDS. BACORR and ACT UP members often shared a political analysis, sexual politics, networks, tactics, and aesthetics. Abortion defense and HIV/AIDS activism were sibling movements in the 1980s and 1990s, and the story of their collaboration is a reminder of the importance of chosen family in a hostile world.

All of which is to say, reproductive justice activists have always also been queer and trans health activists. This is because cis women and queer and trans people of all genders share the lived experience of surviving feminization—the state and the Right's objectification, sexual exploitation, and degradation of them. These fascist forces have always sought to control our bodies and our reproduction.

I don't agree with some people in the movement who believe that we should understand the struggle for abortion access and reproductive justice as being only about defending female sexuality and female reproductive autonomy. That said, I honor deeply the underlying claim they make that people assigned female at birth suffer tremendously all around the world. I would say, additionally, that ours is a struggle to liberate and defend all feminized, oppressed, and policed human sexuality (that of women along with queer and trans people); dismantle patriarchal and racist structures of reproductive control; and help people who have been most often denied body sovereignty—women and nonbinary and trans people—realize body sovereignty. In my mind, these principles are fundamental to a political theory of deep care.

How do we say hands off to the body cops? Study our overlapping histories of struggle. Acknowledge, examine, and deconstruct our internalized misogyny and transphobia. Support each other's demands and share resources. The community self-defense strategies that underground self-helpers and clinic defenders developed would not have been possible without the participation of queer and trans people, whom these strategies also served. And these strategies—the building of secure underground networks, the transfer and sharing of restricted knowledge, and the development of clinic defense tactics—couldn't be more relevant and applicable today.

Have fun

When I go back through my interviews for this book, I am reminded of how many times self-helpers and clinic defenders described each other as laughing, playing, and warmly relating to one another. They had fun, using creativity, humor, and satire to imagine and implement survival strategies that would make their lives more joyful. They insisted that their work be romantic and exciting.

I think of Pat Maginnis's cartoons, making a buffoon of church- and state-enforced patriarchy. And of Alicia Jones, José Alfresco, and Linci animatedly telling stories of Pat Parker telling stories. And of the words of the National Black Women's Health Project, "We cry, laugh, nurture, joke, scream." I think of the Church Ladies for Choice from ACT UP singing hymns at clinic defenses and of the rowdy wedding guests in front of the

San Francisco church spanking their plastic babies. And of underground self-helpers like Izabel expressing the delightfulness of having your body be communal knowledge. And of the warm, intense ritual that was self-help, too, as Cindy described it. The joy of being embodied and sexually happy people, as Max put it, despite the misogyny and queerphobia of the anti-abortion movement. Joy is our revolutionary duty, Linci has said countless times.

I think of self-helpers laughing in each other's beds, limbs overlapping. Clinic defenders laughing on the defense line, limbs overlapping. The curiosity and physicality of those relationships, their deep commitment to consent and respect, their orientation toward the We.

What can we do? Have fun, put ourselves out there physically, and build toward the We.

Self-help is where the power is

And there are many more lessons from self-helpers and clinic defenders:

The personal is political, and silence equals death.

So use all the tools of your being.

Ask questions. Be in your body. Know what your body is.

Claim the liminal space. You have the right to bleed.

Feel your agency and recognize your power.

Your life has meaning, and you get to determine what that is.

Take responsibility for your life. Choose yourself inside of your life.

Slow down. Have a different vibe. Hold intensity. Listen.

Be antihierarchical and interested in process. Be in it for the long haul.

Find your action pack and roam the world with healing intent.

Get your hands into things you normally wouldn't—learning how to put your hands inside of somebody is a good thing to learn how to do.

Learn the steps. Anybody can learn them.

Learn how to do all the jobs.

Learn how to produce what you need.

Become proficient in what will help you help each other.

There's no way to learn except to do.

Allow the best part of you to be present in whatever role you are in.

Allow everyone to become a teacher. No one person is the expert.

Use the collective intelligence of the group.

Look in with curiosity, warmth, and engagement.

Have a sense of humor. You don't know how it's going to unfold, but you're here, so be ready to be really, really open.

Support each other's mutual growth.

Take care of each other. Everyone deserves a place, so make yours a household. Do not leave anyone behind.

Define your work for yourself. Be part of carrying on traditions of resistance.

Bring your razor-sharp analysis. Redistribute knowledge.

Build in the mechanism. And trust rhythm.

Don't say anything you aren't willing to eat.

If they make the law, break the law.

Rage is your bitter fuel.

Learn what it means to defend other people.

Remember that you can learn how to do this, wherever you are.

Be grateful for the lessons.

Acknowledgments

Deep Care has been a highly interactive, collaborative effort. I want to honor and thank the fierce abortion and reproductive justice defenders who generously participated in this project and made the book possible by sharing their stories, archives, lives, and lessons with me. These activists shared time and energy, some over years, offering feedback on my drafts and helping me understand why and how they did what they did. They are my heroes.

I couldn't imagine a better home for this book than AK Press. Thank you to Angelica Sgouros for careful, thorough, incisive editing, which helped breathe more life into these stories, and without which the book would not be what it is; Charles Weigl for his early enthusiasm about the project; and the entire AK Press team for their work to help me bring this project to fruition and into the world.

Thank you to the lawyers Pete Berger and Sam Lachman who, through the ProJourn (Protecting Journalists) program, provided a pro bono legal review, and to the ProJourn program itself for offering to help me. Huge thanks to Denise Tukumnez for reading the manuscript and offering a medical review along with an obstetrician-gynecologist's perspective and critique.

Thank you to Linci Comy, whose heart, mind, words, and life fill this book to overflowing. Immense gratitude to Lysa Samuel, who is not a character in this book, and to Laura Weide and Raven, who are—all of whom read full drafts and engaged with me around the history and politics deeply and over years. Their contributions to this book cannot be overstated. I am grateful to Carol Downer for reading chapters, providing feedback, and helping me begin to understand the politics of population control. Many thanks to Kass McMahon for talking with me at length about the history of clinic defense and for sharing and discussing her extensive BACAOR/BACORR personal archive. Thank you to Robert McBride for reading and commenting on a full draft.

Thank you to friends and collaborators in study and struggle who engaged with me around this project, championed it, offered or held space for me in which to share about it, helped house and feed me, and inspired my mind and heart as I wrote: my East Bay political study group; my environmental humanities/poetics reading group; my antiracism study group led by Judy Grahn and Dianne Jenett; my discomfort practice group facilitated by Suzanne Pegas; and Darrell Alvarez, Priyanka Basu, Drew Belstock, Mei-mei Berssenbrugge, Scott Braley, Charise DeBerry, Breezy DeSilva, Paul Ebenkamp, Mickey Ellinger, Cyrus, Rebecca, Nora, and Kas Farivar, Merle Geode, Judy Grahn, Ben and Rajasree Hawk, Richard Hernandez, Brenda Hillman, Matt Hooley, Elliot James, Ivy Johnson, Lynn Keller, Jasmine, Jesse, Audrey, and Olive Kitses, Leslie Martin, Michelle Niemann, Gillian Osborne, Kaedan Peters, Thane Plantikow, Sonya Posmentier, Samia Rahimtoola, Evelyn Reilly, Frances Richard, Steve Rowell, Jocelyn Saidenberg, Joshua Schuster, Eric Sneathen, Jamie Townsend, Donna Willmott, Laura Woltag, Noelle Yackel, and Stephanie Young. Extra thanks to Lysa Samuel for offering so much support and love while I was writing.

I want to thank my colleagues at the University of Minnesota, Morris, especially Julie Eckerle and Michael Lackey, and at University of California, Berkeley, for support and encouragement. University of Minnesota and the Schlesinger Library granted me generous research funding, and the Santa Fe Women's International Study Center provided me with time and space in which to write. This project would not have been possible without such material support.

Thank you to the librarians and archivists who helped me access this history at Duke University David M. Rubenstein Rare Book & Manuscript Library; Bay Area Freedom Archives; Harvard University Francis A. Countway Library of Medicine; Oakland Public Library; University of Southern California ONE Archives; Radcliffe Institute Schlesinger Library; San Francisco Public Library; Smith College Sophia Smith Collection; Spelman

College Archives; and University of California, Los Angeles Special Collections. Thank you to Sam Tate for interview transcription support at the beginning of the process.

Thank you to my mom, for always encouraging me to ask deep questions and to write; to my grandmother, for being my biggest writing cheerleader; and to all of my other family members who have offered love and support.

Finally, my deepest thanks once again to Linci, for opening the door, and for making my life a different one than it was before

Notes

Preface

1. *Roe v. Wade*, 410 U.S. 113 (1973); *Planned Parenthood of Southeastern Pennsylvania v. Casey*, 505 U.S. 833 (1992).
2. *Dobbs v. Jackson Women's Health Organization* transcript, December 1, 2021, Heritage Reporting Corporation, www.hrccourtreporters.com, https://s3.documentcloud.org/documents/21122957/dobbs-v-jackson-womens-health-transcript.pdf.
3. *Dobbs v. Jackson Women's Health Organization* transcript.
4. Michelle Murphy, *The Economization of Life* (Durham: Duke University Press, 2017), 6–7, 42–43. See also Michel Foucault, *The Birth of Biopolitics: Lectures at the Collège de France, 1978–79*, ed. Michel Senellart, trans. Graham Burchell (Basingstoke, UK: Palgrave Macmillan, 2008).
5. *Roe v. Wade*; Mary Ziegler, *Abortion and the Law in America: Roe v. Wade to the Present* (Cambridge: Cambridge University Press, 2020), 22–23.
6. *Webster v. Reproductive Health Services*, 492 U.S. 490 (1989), Ziegler, *Abortion and the Law*, 23, 105, 117.
7. Claire Cain Miller, Sarah Kliff, and Larry Buchanan, "Childbirth Is Deadlier for Black Families Even When They're Rich, Expansive Study Finds," *New York Times*, February 12, 2023, https://www.nytimes.com/interactive/2023/02/12/upshot/child-maternal-mortality-rich-poor.html; Latoya Hill, Samantha Artiga, and Usha Ranji, "Racial Disparities in Maternal and Infant Health," *Kaiser Family Foundation*, November 1, 2022, https://www.kff.org/racial-equity-and-health-policy/issue-brief/racial-disparities-in-maternal-and-infant-health-current-status-and-efforts-to-address-them.
8. Rachel Anspach, "The Foster Care to Prison Pipeline: What Is It and How It Works," *TeenVogue*, May 25, 2018, https://www.teenvogue.com/story/the-foster-care-to-prison-pipeline-what-it-is-and-how-it-works; and Ruth Wilson Gilmore, *Golden Gulag: Prisons,*

Surplus, Crisis, and Opposition in Globalizing California (Berkeley: University of California Press, 2007).

9. Leslie Reagan, *When Abortion Was a Crime: Women, Medicine, and Law in the United States, 1867–1973* (Berkeley: University of California Press, 1997), 11. See also Jasmine Aguilera and Abigail Abrams, "What the Buffalo Tragedy Has to Do with the Effort to Overturn Roe," *Time*, May 21, 2022, https://time.com/6178135/buffalo-shooting-abortion-replacement-theory.

10. At AidAccess.org, you can order abortion pills before you are pregnant in case you need them in the future. Founded by Dutch physician Rebecca Gomperts, AidAccess.org fulfills requests for abortion pills regardless of the legal status of abortion in the recipient's state or country. See https://aidaccess.org/en/page/2880027/advance-provision.

11. The Jane Collective was an underground abortion referral service and provider in Chicago that operated in the late 1960s and early 1970s. Jane was made up of laywomen, some of whom learned how to do abortions. The group itself provided nearly eleven thousand abortions in the years leading up to *Roe*. See Laura Kaplan, *The Story of Jane: The Legendary Underground Feminist Abortion Service* (New York: Pantheon Books, 1995) and *The Janes*, directed by Tia Lessin and Emma Pildes (HBO Documentary Films and Pentimento Productions, 2022).

12. Reagan, *When Abortion Was a Crime*, 14–16. Prior to criminalization in the nineteenth century, abortion before "quickening" was legal under common law. "Quickening" was when a woman could begin to feel a fetus move, between sixteen and twenty-five weeks. Reagan, *When Abortion Was a Crime*, 8.

13. Reagan, *When Abortion Was a Crime*, 43–44; Association to Repeal Abortion Laws "Self-Induced Techniques" handout, 1967–1968, MC 289, box 4, folder 65, Records of the Society for Humane Abortion (hereafter RSHA), Schlesinger Library on the History of Women in America, Radcliffe Institute, Cambridge, MA (hereafter Schlesinger).

14. Some reproductive rights groups such as Women's March have argued that invoking the danger of self-managed abortion (SMA) prior to *Roe*—through coat hanger imagery, e.g.—perpetuates stigma around SMA. (See Women's March Tweet on October 2, 2021, https://twitter.com/womensmarch/status/1444302751186526210.) While it is true that women have long

practiced and taught SMA, sometimes safely, it is also true that SMA prior to *Roe* was more dangerous than it is today, with abortion pills as an option. It is important that this pre-*Roe* history not be erased. I want to put pressure on these contemporary groups' politics.

In the 1960s, many more Black women than white women died from illegal abortion complications. See Loretta Ross, "African American Women and Abortion," in *Abortion Wars: A Half-Century of Struggle, 1950-2000*, ed. Rickie Solinger (Berkeley: University of California Press, 1998), 161.

15. See Reagan, "An Open Secret," in *When Abortion Was a Crime*, 19-45.

16. Laura Weide introduced me to the language of cultivating "community power and autonomy from the inside" during one of our many conversations about the politics of sex and reproduction.

17. Not long after I started theorizing "deep care," Rupa Marya and Raj Patel introduced the concept of "deep medicine" in their book *Inflamed: Deep Medicine and the Anatomy of Injustice* (New York: Farrar, Straus and Giroux, 2021). They contrast "colonial medicine" with deep medicine, arguing that the former enacts domination while the latter repairs systems damaged by colonization (20-23). I think of deep care as a sibling to deep medicine, with implications, too, for repair.

18. See Mary Ziegler, *Dollars for Life: The Anti-Abortion Movement and the Fall of the Republican Establishment* (New Haven, CT: Yale University Press, 2022).

19. Ninia Baehr, *Abortion without Apology: A Radical History for the 1990s* (Boston: South End Press, 1990), 1.

20. Loretta Ross and Rickie Solinger, *Reproductive Justice: An Introduction* (Oakland: University of California Press, 2017), 9.

21. Patricia Hill Collins develops her concept of Black feminist critical social theory in *Black Feminist Thought: Knowledge, Consciousness, and the Politics of Empowerment,* 2nd ed. (New York: Routledge, [1990] 2000).

Introduction: We Did It Before, and We'll Do It Again

1. See Jennifer Nelson, *More than Medicine: A History of the Women's Health Movement* (New York: New York University Press, 2015); and Shulamith Firestone, quoted in Michelle Murphy, *Seizing the Means*

of Reproduction: Entanglements of Feminism, Health, and Technoscience (Durham: Duke University Press, 2012), 5.

2.   Murphy, *Seizing the Means*, 5.

3.   Pamela Allen, "The Small Group Process," in *Free Space: A Perspective on the Small Group in Women's Liberation* (New York: Times Change Press, 1970), 23–31.

4.   Laura K. Brown, "Blood Rumors: An Exploration of Meaning in the Stories of a Contemporary Menstrual Practice" (PhD diss., California Institute for Integral Studies, 2002), 5–6.

5.   Alondra Nelson, *Body and Soul: The Black Panther Party and the Fight against Medical Discrimination* (Minneapolis: University of Minnesota Press, 2011), 81.

6.   With the support of Tufts Medical School and the Office of Economic Opportunity (OEO), a War on Poverty agency, a doctor named H. Jack Geiger established the first two neighborhood health centers in poor communities in Mississippi. The OEO then adopted the program and began funding neighborhood health centers around the country. See J. Nelson, *More than Medicine*, 16, 23–26.

7.   A. Nelson, *Body and Soul*, 24.

8.   Susan Smith, *Sick and Tired of Being Sick and Tired: Black Women's Health Activism in America, 1890–1950* (Philadelphia: University of Pennsylvania Press, 1995), 18.

9.   Smith, *Sick and Tired*, 20–22, 52.

10. Collins, *Black Feminist Thought*, 33.

11. For a survey of American women's body activism from the nineteenth- to late-twentieth century, see Judith Aliza Hyman Rosenbaum, "Whose Bodies? Whose Selves? A History of American Women's Health Activism, 1968–Present" (PhD diss., Brown University, 2004), 15–31.

12. Sam Gringlas and Justine Kenin, "Dr. Rachel Levine: Transgender Health Care Is an Equity Issue, Not a Political One," *All Things Considered*, NPR, April 1, 2021, https://www.npr.org /2021/04/01/983490883/dr-rachel-levine-transgender-health -care-an-equity-issue-not-political-one.

     More recently, activists have defended trans people against Far-Right harassers who have assaulted them outside of gender clinics. See Andrea Marks, "After Far-Right Harassment, Trans People Are Fighting to Keep Their Health Care," *Rolling Stone*, September 30, 2022, https://www.rollingstone.com/culture/culture-news/trans -health-care-disrupted-right-wing-harassment-1234600910.

13. Alanna Vagianos, "Women Aren't the Only People Who Get Abortions," *HuffPost*, July 6, 2019, https://www.huffpost.com/entry/women-arent-the-only-people-who-get-abortions_n_5cf55540e4b0e346ce8286d3; Anna Brown, "About 5% of Young Adults in the U.S. Say Their Gender Is Different from Their Sex Assigned at Birth," *Pew Research Center*, June 7, 2022, https://www.pewresearch.org/fact-tank/2022/06/07/about-5-of-young-adults-in-the-u-s-say-their-gender-is-different-from-their-sex-assigned-at-birth.

14. Hiʻilei Julia Kawehipuaakahaopulani Hobart and Tamara Kneese, "Radical Care: Survival Strategies for Uncertain Times," *Social Text* 38, no. 1 (142) (2020): 1, 13, https://doi.org/10.1215/01642472-7971067.

15. Sarah Van Gelder, "The Radical Work of Healing: Fania and Angela Davis on a New Kind of Civil Rights Activism," *Yes! Magazine*, February 19, 2016, https://www.yesmagazine.org/issue/life-after-oil/2016/02/19/the-radical-work-of-healing-fania-and-angela-davis-on-a-new-kind-of-civil-rights-activism.

16. Robyn Maynard and Leanne Betasamosake Simpson, *Rehearsals for Living* (Chicago: Haymarket Books, 2022), 243, 248.

17. For more on what has happened to caring, care labor, and care services under neoliberal capitalism, see the Care Collective's "Introduction: Carelessness Reigns," in *The Care Manifesto: the Politics of Interdependence* (New York: Verso, 2020), 1–20.

    Structural critiques of "self-care" discourse are not new: Michel Foucault theorizes how the institution of the "care of the self" started in antiquity in Western society and became increasingly medical in nature over time, ultimately upholding and reifying a moral system and "new erotics" by sacralizing the closed heterosexual marriage. See Michel Foucault, *The Care of the Self: The History of Sexuality*, vol. 3, trans. Robert Hurley (New York: Vintage Books, 1986).

    The concept of self-care has been co-opted by neoliberal "women's health," as Tasha Dubriwny discusses. Dubriwny argues that women are treated as "highly gendered individuals who are empowered to choose among medical treatments, manage their future and current health by altering their lifestyles, and increase or play up their femininity by taking advantage of ever-expanding opportunities to modify their bodies and lifestyles," while at the same time being "part of an inherently at-risk group that must engage in constant monitoring and management of risk." See Tasha

Dubriwny, *The Vulnerable Empowered Woman: Feminism, Postfeminism, and Women's Health* (New Brunswick: Rutgers University Press, 2012), 13.

18.   Hobart and Kneese, "Radical Care," 2, 10.

19.   Linci emphasized to me, "It was Women's Choice lay health care workers who supported the underground self-help groups and provided them with supplies. I take responsibility for that. It was not the medical director, doctors, or nurse practitioners. They ran a compliant health center. They knew nothing."

Chapter 1: Use All the Tools of Your Being

1.   Federation of Feminist Women's Health Centers, *A New View of a Woman's Body: A Fully Illustrated Guide* (Los Angeles: Feminist Health Press, [1981] 1991), 21–22.

2.   Murphy, *Seizing the Means*, 69.

3.   FFWHCs, *New View*, 21.

4.   Murphy, *Seizing the Means*, 28–29, 61–62, 71–72.

5.   Hannah Dudley-Shotwell acknowledges as much in *Revolutionizing Women's Healthcare: The Feminist Self-Help Movement in America* (New Brunswick: Rutgers University Press, 2020), 105.

6.   FFWHCs, *New View*, 123.

7.   Rebecca Chalker and Carol Downer, *A Woman's Book of Choices: Abortion, Menstrual Extraction, RU-486* (New York: Four Walls Eight Windows, 1992), 114.

8.   See Ziegler, *Dollars for Life*, 6.

9.   As Pat Maginnis emphasized, the Therapeutic Abortion Act created obstacles by setting up hospital committees made up of multiple physicians who were tasked with determining whether a woman was eligible for a therapeutic abortion. Pat Maginnis, "Elective Abortion—A Woman's Right," c. 1966–1967, MC 289, box 1, folder 62, RSHA, Schlesinger.

10.   West Coast Sisters, "Self-Help Clinic," 1971, SSC-MS-00394, box 5A, Topical Collection on Women's Health (hereafter TCWH), Sophia Smith Collection, Smith College Special Collections, Northampton, MA (hereafter SSC).

Lorraine and other self-helpers' call for the repeal of all abortion laws dovetailed with that of Pat Maginnis, Rowena Gurner, and Lana Phelan's at that point the well-established Society for

Humane Abortion. See Baehr, "The Army of Three: Making Abortion Public," *Abortion without Apology*, 7-20.

11.   Chalker and Downer, *Woman's Book of Choices*, 114; Brown, "Blood Rumors," 155.

12.   Murphy, *Seizing the Means*, 155-56; Elaine Woo, "Creator of Device for Safer Abortions," *Los Angeles Times*, May 18, 2008, https://www.latimes.com/archives/la-xpm-2008-may-18-me-karman18-story.html; *People v. Karman*, 5583, California Court of Appeal, Second Dist., Div. Three (November 13, 1956).

13.   Dudley-Shotwell, *Revolutionizing Women's Healthcare*, 14-15.

14.   Chalker and Downer, *Woman's Book of Choices*, 115.

15.   Lorraine Rothman, "Menstrual Extraction," *Quest* IV, no. 3 (Summer 1978), reprinted in *Women's Health Movement Papers* (May 1981): 11, Archives of Sexuality and Gender (hereafter ASG), San Francisco Public Library, San Francisco, CA (hereafter SFPL).

16.   Baehr, "Army of Three," *Abortion without Apology*, 7-20.

17.   Chalker and Downer, *Woman's Book of Choices*, 114.

18.   My telling of the first self-help meeting is largely based on Carol's account to me.

19.   Murphy, *Seizing the Means*, 46; Chalker and Downer, *Woman's Book of Choices*, 114-15; Brown, "Blood Rumors," 15.

20.   Dudley-Shotwell, *Revolutionizing Women's Health Care*, 17.

21.   Murphy, *Seizing the Means*, 47.

22.   Chalker and Downer, *Woman's Book of Choices*, 115-16.

23.   Chalker and Downer, *Woman's Book of Choices*, 115-16. The following steps are based on Lorraine Rothman, "How to Put a Del-Em Menstrual Extraction Kit Together," n.d., RL.00427, box 62, folder 1, Feminist Women's Health Center Records (hereafter FWHCR), David M. Rubenstein Rare Book and Manuscript Library, Duke University, Durham, NC (hereafter Rubenstein). I first encountered this document in *Izabel's personal collection.

24.   Suzann Gage, *When Birth Control Fails: How to Abort Ourselves Safely* (Hollywood: Speculum Press, 1979), 17-19.

25.   Chalker and Downer, *Woman's Book of Choices*, 116.

26.   Dudley-Shotwell, *Revolutionizing Women's Health Care*, 20.

27.   View the patent at https://image-ppubs.uspto.gov/dirsearch-public/print/downloadPdf/3828781.

28.   West Coast Sisters, "Self-Help Clinic Part II," 1971, SSC-MS-00394, box 5A, TCWH, SSC.

29.   Feminist Women's Health Centers, "The Four Levels of Self-

Help Clinic," n.d., H MS c261, box 67, "Menstruation: Menstrual Extraction" folder, Boston Women's Health Book Collective Subject Files (hereafter BWHBCSF), Harvard Medical Library, Francis A. Countway Library of Medicine, Boston, MA (hereafter HML).

30. FFWHCs, *New View*, 18; Chalker and Downer, *Woman's Book of Choices*, 118.

31. FFWHCs, *New View*, 18.

32. Feminist Women's Health Centers self-help slideshow, n.d., Linci Comy personal collection.

33. West Coast Sisters, "Self-Help Clinic Part II."

34. Chalker and Downer, *Woman's Book of Choices*, 117.

35. West Coast Sisters, "Self-Help Clinic Part II."

36. Rothman, "Menstrual Extraction."

37. FFWHCs, *New View*, 121.

38. West Coast Sisters, "Self-Help Clinic Part II."

39. FFWHCs, *New View*, 121.

40. Rothman, "Menstrual Extraction."

41. Rothman, "Menstrual Extraction"; FFWHCs, *New View*, 127.

42. West Coast Sisters, "Self-Help Clinic Part II."

43. Debi Law presentation, *Proceedings of the Menstrual Extraction Conference* (San Francisco: Oakland Feminist Women's Health Center, 1974), 34, *Max's personal collection.

44. Murphy, *Seizing the Means*, 160.

45. On May 2, 2022, *Politico* published a leaked draft of the *Dobbs v. Jackson Women's Health Organization* Supreme Court opinion, which stated that "*Roe* and *Casey* must be overruled." Such a leak was unprecedented in Supreme Court history. The leak triggered outrage and protests around the country. Josh Gerstein and Alexander Ward, "Supreme Court Has Voted to Overturn Abortion Rights, Draft Opinion Shows," *Politico*, May 2, 2022, https://www.politico .com/news/2022/05/02/supreme-court-abortion-draft-opinion -00029473.

46. Ann Hibner Koblitz, *Sex and Herbs and Birth Control: Women and Fertility Regulation through the Ages* (Seattle: Kovalevskaia Fund, 2014), 93–94.

47. Koblitz, *Sex and Herbs and Birth Control*, 94–96.

48. Reagan, *When Abortion Was a Crime*, 8–10.

49. Brown, "Blood Rumors," 33, 60. See also Judy Grahn's own *Blood, Bread, and Roses: How Menstruation Created the World* (Boston: Beacon Press, 1993).

50. A number of self-helpers I interviewed for this book cited Barbara Ehrenreich and Deirdre English's *Witches, Midwives, and Nurses: A History of Women Healers* (Old Westbury, NY: Feminist Press, 1973) as an influential text for them. Carol Downer blurbed the book, writing that it "provides a historical background and justification for the self-help movement."

51. Chalker and Downer, *Woman's Book of Choices*, 117–18.

52. Carol Downer and Lorraine Rothman, National Planning Meeting letters, September 3 and 12, 1972, and Feminist Women's Health Centers, "You Are Invited: National Planning Meeting" flyer, 1972, SSC-MS-00394, box 1, TCWH, SSC.

53. For example, the organization Zero Population Growth advocated for the repeal of California's abortion law to help deal with the "population problem." "Zero Population Growth/San Francisco Chapter" letter, 1970, MC 289, box 1, folder 11, RSHA, Schlesinger.

54. Ziegler, *Dollars for Life*, 7–8.
    The Society for Humane Abortion was pro-population control. They reprinted articles such as Princeton University research demographer Irene Taeuber's "Population: From Crisis to Resolution," Senate Government Operations Subcommittee on Foreign Aid Expenditures Hearing, September 22, 1965, MC 289, box 3, folder 56, RSHA, Schlesinger.

55. John Milton, "Resources in America: The Coming Crisis," *Population Reference Bureau (PRB) Newsletter*, no. 23 (May 1968), MC 289, box 1, folder 13, RSHA, Schlesinger.

56. For more about the connections between the eugenics and birth control movements, see Matthew Connelly, *Fatal Misconception: The Struggle to Control World Population* (Cambridge: Belknap Press of Harvard University Press, 2008) and Bonnie Mass, "From Malthus to Sanger: A Social Context for Birth Control," in *Population Target: The Political Economy of Population Control in Latin America* (Toronto: Latin American Working Group, 1976), 15–34.
    Loretta Ross points out that the early birth control movement promoted reproductive rights for all women. But as the movement increasingly relied on the support of the medical institution, it turned to the scientific-seeming language of eugenics to win over doctors. See Ross, "African American Women and Abortion," in *Abortion Wars*, 171.

57. Ross and Solinger, *Reproductive Justice*, 18–24.

58. Mary Ziegler notes that many population controllers who supported abortion rights were much younger than those who were or had been involved in the eugenics movement. Ziegler, *Abortion and the Law*, 36.

59. Connelly, "Populations Out of Control," in *Fatal Misconception*, 18–45.

60. Connelly, *Fatal Misconception*, 25.

61. Mass, *Population Target*, 19; Rebecca Kluchin, *Fit to Be Tied: Sterilization and Reproductive Rights in America 1950–1980* (New Brunswick: Rutgers University Press, 2009), 13.

62. Kluchin, *Fit to Be Tied*, 1–2, 15–17; Ross and Solinger, *Reproductive Justice*, 34–35.

63. Mass, *Population Target*, 36. Also see Matthew Connelly, "How Did the 'Population Control' Movement Go So Terribly Wrong?," *Wilson Quarterly*, Summer 2008, https://www.wilsonquarterly.com/quarterly/summer-2008-saving-the-world/how-did-population-control-movement-go-so-terribly-wrong.

64. The Population Council's funders included the Ford and Rockefeller Foundations and Mellon family. Mass, *Population Target*, 36–37.

65. Mass, *Population Target*, 45–56.

66. Murphy, *Economization of Life*, 62–64.

67. Murphy, *Economization of Life*, 84–85, 78–79.

68. Murphy, *Seizing the Means*, 168–69.

69. Murphy, *Seizing the Means*, 150–51.

70. Chalker and Downer, *Woman's Book of Choices*, 124.

71. Murphy, *Seizing the Means*, 159.

72. Jane Brody, "Physicians throughout the World Are Studying New, Simple Technique for Terminating Pregnancies," *New York Times*, December 20, 1973, https://www.nytimes.com/1973/12/20/archives/physicians-throughout-the-world-are-studying-new-simple-technique.html.

73. Laura Brown, "The Feminist Women's Health Center at Population Planners' Menstrual Regulation Conference," *Feminist Women's Health Center Report* (1974): 6, ASG, SFPL.

74. Murphy, *Seizing the Means*, 156.
   Technology for manual-suction abortions existed in the 1950s in China, too. Amid famine, China sponsored birth control research. Gynecologists in Shanghai developed abortion methods that could be brought to rural places, including a "negative pressure bottle." Illustrations from a Chinese nursing journal made their

way to the United States, and the East Coast Redstockings circulated them in the late 1960s. Murphy, *Seizing the Means,* 155.

75. Murphy, *Seizing the Means,* 163, 168.

76. Murphy, *Seizing the Means,* 172; "global woman power" is from Shelley Farber in November 1974 at the First National Women Controlled Women's Health Clinic Conference, Ames, Iowa.

77. LAFWHC letter, September 17, 1973, MC 512, box 15, folder 3, Records of the Women's Community Health Center (hereafter RWCHC), Schlesinger.

78. Debra Law, "Self Help Clinic Goes to Europe," *Feminist Women's Health Center Report* (1974): 2, ASG, SFPL.

79. Linda Curtis, "Population Control = Control of Women: Japanese Eugenic Protection Law," *Feminist Women's Health Center Report* (1975): 2–3, ASG, SFPL.

80. Judy Rutherford, "I.W.Y. and Imperialism," *Feminist Women's Health Center Report* (1975): 6.

81. Carol Downer, "The Master's Plan," MC 512, box 14, folder 2, RWCHC, Schlesinger. The table cites a memo by Frederick Jaffe, "Activities Relevant to the Study of Population Policy for the U.S.," as its source. Jaffe was a vice president of Planned Parenthood and the founder of the Guttmacher Institute.

82. Downer, "The Master's Plan."

83. Amid recent attempts by the Christian Right to challenge the FDA's approval of the abortion pill mifepristone (see chapter nine for more on the history of medication abortion), some US health workers and activists, such as Joan Fleischman and the MYA Network, argue that primary-care clinicians should be trained in how to perform early abortions using MVA. See Poppy Noor, "'A Gamechanger': This Simple Device Could Help Fight the War on Abortion Rights in the US," *Guardian,* April 18, 2023, https://www.theguardian.com/world/2023/apr/18/abortion-reproductive-rights-manual-uterine-aspiration. See also "Steps for Performing Manual Vacuum Aspiration (MVA)," *Ipas.org,* 2021, https://www.ipas.org/wp-content/uploads/2020/06/PERFMVA-E19.pdf.

84. FFWHCs, *New View,* 18.

85. Carol Downer letter, November 24, 1972, Coll2009-004, "Feminist Women's Health Center" folder, ONE Subject Files Lesbian Legacy Collection (hereafter LLC), ONE Archives, USC Libraries, University of Southern California, Los Angeles, CA (hereafter ONE Archives).

86. Stephanie Caruana, "Great Yogurt Conspiracy," *off our backs*, January 1973, ASG, SFPL.

87. FFWHCs, *New View*, 18.

88. Society for Humane Abortion, "Law, Police and Patricia Maginnis," *Newsletter* 3, no. 1 (January/February 1967), MC 289, box 1, folder 4, RSHA, Schlesinger.

89. Baehr, *Abortion without Apology*, 7; Ziegler, *Dollars for Life*, 7.

90. Baehr, *Abortion without Apology*, 7–8.

91. "Society for Humane Abortion/Association to Repeal Abortion Laws Inventory," 1979, MC 289, box 1, RSHA, Schlesinger.

92. "Citizens Committee for Humane Abortion Laws Resolution," December 1964, MC 289, box 1, folder 1, RSHA, Schlesinger.

93. Dave Swanson, "Speaker Raps Abortions Laws," *Golden Gater*, Summer 1964, MC 289, box 3, folder 59, RSHA, Schlesinger.

94. "Chronological Events of Citizens Committee for Humane Abortion Laws," n.d., MC 289, box 1, folder 1, RSHA, Schlesinger.

95. Baehr, *Abortion without Apology*, 8–10.

96. Pat Maginnis, "Elective Abortion—A Woman's Right," c. 1966–1967, MC 289, box 1, folder 62, RSHA, Schlesinger.

97. Association to Repeal Abortion Laws, "What's Wrong with SB 544?," June 26, 1970, MC 289, box 1, folder 62, RSHA, Schlesinger.

98. Baehr, *Abortion without Apology*, 15.

99. ARAL, "Specialist Kit," MC 289, box 4, folder 70, RSHA, Schlesinger.

100. ARAL, "Specialist Kit."

101. Rowena Gurner, letter to specialist no. 53, October 31, 1967, MC 289, box 5, folder 84, RSHA, Schlesinger.

102. Rowena Gurner, letter to specialist no. 67, April 18, 1968, MC 289, box 5, folder 84, RSHA, Schlesinger.

103. "Society for Humane Abortion/Association to Repeal Abortion Laws Inventory."

104. Baehr, *Abortion without Apology*, 15–16.

105. "A Self Induced Abortion—The Digital Method" handout, c. 1967–1968, MC 289, box 4, folder 65, RSHA, Schlesinger.

106. Society for Humane Abortion, "Law, Police and Patricia Maginnis," *Newsletter* 3, no. 1 (January/February 1967), MC 289, box 1, folder 4, RSHA, Schlesinger.

107. Baehr, *Abortion without Apology*, 17; Keith Walker, "Abortion Backer Arrested," *Redwood City Tribune*, February 21, 1967, MC 935, box 1,

folder 7, Additional Records of the Society for Humane Abortion (hereafter ARSHA), Schlesinger.

108. Baehr, *Abortion without Apology*, 17.

109. Pat Maginnis and Lana Clarke Phelan, "The Abortion Handbook for Responsible Women" (draft), MC 935, box 1, folder 11, ARSHA, Schlesinger.

110. Laura Brown, "Feminist Health Centers Struggle for Survival," *Sojourner* 16, no. 7 (March 1991): 17, ASG, SFPL.

111. Joan McKinney, "Self-Help Clinics: A New Concept," *Oakland Tribune*, April 7, 1973, NA, OPL; Joan McKinney "New Clinic Offers a Choice to Women," *Oakland Tribune*, May 3, 1973, NA, OPL.

112. "Feminist Women's Health Centers" pamphlet, 1973, MC 512, box 14, folder 2, RWCHC, Schlesinger.

113. Chalker and Downer, *Woman's Book of Choices*, 119.

114. "Feminist Women's Health Centers" pamphlet.

115. "Feminist Women's Health Centers" pamphlet.

Chapter 2: Allow Everyone to Become a Teacher

1. Brown, "Blood Rumors," 15; and Judy Grahn, *A Simple Revolution* (San Francisco: Aunt Lute Books, 2012), 158.

2. Penny Righthand, "Feminist Clinic: Health Care by Women," *Montclarion*, July 4, 1979, Newspaper Archive (hereafter NA), Oakland Public Library (hereafter OPL).

3. McKinney, "Self-Help Clinics."

4. Brown, "Blood Rumors," 13–16.

5. Grahn, *Simple Revolution*, 158.

6. Carol Downer presentation, *Proceedings of the Menstrual Extraction Conference*, 6–11, Carol Downer, "Women Professionals in the Feminist Health Movement," April 1974, MC 512, box 14, folder 10, RWCHC, Schlesinger.

7. FFWHCs, *New View*, 79, 123.

8. Grahn, *Simple Revolution*, 116.

9. Susan Stryker and Jim Van Buskirk, *Gay by the Bay: A History of Queer Culture in the San Francisco Bay Area* (San Francisco: Chronicle Books, 1996), 53.

10. Susan Stryker, "At the Crossroads of Turk and Taylor," *Places*, October 2021, https://placesjournal.org/article/transgender-resistance-and-prison-abolitionism-san-francisco-tenderloin. See also

Screaming Queens: The Riot at Compton's Cafeteria, directed by Susan Stryker and Victor Silverman (2005).

11. Grahn, *Simple Revolution*, 117, 123–25.

12. Stryker and Buskirk, *Gay by the Bay*, 57.

13. Grahn, *Simple Revolution*, 161–63.

14. Alondra Nelson, *Body and Soul: The Black Panther Party and the Fight against Medical Discrimination* (Minneapolis: University of Minnesota Press, 2011), xv.

15. A. Nelson, *Body and Soul*, 87–88.

16. Interview with Huey Newton, "In Defense of Self Defense," *Black Panther*, March 16, 1968, Black Panther Party Community News Service Collection (hereafter BPPCNS), Freedom Archives.

17. A. Nelson, *Body and Soul*, 77.

18. Huey Newton and Bobby Seale both had experience working for a War on Poverty Bay Area Community Action Program in summer 1966. Their critiques of the War on Poverty catalyzed their imagination of the Black Panther Party's "survival programs." See A. Nelson, *Body and Soul*, 55, 105.

19. "Black Genocide: Sickle Cell Anemia," *Black Panther*, April 10, 1971, BPPCNS, Freedom Archives.

20. Jennifer Nelson, *Women of Color and the Reproductive Rights Movement* (New York: New York University Press, 2003), 58.

21. Ross, "African American Women and Abortion," in *Abortion Wars*, 169.

22. J. Nelson, *Women of Color*, 64, 76.

23. Ross, "African American Women and Abortion," 168.

24. The case upheld a state's right to forcibly sterilize a person thought to be "unfit to have children" in the name of protecting the "health of the state." See *Buck v. Bell*, 274 U.S. 200 (1927).

25. Ross, "African American Women and Abortion," 170.

26. For an early and detailed discussion of the United States' population control and sterilization campaigns in Puerto Rico, see Mass, "Emigration and Sterilization in Puerto Rico," *Population Target*, 87–108.

27. Cecilia Fire Thunder, National Indigenous Women's Resource Center, et al., "*Dobbs vs. Jackson Women's Health Organization* Brief of Amici Curiae," Supreme Court Press, September 17, 2021, 4, 14–16, https://www.supremecourt.gov/DocketPDF/19/19-1392 /192846/20210917173106773_NIWRC%20Main%20EFILE%20 Sep%2017%2021.pdf; Ross and Solinger, *Reproductive Justice*, 50.

28. Johanna Schoen, *Choice and Coercion: Birth Control, Sterilization, and Abortion in Public Health and Welfare* (Chapel Hill: University of North Carolina Press, 2005), 82, 2–3.

29. Tony Cade, "The Pill: Genocide or Liberation," in *The Black Woman: An Anthology*, ed. Tony Cade Bambara (New York: Washington Square Press, [1970] 2005), 205–6.

30. Frances Beal, "Double Jeopardy: To Be Black and Female," in *The Black Woman*, 119; quoted in J. Nelson, *Women of Color*, 80.

31. "Sterilize Welfare Mothers?" *Black Panther*, May 1, 1971, reprinted from the *Guardian*, BPPCNS, Freedom Archives.

32. "Sterilization—Another Part of the Plan of Black Genocide," *Black Panther*, May 8, 1971, BPPCNS, Freedom Archives.

33. J. Nelson, *Women of Color*, 89.

34. J. Nelson, *Women of Color*, 108.

35. A. Nelson, *Body and Soul*, 89.

36. A. Nelson, *Body and Soul*, 79.

37. Carol Shull, "They're Reducing the Cost and the Trauma of Abortions," *Argus*, May 10, 1973, NA, OPL.

38. Joan McKinney, "New Clinic Offers a Choice to Women."

39. Shull, "They're Reducing the Cost and the Trauma."

40. McKinney, "New Clinic Offers a Choice to Women."

41. Debra Law, "For Immediate Release: Menstrual Extraction, the Five-Minute Period," April 18, 1974, Annah Anti-Palindrome personal collection.

42. Carol Downer presentation, "Proceedings of the Menstrual Extraction Conference," 6–7.

43. See Nancy Langston, *Toxic Bodies: Hormone Disruptors and the Legacy of DES* (New Haven: Yale University Press, 2010).

44. Downer, "Proceedings of the Menstrual Extraction Conference," 7–10.

45. Laura Brown presentation, "Proceedings of the Menstrual Extraction Conference," 14.

46. FFWHCs, *New View*, 157; "A History of Medical Device Regulation and Oversight in the United States," June 24, 2019, *US Food and Drug Administration*, https://www.fda.gov/medical-devices/overview-device-regulation/history-medical-device-regulation-oversight-united-states.

47. Brown, "Proceedings of the Menstrual Extraction Conference," 15.

48. "Proceedings of the Menstrual Extraction Conference," 22.

49. "Proceedings of the Menstrual Extraction Conference," 22–24.

50. "Proceedings of the Menstrual Extraction Conference," 34, 36.

51. Memo, "Phone Conversation—Laura in Oakland to Roberta at Central Office, LA," March 11, 1974, MC 512, box 15, folder 4, RWCHC, Schlesinger.

52. Shelley Farber, memo to Feminist Women's Health Centers, October 24, 1975, and Carol Downer, letter to Department of Investigation of the Bureau of Consumer Affairs, June 30, 1976, MC 512, box 15, folder 1, RWCHC, Schlesinger.

53. Carol Downer, letter to Department of Consumer Affairs, July 8, 1976, MC 512, box 15, folder 1, RWCHC, Schlesinger.

54. FFWHCs, *New View*, 19.

55. Kathy Stoddard letter on behalf of OFWHC/Women's Choice, September 11, 1974, MC 512, box 15, folder 4, RWCHC, Schlesinger.

56. Inez García fact sheet, August 7, 1974, MC 512, box 15, folder 4, RWCHC, Schlesinger. In 1977, Inez was acquitted after a retrial. See "Woman Is Acquitted of Killing, *New York Times*, March 5, 1977, https://www.nytimes.com/1977/03/05/archives/woman-is-acquitted-of-killing-testified-man-aided-in-rape.html.

Chapter 3: The Self-Destruct Mechanism Is the Self-Help Clinic

1. Laura Brown, *The Power of Valuenergy: A Theory of Feminist Economics* (Baltimore: Feminist Economic Network and Diana Press, 1976), 3-4, Barbara Hoke personal collection (hereafter BHPC).

2. Brown, *Valuenergy*, 5.

3. Brown, *Valuenergy*, 6.

4. Brown, *Valuenergy*, 9.

5. Brown, *Valuenergy*, 9.

6. Brown, *Valuenergy*, 3.

7. Brown, *Valuenergy*, 19.

8. Brown, *Valuenergy*, 36-37.

9. Brown, *Valuenergy*, 46.

10. For more on multiple simultaneous second-wave feminisms, which often developed out of experiences of race, see Benita Roth, *Separate Roads to Feminism: Black, Chicana, and White Feminist Movements in America's Second Wave* (Cambridge: Cambridge University Press, 2003).

11. Alice Echols, *Daring to Be Bad: Radical Feminism in America 1967–1975* (Minneapolis: University of Minnesota Press, 1989), 272.

12. FEN binder, BHPC; Grahn, *Simple Revolution*, 238. See also Julie Enszer, "The Whole Naked Truth of Our Lives: Lesbian-Feminist Print Culture from 1969 through 1989" (PhD diss., University of Maryland, 2013), 95–97, http://hdl.handle.net/1903/14038.

13. Joanne Parrent, *Sowing the Seeds of Feminist Economic Revolution* (Baltimore: Feminist Economic Network and Diana Press, 1976), 13, Coletta Reid personal collection.

14. Enszer, "The Whole Naked Truth," 95.

15. Parrent, *Sowing the Seeds*, 14, 8.

16. Enszer, "The Whole Naked Truth," 96.

17. FEN binder.

18. FEN binder; FEN materials, c. 1976–1977, MC 1120, box 34, identifier 427, Papers of Adrienne Rich, Schlesinger. Courtesy of the Adrienne Rich Literary Estate LLC.

19. Grahn, *Simple Revolution*, 239.

20. Chico FWHC, "Position Article on Oakland Feminist Women's Health Center/Cal-Fem Corp.," June 28, 1976, MC 512, box 14, folder 6, RWCHC, Schlesinger.

21. Celine, "fen, credit unions, & the capitali$t system," *off our backs* 6, no. 2 (September 1976): 4, ASG, SFPL.

22. Martha Shelley, "What Is Fen: I Do Not Support the Women of Fen!" n.d., Collection 2135, box 14, folder 12, Diana Press Records (hereafter DPR), University of California, Los Angeles Special Collections, Los Angeles, CA (hereafter UCLASC).

23. LAFWHC, "Why FEN Must Be Opposed and Response to Martha Shelley's Trashing of Fen," February 20, 1977, Collection 2135, box 14, folder 12, DPR, UCLASC.

    For more on "trashing," see Ruth Rosen, "The Politics of Paranoia," in *The World Split Open: How the Modern Women's Movement Changed America* (New York: Penguin Books, 2000), 227–60.

24. Jennifer Woodul, "Trashing Is Garbage: Olivia Records on the Martha Shelley FEN Document" and "What's This about Feminist Business?" n.d., Collection 2135, box 14, folder 12, DPR, UCLASC.

25. Enszer, "The Whole Naked Truth," 77.

26. Kathleen Barry, news release, September 22, 1976, Collection 2135, box 14, folder 12, DPR, UCLASC.

27. Grahn, *Simple Revolution*, 239.

28. Parrent, *Sowing the Seeds*, 17, 19.

29. Echols, *Daring to Be Bad*, 358 (note 139).
30. Echols, *Daring to Be Bad*, 279–80.
31. Grahn, *Simple Revolution*, 240–41.
32. (Presumably) Laura Brown, "Policy Meeting Notes," 1976, Collection 2135, box 15, folder 5, DPR, UCLASC.
33. "Administrative Staff Notes and Agendas," Collection 2135, box 15, folder 7, DPR, UCLASC.
34. Grahn, *Simple Revolution*, 247.
35. Grahn, *Simple Revolution*, 247.
36. Grahn, *Simple Revolution*, 251.
37. "Diana Press" direct mail piece, Collection 2135, box 13, folder 13, DPR, UCLASC.

Chapter 4: Why Would You Not Want to Know What's Up in There?

1. Soon after Rosie's death, Ellen Frankfort wrote a book about her story: *Rosie: The Investigation of a Wrongful Death* (New York: Dial Press, 1979). See also Marlene Fried, "Hyde Amendment: The Opening Wedge to Abolish Abortion," *New Politics*, summer 2007, https://newpol.org/issue_post/hyde-amendment-opening-wedge-abolish-abortion.
2. Ziegler, *Abortion and the Law*, 28–29.
3. Ross and Solinger, *Reproductive Justice*, 39–41. For an in-depth history of reproductive injustice and antiblackness in the United States, see Dorothy Roberts, *Killing the Black Body: Race, Reproduction, and the Meaning of Liberty* (New York: Vintage Books, [1997] 2017).
4. Ziegler, *Abortion and the Law*, 28–29, 41.
5. Cynthia Soohoo, "Hyde-Care for All: The Expansion of Abortion-Funding Restrictions under Health Care Reform," *CUNY Law Review* 15, issue 2 (Summer 2012): 401–2.
6. Ziegler, *Abortion and the Law*, 43, 53. For a detailed analysis of the Hyde Amendment, see Ziegler, "The Hyde Amendment and Its Aftermath," in *Abortion and the Law*, 27–57.
7. Sabrae Jenkins, "Abortion Rights, Poor Women, and Religious Diversity," in *From Abortion to Reproductive Freedom: Transforming a Movement*, ed. Marlene Gerber Fried (Boston: South End Press, 1990), 155.

8. Alyssa Engstrom, "The Hyde Amendment: Perpetuating Injustice and Discrimination after Thirty-Nine Years," *Southern California Interdisciplinary Law Journal* 25, no. 2 (Spring 2016): 454, https://gould.usc.edu/why/students/orgs/ilj/assets/docs/25-2-Engstrom.pdf.

9. Serena Gordon, "Abortion Safer for Women than Childbirth, Study Claims," *U.S. News and World Report*, January 23, 2012, https://health.usnews.com/health-news/family-health/womens-health/articles/2012/01/23/abortion-safer-for-women-than-childbirth-study-claims.

10. See Fried, "Hyde Amendment"; "Reproductive Coercion and Sterilization Abuse," *National Women's Health Network*, October 3, 2022, https://nwhn.org/reproductive-coercion-and-sterilization-abuse; and "Long-Acting Reversible Contraceptives," *National Women's Health Network*, August 24, 2022, https://nwhn.org/larcs.

11. See Shaye Beverly Arnold, "Reproductive Rights Denied: The Hyde Amendment and Access to Abortion for Native American Women Using Indian Health Service Facilities," *American Journal of Public Health* 104, no. 10 (October 2014): 1892–93.

12. "The Never-Ending Maze: Continued Failure to Protect Indigenous Women from Sexual Violence in the USA," *Amnesty International*, May 17, 2022, 7–11, https://www.amnesty.org/en/documents/amr51/5484/2022/en.

13. Arnold, "Reproductive Rights Denied," 1892.

14. "Byllye Avery Interviewed by Loretta J. Ross, July 21–22, 2005," transcript of recording, 10–11, SSC-MS-00535, box 6, Voices of Feminism Oral History Project, SSC, https://compass.fivecolleges.edu/object/smith:1342621.

15. "Avery Interviewed by Ross," 15.

16. Byllye Avery, "Breathing Life into Ourselves: The Evolution of the National Black Women's Health Project," in *The Black Women's Health Book: Speaking for Ourselves*, ed. Evelyn White (Seattle: Seal Press, 1990), 4–5; and "Empowerment through Wellness," *Yale Journal of Law and Feminism* 4, issue 1, article 14 (1991): 147, http://digitalcommons.law.yale.edu/yjlf/vol4/iss1/14.

17. "Avery Interviewed by Ross," 16–18.

18. "Avery Interviewed by Ross," 17.

19. Avery, "Breathing Life into Ourselves," 5–6.

20. "Avery Interviewed by Ross," 25.

21. Avery, "Breathing Life into Ourselves," 6–9.

22. Avery, "Empowerment Through Wellness," 150.

23. Byllye Avery, "Prospectus: Black Women's Health Initiative," 1980, H MS c261, "Black Women's Health Project" folder, BWHBCSF, HML.

24. "Avery Interviewed by Ross," 26–27.

25. June Jackson Christmas, "Black Women and Health Care in the 80s," keynote address, First National Conference on Black Women's Health Issues, Spelman College, Atlanta, printed in *Spelman Messenger* 100, no. 1 (1984): 8–9, Spelman College Archives.

26. Byllye Avery and Sybil Shainwald, letters to conference participants, First National Conference on Black Women's Health Issues Program, June 24–26, 1983, 1–2, SSC-MS-00487, box 3, Black Women's Health Imperative Records (hereafter BWHIR), SSC.

27. "Avery Interviewed by Ross," 30; Avery, "Breathing Life into Ourselves," 9.

28. Dudley-Shotwell, *Revolutionizing Women's Healthcare*, 86.

29. "Avery Interviewed by Ross," 30.

30. Dudley-Shotwell, *Revolutionizing Women's Healthcare*, 90; "Avery Interviewed by Ross," 35–36.

31. "Avery Interviewed by Ross," 36.

32. *National Black Women's Health Project Self-Help Developer's Manual, Revised, 1990*, Pr-15, carton 4, Boston Women's Health Book Collective Printed Material Collection (hereafter PMC), Schlesinger.

33. "The Self-Help Process Is Not Therapy," in *National Black Women's Health Project Self-Help Developer's Manual*, 15.

34. Linda Villarosa, *Body and Soul: The Black Women's Guide to Physical Health and Emotional Well-Being* (New York: HarperPerennial, 1994), xiv.

35. "Unlearning Oppression through Self-Help," *The National Black Women's Health Project Self-Help Developer's Manual*, 15.

36. Dudley-Shotwell, *Revolutionizing Women's Healthcare*, 90–91.

37. "Vision Statement," *National Black Women's Health Project Self-Help Developer's Manual*.

38. Ross and Solinger, *Reproductive Justice*, 58–73.

39. Grahn, *Simple Revolution*, 251–52.

40. Grahn, *Simple Revolution*, 185; Pat Parker, "For Donna," in *The Complete Works of Pat Parker*, ed. Julie Enszer (Dover, FL: Sinister Wisdom, 2016), 40–41.

41. Pat Parker, "Womanslaughter," in *Complete Works*, 155; Papers of Pat

Parker Finding Aid, MC 861, Papers of Pat Parker (hereafter PPP), Schlesinger, https://hollisarchives.lib.harvard.edu/repositories/8/resources/6893.

42. Parker, "Womanslaughter," 156.

43. Pat Parker, journal entry, MC 861, box 8, folder 11, PPP, Schlesinger.

44. For more on Black women's critiques of Black Power, see Roth, *Separate Roads to Feminism*, 82–85.

45. Pat Parker, "Author's Questionnaire [Pit Stop]," MC 861, box 11, folder 16, PPP, Schlesinger.

46. Pat Parker, "Have you ever tried to hide," in *Complete Works*, 55.

47. Pat Parker, "Revolution: It's Not Neat or Pretty or Quick," in *This Bridge Called My Back: Writings by Radical Women of Color*, 4th ed., ed. Cherríe Moraga and Gloria Anzaldúa (Albany: SUNY Press, [1981] 2015), 241.

48. Combahee River Collective, "A Black Feminist Statement," in *This Bridge Called My Back*, 210–18. Also see Barbara Smith, introduction to *Home Girls: A Black Feminist Anthology*, ed. Barbara Smith (New Brunswick: Rutgers University Press, [1983] 2000), xl; Bernice Johnson Reagon, "Coalition Politics: Turning the Century," in *Home Girls*, 343–55; Collins, *Black Feminist Thought*, 42; and also Keeanga-Yamahtta Taylor's interview with Barbara Smith in *How We Get Free: Black Feminism and the Combahee River Collective*, ed. Keeanga-Yamahtta Taylor (Chicago: Haymarket Books, 2017), 29–69.

49. "The First Black Lesbian Conference, October 17–19, 1980" program, MC 861, box 13, folder 22, PPP, Schlesinger.

50. Health center memo, 1985, audiocassette, T-523, PPP, Schlesinger.

51. Parker, "Revolution," 242.

52. This was the argument of the Combahee River Collective, too: "If Black women were free, it would mean that everyone else would have to be free since our freedom would necessitate the destruction of all the systems of oppression." See "A Black Feminist Statement," 215.

53. "Medical, 1987," MC 861, box 1, folder 12, PPP, Schlesinger.

54. Laura Fraser, "Abortion Rights: A Time for Fear," *San Francisco Bay Guardian*, March 29, 1989, NA, OPL.

55. Wendy Simonds analyzes abortion clinic workers' attitudes toward and narratives about their work in a feminist women's health center. See "Feminist Abortion Practice: Getting Graphic," in *Abortion at*

Work: Ideology and Practice in a Feminist Clinic (New Brunswick: Rutgers University Press, 1996), 60–102.

56.   Pat Parker, "Movement in Black," in *Complete Works*, 99.

57.   Collins, *Black Feminist Thought*, 47.

58.   See Angela Davis, "The Approaching Obsolescence of Housework: A Working-Class Perspective," in *Women, Race and Class* (New York: Vintage Books, [1981] 1983), 222–44.

59.   Davis, *Women, Race and Class*, 231.

60.   Collins, *Black Feminist Thought*, 47.

61.   Pat Parker, "maybe i should have been a teacher," in *Complete Works*, 211–12.

62.   "Audre Lorde, Pat Parker 2/7/86 Reading," recorded 1986, San Francisco Poetry Center and American Poetry Archives, San Francisco Public Library, video cassette; and also Poetry Center Digital Archive, https://diva.sfsu.edu/collections/poetrycenter/bundles /238556.

63.   Parker, "maybe i should have been a teacher," 213.

64.   Collins, *Black Feminist Thought*, 46.

65.   "Mode of reproduction" is Martha Gimenez's phrase. See Martha Gimenez, *Marx, Women, and Capitalist Social Reproduction* (Leiden, Netherlands: Brill, 2019). "Means of reproduction" is Shulamith Firestone's, quoted in Murphy, *Seizing the Means*, 5.

66.   Pat Parker, "'Poem: I wish I could be the lover you want,' 1982," MC 861, box 9, folder 44, PPP, Schlesinger.

67.   Pat Parker, "love isn't," in *Complete Works*, 190–91.

68.   Brown, acknowledgements in "Blood Rumors," v.

69.   Parker, "Movement in Black," 95.

70.   Pat Parker, "Movement in Black" drafts, MC 861, box 9, folder 58, PPP, Schlesinger.

Chapter 5: Become a Community Scientist

1.   Sarah Schulman, *Let the Record Show: A Political History of ACT UP New York, 1987–1993* (New York: Farrar, Straus and Giroux, 2021), 19.

2.   Deborah Gould, *Moving Politics: Emotion and ACT UP's Fight against AIDS* (Chicago: University of Chicago Press, 2009), 3.

3.   FFWHCs, *New View*, 33, 47.

4.   FFWHCs, *New View*, 33, 34.

5.   Murphy, *Seizing the Means*, 72, 74.

6. FFWHCs, *New View*, 39–40, 45, 47. The authors' suggestion that the perineum is part of the clitoris is not conventionally accepted even today. Yet conventional medical understandings of the clitoris continue to be superficial, and people continue to sustain debilitating injuries during routine procedures. See Rachel Gross, "Half the World Has a Clitoris. Why Don't Doctors Study It?," *New York Times*, October 17, 2022, https://www.nytimes.com/2022/10/17/health/clitoris-sex-doctors-surgery.html.

7. Gross, "Half the World Has a Clitoris."

8. "The Feminist Women's Health Center Presents: The Participatory Clinic" brochure, n.d., Pr-11, box 4, folder 2, Feminist Ephemera Collection, Schlesinger.

9. Dudley-Shotwell, *Revolutionizing Women's Healthcare*, 40.

10. "Participatory Clinic" brochure.

11. Dudley-Shotwell, *Revolutionizing Women's Healthcare*, 43.

12. "Participatory Clinic" brochure.

13. Dudley-Shotwell, *Revolutionizing Women's Health Care*, 74–77.

14. Alexis Madrigal, "The Surprising Birthplace of the First Sperm Bank," *Atlantic*, April 28, 2014, https://www.theatlantic.com/technology/archive/2014/04/how-the-first-sperm-bank-began/361288; W. Ombelet and J. Van Robays, "Artificial Insemination History: Hurdles and Milestones," *Facts Views Vis Obgyn* 7, no. 2 (2015): 137–43, https://www.ncbi.nlm.nih.gov/pmc/articles/PMC4498171.

15. Madrigal, "The Surprising Birthplace of the First Sperm Bank"; David Pegg, "Principles of Cryopreservation," *Methods in Molecular Biology* 368 (2007): 39–57.

16. Cynthia Daniels and Janet Golden, "Procreative Compounds: Popular Eugenics, Artificial Insemination and the Rise of the American Sperm Banking Industry," *Journal of Social History* (Fall 2004): 13.

17. Kara Swanson, "The Birth of the Sperm Bank," *Annals of Iowa* 71, no. 3 (Summer 2012): 241, 250, 253, https://doi.org/10.17077/0003-4827.1645.

18. Swanson, "The Birth of the Sperm Bank," 253, 256–57.

19. "Baby from Frozen Sperm Expected in Three Months," *New York Times*, December 3, 1953, https://www.nytimes.com/1953/12/01/archives/baby-from-frozen-sperm-expected-in-three-months.html.

20. Elizabeth Mehren, "A Controversial Sperm Bank Where the Women Are in Charge," *Los Angeles Times*, February 6, 1983.

21. Linda Yglesias, "An Open-Door Philosophy," *San Francisco Examiner*, February 7, 1984, Newspapers.com, OPL.

22. Rebecca Salner, "Oakland Feminists Launch Bay Area's 1st Sperm Bank," *San Francisco Examiner*, October 5, 1982, Newspapers.com, OPL.

23. Yglesias, "An Open-Door Philosophy."

24. Daniels and Golden, "Procreative Compounds."

25. Salner, "Oakland Feminists Launch Bay Area's 1st Sperm Bank."

26. Iris Krasnow, "Motherhood by Choice—Without Husbands," *Napa Valley Register*, August 23, 1985, Newspapers.com, OPL. The phrase "compulsory heterosexuality" is Adrienne Rich's. See her "Compulsory Heterosexuality and Lesbian Existence," in *Blood, Bread, and Poetry: Selected Prose 1979–1985* (New York: W. W. Norton & Company, 1986), 23–75.

27. Yglesias, "An Open-Door Philosophy." Notably, in July 1995, Idant Laboratories was ordered to close for repeatedly violating New York State Health Department laws and regulations. See Esther Fein, "Sperm Bank Is Ordered Closed and Denied a License Hearing," *New York Times*, July 19, 1995, https://www.nytimes.com/1995/07/19/nyregion/sperm-bank-is-ordered-closed-and-denied-a-license-hearing.html.

28. Yglesias, "An Open-Door Philosophy."

29. Daniels and Golden, "Procreative Compounds," 6.

30. Daniels and Golden, "Procreative Compounds," 9.

31. Daniels and Golden, "Procreative Compounds," 12.

32. Swanson, "The Birth of the Sperm Bank," 255.

33. Daniels and Golden, "Procreative Compounds," 15.

34. David Plotz, "The 'Genius Babies,' and How They Grew," *Slate*, February 8, 2001, https://slate.com/human-interest/2001/02/the-genius-babies-and-how-they-grew.html.

35. By 1987, the OFWHC sperm bank had begun quarantining sperm and testing for HIV after six months. Dell Richards, "Artificial Insemination and AIDS—How Safe Is It?" *Mom Guess What*, May 1987, AGS, SFPL.

36. Here I borrow Joanna Scheib's language. See https://psychology.ucdavis.edu/people/szschei.

37. For more about Scheib's research, visit https://scheib.faculty.ucdavis.edu/publications.

38. Lawrence Altman, "Clue Found on Homosexuals' Precancer Syndrome," *New York Times*, June 18, 1982, https://www.nytimes.com/

1982/06/18/us/clue-found-on-homosexuals-precancer-syndrome
.html.

39. Gould, *Moving Politics*, 50.

40. Gould, *Moving Politics*, 4, 50–51, 55–56; Steven Epstein, *Impure Science: AIDS, Activism, and the Politics of Knowledge* (Berkeley: University of California Press, 1996), 12.

41. Schulman, *Let the Record Show*, 140.

42. Marion Banzhaf, Tracy Morgan, and Karen Ramspacher, "Reproductive Rights and AIDS: The Connections," in *Women, AIDS and Activism*, ed. ACT UP/NY Women & AIDS Book Group (Boston: South End Press, 1990), 201.

43. ACT UP/NY Women & AIDS Book Group, *Women, AIDS and Activism* (Boston: South End Press, 1990), 2–3.

44. Schulman, *Let the Record Show*, 21, 139–42.

45. Banzhaf, Morgan, and Ramspacher, "Reproductive Rights and AIDS," 201.

46. Schulman, *Let the Record Show*, 251–54, 263, 268.

47. Epstein, *Impure Science*, 8–10.

48. For more about the concept and field of participatory medicine, see the *Journal of Participatory Medicine* at https://jopm.jmir.org.

49. Audre Lorde, *The Cancer Journals* (San Francisco: Aunt Lute Books, 1997), 15.

In the early 1990s, researchers reported a 30 percent increase in breast cancer incidence in American women over the 1980s and evidence of a global rise in the disease as well. See L. A. B. Ries et al., *SEER Cancer Statistics Review, 1973–1991* (Bethesda, MD: National Cancer Institute, 1994); A. N. Gjorgov, "Emerging Worldwide Trends of Breast Cancer Incidence in the 1970s and 1980s," *European Journal of Cancer Prevention* 2 (1993), 423–40.

Activists interpreted HIV/AIDS and breast cancer as structural health injustices and organized around both issues. See Ulrike Boehmer, *The Personal and the Political: Women's Activism in Response to the Breast Cancer and AIDS Epidemics* (New York: SUNY Press, 2000). The Bay Area, where the Women's Cancer Resource Center was founded in Berkeley in 1986, was a center for both grassroots HIV/AIDS and breast cancer activism. See Mairead Sullivan, "A Crisis Emerges: Lesbian Breast Cancer in the Wake of HIV/AIDS," in "Strange Matter: Lesbian Death in Feminist and Queer Politics" (PhD diss., Emory University, 2016), 22–54. Pat Parker herself contributed to an anthology whose political critique reflected that of her activist community: Victoria Brownworth, ed., *Coming Out of Cancer: Writings from the Lesbian Cancer Epidemic* (Seattle: Seal Press, 2000).

50. Reagan didn't request funding for HIV/AIDS research until two years into the crisis. See Gould, *Moving Politics*, 49–50.

51. National Institute of Environmental Health Sciences, "Breast Cancer," https://www.niehs.nih.gov/health/topics/conditions/breast-cancer/index.cfm. Also see Philip Shabecoff, "Reagan and Environment: To Many, a Stalemate," *New York Times*, January 2, 1989, https://www.nytimes.com/1989/01/02/us/reagan-and-environment-to-many-a-stalemate.html.

52. The federal Medical Waste Tracking Act, which was passed 1988, regulated the management of medical waste in some states until 1991, at which point regulation became the responsibility of all individual states. Environmental Protection Agency, "Medical Waste," https://www.epa.gov/rcra/medical-waste.

53. "STDs and HIV—CDC Basic Fact Sheet," Centers for Disease Control and Prevention, https://www.cdc.gov/std/hiv/stdfact-std-hiv.htm.

Chapter 6: Your First Line of Defense Is Self-Defense

1. "Oakland Feminist Women's Health Center" and "Abortion: It's Your Choice" brochures, c. 1983, MC 831, box 409, folder 6, Papers of Bill Baird (hereafter PBB), Schlesinger.

2. Lauren Rankin, *Bodies on the Line: At the Front Lines of the Fight to Protect Abortion in America* (Berkeley: Counterpoint, 2022), 15.

3. Sarah Churchwell, "Body Politics: The Secret History of the US Anti-abortion Movement," *Guardian*, July 23, 2022, https://www.theguardian.com/books/2022/jul/23/body-politics; Carol Mason, *Killing for Life: The Apocalyptic Narrative of Pro-Life Politics* (Ithaca: Cornell University Press, 2002), 36.

4. Kristin Luker, *Abortion and the Politics of Motherhood* (Berkeley: University of California Press, 1984), 127–33; Alesha Doan, *Opposition and Intimidation: The Abortion Wars and Strategies of Political Harassment* (Ann Arbor: University of Michigan Press, 2007), 71–72.

5. Doan, *Opposition and Intimidation*, 73–74.

6. Ziegler, *Abortion and the Law*, 34–35, 42, 49–51; Laura Briggs, *How All Politics Became Reproductive Politics: From Welfare Reform*

to Foreclosure to Trump (Oakland: University of California Press, 2017), 11-12.

The Right's anti-welfare campaign also became a justification for homophobia. Throughout the 1980s the Right resisted funding HIV/AIDS research and care and cultivated massive stigma and homophobia around the disease as it decimated gay men's communities. See David France, *How to Survive a Plague: The Inside Story of How Citizens and Science Tamed AIDS* (New York: Knopf, 2016).

7.   Ziegler, *Abortion and the Law*, 41.

8.   Briggs, *How All Politics Became Reproductive Politics*, 13.

9.   Ziegler, *Abortion and the Law*, 49.

10. See Briggs, introduction to *How All Politics Became Reproductive Politics*, 1-18, for a detailed discussion of the relationship between the Right's anti-welfare ideology and its anti-reproductive justice stance.

11. Rankin, *Bodies on the Line*, 18; National Organization for Women, "NOW v. Scheidler Timeline: The Complete Story," 2014, https://now.org/wp-content/uploads/2014/02/NOW-v-Scheidler-Timeline.pdf.

12. Barbara Raboy and Julie Brutocao, "Women's Choice Clinic," *Women's Voices*, August 1982, ASG, SFPL.

All around the country, clinic escorts have helped make clinic access possible since the beginning of legal abortion in the United States. As journalist and activist Lauren Rankin points out, "A significant reason why legal abortion has largely remained accessible, from the years of bombings to the era of bans, is because of clinic escorts." Rankin, *Bodies on the Line*, 9.

13. Rankin, *Bodies on the Line*, 18.

14. Jeannie Hill, *Sidewalk Counseling Workbook* (Denver: Sidewalk Counselors for Life, Inc., 1986), 2, 5, 16 (my emphasis), Kass McMahon personal collection (hereafter KMPC).

15. Robert Hippler, "L.A. Health Clinic Destroyed in Fire," *Guardian*, April 24, 1985, Coll2009-004, "Feminist Women's Health Center (Los Angeles)" folder, LLC, ONE Archives.

16. Carol McGraw, "Postscript," *Los Angeles Times*, July 14, 1989, Coll2009-004, "Feminist Women's Health Center (Los Angeles)" folder, LLC, ONE Archives.

17. Rankin, *Bodies on the Line*, 21-22.

18. Hippler, "L.A. Health Clinic Destroyed in Fire."

19. Bill Baird and Carol Downer, Pro Choice Defense Fund letter, May 16, 1985, MC 831, box 409, folder 10, PBB, Schlesinger.

20.   Carol McGraw, "Postscript."

21.   Jeff Diamant and Besheer Mohamed, "What the Data Says about Abortion in the U.S.," *Pew Research Center*, January 21, 2023, https:// www.pewresearch.org/fact-tank/2022/06/24/what-the-data-says -about-abortion-in-the-u-s-2.

22.   Kristin Luker's 1984 study of anti-abortion worldviews reveals that the movement was fueled in part by conservative anxieties around changing cultural ideas about "the inherent differences between men and women and about the nature and purpose of sexuality." See Luker, *Abortion and the Politics of Motherhood*, 159–75.

     A 1995 survey of male anti-abortion activists found that, while anger was a motivating factor, the majority of men characterized their motivation as being grounded in a sense of "Christian duty" and the imperative to "act on their beliefs." See Carol Maxwell and Ted Jelen, "Commandos for Christ: Narratives of Male Pro-Life Activists," *Review of Religious Research* 37, no. 2 (December 1995): 117–31.

23.   Clinic Defense Committee, letter, August 6, 1985, in Radical Women, *On the Barricades for Abortion Rights* (Seattle: Radical Women Publications, 1986), 65, Nancy Reiko Kato personal collection (hereafter NKPC).

24.   Clinic Defense Committee, letter, August 6, 1985.

25.   "Protect Reproductive Rights" flyer in Radical Women, *On the Barricades*, 62, NKPC.

26.   Debbie Gregg, "On Saturday, May 10 of Mother's Day weekend," *Women's Echo Newsletter* 2, no. 1 (June 1986): 7, Annah Anti-Palindrome personal collection.

27.   Freedom Socialist Party and Radical Women, Seattle, "Women's Rights In Peril! Open Letter to Delegates to National Ivy Conference Houston" flyer, November 18, 1977, NKPC.

28.   While I don't profile any trade unionists in this book, trade unionists, in addition to labor organizers, played important roles in BACAOR, a point Linci emphasized.

29.   Mary Ann Curtis, "The Abortion War: Feminists vs. the Right Wing," presented at the NWSA Eighth Annual Convention "Reproductive Rights/Public Policy" workshop, Los Angeles Radical Women, June 14, 1986, in Radical Women, *On the Barricades for Abortion Rights*, 11–16, NKPC.

30.   Francis Wilkinson, "The Gospel According to Randall Terry," *Rolling Stone*, October 5, 1989, https://www.rollingstone.com/culture /culture-news/the-gospel-according-to-randall-terry-47951.

31. Wilkinson, "The Gospel According to Randall Terry."

32. Jeff White letter on behalf of Operation Rescue of California, February 26, 1991, KMPC.

33. Jeff White letter, February 26, 1991; Northern California Operation Rescue letter, September 13, 1989, KMPC.

34. Another significant player has been the Federalist Society. See Michael Avery and Danielle McLaughlin, *The Federalist Society: How Conservatives Took the Law Back from Liberals* (Nashville: Vanderbilt University Press, 2013), especially chapter five, "The Jurisprudence of Personal Sexual Autonomy."

35. As Ziegler argues, "To gain control of the Supreme Court, abortion foes joined and ultimately helped to lead a growing fight against campaign finance laws, persuading many social conservatives and GOP leaders to oppose them as well." Ziegler, *Dollars for Life*, x.

36. Rankin, *Bodies on the Line*, 24–25

37. Cathy Cockrell, "Right-to-Lifers Besiege Local Abortion Clinic," *San Francisco Sentinel*, September 23, 1988, KMPC.

38. Elizabeth Fernandez, "Abortion Foes Clash at Clinic," *San Francisco Examiner*, September 18, 1988, KMPC.

39. Cockrell, "Right-to-Lifers."

40. BACAOR, "News Release: Feminists Arrested Defending Abortion Rights; Police Aid Anti-Abortionists," September 18, 1988, MC 831, box 399, folder 9, PBB, Schlesinger.

41. "SFPD: Running Amok," *San Francisco Bay Guardian*, September 21, 1988, KMPC.

42. BACAOR, "News Release," September 18, 1988.

43. Radical Women, National Office Memorandum, "Re: Campaign to Free the Abortion Rights Three," October 12, 1988, KMPC.

    Over the years, BACAOR worked with the Bay Area National Lawyers Guild, or NLG, which provided them with indispensable legal observation, counsel, and representation.

44. "SFPD: Running Amok."

45. Bleys Rose, "Pro-choice Groups Develop New Tactics to Foil Anti-abortion Activists," *Oakland Tribune*, October 5, 1988, KMPC.

46. Radical Women memo, "Re: Campaign to Free the Abortion Rights Three."

47. BACAOR, "STOP Right-wing Attacks on Women's Clinics" flyer, KMPC.

48. Kass McMahon, "10/11/88" and "BACAOR Mtg, Long Haul, 10-12-88" notes, KMPC.

49. Sometimes fake clinics are called "crisis pregnancy centers." Crisis pregnancy centers began to crop up in the early 1970s. See Ziegler, *Abortion and the Law*, 24. In the United States, fake clinics significantly outnumber real abortion clinics. See ReproAction, "The Fake Clinic Database," https://reproaction.org/fake-clinicdatabase. Also listen to Kate Raphael's radio documentary segment on fake clinics on *After Roe: In Search of Reproductive Justice Special,* KPFA, October 31, 2022, https://kpfa.org/area941/episode/after-roe-in-search-of-reproductive-justice-special, 3:20–22:05.

50. For more on how the anti-abortion movement has imagined itself as a "civil rights movement for white people," see Jennifer Holland, *Tiny You: A Western History of the Anti-Abortion Movement* (Oakland: University of California Press, 2020).

51. Pamela Kramer, "2,200 Arrests in Abortion Protests," *San Jose Mercury News*, October 30, 1988, KMPC.

52. Christina Smith, "Inside Operation Rescue," *Coming Up!* 10, no. 3 (December 1988), KMPC.

53. Kramer, "2,200 Arrests."

54. Smith, "Inside Operation Rescue."

55. News staff and wire reporters, "2,200 Arrested in Abortion Protests," *San Francisco Examiner*, October 30, 1988, KMPC.

56. Kramer, "2,200 Arrests." More about Jeff White: Amanda Robb, "Anti-Abortion Extremist Jeff White Sentenced to Prison and $27 Million in Restitution," *Ms.*, March 15, 2021, https://msmagazine.com/2021/03/15/anti-abortion-extremist-jeff-white-prison-restitution.

57. Kramer, "2,200 Arrests."

58. Annie Stuart, "Pro-Choicers Mobilize for Clinic Defense," *Noe Valley Voice*, June 1989, KMPC.

59. Stanton Samuelson, "Charges Dropped against Pro-Choicers," *San Francisco Examiner*, August 2, 1989, KMPC.

60. See *Prairie Fire: The Politics of Revolutionary Anti-Imperialism* (San Francisco: Communications Co., 1974), http://www.sds-1960s.org/PrairieFire-reprint.pdf.

61. Amanda Ream, "AIDS Activism and Beyond: Radical Queer Politics of the '80s and 90s," *Visual AIDS*, April 11, 2013, https://visualaids.org/blog/aids-activism-and-beyond-radical-queer-politics-of-the-80s-and-90s; Anthony Marquez, "Anti-AIDS Protest Closes Golden Gate Bridge, Commuters Angered," *AP*

News, January 31, 1989, https://apnews.com/article/3e23ed98
ab0507a59aea5f6768243a87.

62. In December 1989, Women's Health Action and Mobilization
(WHAM!), a reproductive rights group within ACT UP, led what
Sarah Schulman describes as "an outlandish expression of rage,
alongside humor" in which activists interrupted a Sunday Mass
at St. Patrick's Cathedral in Manhattan, in part by staging a die-in
in the aisles, in protest of the Church's anti-abortion and anti-gay
agenda. See "Collective Leadership: Stop the Church," in *Let the
Record Show*, 136–65.

63. "BACAOR Points of Unity," July 1989.

64. In 1987, the collective called the Silence = Death Project created
the poster that would become a central image and message of ACT
UP. The poster featured the white text "Silence = Death" below a
hot pink triangle on a black background. The triangle invoked the
inverted triangle concentration camp badge that the Nazis would
force men who had been identified as gay to wear. Thessaly La Force,
Zoë Lescaze, Nancy Hass, and M.H. Miller, "The 25 Most Influential Works of American Protest Art since World War II," *New
York Times Style Magazine*, October 15, 2020, https://www.nytimes
.com/2020/10/15/t-magazine/most-influential-protest-art.html.

65. Agnes Sampson, "Sum-up of Saturday, December 10, 1988,"
KMPC.

66. Laura Hagar, "In the Belly of the Beast," *Express*, January 27, 1989,
KMPC.

67. BACAOR, "Press Statement," March 30, 1989, and "BACAOR
Member Victim of Police Brutality," c. April 1989, KMPC.

68. Nina Martin, "Pro-choice Groups Rally for Roe Ruling," *San Francisco Examiner*, April 3, 1989, KMPC.

69. "BACAOR Points of Unity" one-pager, July 1989, KMPC.

70. "Operation Rescue in the Bay Area" report, c. fall 1990, 2, KMPC.

71. "Operation Rescue in the Bay Area."

Chapter 7: No One Person Has the Power

1. Ziegler, *Abortion and the Law*, 88–94, 101–6.

2. *Webster v. Reproductive Health Services*, 492 U.S. 490 (1989).

3. *Webster v. Reproductive Health Services*; Ziegler, *Abortion and the Law*,
105.

4. Linci Comy interview, "Legal Abortion Doesn't Matter if You Can't Get One," *Socialist Worker*, August 19, 2005, https://socialist worker.org/2005-2/553/553_05_LincyComy.php.

5. Chalker and Downer, *Woman's Book of Choices*, 263.

6. *No Going Back: A Pro-Choice Perspective*, directed by the Federation of Feminist Women's Health Centers (Los Angeles: Federation of Feminist Women's Health Centers, 1989).

7. Dudley-Shotwell, *Revolutionizing Women's Healthcare*, 113.

8. Bob Brubaker, Andy "Sunfrog" Smith, et al., "Anarchy in San Francisco: The 1989 Gathering: 3 Views," *Fifth Estate*, no. 333 (Winter 1990), https://www.fifthestate.org/archive/333-winter-1990/anarchy-in-san-francisco.

9. Dudley-Shotwell, *Revolutionizing Women's Healthcare*, 110–11.

10. Ann Japenga, "The New Abortionists," *In Health*, November 1991, 51–52, RL.00427, box 62, folder 1, FWHCR, Rubenstein.

11. Dudley-Shotwell, *Revolutionizing Women's Healthcare*, 113.

12. Janice Perrone, "Controversial Abortion Approach," *American Medical News*, January 12, 1990, 9, 26–27, RL.00427, box 62, folder 1, FWHCR, Rubenstein.

13. Japenga, "New Abortionists," 57.

14. Chalker and Downer, *Woman's Book of Choices*, viii, 129.

15. Karen Houppert, "Civil Cervix—A Woman's Book of Choices," *Village Voice*, January 12, 1993, ProQuest Historical Newspapers, SFPL.

16. Ziegler, *Abortion and the Law*, 115.

17. *Planned Parenthood of Southeastern Pennsylvania v. Casey*, 505 U.S. 833 (1992).

18. *Planned Parenthood v. Casey*; Ziegler, *Abortion and the Law*, 117.

19. *Planned Parenthood v. Casey*.

20. Kiersta Burke, "Self-Helpers Resist States' Intrusion into Health Care," *New Directions for Women*, September-October 1992, ASG, SFPL.

Chapter 8: You Only Need to See the Front Line of Musclebound White Male Thugs to Know What This Struggle Is Really About

1. Thank you to Raven for collaborating with me on the writing of this section about Roots Against War.

2. "Free Tahan K. Jones and All G.I. Resisters," Roots Against War one-pager, c. fall 1990, Raven's personal collection (hereafter RPC). The charges against Tahan were later dismissed.

3. RAW, "Power to the People! Amandla!" trifold brochure, c. 1992, RPC.

4. RAW, "Night of Resistance!" flyer no. 1, January 1991, RPC.

5. RAW, "Night of Resistance!" flyer no. 2, January 1991, RPC.

6. "Power to the People! Amandla!" trifold brochure.

7. People may seek abortions later in pregnancy for medical reasons such as fetal anomalies or maternal life endangerment or because of barriers to care that cause delays in obtaining abortion. See "Later Abortion," *Guttmacher Institute*, November 13, 2019, https://www.guttmacher.org/evidence-you-can-use/later-abortion; and "Working with Dr. Tiller: Staff Recollections of Women's Health Care Services of Wichita," *Guttmacher Institute*, August 10, 2011.

8. "Judge Orders U.S. Marshals to Prevent Closing of Abortion Clinics," *New York Times*, July 30, 1991, https://www.nytimes.com/1991/07/30/us/judge-orders-us-marshals-to-prevent-closing-of-abortion-clinics.html.

9. Rankin, *Bodies on the Line*, 36, 39.

10. Rankin, *Bodies on the Line*, 43.

11. BACORR, "Clinic Defense: A Model," 2nd ed., March 1992, 2–4, KMPC.

12. "America Divided," *LIFE*, July 1992, 34, KMPC.
    Later, Robert Schenck would change his mind about abortion. See Rob Schenck, "I Was an Anti-Abortion Crusader. Now I Support Roe v. Wade," *New York Times*, May 30, 2019, https://www.nytimes.com/2019/05/30/opinion/abortion-schenck.html.

13. NWROC, "We've Got the OR Bigots On the Run!" *Organizer*, April 22, 1992, RPC.

14. Schulman, *Let the Record Show*, 143.

15. Kass McMahon, "Press Release: Local Pro-Choice Forces Return Victorious from Clinic Defense in Buffalo," April 30, 1992, KMPC.

16. Laura for C-ROARR, letter to friends, c. June 1992, RPC.

17. C-ROARR, "Important Information as Clinic Defenders," July 2, 1992, RPC.

18. C-ROARR, "Coalition Ground Rules," June 8, 1992, RPC.

19. BACORR, "Security for Louisiana," c. June 1992, RPC.

20. Laura for C-ROARR, letter to friends.

21. BACORR, "Security for Louisiana."

22. Hillary, "Report Back: Based on Info from R., J., M., D.," July 7, 1992, KMPC; Michael, "A Summary of the July 5th C-ROARR Meeting," July 15, 1992, RJPC.

23. Hillary, "Report Back."

24. "NWROC and the RWL Response to False Charges: Submitted by Marianne and Joyce," July 22, 1992, RPC.

25. C-ROARR, "For Immediate Release: C-ROARR Reports on Operation 'Rescue's' Violent Assaults on Clinic Defenders," July 10, 1992, RPC.

26. Hillary, "Report Back."

27. Meredith, Laura, and Debra, "Between NWROC and a Hard Spot: Over-View of C-ROARR & NWROC Relationship," July 22, 1992, KMPC.

28. As of 2021, more than half of Baton Rouge residents were Black. A little under 40 percent were white. Less than half of residents owned their homes. Almost a quarter of residents had income below the poverty line. See US Census Bureau, https://www.census .gov/quickfacts/batonrougecitylouisiana.

29. Hillary, "Report Back."

30. Churchwell, "Body Politics."

31. Carol Mason writes of how "Klan tactics have crossed over and become pro-life tactics," citing the anti-abortion terrorist group Army of God, which advocated the "removal of abortionists' thumbs." Mason, *Killing for Life*, 36–37.

32. Leading up to the 1999 Seattle WTO protests, Jennifer would also cofound a marching band called Infernal Noise Brigade that would largely occupy this frontline liminal space, aiming, as she put it, to "provide tactical psychological support through a propaganda of sound" and later credited with "keeping WTO protestors energized [and] focused." See Christopher Frizzelle, "R.I.P., INB (1999–2006)," *Stranger*, August 10, 2006, https:// www.thestranger.com/music/2006/08/10/50114/rip-inb -1999-2006.

33. Greg Garland, "Shouted Slurs, War of Words Can Be Jarring," *Baton Rouge Sunday Advocate*, July 11, 1992; Christopher Baughman, "Operation Rescue Ends BR Stay with Revival Gathering," *Sunday Advocate*, July 12, 1992, KMPC.

34. C-ROARR, "C-ROARR Reports on Operation 'Rescue's' Violent Assaults on Clinic Defenders."

35.   Steve Wheeler and Chris Baughman, "Weeklong Protest Here Ends," *Baton Rouge Sunday Advocate*, July 12, 1992, KMPC.

36.   See National American Holocaust Memorial (Christian Patriots for Life), https://www.cpforlife.org/tour.

37.   William Booth, "Doctor Killed During Abortion Protest," *Washington Post*, March 10, 1993, https://www.washingtonpost.com/wp-srv/national/longterm/abortviolence/stories/gunn.htm.

38.   Mason, *Killing for Life*, 37; Larry Rohter, "Towering Over the Abortion Foe's Trial: His Leader," *New York Times*, March 5, 1994, https://www.nytimes.com/1994/03/05/us/towering-over-the-abortion-foe-s-trial-his-leader.html.

39.   Joe Garofoli, "Old Battle, New Tactics," *Contra Costa Times*, c. June 1993, KMPC.

40.   Randall Terry, letter to supporters, April 4, 1993, KMPC.

41.   "Clinic Defense Training Outline," 1993, Laura Weide personal collection.

42.   Kevin Fagan, "Group to Oppose Operation Rescue," *San Francisco Chronicle*, June 23, 1993, KMPC.

43.   William Brand, "Berkeley to Provide Bus Rides for Pro-Choice Demonstrators," *Oakland Tribune*, June 24, 1993, KMPC.

44   March 10 to July 16, 1993, timeline, c. late July 1993, KMPC.

45.   David Sylvester, "Anti-Abortion Group Warns Bay Doctors," *San Francisco Chronicle*, July 8, 1993; Operation Rescue, "Tour of Shame" flyer, c. July 1993, KMPC.

46   Tanya Schevitz Wills, "Clinic Siege a Pro-choice Boon," *San Francisco Examiner*, July 18, 1993, KMPC.

47.   Timothy Ziegler, "37 Arrested in Abortion Protest Unrest," *Oakland Tribune*, July 13, 1993, KMPC.

48.   Tanya Schevitz Wills, "Clinic Siege a Pro-choice Boon," *San Francisco Examiner*, July 18, 1993; Linda Goldston and Brandon Bailey, "Day 9 Proves Troublesome," *San Jose Mercury News*, July 18, 1993, KMPC.

49.   Tom Burghardt for BACORR, "From Operation 'Failure' to Missionaries to the Preborn: What's Next for Bay Area Clinic Defense," July 27, 1993, KMPC.

Chapter 9: Rage Is Your Bitter Fuel

1.   Richard Eder, "Birth Control: 4-Day Pill Is Promising in Early Test," *New York Times*, April 20, 1982, https://www.nytimes

.com/1982/04/20/science/birth-control-4-day-pill-is-promising
-in-early-test.html; Lawrence Lader, *RU 486: The Pill That Could
End the Abortion Wars and Why American Women Don't Have It* (Reading, MA: Addison-Wesley, 1991), 31–32.

2.   One of Baulieu's mentors, Gregory Pincus, was the first to spec-
ulate that "anti-progestins" would inhibit the implantation of a
fertilized egg by acting on cell receptors. Lader, *RU 486*, 29.

3.   Lader, *RU 486*, 30–31; Gabriela Soto Laveaga, *Jungle Laboratories:
Mexican Peasants, National Projects, and the Making of the Pill* (Durham:
Duke University Press, 2009), 2.

4.   Lader, *RU 486*, 32–33.

5.   Lader, *RU 486*, 35.

6.   Eder, "Birth Control."

7.   Lader, *RU 486*, 35–39.

8.   Pam Belluck, "The Father of the Abortion Pill," *New York Times*,
January 18, 2023, https://www.nytimes.com/2023/01/17/health/
abortion-pill-inventor.html.

9.   "Provider Security," National Abortion Federation, https://pro
choice.org/our-work/provider-security.

10.   Shira Hassan emphasizes that harm reduction was introduced
by queer and trans Black, Indigenous, and other people of color
who were themselves drug users, sex workers, and sometimes
unhoused. While harm reduction was and is often thought of
as being focused on mitigating the risks of injection drug use,
in fact it has always been oriented toward community preser-
vation more broadly. See Shira Hassan, *Saving Our Own Lives: A
Liberatory Practice of Harm Reduction* (Chicago: Haymarket Books,
2022).

11.   "History of Health: Needle Exchange in San Francisco," *San Francisco AIDS Foundation*, https://www.sfaf.org/resource-library/
needle-exchange-in-san-francisco.

12.   Ann Devroy, "Clinton Cancels Abortion Restrictions of Rea-
gan-Bush Era, *Washington Post*, January 23, 1993, https://
www.washingtonpost.com/archive/politics/1993/01/23/clinton
-cancels-abortion-restrictions-of-reagan-bush-era/0e145a5a-0b37
-4908-8c4d-44643f62b0a0.

13.   See John Geyman, "Health Maintenance Organizations," in *The
Corporate Transformation of Health Care: Can the Public Interest Still Be
Served?* (New York: Springer, 2004), 36–50.

14.   John Langone, "After-the-Fact Birth Control," *Time*, Octo-

ber 10, 1998, https://content.time.com/time/subscriber/article
/0,33009,968609,00.html.

15. Gina Kolata, "After Large Study of Abortion Pill, French Maker
     Considers Wider Scale," *New York Times*, March 8, 1990, https://
     www.nytimes.com/1990/03/08/us/health-after-large-study-of
     -abortion-pill-french-maker-considers-wider-sale.html; Alan Rid-
     ing, "Abortion Politics Are Said to Hinder Use of French Pill," *New
     York Times*, July 29, 1990, https://www.nytimes.com/1990/07/29/
     world/abortion-politics-are-said-to-hinder-use-of-french-pill
     .html.

16. Riding, "Abortion Politics."

17. Lader, *RU 486*, 7; Elaine Woo, "Lawrence Lader, 86; Activist for
     Abortion Rights," *Los Angeles Times*, May 14, 2006, https://www
     .latimes.com/archives/la-xpm-2006-may-14-me-lader14-story
     .html.

18. Rachael Pine, "*Benten v. Kessler*: The RU 486 Import Case," *Law,
     Medicine and Health Care* 20, no. 3 (1992): 238–39. Under the
     Reagan and Bush administrations, the budgets for birth control
     research at the National Institutes of Health had remained static
     for a decade. See Lader, *RU 486*, 108.

19. Paul, Weiss, Rifkind, Wharton & Garrison, "Memorandum,"
     August 7, 1990, and cover letter to memorandum, August 8, 1990,
     MC 883, box 5, folder 9, Lawrence Lader Papers (hereafter LLP),
     Schlesinger.

20. Pine, "*Benten v. Kessler*," 239.

21. Pine, "*Benten v. Kessler*," 238–39.

22. Pine, "*Benten v. Kessler*," 240.

23. S. J. Diamond, "An Unorthodox 'Everywoman'," *Los Angeles Times*,
     July 23, 1992, https://www.latimes.com/archives/la-xpm-1992-07
     -23-vw-4217-story.html.

24. Pine, "*Benten v. Kessler*," 240.

25. *Benten v. Kessler*, 505 U.S. 1084 (1992).

26. Joannie Schrof, "Reproduction Showdown," *U.S. News and World
     Report* 114, issue 11 (March 22, 1993): 32.

27. See Laveaga, *Jungle Laboratories*.

28. Geyman, *The Corporate Transformation of Health Care*, 78–81.

29. Bill Clinton, "Memorandum on Importation of RU-486," January
     22, 1993, Administration of William J. Clinton, 1993, https://www
     .govinfo.gov/content/pkg/WCPD-1993-01-25/pdf/WCPD
     -1993-01-25-Pg88-2.pdf.

30. "RU-486 Trials to Begin," *FDA Consumer* 28, issue 7 (September 1994): 3.

31. Rachele Kanigel, "Local Clinic to Provide RU 486 Clone," *Oakland Tribune*, August 20, 1996, NA, OPL.

32. Eric Schaff et al., "Protocol to Study a Copy Mifepristone Product Plus Misoprostol for Medical Induction of Early Abortion: Low Dose Mifepristone Trial," May 14, 1996, updated November 11, 1996, 4–5, MC 883, box 6, folder 2, LLP, Schlesinger.

33. Gina Kolata, "Panel Advises F.D.A. to Allow Abortion Pill," *New York Times*, July 20, 1996, https://www.nytimes.com/1996/07/20/us/panel-advises-fda-to-allow-abortion-pill.html.

34. Lawrence Lader, "Statement by Lawrence Lader, President, Abortion Rights Mobilization," July 30, 1996, MC 883, box 6, folder 3, LLP, Schlesinger.

35. Lawrence Lader, letter to Phil Hilts at the *New York Times*, December 13, 1996, MC 883, Box 6, folder 3, LLP, Schlesinger.

36. Eric Schaff et al., "Vaginal Misoprostol Administered at Home after Mifepristone (RU486) for Abortion," *Journal of Family Practice* 44, no. 4 (April 1997): 353–59, MC 883, box 6, folder 5, LLP, Schlesinger.

37. Eric Schaff et al., "Low-Dose Mifepristone 200 mg and Vaginal Misoprostol for Abortion," *Contraception* 59, no. 1 (January 1999): 1–6, https://doi.org/10.1016/S0010-7824(98)00150-4.

38. "FDA Approves Mifepristone for Termination of Early Pregnancy," *FDA Consumer* (November–December 2000): 7.

39. Adam Miller, "Activist Hails U.S. Abort-Pill Approval," *New York Post*, September 30, 2000, https://nypost.com/2000/09/30/activist-hails-u-s-abort-pill-approval.

40. *U.S. v. Hill*, United States Department of Justice, https://www.justice.gov/crt/criminal-section-selected-case-summaries.

41. Booth, "Doctor Killed during Abortion Protest."

42. James Risen, "Shooting Suspect Has Advocated Clinic Violence," *Los Angeles Times*, July 30, 1994, https://www.latimes.com/archives/la-xpm-1994-07-30-mn-21521-story.html; *U.S. v. Hill*.

43. Feminist Majority Foundation, quoted in Charles Clark, "Abortion Clinic Protests," *CQ Researcher* 5, issue 13 (April 7, 1995), https://library.cqpress.com/cqresearcher/document.php?id=cqresrre1995040700.

44. "Testimony of Janet Reno, Attorney General, before the Committee on Labor and Human Resources, United States Senate,

Concerning S. 636, the Freedom of Access to Clinic Entrances Act of 1993, on May 12, 1993," Department of Justice Archives, https://www.justice.gov/archive/ag/speeches/1993/05-12-1993-p.pdf.

45. Rankin, *Bodies on the Line*, 64.

46. David Johnston, "F.B.I. Undertakes Conspiracy Inquiry in Clinic Violence," *New York Times*, August 4, 1994, https://www.nytimes.com/1994/08/04/us/fbi-undertakes-conspiracy-inquiry-in-clinic-violence.html; Pierre Thomas, "U.S. Marshals Dispatched to Guard Abortion Clinics," *Washington Post*, August 2, 1994, https://www.washingtonpost.com/archive/politics/1994/08/02/us-marshals-dispatched-to-guard-abortion-clinics/80067334-dd30-4a0a-9a00-bfa438da968a.

47. Charles Hall and Robert O'Harrow Jr., "Abortion Clinic Violence Probe Was Over at the Start," *Washington Post*, January 26, 1996, https://www.washingtonpost.com/archive/local/1996/01/26/abortion-clinic-violence-probe-was-over-at-the-start/23bec74d-12cd-43e5-9dac-106a35e20a1c.

48. Jim Yardley and David Rohde, "Abortion Doctor in Buffalo Slain; Sniper Attack Fits Violent Pattern," *New York Times*, October 25, 1998, https://www.nytimes.com/1998/10/25/nyregion/abortion-doctor-in-buffalo-slain-sniper-attack-fits-violent-pattern.html.

49. David Staba, "Doctor's Killer Tries to Make Abortion the Issue," *New York Times*, January 13, 2007, https://www.nytimes.com/2007/01/13/nyregion/13abort.html; National Abortion Federation, "Anti-Abortion Extremist James Kopp Convicted of Violating FACE Act," January 26, 2007, https://prochoice.org/anti-abortion-extremist-james-kopp-convicted-of-violating-face-act.

50. See Yardley and Rohde, "Abortion Doctor in Buffalo Slain"; "Provider Security," National Abortion Federation.

51. Roberto Suro, "Justice Dept. Sets Clinic Task Force," *Washington Post*, November 10, 1998, https://www.washingtonpost.com/archive/politics/1998/11/10/justice-dept-sets-clinic-task-force/50801565-9812-48a3-86f6-d0c562daf190.

52. National Task Force on Violence against Reproductive Health Care Providers, https://www.justice.gov/crt/national-task-force-violence-against-reproductive-health-care-providers.

53. Bruce Steir, M.D., *Jailhouse Journal of an OB/GYN: A Memoir* (Bloomington: AuthorHouse, 2008), 267–68.

54. Bruce Steir was prosecuted for second-degree murder in 1997 after a patient died from complications after a later abortion. In 2000, the

American Civil Liberties Union released a study titled "Preventing Unfair Prosecution of Abortion Providers: An Investigation into Political Bias by the Medical Board of California," which found that political bias was to blame for the Medical Board's severe treatment of Bruce Steir. The report revealed that an anti-abortion activist who had a close relationship with the Medical Board had been inappropriately involved in the case. A California Medical Association independent analysis found that Bruce's actions were not criminal. See https://www.aclunc.org/news/aclu-investigates-political -bias-medical-board-california. See also Steir, *Jailhouse Journal*.

55. Steir, *Jailhouse Journal*, 268.
56. Kathleen Kirkwood, "Oakland Abortion Clinic Wants Bulletproof Vests," *Oakland Tribune*, January 8, 1999, NA, OPL.
57. Kirkwood, "Oakland Abortion Clinic Wants Bulletproof Vests."

Chapter 10: No Way to Learn Except to Do

1. Lynn Comella, *Vibrator Nation: How Feminist Sex-Toy Stores Changed the Business of Pleasure* (Durham: Duke University Press, 2017), 12.
2. The idea that people should have the right to sex while also being free to say no to pregnancy was articulated by Second Wave radical feminists. As Jennifer Nelson writes, "Redstockings radical feminists believed that a sexual revolution could not occur if women risked pregnancy, criminal activity, and death every time they had sex." See Nelson, *Women of Color*, 51.
3. *Real Sex*, episode four, "Annie Sprinkle's One-Woman Show," performed by Annie Sprinkle, 1992, HBO.
4. For an extended analysis of the skit, see Terri Kapsalis, "Retooling the Speculum: Annie Sprinkle's 'Public Cervix Announcement,'" in *Public Privates: Performing Gynecology from Both Ends of the Speculum* (Durham: Duke University Press, 1997), 113–33.
5. For more about the Wise Woman Center, see http://susunweed. com/Wise-Woman-Center.htm.
6. D. L. Sackett, W. M. C. Rosenberg, J. A. M. Gray, R. B. Haynes, and W. S. Richardson, "Evidence Based Medicine: What It Is and What It Isn't," *BMJ* 312, no. 7023 (January 1996): 71–72.
7. Christopher Worsham and Anupam Jena, "The Art of Evidence-Based Medicine," *Harvard Business Review*, January 30, 2019, https://hbr.org/2019/01/the-art-of-evidence-based-medicine.

8. S. J. Jejeebhoy et al., "Can Nurses Perform Manual Vacuum Aspiration (MVA) as Safely and Effectively as Physicians? Evidence from India," *Contraception 84*, no. 6 (2011): 615–21, https://pubmed.ncbi.nlm.nih.gov/22078191; quoted at "Vacuum Aspiration: Safety and Effectiveness," *Ipas*, January 28, 2021, https://www.ipas.org/clinical-update/english/recommendations-for-abortion-before-13-weeks-gestation/vacuum-aspiration/safety-and-effectiveness.

Chapter 11: Everyone Deserves a Place

1. A leading developer and practitioner of trauma-informed care was working in the Bay Area during this decade as well. In 2007, Nadine Burke Harris founded the Bayview Child Health Center in the low-income and environmentally burdened San Francisco neighborhood of Bayview, where she began researching the impact of adverse childhood experiences and "toxic stress" on health. See Nadine Burke Harris, *The Deepest Well: Healing the Long-Term Effects of Childhood Adversity* (Boston: Houghton Mifflin Harcourt, 2018).

2. *People v. Garcia*, No. S124003, Supreme Court of California (2005); Fredric Tulsky and Julie Patel, "Convicted Man Acquitted after Eight Years in Custody," *Mercury News*, February 6, 2007, https://www.mercurynews.com/2007/02/06/convicted-man-acquitted-after-eight-years-in-custody.

3. Patrick Hoge, "Beloved Community Activist Slain," *San Francisco Chronicle*, September 1, 2005, https://www.sfgate.com/bayarea/article/RICHMOND-Beloved-community-activist-slain-2578543.php.

4. Annah Anti-Palindrome, "The Pro-Choice Movement Has a White Supremacy Problem—and Anti-Choice Advocates Are Using It to Their Advantage," *Everyday Feminism*, June 16, 2015, https://everydayfeminism.com/2015/06/pro-choice-white-supremacy.

5. Annah Anti-Palindrome, *DNA Hymn* (Little Rock: Sibling Rivalry Press, 2016), 7.

6. Anti-Palindrome, *DNY Hymn*, 31.

7. Parker, "love isn't," in *Complete Works*, 190–91.

8. Rankin, *Bodies on the Line*, 79.

9. Ziegler, *Abortion and the Law*, 150.

10. Rankin, *Bodies on the Line*, 85.

11. Ziegler, *Abortion and the Law*, 179–80.

12. Megan Donovan, "D&E Abortion Bans," *Guttmacher Institute*, February 21, 2017, https://www.guttmacher.org/gpr/2017/02/de-abortion-bans-implications-banning-most-common-second-trimester-procedure; Stephen Chasen et al., "Dilation and Evacuation at >or=20 Weeks," *American Journal of Obstetrics and Gynecology* 190, no. 5 (2004): 1180–83, https://pubmed.ncbi.nlm.nih.gov/15167815; Cassing Hammond, "Second-Trimester Pregnancy Termination: Dilation and Evacuation," *UpToDate*, October 21, 2022.

13. In recent years, anti-abortion advocates have tried to ban D&E, too, the most common procedure for later abortions, as part of their plan to "eliminat[e] access to abortion after the first trimester by banning one method at a time." See Donovan, "D&E Abortion Bans."

14. Ziegler, *Abortion and the Law*, 176–77; Chasen et al., "Dilation and Evacuation at >or=20 Weeks."

15. Lawrence Finer and Stanley Henshaw, "Abortion Incidence and Services in the United States in 2000," *Perspectives on Sexual and Reproductive Health* 35, issue 1 (January/February 2003): 6–15, https://www.guttmacher.org/journals/psrh/2003/01/abortion-incidence-and-services-united-states-2000.

16. Maggie Gilmour, "States Offer Preview of Abortion Law," *Oakland Tribune*, November 5, 2005, NA, OPL.

17. Linci Comy interview, *The Morning Show*, KPFA, November 3, 2005, https://kpfa.org/episode/17735.

18. Rankin, *Bodies on the Line*, 87.

19. Interview with Linci Comy, *Socialist Worker*.

20. Recording of clinic defense training, Oakland, CA, January 19, 2013, Barbara Hoke personal collection (hereafter BHPC).

21. "Guidelines: Clinic Escorting," March 2010, BHPC.

22. Puck Lo, "City Buffer Zone, Separating Abortion Patients from Protesters, Faces Lawsuit in Federal Court," *Oakland North*, November 7, 2009, https://oaklandnorth.net/2009/11/07/city-buffer-zone-separating-abortion-patients-from-protesters-faces-lawsuit-in-federal-court.

23. See *Hoye II v. City of Oakland*, No. 09-16753 (9th Cir. 2011), https://caselaw.findlaw.com/court/us-9th-circuit/1575729.html.

24. Recording of clinic defense training.

25. Brown, *Valuenergy*, 9, 19.

26. "Some Medi-Cal Payments Will Be Frozen until Budget Is OK'd," *California Healthline*, July 24, 2008, https://californiahealthline. org/morning-breakout/some-medical-payments-will-be-frozen- until-budget-is-okd; Angela Hill, "Women's Reproductive Health Clinic Closes," *Oakland Tribune*, April 7, 2009, NA, OPL.

27. Planned Parenthood Action Fund (PPAF), "What Are Trap Laws?" https://www.plannedparenthoodaction.org/issues/abortion/ types-attacks/trap-laws.

28. Guttmacher Institute, "Targeted Regulation of Abortion Provid- ers (TRAP) Laws," January 22, 2020, https://www.guttmacher.org/ evidence-you-can-use/targeted-regulation-abortion-providers -trap-laws.

29. Guttmacher, "TRAP Laws."

30. PPAF, "What Are Trap Laws?"

31. Guttmacher, "TRAP Laws."

32. Guttmacher, "TRAP Laws." For more, see David Cohen and Carole Joffe, *Obstacle Course: The Everyday Struggle to Get an Abortion in Amer- ica* (Oakland: University of California Press, 2020); and *TRAPPED*, directed by Dawn Porter (Independent Lens, 2016).

33. Elizabeth Nash and Joerg Dreweke, "The U.S. Abortion Rate Con- tinues to Drop: Once Again, State Abortion Restrictions Are Not the Main Drive," Guttmacher Institute, September 18, 2019, https:// www.guttmacher.org/gpr/2019/09/us-abortion-rate-continues -drop-once-again-state-abortion-restrictions-are-not-main.

34. "Tracking the States Where Abortion Is Now Banned," *New York Times*, February 10, 2023, https://www.nytimes.com/interactive/ 2022/us/abortion-laws-roe-v-wade.html.

35. Guttmacher, "TRAP Laws."

36. Linci Comy, June 3, 2022, Oakland.

37. Linci Comy, September 3, 2022, Oakland.

Conclusion: All Throughout Your Life You Learn

1. Jejeebhoy et al., "Can Nurses Perform Manual Vacuum Aspiration (MVA) as Safely and Effectively as Physicians?"

2. *Penny, personal interview, August 29, 2021.

3. On this point, see Ziegler, *Abortion and the Law*, 120.

4. A powerful counter to the claim that "abortion hurts women" and testament to the fact that abortion saves lives is the recent

Turnaway Study, conducted at University of California, San Francisco: "The main finding of the Turnaway Study is that receiving an abortion does not harm the health and wellbeing of women, but in fact, being denied an abortion results in worse financial, health and family outcomes." See "The Turnaway Study," *Advancing New Standards in Reproductive Health*, https://www.ansirh.org/research/ongoing/turnaway-study; and Diana Greene Foster, *The Turnaway Study: Ten Years, a Thousand Women, and the Consequences of Having—or Being Denied—an Abortion* (New York: Scribner, 2020).

5. Ziegler, *Abortion and the Law*, 210. Ziegler begins to respond to her own question about the abortion conflict in her more recent *Dollars for Life*.

6. On April 7, 2023, a federal judge in Texas ruled on a case brought by the Christian group Alliance Defending Freedom that the FDA's approval of mifepristone was invalid. The case went to the Fifth Circuit Court of Appeals, which reimposed restrictions on the drug that the FDA had previously lifted. Upon receiving an emergency request from the Joe Biden administration, on April 21 the Supreme Court temporarily stayed (halted) the Texas judge's order and also the restrictions reimposed by the Fifth Circuit Court. As of this writing, the case is back with the Fifth Circuit Court and could make its way back to the Supreme Court. Poppy Noor, "Abortion Pill Case: What Does the Supreme Court Order Mean and What Comes Next?" *Guardian*, April 21, 2023, https://www.theguardian.com/us-news/2023/apr/21/abortion-pill-ruling-mifepristone-supreme-court-explained.

7. Lisa Lerer and Katie Glueck, "After Dobbs, Republicans Wrestle with What It Means to Be Anti-Abortion," *New York Times*, January 20, 2023, https://www.nytimes.com/2023/01/20/us/politics/abortion-republicans-roe-v-wade.html.

8. Kate Zernike, "A Volatile Tool Emerges in the Abortion Battle: State Constitutions," *New York Times*, January 29, 2023, https://www.nytimes.com/2023/01/29/us/abortion-rights-state-constitutions.html.

9. Kiera Butler, "The Anti-Abortion Movement's Next Target: Birth Control," *Mother Jones*, May 5, 2022, https://www.motherjones.com/politics/2022/05/the-anti-abortion-movements-next-target-birth-control.

10. Grace Eliza Goodwin, "Utah Just Banned Gender-Affirming Healthcare for Transgender Kids. These 21 Other States Are Considering

Similar Bills in 2023," *Insider*, February 1, 2023, https://www.insider
.com/states-considering-bills-ban-gender-affirming-healthcare
-transgender-youth-2023-1. The year 2023 has been the fourth
consecutive record-breaking year for anti-trans legislation introduced. See Trans Legislation Tracker, https://translegislation
.com/learn.

11.   The Editorial Board, "A Promising New Path to Protect Abortion
Access," *New York Times*, January 7, 2023, https://www.nytimes
.com/2023/01/07/opinion/abortion-rights.html.

12.   For more ideas and resources, see Robin Marty, *New Handbook for a
Post-Roe America* (New York: Seven Stories Press, 2021).

13.   See "Eliminating Barriers of Parental Involvement Laws and
Judicial Bypass," *If/When/How*, https://www.ifwhenhow.org/get
-involved/strategic-initiatives-2/eliminating-barriers-young
-people-abortion.

14.   "Independent Clinics. The New Landscape of Independent Clinics
in the U.S.," *Abortion Care Network*, 2022, https://abortioncarenet-
work.org/communitiesneedclinics. With ineedana.com, Abortion
Care Network collects data annually on every abortion clinic in the
United States.

List of Interviews

Linci Comy, many interviews, July 17, 2018 to time of publication

Lisa Moore, March 19, 2019

Annah Anti-Palindrome, June 26, 2019

José Alfresco, July 9, 2019; September 19, 2020

Barbara Hoke, July 27, 2019; October 14, 2020

Carol Downer, August 25, 2019; January 4, 2020; March 12, 2021; May 10, 2022; July 3, 2022

Alicia Jones, November 14, 2019; February 27, 2022

*Izabel, August 25 and 27, 2020; January 20, 2021; May 28, 2021

*Simone, September 18, 2020; October 26, 2020; August 8, 2021; April 20, 2022

Laura Weide, many interviews, October 8, 2020 to time of publication

Nancy Reiko Kato, October 14 and 22, 2020; July 28, 2021

Kass McMahon, October 21, 2020, May 15, 2021; June 12 to 17, 2021; September 8, 2022

Coletta Reid, October 29, 2020; June 14, 2021

*Chloe, November 8, 2020; December 22, 2020; May 28, 2021

*Rosie, November 18, 2020; December 3, 2020

Joanna Davis, November 21, 2020

*Fuchsia, December 9, 2020; January 20, 2021; February 22, 2021; May 28, 2021

Arline Hernández, December 21, 2020; June 6, 2022

*Theresa, January 9 and 15, 2021; February 5, 2023

Melissa Moffitt, February 7, 2021

*Max, March 4, 2021; April 27, 2021; May 28, 2021; July 3, 2021; January 4, 2022

*Cindy, March 5, 2021; May 28, 2021
*Lori, March 24, 2021
*Grace, April 12, 2021; June 19, 2021
*Raven, May 10, 2021; September 19, 2021; September 29, 2022
*Vanessa, May 28, 2021; June 16, 2021
*Cecilia, July 21, 2021
*Penny, August 29, 2021
Jane Kaplan, September 9, 2021
Brenda Cummings, October 27, 2021; September 8, 2022
*Mimi, December 7, 2021
Barb Raboy, December 8, 2021; February 10, 2022
*Joe and Agnes Sampson, December 17, 2021; May 4 and 17, 2022
Leona Benten, March 8, 2022
Cherie Harper, May 12, 2022
Marianne Jensen, October 11, 2022
*Dani-Rose, October 20, 2022
Jennifer Whitney, February 2, 2023
Annie Sprinkle, April 15, 2023

*pseudonym

Credits

"A view of the cervix in a mirror" and "The cannula inserted into the uterus" by Suzann Gage, in *A New View of a Woman's Body: A Fully Illustrated Guide* (Los Angeles: Feminist Health Press, [1981] 1991). Reprinted with permission of the artist and the Federation of Feminist Women's Health Centers.

Lorraine Rothman, "How to Put a Del-Em Menstrual Extraction Kit Together" handout, undated, and a self-help group handout, undated, showing two uterine sounds marked with the distance in millimeters from external os to fundus. Courtesy of Izabel.

"maybe i should have been a teacher" by Pat Parker, in *The Complete Works of Pat Parker*, edited by Julie Enszer (Dover, FL: Sinister Wisdom, 2016) Reprinted with permission of the publisher and Anastasia J. Dunham-Parker-Brady.

"Stop Operation Rescue" poster, October 1988, by Joe and Agnes Sampson. Reprinted with permission of the artists.

"Clinic Defense Boards Instructions," July 1989, by BACAOR, and BACAOR bandana, c. 1990. Courtesy of Kass McMahon.

Original Roots Against War napkin drawing by Spie, fall 1990. Reprinted with permission of the artist.

Wedge and bubble formations, "Clinic Defense Training Outline," 1993. Courtesy of Laura Weide.

Index

Page numbers in italics represent illustrations.

#AbortionSavedMyLife, 319–20
#BodyAutonomyForAll, 319–20

40 Days for Life, 301–2
2008 financial crisis, 306

abortion: overview, 322–23, 324–25; admitting to, 20; in Bangladesh, 35–36; banned, 207–8, 321–22 (see also *Dobbs v. Jackson Women's Health Organization*); in China, 346–47n74; digital method, 41; as easy learning, 239–40; funding for, 79–81, 138; as health care, 248–49; history of criminalization, 31 (see also laws); history of reform and appeal in CA, 18–19; ideas shifting, 94; incomplete, 205; in Japan, 34; later abortions, 259, 300–301, 369n7, 375n54, 378n13; as legal, 18, 42–44, 48, 203; as medical procedure, 248–49; vs. menstrual extraction, 2; and population control, 30; pre/post *Roe*, 338–39n14; suction abortion, 19, 20–21, 32 (see also suction devices); and *Webster v. Reproductive Health Services*, 175–76; and welfare, 138, 146. *See also* medication abortion
Abortion Care Network, 328
The Abortion Handbook for Responsible Women (Maginnis and Phelan), 41–42
abortion hotline, 49
abortion pills, 253, 255, 326, 372n2. *See also* RU-486
Abortion Rights Defense Coalition, 225, 254
Abortion Rights Mobilization, 247–48, 250–51
"Abortion Saved My Life" message, 319–20
abortion self-help, defined, 2–3
abortion self-help movement: overview, 2, 3–4, 16–17, 65, 66–67, 323–24; and abortion as legal, 42–44; adaptive responses, 17; as apprenticeship model, 264; clinics as self-destruct mechanism, 66–67; FWHC overview, 12; history told, 183; and HIV/AIDS crisis (see HIV/AIDS); and imperialism, 33–34; intimacy and intensity of, 179–80;

as love, 204; and pelvic exams (*see* pelvic/cervical exams); as resistance, 188–89; secrecy due to laws, 12; self-help tours, 34–35, 48, 188, 285–86; telling history, 11–12. *See also various groups/organizations*

ACCESS Reproductive Justice, 229

ACCESS Women's Health Justice, 229

accumulation of capital, 67, 68, 69–70, 76

ACT UP: overview, 114, 131, 329; Church Ladies for Choice, 216; community-science projects, 133; C-ROARR, 217; Silence = Death, 367n64; WHAM! 132–33, 367n62; women and AIDS conference, 133. *See also* HIV/AIDS; queer and trans people

action list, 325–32

advance provision abortion pills, 326

affinity groups, 264, 282, 327

agency, 249

Agnes and Joe. *See* Sampson, Agnes and Joe

AidAccess.org, 326

AIDS Coalition to Unlock Power (ACT UP). *See* ACT UP

Alfresco, José, 104–5

Alicia. *See* Jones, Alicia

Alito, Samuel, 300

Allen, Lillie, 85–87

Alliance Defending Freedom, 380n6

American Association of Tissue, 126

Anarchist Conference and Festival, 184

anarchists, 152, 154, 169, 176, 207, 221, 230, 241, 246, 249, 264, 278

Angers, Valerie, 68

Ann, 177, 178

anti-abortion movement: overview, 137–39; 40 Days for Life, 301–2; Alliance Defending Freedom, 380n6; as angry men, 142, 146; Army of God, 370n31; bombings, 139–41; campaign finance laws, 365n35; and Clinic Defense Committee, 143–44; and clinics shut down, 142; and defense network, 141; fake clinics, 153, 327, 366n49; and First Amendment, 256–57; hostility overview, 141–42 (*see also* violence); and later-abortion procedures, 300–301; motivations, 364n22; murders by, 90, 225, 234–35, 256, 292; and racism, 153 (*see also* white supremacy); and Radical Women, 145; and RU-486, 347n83; and sexuality, 364n22; TRAP laws, 307; Walk for Life West Coast, 319–21; and *Webster* win, 176. *See also* BACAOR/BACORR; Christian Right; clinic defense; murders; Operation Rescue

Anti-Palindrome, Annah, 292–96

antiwar movement, 207–10

Armour, Norma, 55

Army of God, 370n31

arrests: OR in 1988, 157; ARAL in 1960s, 37, 40–41; BACAOR in 1988, 149–50; BACAOR in 1989, 157; Downer and Wilson in 1972, 36; San Jose 1993, 228; Wichita 1991, 212

art, 154–55, *156*, 158, 367n64

Association to Repeal Abortion Laws (ARAL), 36–42

autoclave, 179

autonomous zones, 2, 18

autonomy, 339n16

Avery, Byllye, 83–86, 87

awareness, 273–74, 316. *See also* fertility awareness method

BACAOR/BACORR: 1988 OR planning, 151, 152–57; overview, 8, 144; Abortion Rights Defense Coalition, 225; as antifascist, 172; bandanas, 158–59, *173*; in Baton Rouge/New Orleans 1992, 216–24, 230–31; in Buffalo 1992, 213–16; on Christian Right and democracy, 137; church protests, 165–68, 169–70; defense boards, 162, *163*; defense training manual, 213; emergency response network, 151, 154, *156*; escorts, 161–62, *163*, 172; first arrests, 148, 149–50; goals articulated, 171–72; growing, 157; logo of, 158; number of defenders, 162, 172; and police, 148–51, 157, 161–62, 217, 218, 221, 222; and RAW, 211, 212; in San Jose 1993, 225–28; slogan of, 159; success, 157–58; and unions, 364n28; video documentation, 154, 159–63, 165–67
Baird, Bill, 141
Bambara, Toni Cade, 53–54
Bangladesh, 32, 35–36
bankruptcy, 142, 306
banner-drops, 319–20
Banzhaf, Marion, 133
Barbara. *See* Hoke, Barbara
Barrett, June and James, 256
Barry, Kathleen, 73
Barton, Julie, 19
BASTA Women's Conference on Imperialism and Third World War, 91
Baton Rouge Delta Clinic, 220–21, 230–31
Baton Rouge, LA, 216–24, 230–31, 370n28

Baulieu, Étienne-Émile, 233–34, 245
Bay Area Coalition Against Operation Rescue (BACAOR). *See* BACAOR/BACORR
Bay Area Coalition for Our Reproductive Rights (BACORR). *See* BACAOR/BACORR
Bay Area Pride march 1978, 83
Bayview Child Health Center, 377n1
Beal, Frances, 53–54
Benten, Leona, 243–52, 253, 255
Benten v. Kessler. See Benten, Leona
Berkeley Free Clinic, 177, 204
Biden, Joe, 380n6
biomedicine, 17
biopsies, 276
birth control: and Black people, 52–55; Dalkon Shield, 60; and eugenics, 30, 31, 345n56; FAM, 119, 121–22, 129; history of criminalization, 31; and IPPF, 32; ME as, 278–79; restrictions, 321. *See also* International Planned Parenthood Federation; population control movement
Birthplace (Gainesville), 84
Black genocide, 52, 53, 54–55, 211–12
Black Nationalism, 52, 53–54, 93, 297
Black Panther Party, 3, 4, 51–52, 54–55, 89, 91, 350n18
Black Panther Party People's Free Medical Clinic (PFMC), 50, 52, 55
Black people: and birth control, 52–55; and harm reduction, 372n10; health activism, 3–4, 51–55 (*see also* Black women's health activism); homeownership, 370n28; leading OFWC,

55; and Operation Rescue, 211–12; parenting, 99–100, 210; and population control/eugenics, 30–31; sexual assaults, 85

The Black Woman (Bambara), 53–54

Black women's health activism, 52–55, 70, 83–84, 85–93, 339n14

Black Women's Health Imperative, 88. *See also* National Black Women's Health Project

Black Women's Health Initiative, 85–86

Black Women's Self-help Collective, 86

Blackmun, Harry, 251

blood, 134

Bodies on the Line (Rankin), 257

Body & Soul (NBWHP), 87

body sovereignty, 5, 14

bombings, 139–41

book overview, 7–9

Boot'em Out of Buffalo! (film), 214–16

boyfriends, 269

brake bleeders, 206

breast cancer, 134, 235, 361n49

Briggs, Laura, 138

Britt, 177

Britton, John Bayard, 256

Brown, Elaine, 55

Brown, Laura: and abortion, 46–47; on Alfresco, 105; and Alicia, 82; on Feminist Institutions, 306; FEN, 67, 68, 71; in Hawaii, 33; and LAFWHC bombing, 140, 141; OFWHC as bankrupt, 142; OFWHC conference 1974, 58, 59–60; OFWHC opening, 42, 45, 46; and Parker, 89, 93; as philosopher, 65–68; philosophy dissertation, 28–29; Reid on, 69; and sperm bank, 123–25; Venice 1971 gathering, 20; Women's Choice opening, 56

Brownworth, Victoria, 365n35

bubble formations, 225, *225*

bubble ordinance, 304–5

Buck v. Bell, 31, 52–53

Buffalo, NY, 213–16

Buffalo United for Choice (BUC), 213–16

bulletproof vests, 260, 303

Bunge, Raymond, 123, 127

Burgess, Fran, 46

Burghardt, Tom, 228

Burt, John, 225

Bush, George H., 134

Bush, George W., 300

Cadden, Wendy, 50

Café Macondo, 208

California Cryobank, 122

California Department of Consumer Affairs of the Board of Medical Examiners, 36

cancer, 59, 89, 134, 235, 361n49

cannulas, 19, 20–23, 96, 197, *198*

capital, 67, 68, 69–70, 76. *See also* Feminist Economic Network Corporation

capitalism: and Black parenting, 99; and body sovereignty, 5; and businesses, 70; co-opting care, 6; debates over (*see* Feminist Economic Network Corporation); and nuclear family, 93; pharmaceutical industrial complex, 252–53; and population control/ eugenics, 31–32; and unpaid housework, 100

care (as term), 7

care of the self, 341n17

Carney, Shawn, 320

Carol. *See* Downer, Carol

Catholicism, 94, 131, 138, 147

Cecilia, 204–6, 275–77, 315

cervical caps, 177

cervical exams. *See* pelvic/cervical exams

cervix, 13–16, *15*, 20–21, 24, 192–93
Chalker, Rebecca, 189
Child of Myself (Parker), 89–90
chlamydia, 323
Chloe, 185–86, 194–95, 200–201, 203–4, 223, 282–83, 314–15
Christian Patriots for Life, 223
Christian Right, 131, 137–38, 142, 146–47, 230, 364n22, 365n34. *See also* anti-abortion movement; Operation Rescue
Christianity, 94
Christmas, June Jackson, 86
Church Ladies for Choice, 216
Churchwell, Sarah, 222
chux pads, 92
Cindy, 177–80, 204, 283, 315, 317
"Cities of Refuge" OR campaign, 225–28
Citizens Committee for Humane Abortion Laws, 38
citizenship, 31
civil rights movement, 229
classism, 72
Clergy Consultation Service, 84
clinic defense, 70–71, 141, 172, 213. *See also* BACAOR/BACORR; Clinic Defense Committee; escorts; Roots Against War
Clinic Defense Committee (CDC), 143–44. *See also* BACAOR/BACORR
clinic escorts. *See* escorts
Clinton, Bill, 236, 242, 252, 253–54
clitoris, 114–17, 271, 359n6
Closed: 99 Ways to Stop Abortion (Scheidler), 141
closure of clinics, 142, 291, 305–6, 307, 322, 328
Coalition to Reclaim Our Abortion and Reproductive Rights (C-ROARR), 217–24
codes, 197, 288–89

Collins, Patricia Hill, 4, 100
colonization, 339n17
Combahee River Collective, 91–92
Comella, Lynn, 263
Coming Out of Cancer (Brownworth), 365n35
commercialization, 33
The Committee for Homosexual Freedom, 49–50
commodification, 33
communism, 230
Community Action Program (CAP), 350n18
community self-defense, 70–71
community-science projects: overview, 113–14; clitoris research, 114–17; fertility, 119–22, 123–27, 128–30; HIV/AIDS, 130–36; participatory clinic model, 117–18
Comy, Linci: overview, 1, 14; and Alfresco, 105; on antis violence, 258–59, 260–61; on autonomy, 263; and OR Benton reaction, 246; buying OFWHC, 142; as capitalist, 242; CDC photo, 143; on challenging extraction, 282, on Cindy, 178; on clinic knowledge, 235; on comfort, 313; on DI program, 126; at East Oakland women's gathering 1989, 184–85; and Fuchsia, 191; Fuschia living room cervical exam, 187; as goal oriented, 308–9; golf course poem, 309–10; on HIV/AIDS crisis, 131, 132, 134–36; and LAFWHC bombing, 139–40, 141; on laypeople, 342n19; mapping Women's Choice office, 57; on Medi-Cal, 243; on medication abortions, 253, 254–55; as mentor, 241; and Moffitt, 244; on National Radical Women, 144; OFWHC's

different sites, 137; on OR, 226; Parker as role model, 93; on Parker's clinic notes, 92; on participatory clinics, 118–19; and police, 258, 260; on Prop 73, 301; and Raven, 214; recruiting, 180; rising poem, 311–12; self-help as continuum, 17; speculum demonstration, 13–14; and sperm bank, 124, 129; on underground's stories, 11–13; on unions, 364n28; on the war years, 141–42; and WCFHP/Women's Choice, 237, 242, 244; WCFHP/Women's Choice closure, 305–6; and WCFHP/Women's Choice purchase, 176; on *Webster*, 196; on women as researchers, 114

confidentiality, 203

Connelly, Matthew, 31

Connie, 169

conscientious objectors, 207

consciousness-raising groups, 2, 47, 84

criminalization, 322

"crisis pregnancy centres," 366n49. *See also* fake clinics

cultural feminism, 68, 73

Cummings, Brenda, 159–60, 161, 163–65, 228–29

cunt self-care, 199

Curtis, Linda, 34

Curtis, Mary Ann, 145

Czarnik, Casey, 68, 71, 75

Dalkon Shield, 60

Danco Laboratories, 255

Daniels, Cynthia, 127–28

Dani-Rose: overview, 211–12; Buffalo defense 1992, 214, 215; Louisiana defense 1992, 218, 220, 230–31; San Jose defense 1993, 226–8

Daring to Be Bad (Echols), 73

Davis, Angela, 6, 100

Davis, Joanna, 239

Day of Action, 184

death, 281

decentralization, 201

deep medicine, 339n17

defense network, 141. *See also* BACAOR/BACORR; clinic defense; Clinic Defense Committee; escorts

Defensive Action, 256

Del-Em Menstrual Extraction Kit, 20–24, *22–23*, 25, 33, 61, 206. *See also* menstrual extraction

democracy, 73, 74, 87, 137, 147, 235

demography, 31

demystification of medicine, 51. *See also* menstrual extraction; pelvic/cervical exams

Department of Consumer Affairs, 61

Detroit, 70

Diana Press, 68, 70, 71, 75–78

die-ins, 367n62

diethylstilbestrol (DES), 59

digital method, 41

dignity, 298

dilation and curettage (D&C), 19

dilation and evacuation (D&E), 301, 378n13

dilation and extraction (D&E), 300–301

discomfort, 315–16

diversity, 315

Djerassi, Carl, 233

DNA Hymn (Anti-Palindrome), 293

Dobbs v. Jackson Women's Health Organization, ix–xi, 313, 344n45

doctors, 82–83, 124, 182, 226, 347n83. *See also* murders

donor-insemination (DI) program, 120, 121–22, 127

Downer, Carol: overview, 18–19; arrested in 1972, 36; and

bombing threat, 140–41; on LAFWHC bombing, 140; learning abortion techniques, 19–20; on ME vs. suction abortion terms, 27; national meeting 1972, 29; OFWHC conference 1974, 58–59; on population control, 30; on racism, 33; self-help tours, 34, 35; and state agency harassment, 61; Venice 1971 gathering, 20–21; as West Coast Sister, 24 (*see also* West Coast Sisters); and *Witches, Midwives, and Nurses*, 345n50; *A Woman's Book of Choices*, 189

drugs causing cancer, 59

Dubriwny, Tasha, 341n17

Dudley-Shotwell, Hannah, 117, 181

Dunham, Martha, 93

Dunham-Parker-Brady, Anastasia, 93

dysmenorrhea, 25

East Coast Redstockings, 347n74

East Oakland women's gathering (1989), 184–85

Echols, Alice, 67, 73, 75

economics, 67, 68, 69–70, 76–77. *See also* Feminist Economic Network Corporation

Edelman, Joan, 84

Ehrenreich, Barbara, 189

embolisms, 21

embryos, 27, 43

emergency response network, 151, 154

emotions, 114

environmentalism, 30

Epstein, Steven, 133

escorts: in 1990s, 172; in 2000s, 300, 302–5; in early 1980s, 139, 363n12; Feminist Women's City Club, 70–71; in late 1980s, 159–62, 163. *See also* clinic defense

An Essay on the Principle of Population (Malthus), 30

eugenics, 30–31, 79, 127–28, 345n56, 346n58

"Every Sperm Is Sacred!" (song), 149

Everywoman's Bookstore, 20

Everywomen's Newsletter, 20

evidence-based medicine, 284

"Expose Fake Clinics" campaigns, 327

fake clinics, 153, 327, 366n49

Falwell, Jerry, 146–47

family conversations, 299, 301

Family Planning Alternatives, 155

Family Planning Specialists, 302, 303–5

Farber, Laura and Shelley, 48

fascism, 321

FBI, 257, 258–60

fear, 136

Federalist Society, 365n34

Federation of Feminist Women's Health Centers (FFWHC), 15, 62, 114–15, 180–81, 188

femininity, 341n17

feminist consciousness raising, 2, 65–68

Feminist Economic Network Corporation (FEN), 67, 68, 69–74

Feminist Federal Credit Union, 68, 71

Feminist Health Educator internship, 235, 236–37, 240–41, 305

Feminist Women's City Club, 70–73

Feminist Women's Health Centers (FWHCs), 12, 42, 62, 72. *See also* OFWHC network; *various FWHC clinics*

fertility awareness method (FAM), 119, 121–22, 129

fetal life, x–xi, 176, 190, 249

firebombings, 139–41

First National Conference on Black Women's Health Issues, 86

Fleischman, Joan, 347n83

Food and Drug Administration (FDA), 61

Food Not Bombs, 184

forced fertility control, 35

forced sterilization, 31, 53, 54–55, 350n24

Ford and Rockefeller Foundations, 346n64

Ford Foundation, 32

Fort Wayne Women's Health Organization, 138–39

Foucault, Michel, 341n17

"Free Inez!" campaign, 62–63

Freedom of Access to Clinic Entrances (FACE) Act, 236, 242, 256–57

Freedom Socialist Party (FSP), 145, 148

Fuchsia, 186–88, 191–92, 197, 269–70, 314, 315

full balloon parties, 195–96

fun, 330–31

Furies, 69

gag rule, 242

Gage, Suzann, *15*, 115, 121–22

Gainesville Women's Health Center, 84–85

García, Inez, 62–63

Gay By the Bay (Stryker and Buskirk), 50

Gay women's liberation movement, 49–50

Geiger, H. Jack, 340n6

gender, 4–5

gender-inclusive language, 5–6

genocide, 52, 53, 54–55, 211–12, 320–21

Golden, Janet, 127–28

Gomperts, Rebecca, 326

Gonzales v. Carhart, 300–301

Gore, Bud, 97, 98, 254, 255

Gould, Deborah, 114, 131

Grace, 265–56, 269

Grahn, Judy: and Diana Press, 77–78; on FEN, 72, 73, 75; on gay liberation, 49, 50–51; and Laura B.'s dissertation, 28; on OFWHC location, 48; and press vandalism, 77–78

great yogurt conspiracy, 36

Gregg, Debbie, 58, 142, 143, 157, 176, 292

Griffin, Michael, 224–25, 256

Gross, Marjorie, 297

Gunn, David, 225, 256

Gurner, Rowena, 19, 37, 38–42

Gwynn, John, 19

Hanson, Boach, 46

harassment. *See* violence

harm reduction, 237–38, 295, 372n10

Harper, Cherie, 296–300

Harris, Nadine Burke, 377n1

Hassan, Shira, 372n10

health centers vs. self-help clinics, 66–67

health maintenance organizations (HMOs), 242

Heiman, Elaine, 19

Helms, Jesse, 138

herbs for menstruation, 27, 28

Hernández, Arline, 94–97, 100, 105–6

Hill, Jeannie, 139

Hill, Paul, 256

Hindin, Roanne, 149, 150–51

Hinton-Hoytt, Eleanor, 85–86

hiphop, 210

HIV/AIDS: overview, 130–36; funding from Reagan, 362n50; in women, 132–33, 297; needle exchanges, 237–38; and participatory clinic model, 119; screening sperm donors, 129, 360n35; and sex concept, 267; stigma and research, 363n6; as structural health injustice, 361n49. *See also* ACT UP

Hobart, Hiʻilei Julia Kawehipuaakahaopulani, 6

Hoechst, 245, 252

Hoke, Barbara: overview, 47–48; as escort in 2000s, 302–4, 305; FEN, 68, 71, 75; OFWHC house, 48–49; on OFWHC work, 62; on self-help, 56–57

homophobia, 126, 150, 229, 363n6

Hornstein, Francie, 58, 121–22

hospital admitting privileges, 307

household formations, 50–51

Huerta, Dolores, 150

Hyde Amendment, 79–80, 138, 147–48, 243

Idant Laboratories, 126, 360n27

identity-release sperm donors, 129, 130

Ifateyo, Ajowa, 86

imaging, 287

immigration, 31, 205

imperialism, 30, 32–34. *See also* racism

incomplete abortions, 205

Indian Health Service (IHS), 53, 80

Indigenous Peoples, 30–31, 53, 80–81

Industrial Workers of the World (IWW), 217

Infernal Noise Brigade, 370n32

insurance costs, 235

intact D&E, 300–301

International Planned Parenthood Federation: critiquing, 29; disapproving of ME, 188; and feminism, 296; and forced fertility control, 35; funding for, 32; vs. independent clinic

abortions, 328; and Karman's suction device, 33; *Planned Parenthood of Southeastern Pennsylvania v. Casey*, 190, 213, 344n45; in San Jose, 228

intersectionality, 208

Ipas, 35–36, 188

irony, 149

isolation, 2, 34

IUDs, 60

Izabel: overview, 186–87; on authority, 317; on body sharing, 265; June 2021 interview, 314; menstrual extraction, 197–98, 269–70; pelvic exam practices, 191–92

Jane collective, 338n11

"Japanese Eugenic Protection Law" (Curtis), 34

Japanese internment camps, 145

Japenga, Ann, 188

Jenkins, Sabrae, 79–80

Jensen, Marianne, 151–52, 158, 159, 162, 214, 219

Jiménez, Rosie, 77–78, 80

Jo, 177

Johnson, Lyndon B., 3

Jones, Alicia, 81–83, 89, 100, 101, 105–6, 118

Jones, Talian K., 207–8

joy, 330–31

Judy. *See* Grahn, Judy

Kaplan, Jane, 304

Karman, Harvey, 19, 20, 33, 35

Kathy, 149–50, 151

Kato, Nancy Reiko, 144–45, 150, 157, 320

Kennedy, Anthony, 175

Kessler, David, 250

Kiessling, Rebecca, 319–20

Kneese, Tamara, 6

Koblitz, Ann Hibner, 28

Koonz, Bob, 214

Kopp, James Charles, 258

Ku Klux Klan (KKK), 221–22, 225, 228, 370n31

Laden, Vicki, 304
Lader, Lawrence, 247–48, 250–51, 254
"Ladies Against Women," 149
Ladies Center Clinic, 256
LAFWHC. *See* Los Angeles Feminist Women's Health Center
Lake, Terry, 143
language, 5, 95
later abortions, 259, 300–301, 369n7, 375n54, 378n13
Latin America, 32
Latinx, 95–96
Laura (cervical exam instructor), 13–14
Laura (clinic defense). *See* Weide, Laura
Law, Debi, 26, 34, 46, 61, 73
laws, 37, 39, 41, 42. *See also* Association to Repeal Abortion Laws; Society for Humane Abortion
lawsuits, 250
laypeople, 237, 239–40, 317–18, 342n19
Leaks, Linda, 86
lesbians. *See* queer and trans people
Levy, Judy, 84
LGBTQ+. *See* queer and trans people
Libbey, Cheryl, 19
liberalism, 5, 73, 235
liberation, 130–31
liminal experiences, 29
"The List of Abortion Specialists" (ARAL), 39
lived experience, 2
Long Haul Info Shop, 152, 153
Lorde, Audre, 134
Lori, 278–82
Los Angeles Feminist Women's Health Center (LAFWHC): DI

program, 122; Farbers's tour in Tampa, 48; and FFWHC, 62; firebombed, 139–41; legal abortions first performed, 42; and OFWHC politics, 72; opening of, 24; raided in 1972, 36; and *Roe v. Wade*, 42; sold, 142; and state agency harassment, 61
Los Angeles State Health Department, 61
Los Angeles Women's Center, 24
love, 103–4, 204, 244–45
"love isn't" (Parker), 103
Luker, Kristin, 364n22

Maginnis, Pat, 19, 36–42, 58, 303, 342n9
Malthus, Thomas, 30
managed care, 242–43
manual vacuum aspirator (MVA), 33, 35–36, 285, 347n83
Marker, Russell, 233
Marya, Rupa, 339n17
masculinity, 91
Mason, Carol, 370n31
"The Master's Plan" (pamphlet), 35
Max: overview, 181–82; on awareness, 273–74, 316; cervical exams, 183–84, 271–72; on continuing knowledge, 317; on DIY, 314, 315, 318; and Fuchsia and Izabel group, 186–87; menstrual extraction, 199–200, 203–4; on sexuality, 265, 272–73; on sharing skills, 285–87; on third space for queers, 271–72; Vanessa joining group, 264
"maybe i should have been a teacher" (Parker), 100–101, 107–11
Maynard, Robyn, 6
McMahon, Kass: overview, 147–48; on ACT UP message, 168;

BACAOR bandana, 159-60; as BACAOR first arrests, 148-51; BACAOR planning 1988, 152-53; in BACAOR video, 161-62; Buffalo defense 1992, 214-15, 216; on "Cities of Refuge," 226; in San Jose 1993, 226-27; on South Bay and Sacramento clinics, 158; on OR in Sunnyvale, 155

media coverage, 153-54, 188-90, 250-51

Medicaid, 79, 80, 138

Medi-Cal, 242-43, 297, 306

Medical Board of California, 376n54

medical civil rights movement, 3

Medical Device Regulation Act, 60

medical procedures, 248-49

medical supplies, 178-79

Medical Waste Tracking Act, 362n52

medication abortion, 245, 253. See also abortion pills; RU-486

Mellon family, 346n64

menstrual cycles, 24

menstrual extraction (ME): as abortion, 175, 193, 200 (see also pregnant MEs); and abortion as legal, 42-43, 203; and abortion self-help, 2-3; as birth control, 278-79; and boyfriends, 269; and Cindy's group, 179-80; vs. clinical abortion, 2, 25-27, 181; as collective learning, 26; defined, 12; disapproval of, 188; and everyone knowing how, 281-82; as exchange, 200; explained by Chloe, 196-97; explained by Fuchsia, 197; explained by Izabel, 198; Fuschia on, 191; as life changing, 48; Max's experience, 199-200; as menstrual regulation, 29; vs. menstrual regulation, 32-33;

Mimi's experience, 275-78; No Going Back, 180-81; objective of, 26; at OFWHC, 48-49, 56; OFWHC conference 1974, 60-61; and pain threshold, 269; preliminary interviews, 204; Rosie's experience, 202-3; with septum uterus, 287; Simone/Chloe/Rosie group, 195-96; Theresa's views, 283-85; and younger generation, 240. See also Del-Em Menstrual Extraction Kit; pregnant MEs; suction devices

menstrual regulation, 28-29, 32-33

menstruation, 25, 27-29, 43. See also menstrual extraction

Mexico, 34-35

Michigan Organization for Human Rights, 147

"middle c" (Anti-Palindrome), 293-94

Mifeprex. See RU-486

mifepristone. See RU-486

military, 207-10

Mimi, 275-78

minors, 301

misogyny, 90-91

misoprostol, 234, 245, 254-55, 326

Mitsu, Tanaka, 34

Miyuki, Takeda, 34

mock wedding, 165-68

Moffitt, Melissa, 236, 238-40, 241-42, 244-45

Moore, Lisa, 105-6

Moral Majority, 146-47

Morgan, Tracy, 133

"Movement in Black" (Parker), 99, 105-6

murders, 90, 225, 234-35, 256, 292

Murphy, Michelle, 2, 16-17, 26, 32, 33-34, 115

mutilation, 116

MYA Network, 347n83

Nadel, Nancy, 304
Naeko, Wakabayashi, 34
National Abortion Federation
(NAF), 140
National Abortion Rights Action
League (NARAL), 147, 247
National Black Women's Health
Project (NBWHP), 87–88
National Organization for
Women (NOW), 18–19, 25,
70, 139
National Radical Women, 144–45
National Right to Life Commit-
tee, 300
National Women and AIDS
Conference, 133
National Women's Rights Orga-
nizing Coalition (NWROC),
172, 219–20
nationalism, 52
needle exchanges, 237–38
Nelson, Alondra, 3, 51, 55
Nelson, Jennifer, 52, 55, 370n32,
376n2
neoliberal "women's health,"
341n17
neoliberalism, 16–17, 138
New Orleans, 216–24
New Right, 147. See also Christian
Right
A New View of a Woman's Body
(FFWHC), 15, 114–17, 198
New York Center for Reproduc-
tive Law and Policy, 250
Newton, Huey, 350n18
Night of Resistance, 208–9, 209,
210–11
No Going Back (film), 180–81, 188
nonbinary people, 5
non-governmental organizations
(NGOs), 16–17. See also various
organizations
nonhierarchical model, 7, 178,
316

Noriko, Fujisawa, 34
nuclear family, 65, 93, 104
Nurses' Training School, 3

off our backs (newspaper), 36, 69
Office of Economic Opportunity
(OEO), 3, 340n6
Office of Medical Devices, 61
OFWHC network, 137, 142, 143.
See also individual clinics
OFWHC/Women's Choice: overview, 62; abortion prices, 56;
and AIDS personal protection,
135; and AIDS testing, 132;
Alfresco working at, 104–5; Alicia's memories, 82–83; as bankrupt, 142; Black women leading,
55; conference 1974, 58–59; DI
program, 120, 121–22, 123–27,
128–30; and Diana Press, 75–78;
FAM, 119, 121–22, 129; FEN,
68; and FFWHC, 62; finding,
45–46; Hernández's memories,
94–99; leaders of, 4; and Linci,
1; and Moore's queerness, 106;
name changed to WCFHP,
142; opening of, 42, 46,
56–57; and other FWHC, 72;
participatory clinic model, 118;
and personal protection, 135;
and Roe v. Wade, 48; salaries,
62; second-trimester abortion
care, 96–97; shared parenting,
100–101; sperm bank, 119–20,
122, 123–27, 128–30; vandalism,
77–78
Olivia Records, 72–73
one-way valves, 21
Operation Rescue (OR): overview, 148–50; Baton Rouge/
New Orleans 1992, 216–24;
and Benton abortion reaction,
246; and Black people, 211–12;
in Buffalo 1992, 213–16; and
Catholic Church, 131; and
clinic defense changes, 145–46;

infiltration of, 169–71, 217; San
Jose 1993, 225–28; Southern
California 1988/89, 155–57;
Wichita 1991, 212–13. *See also*
anti-abortion movement;
BACAOR/BACORR
operation VAAPCON, 257
orgasms, 115, 116
ownership, 202–4

pain, 276, 315–16
palindromes, 293
parental notification, 301
parenting, 99–101
Parker, Pat: overview, 89–91, 93;
and Alfresco, 104; as auntie,
100; BASTA conference,
91–92; on Black National-
ism, 93; and clinic defense,
142–43; in *Coming Out of Cancer*,
362n49; and Diana Press, 77;
First Black Lesbian Conference, 92; as internal medical
director, 92–93; and Linci,
1; on love, 103–4; "maybe i
should have been a teacher,"
100–101, 107–11; "Movement in
Black," 99, 105–6; on parenting,
99, 100–101; on pregnancy,
101–2; at Richmond FWHC
rally, 143; on *Roe v. Wade*, 94;
"Womanslaughter," 90–91;
Womanslaughter, 77
Parrent, Joanne, 68, 70, 71, 73–74
Parrish, Margaret, 84
partial-birth abortion, 300
Partial-Birth Abortion Ban Act,
300
participatory clinic model, 7,
117–19
passivity, 252
pasta dinners, 288
Pat. *See* Parker, Pat
Patel, Raj, 339n17
patents, 24, 33
patriarchy: and anti-abortion

movement, 146, 229; democracy as, 73; and economics, 73;
and HIV/AIDS crisis, 132; and
isolation, 2, 34; and medical
categories, 27; vs. valuenergy, 67
pelvic/cervical exams: overview,
16–17; to achieve pregnancies,
181; Alicia as model, 82; and
arrests, 36; Barb's memories,
120; as better objectivity,
115–16; and clits, 271; at East
Oakland women's gathering
1989, 184–85; explained by
Fuchsia, 191–92; Linci and
Laura 1977, 13–14; Max's experience, 183–84; at OFWHC,
49; ongoing practicing, 191,
192–93; participatory clinics,
117–18; right to self-exam, 36;
Simone/Chloe/Rosie group,
194–95; and Sprinkle, 267–68;
in Tampa, 48; and uterus,
271–72; Venice 1971, 20–21;
view in mirror, 15; West Coast
Sisters, 24
Pensacola Medical Services, 225
people of color. *See* Black people;
Roots Against War
perineal sponge, 116
personal protection, 134–35
Peskin, Ellen, 121–22
Petrinovich, Mary, 19
pharmaceutical industrial complex, 252–53
Phelan, Lana Clarke, 19, 37, 38,
40–42, 58
phone tree, 151
"The Pill: Genocide or Liberation?" (Bambara), 53–54
Pincus, Gregory, 372n2
Pine, Rachael, 247, 250, 251, 252
pink triangles, 367n64
PlanCPills.org, 326
Planned Parenthood. *See* Inter-
national Planned Parenthood
Federation

Planned Parenthood of Southeastern Pennsylvania v. Casey, 190, 213, 344n45

police: and ARAL, 41; and BACAOR escorts video, 161–62; in Baton Rouge 1992, 217, 218, 221, 222; Bay Area Sept. 1988, 148–51, 157; harassment, 50; infiltrators arrests, 171. *See also* FBI

population control movement, 29–34, 345n54, 346n58

Population Council, 32, 254, 346n64

Population Reference Bureau, 30

porn, 267

"Post Porn Modernist," 267

poverty: and abortion bans, 322; in Baton Rouge, 370n28; and environmental carcinogens, 134; poor women's reproduction, 79–80; and racism, 86, 134; and *Roe v. Wade*, 144

power, 178

The Power of Valuenergy (Brown), 65–68

Prairie Fire, 164

preferred provider organizations (PPOs), 242

pregnancy, 25–29, 35–36, 376n2

Pregnancy Consultation Center (San Jose), 148–49, 159–60, 228

pregnant MEs: overview, 25–29, 182–83; as birth control, 279; Chloe's group, 200–201; engaging in process, 280; Izabel and Fuchsia's groups, 269; Max's views, 200–201; Rosie's experience, 202–3

presence, 273–74

"Preventing Unfair Prosecution of Abortion Providers" (ACLU), 376n54

Prevention Point, 237–38

privilege, 72

professionalism, 48–49, 239–40

Pro-Life Action Network, 139

Proposition 73, 301

protests: anti-Bush 1988, 150; BACAOR OR church protests, 165–68, 169–70; creativity in, 149; fake clinics, 327; Hancock Park 1969, 20; Hyde Amendment, 147–48; "Ladies Against Women," 149; over Feminist Women's City Club, 72; RAW 1991, 210–11; Richmond FWHC rally, 143; Stop AIDS Now Or Else, 165; against Walk for Life, 320–21; WHAM! church protest, 367n64; WTO Seattle protests, 370n32. *See also* anti-abortion movement; Operation Rescue

psychological self-help, 87

psychological terror, 228

"Public Cervix Announcement," 267–68

Puerto Rico, 53, 95

queer and trans people: in BACORR, 217; banding with, 329–30; Bay Area Pride march 1978, 83; dyke household formations, 50–51; Furies, 69; Gay women's liberation, 49–50; and harm reduction, 372n10; HIV/AIDS stigma, 363n6; Laura B. interviewing Alicia, 82; links to self-helpers, 5, 329, 330; and Moore at OFWHC, 106; riots, 50; and third space, 271; transphobia, 321–32, 340n6. *See also* ACT UP

"quickening," 338n12

Raboy, Barb, 119–22, 123–27, 128–30

racism: at Alameda County Welfare Department, 81; and anti-abortion movement, 153 (*see also* white supremacy);

in antiwar movement, 207;
Downer on, 33; and poverty,
86; and responsible reproduc-
tion, 79; in women's move-
ment, 91. See also xenophobia
Radcliffe, Lisa, 124
radical care. See self-care concept
Radical Feminist Conference
(Tampa), 47
radical social justice work, 6
Radical Women (RW), 144–45,
148
Ramos, Yvonne, 142, 292
Ramspacher, Karen, 133
Rankin, Lauren, 257, 300, 363n12
Raven: overview, 207–8; on
Baton Rouge Delta Clinic
protest, 217, 221, 222–23; Buf-
falo defense 1992, 214–15; on
Louisiana safety, 218; protest
against Walk for Life, 320; on
RAW, 210–11; in San Jose 1993,
226–28; on Wichita protest,
213
Reagan, Ronald, 134, 137–38, 175,
362n50
Real Sex (TV show), 267
red balloon parties, 195–96
Redding FWHC, 259
referral kits, 39
referrals, how to, 325–26
reformism, 39, 66–67
Refuse and Resist, 217
Reid, Coletta, 68–70, 71, 72, 75
Reno, Janet, 256–57
Rescue America, 225
research, 284–85
responsibility, 249
revolution, 91, 195
"Revolution: It's Not Neat or
Pretty or Quick" (Parker), 91
Revolutionary Workers League
(RWL), 143, 151, 219–20
Richmond FWHC, 143
right to bleed, 26, 28, 331
riots, 50

Roberts, John, 300
Roe v. Wade: and Catholicism,
138; as illusion, 144; and
LAFWHC, 42; and OFWHC,
48; overturning, 175, 344n45;
Parker's foreshadowing, 94;
and Planned Parenthood of Southeastern Pennsylvania v. Casey,
190; and self-help movement,
42–44; and Webster, 175–76
Roots Against War (RAW),
208–11, 209, 220
Rosie, 185–86, 194–95, 201–2,
289
Ross, Loretta, 30–31, 52, 87, 252,
343n56
Rothman, Lorraine: overview, 18;
inventing ME kit, 21–24, 22–23,
25; national meeting 1972, 29;
in No Going Back film, 180–81;
OFWHC conference 1974, 58;
opening Santa Ana clinic, 42;
patenting Del-EM, 24, 33;
self-help tours, 34; Venice 1971
gathering, 20; as West Coast
Sister, 24 (see also West Coast
Sisters)
Roussel Uclaf, 234, 245, 253–54
RU-486: overview, 234; AidAc
cess.org, 326; and Alliance
Defending Freedom, 380n6;
approval challenged, 347n83;
approved in France, 245;
Benten challenging laws
against, 246–52, 253; licensing,
253–55; in Woman's Book of
Choices, 189
Rubin, Rachel, 117

Sackett, David, 284
safety/security, 218, 253, 260,
270, 283, 287–89. See also clinic
defense
salaries, 62, 76
Sampson, Agnes and Joe:
BACAOR overview video, 159;

BACAOR think tank, 169; bandanas, 158; Buffalo defense video, 214; First Orthodox Presbyterian church protest, 165–66, 168; "Stop Operation Rescue" poster, 155, *156*; video overview, 154

San Francisco Archdiocese, 126, 127

San Francisco Police Department, 148–51

San Jose, CA, 225–28

Sanger, Margaret, 30

Santa Rosa FWHC, 139, 142

Scalia, Antonin, 175

Schaff, Eric, 254, 255

Scheib, Joanna, 130

Scheidler, Joseph, 138–39, 140–41

Schenck, Robert, 215, 369n12

Schoen, Johanna, 53

Schulman, Sarah, 113–14, 367n62

Seale, Bobby, 52, 350n18

Seattle WTO protests, 370n32

Second Wave radical feminists, 376n2

secrecy, 12, 201, 253

self-care concept, 6, 341n17

self-defense. *See* clinic defense

self-health, 51–52, 55

self-help classes, 117–18

Self-Help Developers Manual (NBWHP), 87

self-selection, 73

Selina, 181

settler colonialism, 6

sexual assaults, 40, 80–81, 85

sexuality: and anti-abortion movement, 364n22; asserting rights, 266; awareness and presence, 273–74, 316; challenging narratives on, 263; discussing, 202; and health, 271–72, 299; misconceptions, 272–73; normalizing, 264–65; and pelvic exams, 271; and pregnancy, 376n2; Sprinkle on, 267, 268

sexualization, 265, 266

Seymour, Frances, 127

She Who (Grahn), 77

Shelley, Martha, 72

Sherman, Jerome, 123, 126

sickle cell anemia, 52

Sidewalk Counselors for Life, Inc, 139

"Siege of Atlanta," 147

Silence = Death, 367n64

Simone, 186, 194–95, 240–41, 317–18

SisterSong Women of Color Reproductive Justice Collective, 88

slavery, 30–31, 99–100

Slepian, Barnett, 256–57, 258, 260

Smith, Christina, 156–57

Smith, Susan, 3

Smutfest, 267

Society for Humane Abortion (SHA), 4, 19, 36–42, 345n54

Society of Women Accountants, 70

Solinger, Rickie, 30–31

sounding, 193

South Asia, 32

Sowing the Seeds of Feminist Economic Revolution (Parrent), 70, 71, 73–74

specialists and referral kits, 39–40

Sperm Bank of California, 119–20, 122, 124–27, 128–130, 360n35

sperm banks, 122–23. *See also* Sperm Bank of California

sperm quarantining, 129, 360n36

Spie, 208, *209*

Sprinkle, Annie, 267–68

state agency harassment, 61

Steinem, Gloria, 71

Steir, Bruce, 259, 375–76n54

sterility, 196, 197
sterilization: overview, 31; and abortion bans, 80; and Black people, 54–55; and "health of state," 350n24; numbers of people, 53; and reproductive health injustice, 95; and Richmond FWHC rally, 143
"Sterilize Welfare Mothers?" (Black Panther Party), 54
steroids, 233–34. See also abortion pills
Stevens, John Paul, 251
stink-bombs, 170–71
stocks, 71
Stop AIDS Now Or Else, 165
street theatre, 149, 165–68
Stryker, Susan, 50
Student Nonviolent Coordinating Committee, 3
suction devices: Celia's, 206; commonality of, 188; Karman's, 20–21, 33, 35–36, 188; Lorraine's, 21–24, 22–23, 25; menstrual regulation device, 32. See also menstrual extraction
Suki, 170–71
Supreme Court, 247, 250, 251–52, 344n45, 365n35, 380n6
Syntex, 233

Taeuber, Irene, 345n54
Tampa Women's Center, 47
Targeted Regulation of Abortion Providers (TRAP) laws, 307
Task Force on Violence Against Health Care Providers, 258
telemedicine abortion services, 328
Terry, Randall, 146, 216
theatre, 149, 165–68
Therapeutic Abortion Act, 18, 342n9
Theresa, 282–84, 287–88
third space, 271

Thomas, Clarence, 212
threats, 140–41
Tijerina, Lyn, 46
Tiller, George, 212
Tillery, Linda "Tui," 105
training videos, 159–60. See also video documentation
trans people, 50, 321–22, 340n6. See also queer and trans people
trauma-informed care, 291, 300, 377n1
trust, 203, 205, 264
tubal ligations, 31
tubal pregnancies, 323
Tufts Medical School, 340n6
Turnaway Study, 380n4
twins, 277–78

underground abortion. See abortion self-help movement
undocumented people, 205
unions, 145, 364n28
United Auto Workers (UAW), 152
United Farm Workers, 150
urethral sponge, 116
US Agency for International Development (US AID), 32, 33
uterus: and abortion pills, 233; changes in, 194; clearing, 96–97; during MEs, 193, 280; and pelvic exams, 16, 192; with septum, 287; as site of pregnancy, 102; sizing, 271–72; and suction devices, 21

VAAPCON (Violence Against Abortion Providers Conspiracy), 257
Van Buskirk, Jim, 50
vandalism, 77–78
Vanessa, 169–71, 184, 185, 187, 264–65, 314
vasectomies, 31, 62
video documentation, 154, 159–63, 165–67
Vietnam war, 14

Villarosa, Linda, 87
violence: antis in 1992, 220, 222; antis in 1994, 256, 259; Christian Right justifying, 230; domestic, 90; Task Force on Violence Against Health Care Providers, 258, 260; against trans people, 50; VAAPCON inquiry, 257. See also murders; sexual assaults

Walk for Life West Coast, 319–21
Walters, Ron, 259
War on Poverty, 3, 340n6, 350n18
Washington, Booker T., 3
WCFHP/Women's Choice: arms of, 176; and Benten, 252; bulletproof vests, 260; Cherie's experience, 297–300; closure of, 291, 305–6; donations, 242, 244; Feminist Health Educator internship, 235, 236–37, 240–41, 305; harm reduction, 237–38, 295; insurance costs, 235; and laypeople, 237, 238–40; and Medi-Cal, 242–43; and mifepristone, 235–36; mifepristone/misoprostol trial, 254–55; move to 14th Street, 291; move to 30th Street, 243; as OFWHC name change, 142; patient involvement, 295; and Simone/Chloe/Rosie group, 194–95; and Steir, 259. See also OFWHC/Women's Choice
Webster v. Reproductive Health Services, 94, 168, 175–76, 196
wedge formations, 225, 225
Weide, Laura: overview, 153–54; "Abortion Saved My Life" banner drop, 319; on anarchism, 230; autonomy, 339n16; on homophobia, 229; Louisiana defense 1992, 217–19, 221–24; on "Stop Operation Rescue"

poster, 155; Sunnyvale 1988 defense, 157
welfare, 138, 146
West Coast Feminist Health Project. See WCFHP/Women's Choice
West Coast Feminist Health Project,. See OFWHC/Women's Choice
West Coast Sisters, 24–26, 32–33, 42, 43
White, Jeff, 157, 227
white supremacy, 138, 218, 221–22, 320–21, 370n31
Whitney, Jennifer, 221, 222–23
Wichita, KS, 212–13
Wiley, Jane, 55
Williams, Faye, 86
Willow, 170–71
Wilson, Colleen, 36
Wise Woman Center, 267
A Woman's Book of Choices (FWHC), 189–90
"Womanslaughter" (Parker), 90
Womanslaughter (Parker), 77
Women, AIDS & Activism (WHAM!), 133
Women Against Imperialism, 143
women in medicine, 59
Women Lawyers Association, 70
Women of African Descent for Reproductive Justice, 88
Women's Choice. See OFWHC/Women's Choice; WCFHP/Women's Choice
Women's Choice Medical Clinic, 157
Women's Health Action and Mobilization (WHAM!), 132–33, 367n62
Women's March, 338n14
Women's Press Collective, 75
Woo, Merle, 143
Woodul, Jennifer, 72
workshop tours, 34–35, 48, 188, 285–86

World Health Organization
    (WHO), 245
WTO Seattle protests, 370n32

xenophobia, 210

Ziegler, Mary, 146–47, 190,
    346n58, 365n35

AK PRESS is small, in terms of staff and resources, but we also manage to be one of the world's most productive anarchist publishing houses. We publish close to twenty books every year, and distribute thousands of other titles published by like-minded independent presses and projects from around the globe. We're entirely worker run and democratically managed. We operate without a corporate structure—no boss, no managers, no bullshit.

The **FRIENDS OF AK PRESS** program is a way you can directly contribute to the continued existence of AK Press, and ensure that we're able to keep publishing books like this one! Friends pay $25 a month directly into our publishing account ($30 for Canada, $35 for international), and receive a copy of every book AK Press publishes for the duration of their membership! Friends also receive a discount on anything they order from our website or buy at a table: 50% on AK titles, and 30% on everything else. We have a Friends of AK ebook program as well: $15 a month gets you an electronic copy of every book we publish for the duration of your membership. *You can even sponsor a very discounted membership for someone in prison.*

Email **friendsofak@akpress.org** for more info, or visit the website: **https://www.akpress.org/friends.html**.

There are always great book projects in the works—so sign up now to become a Friend of AK Press, and let the presses roll!